Ottoman Athens:
Topography, Archaeology, History

Ottoman Athens:
Topography, Archaeology, History

Edited by
Maria Georgopoulou
and
Konstantinos Thanasakis

Athens 2019

With the support of the Association of the Philoi of the Gennadius Library

The Gennadius Library,
American School of Classical Studies at Athens
61 Souidias Street
Athens 106 76, Greece
www.gennadius.gr

The Aikaterini Laskaridis Foundation
169 Praxitelous Street
Piraeus 185 35, Greece
www.laskaridisfoundation.org

ISBN: 978-960-99945-3-8 (Gennadius Library of the American School of Classical Studies at Athens, hardcover)
ISBN: 978-618-83019-8-6 (Aikaterini Laskaridis Foundation, hardcover)

ISBN: 978-960-99945-4-5 (Gennadius Library of the American School of Classical Studies at Athens, paperback)
ISBN: 978-618-83019-9-3 (Aikaterini Laskaridis Foundation, paperback)

Copyright © 2019 The Gennadius Library of the American School of Classical Studies at Athens and the Aikaterini Laskaridis Foundation

Reprinted 2024

All rights reserved. No part of this publication may be reproduced, distributed, or transmitted in any form or by any means, electronic or mechanical, including photocopying, recording, or by any information storage or retrieval system, without the prior written permission of the Gennadius Library of the American School of Classical Studies at Athens and the Aikaterini Laskaridis Foundation.

The content of each article is the sole expression and opinion of its author(s), and not necessarily that of the publisher. The illustrations in the book have been selected by the authors, who have secured the permissions for the images' reproduction.

Cover: "The Bazar of Athens," etching and aquatint, 38.1 x 24.1 cm, by Edward Dodwell, from his *Views in Greece, from Drawings*, London 1819. American School of Classical Studies at Athens, Gennadius Library.

Cover background: Detail of "Atina kalesiyle varoşunun krokisi" [Plan of the castle and "suburb" of Athens]. Courtesy of the General Directorate of State Archives of the Prime Ministry of the Republic of Turkey, Istanbul.

Contents

Contributors   7

Foreword   9
Panagiotis C. Laskaridis

Acknowledgements   11
Maria Georgopoulou

List of Illustrations   13

Introduction   19
Maria Georgopoulou and Konstantinos Thanasakis

The Ruined City Restored: Athens and the Fabric of Greece in Renaissance Geography   23
George Tolias

Reconsidering Documents about Athens under Ottoman Rule: The Vienna Anonymous and the Bassano Drawing   49
Tasos Tanoulas

The Parthenon Mosque, King Solomon, and the Greek Sages   67
Elizabeth Key Fowden

An 18th-century Take on Ancient Greece: Mahmud Efendi and the Creation of the *Tarih-i Medinetü'l-Hukema*   97
Gülçin Tunalı

The Neighborhood of Karykes and the Fountain of the Exechoron   123
Dimitris N. Karidis

The Restoration of the Benizelos Mansion: The Sole Preserved Athenian Residence of the Ottoman Era   135
Yannis Kizis

Documenting the Ottoman Baths of Athens: A Study on Topography   151
Eleni I. Kanetaki

Travelers' Narratives Describing the Hammams of Athens 167
Aliki Asvesta and Ioli Vingopoulou

Broken Pots from Ottoman Athens: A New View from the Agora Excavations 179
Joanita Vroom

Putting Athens on the Ottoman Map: Preliminary Observations 213
Katerina Stathi

Early 19th-century Athens, the Great Powers, and the Parthenon Sculptures 227
Elena Korka and Seyyed Mohammad Taghi Shariat-Panahi

Revolutionary Athens through Ottoman Eyes (1821–1828): New Evidence 243
from the Ottoman State Archives
H. Şükrü Ilıcak

Archival Sources 261

Bibliography 262

Contributors

Aliki Asvesta is a historian and Research Associate at the Gennadius Library, American School of Classical Studies at Athens (ali.asve@yahoo.gr).

Elizabeth Key Fowden is a historian and Senior Researcher, Impact of the Ancient City ERC Project, Faculty of Classics, University of Cambridge (ekf31@cam.ac.uk).

H. Şükrü Ilıcak is a historian–Ottomanist and Research Associate at the Aikaterini Laskaridis Foundation (ilicak@gmail.com).

Eleni I. Kanetaki is an architect–engineer and Adjunct Assistant Professor in the Department of Architectural Engineering at Democritus University of Thrace and in the Department of Civil Engineering at the University of West Attica (eleni.kanetaki@gmail.com).

Dimitris N. Karidis is Professor Emeritus of the National Technical University of Athens (karidis@central.ntua.gr).

Yannis Kizis is Professor Emeritus of the National Technical University of Athens (yannis.kizis@gmail.com).

Elena Korka is Honorary Director General of Antiquities and Cultural Heritage, Hellenic Ministry of Culture and Sports (ekorka@culture.gr).

Seyyed Mohammad Taghi Shariat-Panahi is Assistant Professor, University of Thessaly (sshariatpanahi@gmail.com).

Katerina Stathi is a historian–Ottomanist (katstathi@yahoo.co.uk).

Tasos Tanoulas is the architect in charge of the Propylaea Restoration Project, Hellenic Ministry of Culture and Sports (atano@otenet.gr).

George Tolias is a Research Director of the Institute of Historical Research/NHRF, Athens, and a Director of Studies at the École pratique des hautes études, Paris Sciences et Lettres (gtolias@eie.gr).

Gülçin Tunalı is a historian and children's book author (gultunali@yahoo.com).

Ioli Vingopoulou is a historian–researcher, formerly of the Institute of Historical Research/NHRF, Athens (iovingo@yahoo.gr).

Joanita Vroom is Professor of the Archaeology of Medieval and Early Modern Eurasia, Faculty of Archaeology, Leiden University (j.a.c.vroom@arch.leidenuniv.nl).

Foreword

Although Ottoman studies have flourished significantly over the last decades, the Ottoman past of today's Greece remains little examined. Partially due to the lack of primary sources, or, as modern scholarship shows, the lack of known and well-preserved and catalogued sources, knowledge of many aspects of the Ottoman presence in the Greek territory, including architecture, administration, and everyday life, is scarce. Secondly, and perhaps most importantly, the Ottoman past had been systematically neglected. Traditional historiography of the 19th and early 20th centuries associated the Ottoman occupation with mere vandalism and perceived the Ottoman centuries as the dark ages of "Greece." Despite the attempts of several scholars to disentangle Ottoman history from such approaches, it is only very recently that the field has shifted towards a new and more concrete understanding of the Ottoman centuries. Instead of considering the Ottoman past as alien, modern scholars capable of conducting research in both Greece and Turkey focus on continuities and try to make sense of the Ottoman administration in today's Greece, outside ideologically biased perceptions.

Strikingly, however, this has not been the case with Ottoman Athens. As Athens was considered a marginal city on the Ottoman periphery, the years of the Ottoman administration and the Ottoman footprint had been overlooked. This current edition seeks, therefore, to reappropriate the Ottoman character of the city and to contribute to a better understanding of the history of Athens altogether. Inspired by the relevant conference held at the Gennadius Library of the American School of Classical Studies at Athens, this volume is the outcome of joint efforts to reevaluate the history of Athens through its Ottoman self. Completely harmonized with the overall intention of the Aikaterini Laskaridis Foundation to reappraise history (teaching and learning) and uncover historical existences little known, *Ottoman Athens: Topography, Archaeology, History* aims to inform but also inspire its audience for future studies. This has also been the philosophy behind the master databases that the Aikaterini Laskaridis Foundation has launched, *Travelogues* and *TravelTrails*, the latter in fact another joint project with the Gennadius Library. The first, a massive database of the iconographic elements in travelers' editions from the 16th century onwards, and the second, a detailed indexing of travelers' works based on a large project initiated at the Gennadius Library in the 1990s, attempt both to shed light upon the "dark ages" of Greek historiography and to reveal that, contrary to what has been highly argued, continuities surpass discontinuities.

Ultimately, and gross classifications aside, we believe that this volume will deepen our knowledge and understanding of Greek history, especially now, on the eve of the celebrations for the bicentennial of the Greek War of Independence.

Panagiotis C. Laskaridis
President of the Aikaterini Laskaridis Foundation

Acknowledgements

An edited volume is by definition a complex collaborative undertaking that would not succeed without the hard work of many individuals. We are indebted to all the colleagues who supported this endeavor.

The project was conceived around the exhibition *Ottoman Athens, 1458-1833*, shown at the Gennadius Library from February 10 to June 30, 2015. I would like to thank the historian Aliki Asvesta for all her help in curating this show. Her exceptional knowledge of the early travelers' books at the Gennadius Library constituted the basis of the exhibition and the starting point of this book.

In the exhibition the collections of the Gennadius Library were supplemented by unique archaeological material from the Excavations in the Athenian Agora of the American School of Classical Studies. We thank the Director, Professor John McK. Camp II, Sylvie Dumont, and Craig Mauzy, as well as the Ephorate of Antiquities of Athens and the General Directorate of Antiquities and Cultural Heritage of the Hellenic Ministry of Culture and Sports, for giving us the opportunity to showcase several Ottoman finds excavated in Athens. Additional thanks go to Joanita Vroom for selecting objects excavated at the Ancient Agora (published as a group in this volume), and her two graduate students from Leiden University, Charalambos Maliopoulos and Iulian Ganciu, who served brilliantly as curatorial interns for the exhibition in 2015. Joanita Vroom also curated an interesting photographic exhibition entitled *Life among Ruins: Pictures of the 1930s and 1940s from the Excavations at the Athenian Agora Conducted by the American School of Classical Studies at Athens*, shown at the Netherlands Institute at Athens.

The rich collections of the Benaki Museum and of the Museum of the City of Athens–Vouros-Eutaxias Foundation acted as bookends to the Gennadius Library's exhibition by showcasing important travelers' texts and famous works of art that illustrate different moments in the life of Ottoman Athens. I would like to thank the late Angelos Delivorrias, then Director of the Benaki Museum, as well as Polina Kosmadaki, Curator of the Department of Paintings, Drawings, and Prints at the Benaki, who responded to my call for collaboration with swiftness and professionalism. Equally important was the willingness of the Museum of the City of Athens–Vouros-Eutaxias Foundation, especially Aglaia Archontidou-Argyri, who was then the Museum's Director, and the historian–archaeologist Leonidas Argyros, to support the project with material, as well as tours of the Museum's significant collections. We owe special gratitude to the Museum of the City of Athens–Vouros-Eutaxias Foundation for the permission to use the iconic painting of the visit of the Marquis de Nointel in Athens in 1674 in this book.

Several public lectures and a symposium entitled "The Topography of Ottoman Athens: Archaeology and Travel," held at the Gennadius Library on April 23–24, 2015, led to this collection of essays. In addition to the essays that are presented in this volume, several other eminent scholars, who for a variety of reasons are not included here, shared their expertise with varied audiences at the

Gennadius Library. For their erudite lectures I would like to thank the late Charalambos Bouras, John Camp, Edhem Eldem, Machiel Kiel, Yiannis Kokkonas, Manolis Korres, and Dimitris Loupis.

The late Elizabeth Zachariadou provided encouragement and guidance from the beginning of this project, while the thoughtful advice of Evangelia Balta was key in defining its parameters. Panagiotis Poulos, Nikos Nikolaidis, and Dimitris Loupis shared their knowledge of the Ottoman monuments of Athens with great enthusiasm, and I am grateful to them for their willingness to be part of our efforts.

When it comes to the production of this book, to the authorial voice of the Director of the Gennadius Library is added that of the co-editor, Ottoman historian Konstantinos Thanasakis. For her excellent translation skills and keen editorial eye, we thank Stefanie Kennel, who molded the first batch of essays into a coherent body. The latter editorial process, including the bibliography and images, was entrusted to the capable hands of Alexandra Pel, whom we thank for the long hours she put into this seemingly non-ending project. We are grateful to Olga Antonea's skillful design work that produced this beautiful book and to Menandros Press for the printing.

This edition would not have been possible without the tangible support of the Association of Friends of the Gennadius Library (the Philoi), who back many of the activities of the Gennadius Library, and without the financial support of the Aikaterini Laskaridis Foundation and the personal interest of its President, Panagiotis C. Laskaridis. We are indebted to both for their steadfast support of scholarly publications that take a very long time to gestate. Most importantly, we would like to thank the contributors to this volume for their patience and their erudition.

Maria Georgopoulou
Director, Gennadius Library,
American School of Classical Studies at Athens

Note on Ottoman Turkish and Greek

For reasons of clarity, Ottoman Turkish terminology appears in a simplified form, without the use of diacritics and special characters. Likewise, polytonic Greek has been used selectively, where necessary, for some citations and quotations from earlier Greek texts.

List of Illustrations

1.1. Nikolaos Sophianos, "Descriptio nova totius Graeciae," Basel: Johannes Schroeterus, 1601. Reissue of the 1544 edition by Johannes Oporinus. Basel, Öffentliche Universität Bibliothek, AA 89. *page* 29

1.2. Detail with the vignette of Athens. Nikolaos Sophianos, *Totius Graeciae descriptio … Romae in templo Boni Eventus.* M.D.LII, [Rome: Antonio Blado, 1552]. London, British Library, Maps M.T. 6.g.2.(4). 30

1.3. Christoph Zweicker, "Athenae." Gerbel 1545, p. 19. American School of Classical Studies at Athens, Gennadius Library. 30

1.4. Statue of Achilles found in Athens. André Thevet, *Cosmographie du Levant*, Lyon 1556, p. 94. American School of Classical Studies at Athens, Gennadius Library. 34

1.5. Antiquities of Athens. Thevet 1575, fol. 795v. Paris, Bibliothèque de l'Arsenal, FOL-H-78 (2). 35

1.6. Johannes Lauremberg, "Achaia quae et Hellas" [Achaia which is Hellas]. Lauremberg 1660. American School of Classical Studies at Athens, Gennadius Library. 42

1.7. Johannes Lauremberg, "Attica." Lauremberg 1660. American School of Classical Studies at Athens, Gennadius Library. 43

1.8. Plan of Athens drawn by the French Capuchin monks in Athens ca. 1670, after a manuscript preserved in the Bibliothèque nationale de France (Département des manuscrits, supplément français, 19). Laborde 1854a. American School of Classical Studies at Athens, Gennadius Library. 45

2.1. View of the Horologion of Andronikos (the "Tower of the Winds"). Stuart and Revett 1762, ch. 3, pl. 1. 50

2.2. Top: View of the Arch of Hadrian from the north-west. Stuart and Revett 1827, ch. 2, pl. 16. Bottom: View of the Temple of Olympian Zeus as seen from the Temple of Artemis Agrotera by the Ilissos River. Stuart and Revett 1827, ch. 3, pl. 19. 52

2.3. View of the Temple of Artemis Agrotera by the Ilissos River from the south-west. Stuart and Revett 1762, ch. 2, pl. 1. 53

2.4. The Propylaea and the western access of the Acropolis, ca. 1204. Drawing T. Tanoulas. 56

2.5. Ground plan of the duke's residence in the Propylaea in 1458. Drawing T. Tanoulas. 57

List of Illustrations

2.6. Cross-section of the duke's residence along the central passageway of the Propylaea central building in 1458, looking north. Drawing T. Tanoulas. — 57

2.7. Plan of the Acropolis in 1458. Drawing T. Tanoulas. — 58

2.8. Top: View of the Acropolis from the south-west in 1670, unknown artist, pen and ink on white paper, 30 x 45 cm. Bassano del Grappa, Museo Civico, Collezione RIVA, 11599. Photo Museo Civico di Bassano del Grappa. Bottom: Model representing the Acropolis, ca. 1500, view from the south-west. Reconstruction T. Tanoulas, model made by P. Dimitriadis, 1985. — 61

2.9. Top: View of the Acropolis from the south-west after the 1687 explosion in the Parthenon, Francesco Fanelli, after a drawing by G. M. Verneda. Fanelli 1707. Bottom: View of the Acropolis from the north-east during the 1687 explosion in the Parthenon, Francesco Fanelli, after a drawing by G. M. Verneda. Fanelli 1707. — 63

2.10. View of the Acropolis from the south-west in 1674, unknown artist, probably pen and ink on paper, 20 x 30 cm. Bowie and Thimme 1971, fig. 8. Paris, Bibliothèque nationale de France. — 64

3.1. Throne of Belkis / Palace of Hadrian and walled town, by an unknown artist in the Nointel suite, 1674, red and black pencil, 26.6 x 45 cm. Paris, Bibliothèque nationale de France, Cabinet des Estampes, album Fc 3a (Réserve), no. 10, fol. 27. — 73

3.2. "Vue d'Athènes dont une partie est cachée derrière la colline." Babin 1674. American School of Classical Studies at Athens, Gennadius Library. — 75

3.3. The minaret rises at the south-west corner of the Parthenon, which is shown surrounded by houses constructed within the citadel walls (detail of Fig. 3.4). — 79

3.4. Charles-Marie-François Olier, Marquis de Nointel, with his suite in Athens in 1674, unknown artist, oil on canvas, 2.60 x 5.20 m. Chartres, Musée des Beaux-Arts, on permanent loan to the Museum of the City of Athens–Vouros-Eutaxias Foundation. — 85

3.5. Throne of Belkis / Palace of Hadrian by an unknown artist in the Nointel suite, 1674, red and black pencil, 26.6 x 45 cm. Paris, Bibliothèque nationale de France, Cabinet des Estampes, album Fc 3a (Réserve), unnumbered, fol. 28. — 86

3.6. "Le Temple de Jupiter Olympien et l'Acropolis d'Athènes" by Louis Dupré. Dupré 1825, pl. 22. American School of Classical Studies at Athens, Gennadius Library. — 87

3.7. Section drawing from the north and plan of the second Parthenon mosque, after the 1687 explosion. Drawing John Travlos. Travlos [1960] 1993, p. 203, fig. 137. — 91

3.8. "Grèce. Le Parthénon à Athènes," showing the second Parthenon mosque in September 1839, before its demolition in 1843, aquatint copy, 1842, of a daguerreotype by Pierre-Gustave Joly de Lotbinière, 15.1 x 20.3 cm. Digital image courtesy of the Getty's Open Content Program. — 93

5.1. The street layout in Ottoman Athens, topographical survey by Stamatios Kleanthes and Gustav Eduard Schaubert, 1832. Redrawing D. N. Karidis. — 124

5.2. Detail of Georg Gropius's panoramic view of Athens, ca. 1810, pencil drawing, 0.41 x 2.22 m. London, British Library, Department of Manuscripts. Photo © Trustees of the British Museum.   125

5.3. "The French Capuchin Monastery at Athens" by W. Page, also showing the Monument of Lysicrates, copper engraving, 9.3 x 6.5 cm. *Forget Me Not: A Christmas and New Year's Present for 1826*, London 1826, p. 293. Private collection.   126

5.4. "Mercato d'Atene," colored copper engraving, 11.5 x 17 cm. Giulio Ferrario, *Il costume antico e moderno ...*, Florence 1828. Private collection.   127

5.5. The Tower of the Winds and the newly opened Aiolou Street (in the background), unknown artist, 1843, lithograph, 10 x 18 cm. Private collection.   128

5.6. Decoding urban design principles in the first Athens plan. Karidis 2014, p. 105, fig. III.3.   130

5.7. Stamatios Kleanthes and Gustav Eduard Schaubert, Plan of Athens (detail). Karidis 2014, p. 107, fig. III.4.   131

5.8. "Modern Athenians," artist and date unknown, lithograph, 25 x 18 cm. Private collection.   133

5.9. "The Prince of Wales Leaving Athens." *The Illustrated London News* (November 13, 1875, special supplement).   134

6.1. The Benizelos mansion and its neighbors (detail of Fig. 3.4).   137

6.2. View of the Acropolis during the 1687 explosion in the Parthenon, drawing by Giacomo Verneda (detail). Tsigakou 2000, p. 288.   138

6.3. The residence of the Bishop of Athens and its grounds, just north of the church of the Panagia Gorgoepikoos, drawing by Vasilij Grigorovich Barskij, 1745. Gennadius–Benaki 1979, p. 39.   139

6.4. The restored Benizelos mansion: *hayati* and south side. Photos Y. Yerolymbos.   142

6.5. The Benizelos mansion: views of the stairway on the east side of the courtyard leading up to the *hayati* in 1979 and 2017. Photos Yannis Kizis and Y. Yerolymbos.   144

6.6. The Benizelos mansion: floor plan of the upper story as restored in 2010. Kizis Studio.   145

6.7. The upper floor of the restored Benizelos mansion, showing the central intervening seating area [orta-sofa] furnished with modern seating and an interactive digital application. Photo Y. Yerolymbos.   148

6.8. The upper floor of the restored Benizelos mansion: the winter room as a "living painting." Photo Y. Yerolymbos.   148

7.1. "Map of the Athenian Old City" by Kostas Biris, depicting the buildings which existed during the first decade of the 20th century. Biris 1959, pp. 44–45.   152

7.2. To the right, the Oula Bey Hammam in 1870. Photo P. Moraitis © Benaki Museum.   155

List of Illustrations

7.3. The Roman Agora from the east in 1877, showing the Tower of the Winds and, to the left, the semi-ruined Oula Bey Hammam. Mallouchou-Tufano 1998, p. 66 (DAI Athens, B.113).	156
7.4. Remains of the Oula Bey Hammam. Photo E. Kanetaki.	156
7.5. Ground-floor plan of the Haçi Ali Hammam. Travlos [1960] 1993, p. 185.	158
7.6. Ground-floor plan of the Abid Efendi Hammam. Kanetaki 2008, p. 81.	159
7.7. "Plan d'Athènes, levé en 1826 par ordre du Général Gourrhas, par J.-F. Bessan," lithograph, 40.5 x 52 cm. Bessan 1835.	161
7.8. Detail of the "Plan der Neustadt Athen" by Leo von Klenze, 1834. Von Klenze 1834.	162
7.9. Detail of the plan of Athens by Friedrich Stauffert and Gustav Eduard Schaubert with the help of Christian Hansen, 1836, showing the Oula Bey Hammam. Korres 2010a, p. 222.	163
7.10. Detail of "Athens mit Umgebung-Karten von Attika, Bild I" by Johann August Kaupert, 1875, as evidence for the demolished Oula Bey Hammam. Curtius and Kaupert 1903.	164
7.11. Baron Jean Antoine Théodore Gudin, *View of Athens with the Tower of the Winds and the Agora*, oil on card laid on panel, 36.5 x 61.5 cm. France, private collection.	165
8.1. A relaxing massage in the men's bath. Thévenot 1725, p. 9.	168
8.2. "Cooling Room of a Hammam." Pardoe 1838, opposite p. 15.	171
8.3. "Les Bains," a scene of bathers, serving women, and a small boy inside a public bath. Guys 1783, p. 224.	172
8.4. "Bain public des femmes mahométanes." D'Ohsson 1788, vol. 1, pl. 13.	175
9.1. Map of the Athenian Agora with Ottoman contexts. Drawing J. Vroom and E. Tzavella. American School of Classical Studies at Athens, Agora Excavations.	182
9.2. Map of the Athenian Agora with Ottoman wells only. Drawing J. Vroom and E. Tzavella. American School of Classical Studies at Athens, Agora Excavations.	184
9.3. Map of the Athenian Agora with finds of Kütahya ware. Drawing J. Vroom and K. Berghuis. American School of Classical Studies at Athens, Agora Excavations.	191
9.4. Miniature with a depiction of a coffee cup and saucer. Istanbul, Topkapı Palace Museum Library, H. 2164 (fol. 12a), early 18th century. Atasoy and Raby 1989, fig. 26, and Vroom 2003, fig. 12.15.	192
9.5. Map of the Athenian Agora with finds of tobacco pipes. Drawing J. Vroom and K. Berghuis. American School of Classical Studies at Athens, Agora Excavations.	193
9.6. Graph with dates of several tobacco pipes recovered in the Athenian Agora. J. Vroom and K. Berghuis.	193
9.7a–b. Dish, Italian-influenced sgraffito ware, Athenian Agora P 5673. Photo C. Mauzy. American School of Classical Studies at Athens, Agora Excavations.	197
9.8a–b. Bowl, locally made, Athenian Agora P 9022. Photo C. Mauzy. American School of Classical Studies at Athens, Agora Excavations.	198

9.9a–c. Jug, Italian import, Athenian Agora P 7610. Photo C. Mauzy. American School of Classical Studies at Athens, Agora Excavations. 199

9.10a–c. Small bowl, locally made, Athenian Agora P 6650. Photo C. Mauzy. American School of Classical Studies at Athens, Agora Excavations. 200

9.11a–c. Small bowl, locally made, Athenian Agora P 2179. Photo C. Mauzy. American School of Classical Studies at Athens, Agora Excavations. 201

9.12a–c. Dish, locally made, Athenian Agora P 12079. Photo C. Mauzy. American School of Classical Studies at Athens, Agora Excavations. 201–202

9.13a–c. Jug, locally made, Athenian Agora P 7092. Photo C. Mauzy. American School of Classical Studies at Athens, Agora Excavations. 203

9.14a–d. Jug, locally made, Athenian Agora P 1902. Photo C. Mauzy. American School of Classical Studies at Athens, Agora Excavations. 204–205

9.15a–c. Dish, Iznik ware, Athenian Agora P 10150. Photo C. Mauzy. American School of Classical Studies at Athens, Agora Excavations. 205–206

9.16a–b. Jug, Iznik ware imitation, Athenian Agora P 12493. Photo C. Mauzy. American School of Classical Studies at Athens, Agora Excavations. 207

9.17a–c. Coffee cup, Kütahya ware, Athenian Agora P 23893. Photo C. Mauzy. American School of Classical Studies at Athens, Agora Excavations. 207

9.18a–c. Coffee cup, Kütahya ware, Athenian Agora P 5517. Photo C. Mauzy. American School of Classical Studies at Athens, Agora Excavations. 208

9.19a–c. Coffee cup, Kütahya ware, Athenian Agora P 5518. Photo C. Mauzy. American School of Classical Studies at Athens, Agora Excavations. 208

9.20a–c. Coffee cup, Kütahya ware, Athenian Agora P 34943. Photo C. Mauzy. American School of Classical Studies at Athens, Agora Excavations. 209

9.21a–b. Saucer, Kütahya ware, Athenian Agora P 12475. Photo C. Mauzy. American School of Classical Studies at Athens, Agora Excavations. 209

9.22. Tobacco pipe, Athenian Agora MC 1277. Photo C. Mauzy. American School of Classical Studies at Athens, Agora Excavations. 210

9.23. Tobacco pipe, Athenian Agora MC 1322. Photo C. Mauzy. American School of Classical Studies at Athens, Agora Excavations. 210

9.24. Tobacco pipe, Athenian Agora MC 1279. Photo C. Mauzy. American School of Classical Studies at Athens, Agora Excavations. 210

9.25. Tobacco pipe, Athenian Agora MC 1285. Photo C. Mauzy. American School of Classical Studies at Athens, Agora Excavations. 211

9.26. Tobacco pipe, Athenian Agora MC 1324. Photo C. Mauzy. American School of Classical Studies at Athens, Agora Excavations. 211

9.27. Tobacco pipe, Athenian Agora MC 1303. Photo C. Mauzy. American School of Classical Studies at Athens, Agora Excavations. 211

9.28. Beaker, Athenian Agora G 616. Photo C. Mauzy. American School of Classical Studies at Athens, Agora Excavations. 212

List of Illustrations

10.1. "Atina kalesiyle varoşunun krokisi" [Plan of the castle and "suburb" of Athens]. Istanbul, Başbakanlık Devlet Arşivi Genel Müdürlüğü [General Directorate of State Archives of the Prime Ministry of the Republic of Turkey], Başbakanlık Osmanlı Arşivi [Ottoman State Archives], Hatt-ı Hümayun [Imperial decrees], 946.40721. Photos in Figs. 10.1-6: Courtesy of the General Directorate of State Archives of the Prime Ministry of the Republic of Turkey, Istanbul.	214–215
10.2. The compass rose (detail of Fig. 10.1).	217
10.3. The center of Athens (detail of Fig. 10.1).	219
10.4. The Acropolis rock (detail of Fig. 10.1).	220
10.5. The small defensive wall facing the Propylaea (detail of Fig. 10.1).	221
10.6. Legend in the upper-right corner (detail of Fig. 10.1).	222
10.7. Georeferenced version of the Ottoman map on top of modern satellite imagery of the center of Athens. National Cadastre & Mapping Agency [NCMA] S.A. Photo © Dipylon.	225
11.1. View of the south-east corner of the Parthenon showing the scaffolding for removing the sculptures, drawing by William Gell, 1801. London, British Museum. Photo © Trustees of the British Museum.	231
11.2. "The Acropolis as seen from the Home of the French Consul M. Fauvel," engraving after Louis Dupré. Dupré 1825, pl. 19. American School of Classical Studies at Athens, Gennadius Library.	234

Introduction

The history of Athens during the Ottoman period is of central importance for the Gennadius Library. The founder of the Library, Joannes Gennadius, was interested in an expansive vision of Hellenism through the ages. His collections are particularly significant in holdings of the Ottoman period, and he was especially drawn to materials on Athens, for he was a descendant of the prominent Athenian Benizelos family. Not only is the family's mansion the sole surviving residence of the Ottoman period, as the essay of Yannis Kizis demonstrates, but the Gennadius Library owns two works in manuscript form authored by Joannes Gennadius's ancestor Ioannis Benizelos (1730–1807).[1] The similar interests of the Aikaterini Laskaridis Foundation have secured the publication of this volume, a joint effort of two institutions that respect the exploration of history.

It is common knowledge that the grandeur of Classical Athens has dwarfed attempts to study the city in the medieval and early modern periods. In comparison to the brilliance of Athens in Antiquity, post-Classical Athens seems an insignificant village not worthy of any attention. Similarly, for the Ottomans, Athens was not a city crucially important for their concerns: there are scant sources that offer insights into the history and workings of Athens during the Ottoman period. If, however, Ottomanists have little archival information at their disposal in Athens and Istanbul (at least based on what we know of today), the important position that the city of Athens acquired in the imagination of early modern European and Ottoman travelers, antiquarians, topographers, poets, and artists produced works that offer a lively picture of the city during the Ottoman period. In addition to the travelogues and artworks that are relatively well-known [we cite here as an example just one recent compilation by Aikaterini Koumarianou (2005)], this book explores chronicles, archaeological finds, architectural remains, inscriptions, maps, and archival materials to study the topography, monuments, and history of Ottoman Athens.

This volume grew out of a symposium entitled "The Topography of Ottoman Athens: Archaeology and Travel" held at the Gennadeion in the spring of 2015 to accompany an exhibition on Ottoman Athens. The rich library of travel books, engravings, maps, and manuscripts that formed the core of Joannes Gennadius's collecting in late 19th-century London and the historical index of the Library's *Geography and Travel* collection compiled in the past decades by Aliki Asvesta provided the impetus for the exhibition, which sought to highlight lesser-known materials relating to Ottoman Athens. As examples, let us mention an album of drawings attributed to the French consul Louis-François-Sébastien Fauvel (1753–1838), who was an amateur archaeologist, and a manuscript containing the English translation of Angelos Christophoros's account of his sufferings at the hands of the Ottoman

---

[1] These are the *Ιστορία των Αθηνών* [History of Athens] (MS 220), which was eventually published in 1986, and the *Εφημερίδες* [Ephemerides] (MSS 221).

Turks before he fled Athens for England in 1608, accompanied by a crude drawing of his flogging; the Greek original is kept at Corpus Christi College, Oxford. What made the exhibition truly shine, however, was the inclusion of Ottoman finds from the excavations of the Athenian Agora, many of them unknown. An Ottoman grave stele from the Archives of the American School reminded us of the fact that relics of all periods are important for archaeologists. Once the core material was in place, further research into the unique materials from the Gennadeion offered the opportunity to devise a narrative thread that brought the objects together to highlight various aspects of Ottoman Athens: antiquities, monuments, architecture, relations among various ethnic groups, commerce, religious life, customs, and everyday activities. In order to muster additional materials, visitors to the exhibition were encouraged to visit the Benaki Museum's important collection of paintings by European travelers to Athens, as well as the Museum of the City of Athens–Vouros-Eutaxias Foundation, where the majestic oil painting of the Marquis de Nointel's suite hangs.

This was an endeavor meant to showcase Ottoman Athens. The objective was not to reiterate the rivalries between Greeks and Turks, nor to find fault with the Tourkokratia (the Turkish domination of Greece, as it is referred to in Greek historiography). By exploring the city's monuments, topography, and archaeology through the lens of Greek, Ottoman-Turkish, and western European sources, the contributors to this volume offer a panoramic vision of various layers of the early modern city.

True to its celebrated Classical heritage, the Acropolis of Athens and its antiquities held center stage in travelogues and sketches, but also in the imagination of travelers and locals as well. George Tolias explains the ways in which Athens was portrayed by Renaissance geographers as a silent ruin and then recontextualized by the Enlightenment through ancient texts in order to gain its position as the metropolitan center of Greece. The monuments offer multiple ways to anchor the discussion. Denuded, spoliated, reclaimed, but surely widely admired by all, the most significant landmark of Athens, the Parthenon, was Ottomanized as "the most beautiful mosque in the world." Tasos Tanoulas uses his intimate knowledge of the architectural history of the monuments on the Acropolis to explain its complex building history based on European accounts.

Elizabeth Key Fowden traces the complicated history of the Parthenon in the eyes of the Ottomans based on the description of the city in the *Seyahatname* [Book of travels] by Evliya Çelebi (1611–1682) as a foil to European accounts. A second Ottoman text, the chronicle of Mahmud Efendi entitled *Tarih-i Medinetü'l-Hukema* [The history of the city of the sages], the only history of ancient Athens written in Ottoman Turkish, is shown to have strong ties with the history of Athens of Georgios Kontares (published in Venice in 1675). The help given to Mahmud Efendi by two "profound" Greek abbots, Theophanes Kavallares and Gregorios Soteres, who translated sources from the ancient Greek, Latin, and French, has allowed Gülçin Tunalı to trace the genealogy of this text, which fits into a local tradition related to the city of Athens, and to stress the interaction of Ottoman and Greek cultures. The use of Ottoman terminology and transference of rituals onto a well-known custom allowed the Ottomans a clearer picture of the world of ancient Athens.

To supplement the historical accounts, the architectural traces of monuments and urban patterns tell us much about the growth of the city after 1460. Numerous engravings confirm the multicultural character of the urban fabric in many neighborhoods of Ottoman Athens. The area around the Tzistarakis Mosque (in Monastiraki Square), housing Hadrian's Library (where the first Greek school, the Seminary of Greek Studies, was established in 1717, as we learn from Gülçin Tunalı) and the church of the Great Panagia, showcases how in the pre-modern city diverse religions, different confessional elements, and various histories could blend together and coexist side by side. In a similar fashion, the western travelers noticed the practices of the Orthodox, as we see in a drawing published by James Stuart and Nicholas Revett (1787, vol. 2, ch. IV, pl. I) that shows an Orthodox family holding candles as they go to worship at the church of Panagia Spiliotissa on the south slope of the Acropolis.

Starting with a careful consideration of the detailed urban planning of Athens after the Greek War of Independence, Dimitris Karidis provides a rich canvas of the topography of the city in the earlier period while discussing the prominence given to the vistas of ancient monuments in the plans for the city when Athens was conceived as the capital of the nascent Greek state. Despite its perceived non-importance for the Ottomans, Athens was well-equipped architecturally, as the essays by Eleni Kanetaki and Yannis Kizis make clear. It was endowed with mosques and a madrasa (next to the Tower of the Winds), as well as hammams, fountains, fine residences for the wealthy residents, simple houses for the garrison on the Acropolis, and churches and monasteries, both Orthodox and Latin.

Competing and complementary accounts of Greeks, western Europeans, and Ottoman Turks project a pluralistic view of a society that interacted in deep but also in superficial ways. The reports of travelers on the public bath houses presented by Aliki Asvesta and Ioli Vingopoulou provide voyeuristic, if comical, references to an exotic culture in which bathing was a normal pastime and ritual for locals of every confession. The oft-quoted description of the ritual dance of the swirling dervishes in the Tower of the Winds so evocatively drawn by Edward Dodwell is another example of the fascination that foreign customs held for Europeans.

How about everyday life in Ottoman Athens? We hear about the bazaar from a variety of travelers and especially about honey, olive oil, and other commodities. The busy marketplace, so vividly portrayed by Edward Dodwell, accentuates the variety of peoples, materials, and dress, all items that constituted the very essence of the Athenian economy. Thankfully, the Ottoman material unearthed since 1931 in the excavations of the Athenian Agora of the American School of Classical Studies at Athens offers a lens into the archaeology of the area. The pottery, published here for the first time as a group by Joanita Vroom, showcases local production, as well as imports from Italy and Turkey. The clay pipes and coffee cups bring to light important customs associated with the Ottomans at the time. Coffee cups from Kütahya and chibouk pipes are often included in the travelers' drawings, as if to add some local color to the depictions. They remind us of the mysterious atmosphere that Athens held for western Europeans.

Finally, a look at archival material from Istanbul offers some correctives and new perspectives. The topography of the city on the eve of the Greek War of Independence is made palpable by a newly discovered Ottoman map from the Ottoman State Archives in Istanbul, presented here by Katerina Stathi. Hidden moments in the history of the infamous despoliation of the Parthenon by Lord Elgin are fleshed out in the archival research of Elena Korka and Seyyed Mohammad Taghi Shariat-Panahi. Şükrü Ilıcak brings to the fore new archival materials from the Archives in Istanbul that bear upon the siege of the Acropolis during the Greek War of Independence.

Pulling together sources that highlight unknown facets of Ottoman Athens, piecing together little-known accounts and archaeological artifacts alongside better-known engravings and travelogues, this volume seeks to encourage us to take a fresh look at early modern Athens from 1460 to 1827. Even though the Ottoman Archives do not contain the wealth of information that exists for other parts of the Ottoman Empire, the fame of the ancient city of Athens inspired many visitors to compose travelogues, histories, and chronicles, as well as poetry. The renewed interest in the restoration and reuse of Ottoman monuments in the past decades has surely changed the ways in which the urban space of Athens is viewed by the broader public as well. By insisting on the complexities of the different "readings" of the city by natives, and visitors, we hope that this volume offers new perspectives for a more nuanced study of early modern Athens.

Maria Georgopoulou
Director, Gennadius Library,
American School of Classical Studies at Athens
(mgeorgopoulou.genn@ascsa.edu.gr)

Konstantinos Thanasakis
Scientific Advisor, Aikaterini Laskaridis Foundation
(thanasakis@laskaridisfoundation.org)

The Ruined City Restored:
Athens and the Fabric of Greece in Renaissance Geography

George Tolias

The Silenced City

A reassessment of the early modern perceptions of Athens is essential, as a void of two centuries persists in older and more recent literature on the history of the recovery of the city. Directly or indirectly, scholars consent to its absence until the late 17th century, as trustworthy descriptions and reliable surveys are unknown between Cyriac of Ancona's description and the antiquarian travels undertaken by the Marquis de Nointel, Jacob Spon, and George Wheler.[1] These interpretations rely chiefly on the material assembled by Léon de Laborde in the mid-19th century and on the prevailing historical positivism of the age, with its faith in facts and accuracy.[2] Aiming to trace the misfortunes of the Athenian monuments during the first centuries of the Ottoman era, Laborde discarded the corpus of the early modern descriptions of the city as verbiage and even considered the Athens of his day a "silenced and ruined city."[3]

However, Athens was not always seen as a ruin. In early Humanism, the city and its monuments were celebrated by Cyriac of Ancona, or the anonymous Greek author of 1460 who portrayed the citadel of the Acciaiuoli as a humanist's dream of living memory.[4] Athens appears to fall into oblivion from the Ottoman conquest (1456) until the wave of Enlightenment antiquarian travelers

---

* My warmest thanks to Maria Georgopoulou for her kind invitation to the symposium. Special thanks are due to Anca Dan for her valuable suggestions and to Stefanie Kennell, Alexandra Pel, and Konstantinos Thanasakis for their help. All translations of quotations are my own, unless otherwise indicated.

[1] Paton 1951, p. 9; Weiss 1969, p. 144; Etienne 1990, pp. 31–41; Shanks 1996, p. 55; Yakovaki 2006, p. 170; Stoneman 2010, pp. 56–80.

[2] Laborde 1854a.

[3] Laborde 1854a, vol. 1, pp. X–XI. Certainly, first-hand evidence and precise measurements are useful tools in the study of the history of Athenian urbanism and monuments. Nonetheless, they do not help us to grasp complex issues such as cultural constructs and the workings of intellectual history, let alone the fact that in cases such as that of early modern Athens, with its radical political change and the absence of public systems of spatial management and the concomitant archiving bureaucracy, these approaches are products of external and piecemeal initiatives.

[4] For Cyriac's visits in 1436 and 1444, see the classic studies by Edward W. Bodnar (1960 and 1970); for the anonymous Greek description of Athens of ca. 1460, see Laborde 1854a, vol. 1, pp. 17–25. Marco Di Branco has recently argued that this text may have been composed in the 12th century (Di Branco 2005), a period when the city was a center for visitors and pilgrims (Kaldelis 2009). To the early modern praises of Athens should be added Niccolò de Matroni's account (1394–1395) published by Léon Le Grand (1895), the anonymous Venetian traveler of 1470 published by E. Ziebarth (1899), and Laonikos Chalkokondyles's praise of the wise and moderate rule of Antonio Acciaiuoli, who "embellished the city as much as possible" (Chalkokondyles 2014, 4.59). See also the anonymous Greek lament of ca. 1456, "On the Destruction and the Captivity that Occurred under the Persians in Athens of Attica," in which the city is portrayed as a "skillfully built city," "with its marble glistening in the sun" (Van Steen 2014, p. 236).

ushered the city's revival. The intervening period remains a "dark age," an uncharted time of imperceptible, though fundamental transformations. Indeed, for Athens to be praised, then vanish, and finally re-emerge as an attraction for antiquarian travelers and the object of systematic survey, a series of essential conceptual readjustments had to occur. It would take all the efforts of a series of humanists for Athens to be considered as a silenced ruin and then retrieved as the cornerstone of the early modern conception of ancient Greece.

In the following pages, we shall turn our attention to this era of transitions, in an effort to explore the early modern perceptions of Athens. In order to set the discussion on a consistent corpus of evidence with internal coherence, we shall focus on the material offered by Humanism's geographical lore. By following the descriptions and representations of the city, and by analyzing the processes of their creation, standardization, and dissemination, an attempt will be made to trace the place of the city in the early modern perception of Greece and to interpret its structural function.

The City as Ruin

Renaissance geography combined knowledge of people and places, historical and anthropological curiosity, political reflection, and moral meditation. It sought to confront ancient and modern information on places in order to connect the past with the present and to "revive the memory" of places.[5] The reasons behind this pursuit were many and operated simultaneously: the desire for a deeper understanding of the geographical setting of ancient texts; the new spatial awareness triggered by the proliferation of communication networks; the aspiration to confront new data and ancient authority in order to renew global knowledge; but chiefly the rise of national sovereign states and the need for their legitimation through defining a historic fatherland and establishing genealogical links of origin.[6] Although initiated in the time of Petrarch, these learned endeavors achieved their final form during the second half of the 15th century and climaxed in the 16th. The inhabited world was gradually perceived as an aggregation of territorial entities, each one with its own history and culture, its own regional organization, and capital city.[7] Within this framework, the Greeks also found their country, a Greece twice lost, once in the antique past and then again with the Ottoman conquest of the Eastern Roman Empire.[8]

Ottoman expansion changed the rhythm of history, upset long-standing geopolitical equilibria, and entrenched a new cultural polarization. The conquest of Constantinople was immediately felt as the major event of the age. Humanists' geographical descriptions focus on the utter demise of Greece and meditate on the vicissitudes of fortune and the uncertainty of the human condition. Many writers spoke about the fall of the city and the imminent Turkish threat to Christianity.[9] One of the most prominent among them was the cosmographer–pope, Enea Silvio Piccolomini (Pius II, 1458–1464). In his celebrated letter to Pope Nicholas V, dated July 12, 1453, he grieved the loss of Constantinople, which he presented as the successor of Athens. The fall of Constantinople, according to him, was the second and final death of Greek culture: "It is a second death for Homer, a second passing for Plato.

---

[5] Milanesi 2001–2002; Gautier Dalché 2012.
[6] On the early modern geographical notions of the sovereign state, see Akerman 1984; Biggs 1999; Mukerji 2006; Branch 2011.
[7] Tolias 2014–2015.
[8] For the early modern cartographic definitions of Greece, see Tolias 2012, pp. 61–102; for the territorialization of Hellenism proposed by Greek emigrant scholars in the early 16th century, see Lamers 2016, pp. 233–269.
[9] See Pertusi [1976] 2007; also Vatin and Déroche 2016.

Where now shall we seek the genius of philosophers or poets? The fount of the Muses has been exhausted."[10] Enea Silvio endorsed the notion of *translatio studii* from Athens to Constantinople, a concept closely linked to *translatio imperii*, the transfer of political power from one center to another.[11] The idea of Constantinople as successor of Athens is persistent in his texts on the Ottoman conquest. In another letter, addressed to Cardinal Nicolaus Cusanus and dated a week later (July 20, 1453), he returned to the parallel of the two cities and presented Constantinople as the source of Greek learning for the Latin West, just as Athens was for ancient Rome.[12]

In 1458, the year of his election to the papacy, Enea Silvio composed *Europa*, which, together with *De Asia* (written in 1461), formed the two parts of his *Cosmographia*, the first modern global geographical narrative.[13] Geopolitical concerns on a worldwide scale underlie its composition: as the Ottoman specter was haunting Europe, the humanist pope offered the ruling elites of Western Christendom a tool for global reflection. Enea Silvio did not venture a formal geographical definition of Greece. His description vacillates between the Late Antique and medieval geographical traditions that defined Greece as the Roman province of Illyricum[14] and the common assumption that recognized Greece as the Eastern Roman Empire, with Constantinople as its capital. In his description of Athens, Enea Silvio deplores its degeneration into a desolate village and curses Francesco Acciaiuoli, the last Florentine lord of Athens, for surrendering the city to the Turks:

> In this place [Greece/Attica] was the city of Athens, once most noble, in need of no praise so greatly did its glory abound. The same city, in our own time, has the appearance of a small hamlet. Nevertheless, on that rock where the ancient temple of Minerva was is what is called the citadel throughout all Greece, both for the magnificence of its fortifications and for the difficulty of besieging it. A certain Florentine handed this citadel over to Mehmed when he found no one to aid him, after having implored […] for reinforcements. Country estates were handed over to him on account of this; in them may he lead a dishonorable life.[15]

Pius's vision of the decay of Athens became a commonplace, a warning that every country in the Christian West could soon await a similar fate. Its echo resonated not only in the ensuing descriptions of the humanists' geographies, but also pervaded the political analyses and moral discourses of the age. Even a century later (1556), Philip Melanchthon, speaking at the University of Wittenberg about the fall of Constantinople, adopted Pius's notion of *translatio studii* from Athens to Constantinople and mourned the destruction of Athens by Mehmed II:

---

[10] See Pertusi [1976] 2007.

[11] "*Hic oratoria, hic philosophia, et omnium bonarum artium studia, postquam consenuerunt et extinctae sunt Athenae, unicum domicilium et certissimum templum habuere.*" Cf. Cotta-Schönberg 2014, pp. 38–39. On the notions of *translatio studii* and *translatio imperii*, cf. Stierle 1996, esp. p. 56, and Gertz 1987.

[12] Petrusi [1976] 2007, 2:52; cf. also Bisaha 2004, p. 65.

[13] The two works were published jointly in 1509 as the *Cosmographia* by Henricus Stephanus (Piccolomini 1509). For *Europa*, see Piccolomini 2001; for *De Asia*, see Piccolomini 2004.

[14] Cf. Isidore of Seville *Etym.* 14.4.7: "*Graecia a Graeco rege vocata, qui cunctam eam regionem regno incoluit. Sunt autem provinciae Graeciae septem: quarum prima ab occidente Dalmatia, inde Epirus, inde Hellas, inde Thessalia, inde Macedonia, inde Achaia, et duae in mari, Creta et Cyclades. Illyricus autem generaliter omnis Graecia.*"

[15] Piccolomini 1509, fols. 100v–101r: "*In hac civitas Atheniensis quondam nobilissima fuit nullius indiga praeconii: tanta eius superfuit claritas. Eadem nostro tempore parui opidi speciem gerit. In eo tamen saxo quo vetustum Minervae templum fuit. Arx est per omnem Graeciam nominata cum operis magnitudine: tum difficultate oppugnationis: hanc Florentinus quidam: Maumeti tradidit: cum imploratis Latinorum auxiliis nullius opem inveniret. Rura ei ob eam rem tradita in quis aeuum ignobile ducat.*" See also Casella [1972] 1974; Piccolomini 2001, p. 88 (*Europa*, §50).

> Now only ruins are left, fishermen's shacks and the dregs of wandering foreigners who have flocked there by chance from barbarian nations. This is the fall of the city that has had both eminent instances of virtues, and was the abode of the sciences, and with wisdom and bravery performed great and honorable deeds against the Persians, and in its rule was more temperate than the Spartans and the Thebans. And there are two thousand years from Solon to this Mehmed, the destroyer of Athens.[16]

The descriptions of Athens were accompanied by a melancholic aura. The image of a once glorious city brought low prevails in the geography compositions that followed. In his *Septe giornate della geographia* (1482), a cosmographical poem and cultural geography, Francesco Berlinghieri stressed Athens' ancient glory and present demise. He devoted a fair number of verses to the city, in which its ancient splendor and the patriotism of its inhabitants are highlighted by the repetition of the word "fatherland" [*patria*] at the beginning of several verses; and he concluded his description with an Ovidian reflection on the impermanence of power: "[...] Today it is called Sethine and has lost all its power. / Look now at Oinoe and Rhamnous / which fortune adored for its power, / then wanted to crush [...]"[17]

An Ancient Country and Its Capital (1500–1550)

The new geography that Piccolomini launched had a conspicuous career during the 16th century. A series of regional or universal geographical narratives ensued, steadily converting the regions of the world into spaces of power. Within this context, a Greek territorial identity was gradually conceived, blending elements of the antique geographical descriptions of the Greek lands and medieval reminiscences of the Roman Illyricum with the imperial notion of Byzantium. However, the transition from the historical ethnocultural reality of Hellenism to the modern geographical construct of Greece as a country was long and tortuous, as the Greeks were dispersed in a wide geographical area, and Greece as a political territorial entity had never existed in ancient times. Furthermore, great confusion reigned thanks to the elusiveness of the ancient sources and their ambiguity on the regional designations of Greece. This was due to the uncertainty of whether the term Greece [Ἑλλάς] denoted the whole of the lands inhabited by the Greeks, or a specific historical region, dating back to the Homeric era, which Strabo situated in south-eastern Thessaly, or the area located above the Isthmus of Corinth, also named Achaia, as Ptolemy, Pliny, and Isidore of Seville defined it.[18]

---

[16] Melanchthon 1844, cols. 153–161, at 155: "[...] Nunc tantum ἐρείπια reliqua sunt, casae piscatorum et colluvies peregrinorum hominum, qui ex barbaris gentibus casu eo confluunt. Hic est urbis finis, quae et exempla virtutum egregia habuit, et domicilium fuit doctrinarum, et res honestas ac magnas sapienter et fortiter gessit contra Persas, et in imperio modestior fuit Spartanis et Thebanis, suntque duo millia annorum a Solone usque ad hunc Mahometum eversorem Athenarum." For Melanchthon's opinions regarding Greece, see Ben-Tov 2013.

[17] Berlinghieri 1482, fols. 58r-v (3.26): "[...] / In Attica hora Athene vedera amata / patria a tanti philosophi & a tanti / poeti chiara & di celeste fama / patria di tanti duci & si prestanti / patria di tanti studii et tanti regii / patria di tanti ogni suo ben zelanti / patria di tanti cictadini egregii / che la tua liberta ti conservano / onde hoggi sono intra edivin collegii. / Quante le tue victorie & quanto chiaro / lhonore & ilnome tuo quanta potenza / hor giaci & lesser nostro quindi apparo / [...] / Hoggi e decta Sethine et dallei scossa / ogni Potenza hor mira Enoe et Rhanno / che la fortuna adora per sua possa / Chi lo pone in macrina alla qual danno / [...]" For the modern toponymy, Berlinghieri resorted to the portolan charts of his day, where Athens appears as Settine or Sethine, a corruption to εἰς Ἀθήνα [in Athens].

[18] Strabo 9.5.6: "As for Phthia, some say that it is the same as Hellas and Achaia, and that these constitute the other, the southern, of the two parts into which Thessaly as a whole was divided; but others distinguish between Hellas and Achaia;" Ptolemy *Geography* 3.14.1: "The part of Achaia, which is neighboring the mentioned provinces down to the isthmus of the Peloponnese, is called Greece;" Pliny 4.11: "At the narrow neck of the isthmus, Hellas begins, by our people known as Graecia. The first state that presents itself is Attica, anciently called Acte;" Isidore *Etym.* 14.4.10: "Attica [...] is the true Greece, where the city of Athens was located, the mother of the liberal arts and the nurse of philosophers; there was nothing nobler and more illustrious in all of Greece."

An early attempt to reconcile these conflicting elements and to proceed to a "national" geographical designation of ancient Greece occurred in 1509, in Sebastiano Compagni's world geography. The Ferrarese geographer blended the available ancient descriptions into a novel designation of an antique "nation-state," with its founding myth, its origins, its historical development, and its cultural and political center:

> The region of Achaia begins after Epirus, and some believed that it was named after the frequent inundations that occurred there, [or after] one of the three leaders of the Pelasgians, Achaios, son of Larissa and Neptune, who spent many years there with a Pelasgian army. Originally, the region was called Daona [sic] and then Greece, a name that is still retained, after the king, Graecus, successor of Cecrops who ruled in Attica, as attested by some authors. Greece was small, as Cicero affirms, adding that it was inhabited by three tribes. And the whole of Greece, which flourished so greatly with fame, with glory, with learning, with many arts, and even with wide dominion and military renown, occupies (as you know) and has always occupied but a small part of Europe, and subsequently extended its borders so greatly, so that the Peloponnese and parts of Macedonia, and as far as the Axios River in the east, and the Thesprotians, and all the islands of the Aegean are now called Greece.[19]

Compagni's perception of Greece, strongly impregnated with Strabo's historical and cultural understanding of human settlements, is a remarkable testimony to Humanism's creative ability. By combining elements extracted from Ptolemy, Strabo, Pliny, Isidore, and Cicero, Compagni reads the shifting of the name "Greece" as a dynamic historical growth of a country, promoting the area of Attica (and of Athens) as its historical core.[20] However, this was not a gratuitous performance of philological virtuosity. Throughout Compagni's effort to extract data from the ancient sources related to the territorialization of Hellenism, there echoes the slow process of Hellenization, understood as a course of territorial expansion.

Compagni's work occupies an irregular place in the corpus examined here. It remained unpublished until 1557, when Wolfgang Wissenburg edited a version of the text in Basel, under the name of the obscure Domenicus Marius Niger.[21] We have to assume that Compagni's manuscript was not widely disseminated, since there are no traces of his audacious conversion of the spread of Hellenism into an ever-expanding Greece in subsequent geography editions. Thus, in 1534, the Reformed theologian and cosmographer Joachim Vadianus [Joachim von Watt] made a fresh attempt to elucidate the elusiveness of the ancient texts. He confronted the contradictory ancient sources and

---

[19] Niger [Compagni] 1557, p. 298: "*Achaia regio post Epyrum initium capit, dicta ut nonnulli existimant a crebra acquarum inundatione. Quidam ab uno trium ducum Pelasgorum Achaio Larissae et Neptuni filio qui ibi cum Pelasga manu multo aevo degit. Prius Daona vocata ac deinde Graecia, quod nomen adhuc retinet a rege Graeco dicto Cecropis successore qui Atticae tantum reginio imperavit, ut quidam volunt. Quam olim modicam fuisse e his verbis probat Cicero, qui quum tria Graecorum genera esse meminissit et subiunxit. Atque haec cuncta Graecia quae fama, quae gloria, quae doctrina, quae plurimis artibus quae etiam imperio et bellica laude floruit, parvum quendam locum (ut scitis) Europae tenet, semperque tenuit, hic ille postea fines suos adeò ampliavit, ut et haec, et Peloponesus, et partes Macedoniae quae ad auroram vergunt ab Axio amneusque ad Thesprotas, et omnes Aegei maris insulae, quemadmodum et nunc Graecia nuncupata est.*"
[20] In his definition of Greece, Compagni combines Ptolemy's regional arrangement, as described in Book III (3.14.1) and visualized in *Tabula Europae X*, and Strabo's image of Greece as a succession of juxtaposed peninsulas from the Peloponnese to the mouths of the Axios River in the Thermaic Gulf (8.1.3). To these he adds etymological information from Pliny (4.11) and Isidore (14.4.7), as well as Cicero's praise of Athens (*Pro Flacco*, 64).
[21] Bouloux 2016, pp. 29–37.

identified Greece solely as Attica, upholding Athens as its capital by reason of the autochthony of its inhabitants, its political power, and its cultural importance:

> Greece is therefore said by Pliny to be called after King Graecus, born there. It is Hellas, however, as for instance in Book VIII of Strabo, who explains [that it was] from Hellen, son of Pyrrha and Deucalion. Ptolemy in Book III, greatly diverging from Pliny, calls this whole territory Achaia, although Pliny by this name includes not Greece but the Peloponnese. It is also called Attica, meaning Greece, because Attis was the most famous of the regions of Achaia. Athens itself was its principal city, not only because of its one-time imperial power, but also as fostering every kind of arts and the most outstanding intellects [...] Today, in place of so great a city, they report that it is a humble fort. Many prominent vestiges of Athens survive, among them the citadel once sacred to Minerva, still very well fortified, which in the recollection of our fathers a certain Florentine from the family of the Acciaiuoli, when no help came [...] although he had often and strongly besought it, handed it over to Mehmed, Emperor of the Turks, by the intermediation of an agreement. This is Athens, which, for so many centuries celebrated for the renown of its wisdom, Paul was the first to enlighten with true wisdom [...].[22]

Vadianus described the modern city based on Piccolomini; yet, he stressed the survival of outstanding antique vestiges, such as the Parthenon. In his description of the ancient city, he emphasized the rule of law (Draco and Solon) and its evangelization by St. Paul and Dionysius the Areopagite.

Nonetheless, the uncertainty of the geographical term persisted, affecting even earlier works, as attested by the 1531 Basel edition of Piccolomini's cosmography, where the chapter on Attica bears the title "*De Hellade qua et Graecia et Attica est dicta.*" The confusion reached its climax in 1540, when two conflicting modern ethnocultural geographic designations of Greece appeared simultaneously: the Basel edition of Ptolemy's *Geographia* by Sebastian Münster and the publication in Rome of the antiquarian map of Greece by the Corfiot humanist Nikolaos Sophianos.[23] In his effort to identify modern states and Ptolemy's regional maps, Münster recognized Greece in the regions included in Ptolemy's *Tabula Europae X* (Macedonia, Epirus, Thessaly, Achaia, the Peloponnese, the Cyclades and Crete), an option also adopted in the Italian adaptations of the book by Giacopo Gastaldi (1548) and Girolamo Ruscelli (1561). This territorially narrow option for ancient and modern Greece was challenged by Sophianos's map charting the historical spread of Hellenism from the sack of Troy to the foundation of Constantinople in a broad geographical zone in the north-east Mediterranean and, at the same time, puts Athens forward as the chief urban center (Fig. 1). The city, a large

---

[22] Vadianus 1534, pp. 43–44: "*Graecia igitur a Graeco rege ibi nato dicta est Plinio. Hellas autem quemadmodum libro VIII, Strabo tradit ab Hellone Deucalionis et Pyrrhae filio. Ptolemaeus lib. III longe a Plinio diversus totum eum tractum Achaiam vocat, cum hoc nomine non Hellada sed Peloponnesum Plinius ambiat. Dicitur et Attica, quae Graecia, quod Attis omnium Achaiae regionum celeberrima fuerit, ipsasque Athenas principem urbem, non imperii solum late quondam dominantis, sed et artium omne genus et ingeniorum praestantissimorum alumnam habeat [...] Hodie tantae urbis loco humilie castellum esse tradunt. Athenarum vestigia magis insignia extant, cum arce quondam Minervae sacra, etiamnum munitissima, quam patrum nostrorum memoria Florentinus quidam ex Aciaolum familia, quum saepe multumque Latinorum auxilia implorasset, nec impetraret, Mahometum Turcarum Imperatori pacto interveniente contradidit. Haec sunt Athenae quas sapientiae fama tot saeculis celebres, primum Paulus vera sapientia illustravit [...]*" On Vadianus, see Strauss 1958.

[23] For Greece in Münster's edition of Ptolemy, see Tolias 2012, p. 39; for Sophianos' map, see Tolias 2006.

imaginary vignette that covers a significant part of Attica, is represented by the Acropolis, the city walls, and the double harbor of Piraeus (Fig. 2). A smaller vignette, again imagined, is dedicated to Byzantium/Constantinopolis, while the remaining cities on the map are indicated only by a conventional cartographic symbol. The vignette of Athens, in all probability drawn by Sophianos,[24] inspired the view of the city that Christoph Zweicker of Strasbourg drew for Nikolaus Gerbel's 90-page introduction to the 1545 Basel edition of Sophianos's map (Fig. 3).[25] These images were intentionally imaginary: they portray the lost antique city unfettered by its actual topographical reality or its material remains; they are based exclusively on a reading of the ancient texts, which they loosely try to illustrate.

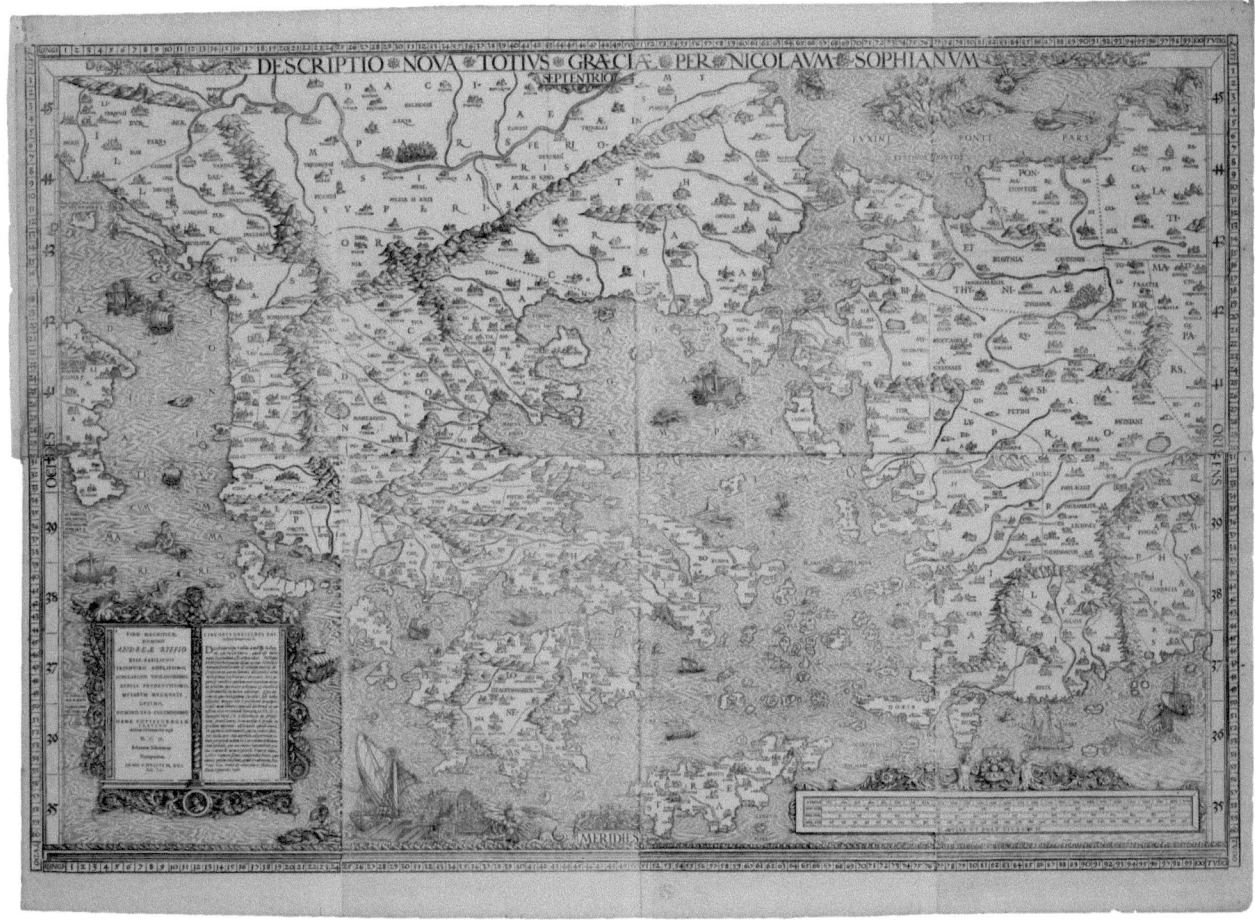

Figure 1. Nikolaos Sophianos, "Descriptio nova totius Graeciae," Basel: Johannes Schroeterus, 1601. Reissue of the 1544 edition by Johannes Oporinus. Basel, Öffentliche Universitat Bibliothek, AA 89.

---

[24] The vignette of Athens exists in all the surviving editions of the map that were printed in Sophianos's lifetime; no artistic collaborator is mentioned in the first editions of the map.
[25] Cf. Gerbel 1545, p. 19.

Figure 2. Detail with the vignette of Athens. Nikolaos Sophianos, *Totius Graeciae descriptio … Romae in templo Boni Eventus*. M.D.LII, [Rome: Antonio Blado, 1552]. London, British Library, Maps M.T. 6.g.2.(4).

Figure 3. Christoph Zweicker, "Athenae." Gerbel 1545, p. 19. American School of Classical Studies at Athens, Gennadius Library.

The difficulty of defining ancient Greece as a single country led Gerbel to adopt a mosaic composition for the structure of his narrative. He presented a constellation of 21 significant cities [*celebri urbes*], each one constituting a chapter introduced by an imaginary vignette. Five years later, the work went through a second, enlarged edition of 297 pages, fully revised and restructured, this time adopting Ptolemy's regional layout.[26] The description of Athens, identical in both editions, occupies a central position in the former as the second of the 21 famous cities of Greece (the first one is Tarentum [modern Taranto] in Magna Graecia). Following Pausanias, Gerbel commenced his description of the cities of the Greek mainland with Athens; he stressed its cultural importance and repeated Aelius Aristides' rhetorical celebration of Athens as the core of a series of concentric geographical circles embracing the entire world:[27] "For those beginning the journey from the rising of the sun [the east], Attica comes first of all. Although this is not shown on the map, yet the place where Athens is located will have to be marked by learned men in capital letters. For as Greece is central in the world, so in Greece itself Attica is central, and in the center of Attica is Athens, most renowned of cities."[28]

With continued reference to Aelius Aristides, Gerbel described Athens as the strongest and most important city of the Greeks.[29] Furthermore, he alluded to the autochthony of the Athenians and the purity of their language, and presented the city as a metropolis of the Greek colonial diaspora, images reinforced with an epigram by Ausonius that is quoted at the end of his description.[30] The splendor of the first city of ancient Greece is contrasted to its actual desolation. Gerbel quotes Piccolomini's description of the modern city as a humble village surrendered to the Turks and rounds off his account with a lament on its ruin and loss:

> [...] As Ovid too truly said, "What remains of Pandion's Athens, but a name?" O miserable changes of human affairs! O tragic transmutation of human power! A city once most thriving in its walls, dockyards, buildings, weaponry, wealth, men, prudence, and every sort of wisdom, has been reduced to a small town, or rather a village. Once free and living by its own laws, it is now bound to ferocious beasts by the yoke of servitude. Go to Athens and, in place of magnificent edifices, see rubble and deplorable ruins. Do not, do not rely too much on your own strength, but trust in him who says, I AM THE LORD YOUR GOD.[31]

---

[26] Gerbel 1550, p. 37: "*Positis igitur Graeciae quatuor praecipuis partibus: Macedonia, Epiro (cui Graecia magna insertabitur) Achaia, Peloponneso [...]*"

[27] Aristid. *Or.* 1.15: "[...] for just as in the case of a shield with circles falling within circles, a fifth, the fairest of all, constitutes the central boss; if indeed Hellas lies in the center of the whole earth, then Attica lies in the center of Hellas, the city in the center of the country, and the Acropolis in the center of the polis" [(...) ὥσπερ γὰρ ἐπ' ἀσπίδος κύκλων εἰς ἀλλήλους ἐμβεβηκότων πέμπτος εἰς ὀμφαλὸν πληροῖ διὰ πάντων ὁ κάλλιστος, εἴπερ ἡ μὲν Ἑλλὰς ἐν μέσῳ τῆς πάσης γῆς, ἡ δ' Ἀττικὴ τῆς Ἑλλάδος, τῆς δὲ χώρας ἡ πόλις, τῆς δ' αὖ πόλεως ἡ ὁμώνυμος].

[28] Gerbel 1545, p. 17: "*Ab exortu solis iter ingredientibus, prima omnium Attica occurrit. Quae quamvis in pictura non sit expressa, tamen a studiosis eo loci ubi Athenae positae sunt, grandiusculis literis erit annotanda. Ut enim in orbe terrarum media est Graecia, ita in ipsa Graecia media est Attica: in media Attica, urbium clarissima Athenae.*"

[29] Gerbel 1545, pp. 18–19: "*Fuere in Attica multae preclarae urbes, sed omnium nobilissima Athenae [...] Aristides in Panathenaico scribit, hunc situm, urbis imperium & dignitatem indicare, eamque veluti commune quoddam totius Graeciae ὁρμητήριον extitisse, in quod vicinae urbes bellicis terroribus, aut aliis malis adflictae confugiebant.*"

[30] Auson. *Ordo nob. urb.* 15: "*Nunc et terrigenis partibus memoremus Athenas / Pallados et Consi quondam certaminis arcem, / pacifirae primum cui contigit arbor olivae, / Attica facundae cuius mera gloria linguae, / unde per Ioniae populos et nomen Achaeum / versa Graia manus centum se effudit in urbes.*" On the political uses of autochthony in ancient Athens, cf. Loraux 1996.

[31] Gerbel 1545, p. 21.

George Tolias

Ruins of Ruins (1550–1570)

The mourning for the city's collapse is a commonplace of the age and left traces in the cartographical image of Greece. In the vignettes adorning the maps of the land, we often encounter humanists sitting among the ruins, studying works of art and reading ancient authors, a reminder that Greece belonged to the realm of books and was a region in the Republic of Letters.[32] To see Athens, no one needed to travel, for he would find merely silent ruins. It was preferable to avoid such grief and to turn instead to the ancient authors, as the title page of Abraham Loescher's Latin translation of Pausanias' *Periegesis* (1550) specifically advertises.[33] It made no sense to include Athens in the series of important cities in Europe and the Mediterranean that the learned ought to know and, if possible, to visit. In fact, Athens is absent from the town atlases published in Italy, Germany, and France that were widely circulated in the 16th century. However, the ruins of renowned cities of the past were present in the world's memory, venerated and feared as omens of the mutability of fortune and the uncertainty of the human condition, as Sebastian Münster reminded his readers in the opening chapters of his *Cosmographia universalis*:

> There were once great cities in the world and flourishing, and if you sought them now, you would find but their ruins [...] These testify enough for Troy the great, Alesia in Burgundy, Tyre in Palestine, Corinth in the Peloponnese, Babylon in Shinar, Athens in Attica, and other famous cities, which were deserted a long time ago. And yet, as Strabo writes, man takes pleasure in seeing the places and the ruins where such magnificent cities were located, as we gladly visit the vaults where the bones of the great and excellent personages rest [...] That is how all things go up and down in this world, and there is nothing that is everlasting or stable under the sun and the moon. The kingdoms are turned into provinces, one city rises in honor and wealth, and the other falls. People are transferred from region to region, a flourishing province is spoiled, the other endures some adversity, so many changes, so many defeats and calamities happen in the world that no one could count them, and what is even more miserable, we perish with the world, and deteriorate the same as it [...][34]

First published in German in 1544, Münster's *Cosmographia universalis* is a tool for political, historical, and moral reflection, inspired by Strabo's ethical, cultural, and historical approach. The book was quite influential. It was soon translated into Latin and many vernacular languages and went through dozens of expanded editions until the early decades of the 17th century. The *Cosmographia* standardized the image of the inhabited world as a sequence of political territories, each

---

[32] Among the first allegorical figures encountered in maps of Greece is the mourning figure who adorns the title of the map in the Medici Guardaroba in the Palazzo Vecchio in Florence, a work of Stefano Buonsigniori (1586). We find corresponding hints in Gerardus Mercator's map of the northern regions of Greece (1589), in which a skull crowns the map's title. The atlas of the Aegean by Olfert Dapper (1688) and Pieter van der Aa's atlas of 1728 both present scenes from the destruction of Troy; see Tolias 2007.

[33] Pausanias 1550, title page: "Cease, there is no need, forget the swift keels, / Read Pausanias; what you seek you will bring thence. / Read Pausanias, nor in just one part will you see / Whatever was pre-eminent in the Greek world. / Read Pausanias; the footsteps of primeval praise / Will you discern; thence is primeval honor glimpsed." [*Desine, non opus est, celeres omitte carinas, / Perlege Pausaniam: quod petis, inde feres. / Perlege Pausaniam, nec in una parte uidebis, / Praeclarum Graeco quicquid in orbe fuit. / Perlege Pausaniam, priscae uestigia laudis / Agnosces, priscum cernitur inde decus.*]

[34] Münster 1552, pp. 38–39. The opening lines were inspired by Piccolomini's lament on lost cities; see Schnapp 1993, p. 141. On the meditation on ruins, see Labate 1991; Barbanera 2009; Schnapp 2015.

endowed with its own internal regional divisions, capital, history, and noteworthy men. The two cornerstones of this global narrative were Greece and Germany, the two heads of the Eagle of Rome,[35] around which the regions of the world were arranged. The book is organized on the basis of the capital cities and significant urban centers of each country, to all of which large double-page views are dedicated. The description of Greece opens with a large view of Constantinople, the country's capital city, while the relatively extensive description of Athens, compiled after Isidore, Thucydides, Strabo, and Pliny, mentions its actual decay and stresses the city's important position in the ancient Greek world, its literary and scientific achievements, and the prevailing rule of law.[36]

Athens is the ruined capital city of ancient Greece in Antoine du Pinet's *Plantz, pourtraitz et descriptions de plusieurs villes et forteresses*, published in Lyon in 1564, a blend of cosmography and town atlas. Probably inspired by the recent edition of Compagni's geography by Domenico Negri (1557), du Pinet presents the city as the former "head of Greece and of the Morea, but also of numerous foreign nations,"[37] and, paraphrasing Gerbel, he describes the modern city as "a little castle and a small town that are not even safe from foxes and wolves," where "one sees only ruins and the look of a lonely place."[38] Athens also remained a fallen city for André Thevet, the cosmographer to the last kings of the house of Valois.[39] The city, this time together with Sparta, represents the now-blind eyes of Greece.[40] Thevet claimed that he had visited Athens during his tour of the Levant (1549–1551), though he never ventured into continental Greece. He also maintained that he saw a marble statue of Achilles, unearthed long before his visit; he described and reproduced it (Fig. 4) as a preamble to his description of the ruins of Athens:

> Now Athens is in ruins, and beautiful antiquities may still be seen at present, and things that were formerly of great eminence, that still delight and refresh those who contemplate them up close [...] In truth, there are some columns and obelisks, but they are all falling into ruins; as well, some vestiges of numerous schools where (according to the view common among the inhabitants of the place) Plato used to

---

[35] Münster 1552, p. 41: "[...] l'empire de Romme a este transporte en Grece soubz l'empereur Constantin, et puis apres que l'empire nouveau a este institue par Charles maigne en Germanie, et que l'aigle de Romme a eu deux testes [...]"

[36] Münster 1552, pp. 1148–1150: "[...] En Attique a esté la region d'Athènes mere des philosophes & des lettres liberales. Il n'y a rien eu si excellent ne si noble en toute la Grèce. La seulle assiette de ceste ville estoit de grand respect. C'estoit comme une forteresse & refuge commun de toute la Grece, où les villes voisines se retiroient, estant affligees de guerres ou d'autres adversitez. C'a esté aussi une seure retraicte pour les navigeantz. C'a esté l'exercice des lettres, & l'estude universelle de tout le monde. On ne tenoit point un homme pour sçavant, s'il n'avoit estudié en Athenes. Strabon escrit que Athenes a esté un rocher situé en plaine, habité tout a l'environ, auquel il y a eu un temple de Minerve, & en ce temple y avoit une statue que les habitantz croioient estre descendue du ciel, ou le feu estoit perpetuellement entretenu par les vierges qui estoyent dediees a cela [...] Au reste cest belle ville qui a esté si florissante autresfois, de murailles naturelles, de bastimens, d'armes, de richesses, d'hommes, de prudence & toute sagesse, a grand poine [sic] est ce de nostre temps une villette, & se nomme Sethine [...]." The French edition of the *Cosmographia universalis* (1552) is the fullest version published during Münster's lifetime.

[37] du Pinet 1564, p. 230.

[38] du Pinet 1564, p. 230: "[...] Touchant les villes de terre ferme dependentes de ladite Duché y à Enone, & le chasteau de Setiné relique de la grande & tant renommee cité d'Athenes, chef iadis non seulement de toute la Grece & de la Moree, mais aussi de plusieurs nations estranges: ayant d'ailleurs esté Merenourrisse de tous ars & disciplines. Et maintenant ô Dieu, il n'y a de reste qu'un petit chasteau & une bourgade, qui n'est mesmes asseuree des renardz & des loups, ny des autres bestes sauvages. En quoy certes on peut bien voir le Jugement de Dieu, d'avoir mis ceste desolation en lieu tant illustre pour le mespris de sa parolle. Car si onques ville fut bien assise & bien policiee, ceste-cy l'estoit: & neantmoins on n'y voit que ruyne & apparence de lieu desert [...]"

[39] Thevet designated Constantinople as the former capital of the Greeks (Thevet 1554, p. 85: "[...] Quand à la condition des habitans de ladite Grèce, ilz ont tous esté esclaves depuis la prinse de Constantinoble, qui estoit leur ville principale & capitale, faite par Mehemet second de ce nom, Empereur cruel en guerre, & mesme contre son propre sang tirant & inhumain [...]").

[40] Thevet 1554, p. 86: "[...] en tout ce grand & spacieux corps y ha deux penetrans yeux. Que dy-ie, y ha ! mais anciennement furent. O inconstance & mutacion des choses! que ce corps qui ha esté tant celebre, tant noble, & tant lumineux, maintenant soit aveuglé & plein de tenebres!"

lecture, made in the shape of the Roman Colosseum. This city (once so famous and so renowned) is now inhabited by Turks, Greeks, and Jews, who have little attention and respect for such memorable antiques.[41]

Thevet reassured his readers that the city still exists, and that beautiful relics may be seen, to the delight of lovers of antiquities. Nonetheless, the decay of the city is equally apparent in the neglect of its residents, who have little respect for such ruins. Twenty years later, Thevet returned to the collapse of Athens, which he saw as retribution for the depravity of its inhabitants, in his *Cosmographie universelle*, published in 1575.[42] There, he insisted on the presence of a great many

Figure 4. Statue of Achilles found in Athens. André Thevet, *Cosmographie du Levant*, Lyon 1556, p. 94. American School of Classical Studies at Athens, Gennadius Library.

---

[41] Thevet 1554, pp. 90–94: "*Or est Athenes maintenant ruïnée, & y voit ont encores à present belles antiquitez, & choses qui ont esté autrefois de grande excellence, qui encores resiouissent & recreent ceux qui de près les contemplent. Mesme du temps que i'estois en ladite ville, un Chrestien renié me mena dens sa maison pour voir une statue qui n'agueres avoit esté trouvee bien profond déns terre: laquelle estoit de marbre blanc bien poli, de la grandeur d'un enfant de trois ans [...] & avoit à ses piez un escriteau, dens lequel estoit escrit en caracteres Grecs Ἀχιλλῇ φιλτάτῳ, cestadire, à Achilles le tresaymé. Outre cela ie ny ay veu chose qui merita le descrire. Vray est qu'il y ha quelques Colomnes & Obelisques: mais elle tombent toutes en ruïne: aussi quelques apparences de plusieurs collieges, ou (selon la commune opinion des habitans du lieu) Platon lisoit, faits en forme du Colisee Rommain. Or est ceste cité (iadis tant celebre, & tant renommee) habitee des Turqs, Grecs, & Juifs, qui ont peu d'esgard & de reverence à telles memorables antiquailles.*"

anonymous ruins, illegible inscriptions, and spoiled monuments that had lost their names and whose uses had been forgotten. They were "ruins of ruins,"[43] a perception endorsed by the view of the city included in the book, in which Athens is portrayed as a great mass of ruins (Fig. 5):

> Now is that city in ruins, but not so greatly, as some say, that there is no remnant of the memories of its excellence in its destruction. For you can still see this portico, which is made like Rome's Colosseum, where it is held that Plato ran his school.

Figure 5. Antiquities of Athens. Thevet 1575, fol. 795v. Paris, Bibliothèque de l'Arsenal, FOL-H-78 (2).

[42] Thevet 1554, p. 93.
[43] "Ruines, ruine de ruines," as Benjamin Péret put it (Péret 1939), quoted by Alain Schnapp (2015, p. 169).

Which I quite easily believe, having seen the marbles that are about, with the inscriptions of all those who had them set up, almost invisible, whether because the barbarians have scraped them off, or because this has been done by the assaults of time. And together with all this is still a quantity of columns and obelisks, into which Greek letters have been driven that one cannot read from a distance because the greatest part of them has been obliterated. Still visible are a great number of houses and colosseums, arches, capitals, cavernous underground places which today serve only as a refuge for owls, tawny and common. The plan, following my observations, is just as I am representing to you. The place is not so depopulated that one does not find quite a large number of Greeks, and a *caravanserai*, and a Turkish officer who is in command of the entire region of Athens. Both in the city and in the neighboring localities more than a hundred Greek churches are still to be found, which should make us think that it is a great shame that this city has been so ruined, seeing the order, the beauty, and the magnificence which once existed in it.[44]

Standardization of Athens as the Ancient Capital of Greece (End of the 16th Century – Beginning of the 17th)

The 16th century ended with a milestone in the history of geography—the publication of the first atlas in the modern sense of the term, Abraham Ortelius's *Theatrum orbis terrarum*. Initially published in Antwerp by Christoph Plantin in 1570, the *Theatrum* was frequently enlarged through the edition of supplements up to Ortelius's death in 1598. Ortelius's atlas represented the culmination of a long chain of conceptual adjustments in Humanism's spatial awareness, the final conversion of the world's ethnocultural regions into a series of political territories. Once again, the enterprise to integrate Greece into this global pattern was not easy. Well aware of the particularities of Hellenism, and of the divergence between the ancient and the modern state of the country, Ortelius included two maps of Greece in the *Theatrum*, reproducing Sophianos's antiquarian map of 1540 for the extensive ancient Greece, and the map drawn by the Venetian cosmographer Giacomo Gastaldi (ca. 1560) for modern Greece, which followed Münster's definition and was limited to the provinces included in Ptolemy's *Tabula Europae X*. He later enhanced these two versions of Greece with maps detailing the diffusion of Hellenism, such as Greek colonial expansion in Magna Graecia and the Black Sea, but also with maps displaying the journeys of the Argonauts, Ulysses, and Pytheas, and of Alexander's expeditions.

Ortelius's maps were provided with succinct geographical descriptions summing up the available information on each area. No mention of Athens is made in the description of the map of modern Greece, which is depicted as a crushed and torn country, subjugated to foreign rules.[45] In his description of Sophianos's map of Greece, Ortelius stressed the fluidity of the definitions of the country and, with

---

[44] Thevet 1575, vol. 2, leaf 795v. Thevet had access to first-hand accounts, and the identification of the Odeon of Herodes Atticus (the "portico") with Plato's Academy was part of the local tradition in 16th-century Athens.

[45] Ortelius 1598, fol. 92r (a French edition of the *Theatrum*, the last to be supervised by the author): "*Le pays de Grèce. Qui par la lecture des histoires anciennes a peu cognoistre de quelle façon ce pays a fleury iadis en tous arts et sciences, et de quelle estendue a esté son gouvernement, celuy là voit tout ainsi en mirouër les effects de l'inconstante Fortune. Car au lieu qu'alors ilz auoyent domination par dessus autres Nations et pays, il est maintenant rendu esclave soubs le ioug du Turcq, (qui s'en est saisi) ou sous la servitude des Venitiens, qui en tiennent quelques isles situées és environs.*"

his usual subtlety, alluded not only to the central place of Athens, but also to the city's key function in establishing the origins and the fundamental designation of Greece:

> The ancient country of Greece. What the Latins have called Graecia, the Greeks name Hellas, but its borders and frontiers are described by several writers in different ways. The principal and true Greece is the one that Ptolemy, Pliny, and Mela call Attica, in which the city of Athens is located. It is a free city, as Pliny calls it, and needs no further recommendation, so noble and renowned is it. It appears, however, that not only modern authors, but also Strabo himself, the prince of geographers, are of the opinion that under the name of Greece or Hellas many other regions are encompassed, such as Macedonia, Epirus, the Peloponnese, and other provinces contained under this name [...][46]

Strabo's assertion of the versatility of the terms "Greece"/"Hellas," "Greeks"/"Hellenes," and "Panhellenes" had already attracted the attention of other geographers.[47] As mentioned above, in 1509 Compagni had noticed the expanding character of the "national" designation, first given to Attica and gradually encompassing other regions, such as the Peloponnese, Epirus, Macedonia, and the Aegean islands; in 1540, Sophianos defined Greece as extending from Calabria and the entire Balkan peninsula to western Asia Minor, with Athens as its principal city; and in 1564, du Pinet had also alluded to the power of Athens, extending over Greece and the Morea, as well as many foreign nations. Ortelius authenticated this understanding of Athens as the cornerstone in the origins and the foundation of Greece, a notion that was further elaborated by Giovanni Antonio Magini in 1598. In his ancient and modern geography, an influential work comprising an updated edition of Ptolemy's *Geographia* and supplemented by a volume containing modern geographical descriptions, Magini considered Athens as the cradle of an ever-expanding Greek Empire. In line with Compagni, Magini understood Strabo's stoic geographical vision of Hellenism as a progressive expansion of Greece.[48] He described the shifting of the term "Greece" as a progressive growth of the country, from its origins in the area of Attica and the city of Athens to a wide territorial extent, steadily integrating the adjacent provinces: first Achaia, the Peloponnese, Thessaly, Epirus, and Macedonia, then Thrace, and then western Asia Minor and also southern Italy.[49] As for the actual condition of the city of Athens, Magini subscribed to Piccolomini's and Gerbel's image of desolation, as did Ortelius in his geographical dictionary, the *Thesaurus geographicus*.[50]

---

[46] Ortelius 1598, fol. 119r: "*L'ancien pays de la Grèce. Ce que les Latins ont dit Graecia, les Grecz le nomment Hellas, mais les termes et frontiers de cette region sont descrites de plusieurs en diverses sortes. La principale et vraye Grece est celle laquell Ptolemée, Pline, et Mela appellant Attica, en laquelle est la ville d'Athènes, ville libre comme l'appelle Pline, et n'a besoin d'autre louenge, tan test elle noble et renommée. Il appert toutefoys que non seulement les auteurs vulgaires, mais aussi Strabo le Prince des Geographes sont d'avis, que sous le nom Hellas ou Graecia plusieurs autres regions sont comprises: comme Macedoine, Epire, Peloponnese, et autre provinces continues sous icelles. De sorte que tout le pays de Grèce est assailli de troys mers, à scavoir de la mer Ionique, de la mer Aegée et de la mer Libyque [...]*"

[47] Strabo 8.6.6. Cf. Dandrow 2017, p. 117.

[48] On Strabo's stoicism, see Hatzimichali 2017.

[49] Magini 1598, p. 106r: "*Il nome della GRECIA usurpasi diversamente presso gli Scrittori, percioche prima, propria e vera Grecia è da Tolomeo, e de Plinio chiamata quella Provincia, che ATTICA si nomina, in cui è la famosissima città d'Atene; poi, sotto cotal nome largamente, e per commune vocabolo, cadono quattro Provincie, la Macedonia, l'Epiro, l'Acaia, il Peloponnesso, e l'altre regioni, che sono in esse comprese; terzo l'Isole del Mar Ionio, e dell'Egeo. Ultimamente, può anco il nome della Grecia prendersi larghissimamente, si come abraccia la Tracia, e la non minima portione dell'Asia, già, senza le dette Provincie, posseduta da' Greci, nellaquqle mandarono le loro colonie; e di più, quella parte dell'Italia, dianzi addimandata Magna Grecia, ma hora Calabria Superiore.*"

[50] Magini 1598, p. 122r; Ortelius 1596, "AT–AT", n.p.: "*ATHENAE, ἀθῆναι, Graeciae nobilissima urbs, & omnis eruditionis fons. Splendidissimam urbem omnium quibus illucet Jupiter, vocat Athenaeus. Idem & Graeciae Museum. Nunc tantùm casulae supersunt quaedam. Locus Satine hodie dicitur, Sophiano & Favolio testibus, Sethine est in itinerario Scepperi M.S. ASTY ἄστυ, per excellentiam, & eius incolae ASTI ἀστοί, & ASTICI ἀστικοί, dicti fuere, ut Stephanus tradit.*"

By the end of the 16th century, Greece was recognized as a country of Antiquity, with Athens as its capital city. In the years to follow, geography passed the torch to historiography, and several essays on the ancient city's history and institutions were produced. One of the most prolific and influential authors on Athens was the Dutch classical scholar and antiquarian Johannes Meursius, professor of Greek language and history at Leiden University and historiographer of the Republic of the Seven United Provinces and then to the king of Sweden. Among his many works dedicated to Athens, mention should be made of his *Fortuna Attica*, published in 1622, a historical essay that summarizes in 114 pages in quarto the rise, grandeur, decline, and fall of Athens from its mythical origins to the end of the 16th century. Meursius also compiled two books dedicated to Athenian monumental topography: the *Cecropia*, a small volume of 93 pages also published in 1622, describing the monuments of the Acropolis, and its sequel published in 1624, *Athenae Atticae sive de praecipuis Athenarum antiquitatibus libri III*, an extensive description of the monuments of Athens in 200 pages in octavo. Meursius's principal source in both works was Pausanias, supplemented with information gathered from extensive readings, especially of Athenaeus, Hesychius, Plutarch, Pliny, Thucydides, and the so-called Suidas.

Meursius focused on the history and functions of each monument he described and did not venture on to ambitious appreciations of the city's standing in the foundation of Greece's ethnocultural identity. He presented his work as an attempt to restore the city,[51] while in his preface he meditated on the downfall of Athens' mighty power. He considered the city as utterly extinct and, quoting Synesius of Cyrene, he compared its ruins to the decomposed skin and bones of a carcass.[52]

From High to Low Culture: Athens in Geography Textbooks (1590–1660)

Geography became part of the curriculum towards the end of the 16th century. This occurred first in Reformed Germany thanks to Melanchthon's educational reorganization adopted in the Protestant countries. An early German geography textbook was compiled by the Greek scholar Michael Neander [Neumann], a disciple of Melanchthon and prolific author of teaching manuals who served as teacher

---

[50] Magini 1598, p. 122r; Ortelius 1596, "AT–AT", n.p.: "*ATHENAE, ἀθῆναι, Graeciae nobilissima urbs, & omnis eruditionis fons. Splendidissimam urbem omnium quibus illucet Jupiter, vocat Athenaeus. Idem & Graeciae Museum. Nunc tantùm casulae supersunt quaedam. Locus Satine hodie dicitur, Sophiano & Favolio testibus, Sethine est in itinerario Scepperi M.S. ASTY ἄστυ, per excellentiam, & eius incolae ASTI ἀστοί, & ASTICI ἀστικοί, dicti fuere, ut Stephanus tradit.*"

[51] Meursius 1624, p. 3: "*Equidem induxi animum, denuo illustrare urbem, et collapsam tot jam annos, ex auctorum monumentis, quantum stylo fieri potest, instaurare.*"

[52] Meursius 1624, epistola: "*Qui incerta rerum humanrum volet contemplari, viri amplissimi, ac prudentissimi, is Athenas mihi videat; illas olim tam ingentes, ut ducenta ferem stadia in circuitu continerent: tam potentes, ut sibi ipsos quoque reges tributarios haberent: tam illustres, ut splendore, gloriaque, plurimas rerumque superarent, ipsae a nullam vincentur: at nunc ita imminuta est magnitudo, ut consupti animalis ossa, ac pellis, quod Synesius olim eleganter dixit, tantum esse videatur: et potentia, adeo illis nulla restat, ut miserrimam contra servitutem serviant, sub Turcarum imperio sitae: gloriae, item par fortuna est; et vix nomen nunc sciretur, nisi historia id serasset. Ego, seu reliques quasdam in ciners redacti corporis, quae legendo apud auctores singularia quodam in urbe observavi, in volumen hoc colligere animum induxi; ut sic quasi instaurarem urbem, indignam, quae tam miserem intercideret. Huic operi cum patronos circumspicerem, quibus rectem dedicarem, vos inprimis occurristis; qui, ut benem erga humaniiores literas animati ipsi estis, ita earum dignitatem, quantum in vobis perbenignem defendandam existimatis. Atque ut publica ista causa, sic privata quaedam mea est. Ego, qui in territorio vestro natus, et educatus, prima quoque literarum tyrocinia quadriennium in gymnasio vestro feci, monumentum aliquod meae observantiae vobis exhibendum statui. Itaque nunc hoc tenere; et me, civem, non indignum quem ametis, quasque offero Athenas, ut benignem complectamini, pro humanitate vestram singulari, etiam atque etiam rogo. Lugduni Batavorum, ad diem IV Octobris 1624.*" The reference to Synesius of Cyrene is from a letter to his brother (Letter 136). Synesius visited Athens at the beginning of the 5th century, after the Visigoths under Alaricus had devastated the city. However, his remark refers more to the state of the teaching of philosophy in Athens than to the condition of the city. See Cameron and Long 1993, pp. 409–410.

and rector for 45 consecutive years of the trilingual (Greek, Latin, and Hebrew) gymnasium in Ilfeld (Thuringia).[53] It is the *Orbis terrarum divisio compendiaria*, first published in Eisleben in 1583, a textbook that went through several enlarged editions, published in Leipzig until the end of the century.[54]

Neander's description of Greece is extensive.[55] The country is presented with an internal regional arrangement that comprises Thrace, Macedonia, Thessaly, Epirus, Magna Graecia, and *vera* or *propria Graecia*. Constantinople is presented in the opening of the narrative as the first city of Thrace, and its brief description focuses on the preaching of the Church Father St. John Chrysostom, Archbishop of Constantinople. Athens is the principal city of *vera Graecia*, which includes the regions of "Hellada" and the "Peloponnesus." The notion of "true Greece," already present in the *Etymologies* of Isidore as an alternative for "proper Greece,"[56] is understood by Neander as founded on the purity of Athens' language, its political power, and dynamism, promoted as the hub from which many ancient colonies sprang.[57] Quoting a multitude of ancient authors, Greek and Latin (Pomponius Mela, Euripides, Thucydides, Diodorus of Sicily, Strabo, Aelius Aristides, Demosthenes, Cicero, Plutarch, and Ovid), he described the ancient city as the core of the Greek world and followed its history up to its present decay. Referring to Martin Crusius's recently published *Turcograecia*,[58] Neander presented the modern city as a barbarous Turco–Greek village with a boundary no larger than six German miles, on whose gate could be read, as on a gravestone: "Here lies Athens, once the city of Theseus."[59]

Neander's account reflects the average educated perception of Athens in late 16th-century Protestant Germany and is evidence of the rise of the German obsession with Greece. Neander insisted on Greece's complete demise and presented Germany as its true successor, stressing the achievements of Greek learning in Germany, as attested by the philological works of the numerous German Hellenists, and stating that Athens' "eternal light" had been transplanted to Germany, especially in Neander's own

---

[53] On the teaching of geography in 16th-century Protestant Germany, and especially on Neander, see Chassagnette 2018, ch. 6: "La géographie dans les écoles protestantes du saint empire"; Brown, Kristeller, and Cranz 1992, p. 176.

[54] It is a pedantic and Christianized cosmographic compilation, crammed with Greek and Hebrew quotations, and focuses on the Christian Antiquity of each region. With his Reformed neophyte's enthusiasm, Neander followed the process of each region's evangelization; he quoted extensively from the Church Fathers and determined the geographical location of each place according to its distance from Jerusalem.

[55] It fills 20 folios in 8v° in the last edition published in the author's lifetime (Neander 1589, fols. 121–141).

[56] Isidore *Etym.* 14.4.10: see n. 18 above.

[57] Neander 1589, fol. 127r: "*Sequitur nunc Graecia vera dicta. Superioris namque Graeciae regiones quinque ad Graeciam propriè non pertinebant, quod lingua principio à Graeca diversa uterentur, donec per colonias Graecorum, et commertia cum illis frequentia, ipsa quoque linguam Graecorum discere et illa uti inciperent.*"

[58] In spring 1576, Martin Crusius corresponded with the Greek scholars Symeon Kavasilas and Theodosios Zygomalas, seeking first-hand information about the actual condition of Athens and its monuments. He was delighted to learn that the city and its ancient ruins still existed and published descriptions of them in his *Turcograecia* (Crusius 1584). His reply to Zygomalas mentions the widespread opinion among German scholars that Athens was destroyed, despite Chalkokondyles's testimony of its survival, his description of Mehmed II's visit to Athens, and his admiration for the city's antiquities; Crusius ended by expressing a desire to acquire a faithful image, an eyewitness view of the city, to support his teaching of Thucydides' *History*. Cf. Crusius 1584, p. 446a. Neander borrowed Zygomalas's comments on the corruption of the language in Athens, an irrefutable proof of the demise of the city, from Crusius's *Turcograecia*. Neander returned to the "Scythian" and "semi-barbarous" Greek of contemporary Athenians in his *Chronicon*, a manual of universal history also first published in 1583 and reissued with substantial additions three years later. In this work he recalled the ancient oracle that prophesied the city's destruction and quoted Melanchthon's portrait of Mehmed II as the destroyer of Athens. See Neander 1583, fol. 133r, fol. 121r, fol. 143 (*Nullae Musae in Helicone hodie*); Neander 1586, fol. 162r. For Neander's *Chronicon*, cf. Bodnar 1960; Ben-Tov 2013.

[59] Neander 1589, fols. 132r–133v: "*Urbs Athenae quae abfuisse produntur Hierosolymis spatio milliarium Germanicorum 182. Pomponio libro 2. clariores quam ut indicari egeant. Euripidi apud Athenaeum Ἑλλάδος Ἑλλὰς, Graeciae Graecia, seu compendium Graeciae. Thucydidi πόλις πρώτη ἐν τοῖς ἕλλησι, καὶ παίδευσις schola Ἑλλάδος. Et Diodoro Siculo κοινόν πάντων ἀνθρώπων παιδευτήριον. Communis Schola generis humani. Straboni σόφων οἰκητήριον. Aristidae Adrianaeo σοφίας πρυτανῦον. Demostheni ψυχὴ καὶ ἥλιος, καὶ ὀφθαλμὸς Ἑλλάδος. Valde praedicat illam urbem Cicero oratione pro L. Flacco. Inde, inquit, humanitas, doctrina, religio, fruges, iura, leges ortae atque in omnes terras distributae putantur. Ac lib. 2 de legibus. Unde non solum cum laeticia vivendi rationem accipimus, sed etiam cum spe meliore vivendi. In Dialogo vero de partitione oratoria,*

college (where "it shines with no interruption").[60] He discussed the similarities between the two languages and gave a list of German words that derive directly from Greek rather than being later loans through Latin, and he went as far as to grant Greek origins to some German towns, such as Kraichgau in Baden-Württemberg or Speyer in Rhineland-Palatinate. The identification of Germany with ancient Greece is also implicitly made in the opening lines of his description of Greece, where he reminded his students that Greece (and also Germany) was originally a barbarous land: according to Strabo, "σύμπασα κατοικία βαρβάρων τὸ παλαιὸν fuerit."

Neander's teaching manual was widely circulated, and excerpts from it were quoted (though not accredited) in the pedagogical handbooks that followed. For reasons of clarity, subsequent schoolbooks abandoned Neander's pedantic erudition and adopted a simplified scheme in order to present the past and present conditions of each country. This was achieved through the publication of historical school atlases and the compilation of comparative geography textbooks. Indeed, comparative geography was applied as the method *par excellence* for teaching geography. Magini's 1598 ancient and modern geography provided an early scholarly model for this. It was adopted by Philipp Cluver in his handbook of comparative geography, published posthumously in 1624.[61] The comparative approach was further elaborated in *Parallela geographiae veteris et novae*, a three-volume handbook compiled by the Jesuit educator Philippe Briet in 1648–1649.[62]

Briet's work is distinguished by its systematic character and instructional clarity. It is divided into short thematic chapters that recur in each regional description, while the details of ancient and modern geography are summarized in mnemonic diagrams and further simplified in the 144 maps that accompany the texts. The maps are plain and contain a plan of each country's capital in an inset. Through a skillful and deliberate misuse of his sources, the Jesuit pedagogue proposed a definition of ancient Greece as a country that comprises Thrace, Macedonia, Epirus, Achaia, the Peloponnese, and the islands.[63] As clearly summarized in the diagram, Briet's ancient Greece is divided in two parts, the Kingdom of Macedonia and the "True Greece," with Athens and Corinth as chief cities of Achaia and the Peloponnese, respectively. The accompanying text focuses on the city's central location and enumerates its demes and monuments, which are marked on the relevent plan (in an inset). In contrast, modern Greece is identified with imperial Byzantium and its Ottoman successors. It is given the names

---

omnium doctrinarum inventrices nuncupat. Et lib. 4. Epistolarum familiarum nobilissimum orbis terrarum gymnasium cognominat. Nihilominus tamen de Athenis tantopere praedicatis, Plutarcho teste dici solebat: πάντα καλὰ παρὰ τοῖς Ἀθηναίοις, quasi ibi prorsus nullum esset studium honestatis, et virtutis. [...] Tametsi autem Ovid. sua etiam aetate scripserit : Quid Pandioniae restant nisi nomen Athenae : Tamen contra multorum magnorum virorum non veras narrationes annis superioribus scribitur a Graecis Christianis, e Graecia Turcica nunc et barbara ad Martinum Crusium professorem linguarum et eloquentiae in Academia Tubingensi celeberrimum, amicum nostrum optimum et veterem, Athenas etiamnum frequentissime habitari a variis gentibus Christianis etiam, iisque non parvo numero, et complecti in ambitu sex milliaria Germanica, quarum portis etiam hodie praescriptum legatur hoc Monostichon.—Αἱ δ᾿εἰσ᾿Ἀθῆναι, Θησέως ἡ πρὶν πόλις."

[60] Neander 1589, fol. 133v: "Strabo lib. 9. qui totus occupatus est in laude Athenarum, Athenis in templo fuisse λύχνον ἄσβεστον, id est, aeternum ignem, Lampadem perpertuam [sic], quae nunquam exstingueretur, cum Parthenone id est, coetu virginum, sive Vestalium, quae illum ignem servarent, et perpetuum custodirent. Talis lux aeterna etiam olim conservata fuit, in collegio Ilfeldensi non parvis sumptibus, die noctuque sine intermissione lucens."
[61] Cluver's work identifies Greece with Illyricum and the Eastern Roman Empire, and Athens is highlighted as the most significant of the cities of ancient Greece, while Thessaloniki, Dyrrachium [Durazzo], and Croia [Krujë] received mention as noteworthy cities of modern Greece. Cluverius 1624.
[62] Briet 1648–1649. On Briet's geographical work, see Tolias 2017.
[63] Briet 1649, vol. 3, p. 90: "*De Graecia antiqua. Regionem describemus hoc libro viribus, et dignitate orbis terrarium principem, inquit ex Trogo Iustinus lib. 8 quae hoc versu reddit Manilius, Maxima terra viris, et foecundissima doctis urbibus. Ex quam, ait Plinius, omnis litteratum claritas essulsit: ideomque non leviter videtur attingenda. Porri totum hunc ingentem tractum uno Graeciae nomine appellavimus: quoniam Aristoteles I. Meteorum

Nova Graecia, Rumelia, and *Europa inferior,*[64] and Constantinople, to which a topographical drawing is devoted as an insert on the map of Thrace, is recognized as its capital. Modern Athens, however, is described as a noteworthy settlement with a castle, in which many vestiges of Antiquity are still present.[65]

The consecration of ancient Greece as a sovereign country with Athens as its metropolitan center was enhanced by the first atlas of ancient Greece, Johannes Lauremberg's *Graecia antiqua.* This was the second work on geography to be dedicated exclusively to Greece since Gerbel's introduction to Sophianos's map. The work was composed around 1650 and remained unpublished until the death of its author in 1658. The young Samuel Pufendorf found it among Lauremberg's literary remains at Sorø (south-west of Copenhagen) and had it published in Amsterdam in 1660.[66] As in Sophianos's map, Athens is represented as the principal city of the country with a special vignette in Lauremberg's maps, while the city's fortifications are depicted on the map of Attica (Figs. 6-7).

Lauremberg considers Greece originally confined to the region of Attica and the city of Athens. The country gradually extended its power and created colonies throughout the known world, disseminating its laws and virtues: this was the Universal Greece, the *Graecia universa*, as the title of Lauremberg's preface indicates.[67] At once lyrical and pedantic, he presents his atlas as an aerial journey guided by the spirits of Ptolemy and Pausanias, whose regional scheme he followed by beginning his description with the region of Attica and the city of Athens. Lauremberg also adopted Aelius Aristides' image, repeated by Gerbel, and viewed Athens both as the center of Attica, of Greece, and of the world. Referring to Pindar, Thucydides, and Aelius Aristides, he described it as the main city of ancient Greece.[68] However, Greece was no more. It had declined to a state of complete debilitation and mutilation: "Once there was Greece, there was Athens; now, neither in Greece is there an Athens, nor in Greece itself a Greece."[69]

Macedoniam, Epirum, Achaiam, et Peloponnesum Graecia ἀρχαίαν vocat, quibus et in Politicis adiungit Cretam. Posterioribus autem temporibus in Thraciam Constantinopolis condita, Thraciam quoque adiuxxit Graeciae. Nos autem methodi gratiam hanc Regionem in duas partes distribuemus, Macedonicum Regnum, et Graeciam Veram, quae huic libro materiam sufficient; et Graeciam recentiorem, que libro sequenti." Aristotle's mention of "ancient Greece" in the *Meteorologica* refers solely to the area of Epirus, "the country about Dodona and the Achelous," where "the Selli dwelt and those who were formerly called Graeci and now Hellenes;" the inclusion of Crete in the Greek regions is deduced by Aristotle's comparison of the Cretan and the Spartan political systems in his *Politics.* Trogus confined Greece solely to Achaia and the Peloponnese, while Marcus Manilius's "most noble part of the world, fertile in heroes and learned cities" (*Astronomicon* 4.684) refers to Europe and not to Greece.

[64] Briet 1648–1649, p. 450: "*DE NOVA GRAECIA* [...] *RUMELIA dicitur à Turcis, quasi Romania, vel potius RUM-URLAGET* [...] *In titulis Imperatoris Turcici Graecia cum Hungariae regno dici videntur uno nomine EUROPA INFERIOR, itémque Imperium Orientale, seu Novae Romae, ex quo Ottomani Constantinopoli, & Graeciâ potiti, urbem illam Imperii sui sedem constituere.*"

[65] Briet 1648–1649, p. 476: "*SETINES: Athenae, urbs seu burgus iam amplissimus, cum castro in colle ubi soli Turcae degunt, in reliquis partibus Turcae Graecis permixti viuunt: in eô burgo multa ostenduntur vestigia antiquitatis, ut Areopagi, Academiae, &c. Capta fuit à Mahumeto anno Christi 1455.*"

[66] Lauremberg 1660. Lauremberg's lexicon of obsolete words should be mentioned among his other works on Classical Antiquity (Lauremberg 1622).

[67] Lauremberg 1660, p. 3: "*Graecia sanem saepe nomen suum immutans certissimum dare videbatur praesagium immutandae potentiae, et imperii ad finem tendentis, quae antem ex minima gente in tam amplum accrevit numerum, tantamque multitudinem, ut cum proprii regni finibus et terminis comprehendi non posset, in totum terrarum orbem dissiparentur, multasque urbes conterent legibus et praeclaris institutis instructas. In Italiam enim Graeci coloniam deducentes, utrusque occuparunt littus, et oppida Crotonem, Brundusium, Tarentum, et Locros extruxerunt. In Gallia itidem Phocaeorum colonia est Marsilia. In Lybia Duce Batto Cyrenem considerunt. Athenienses indigenis aucti divitiis, Peloponnesum rerum et fortunam suarum sedem ceperunt: eamque terram primum Aigialiam vocatam, Ioniam appellentur. At Heraclidae cum istuc descendissent, eorum socii Achaei Athenienses ejecerunt; qui Duce Androclo in Asiam commigranrunt.*"

[68] Lauremberg 1660, p. 20: "*ATTICA. Medium mundi locum obtinet Graecia, medium Graeciae Attica, medium Atticae omnium urbium urbs illustrissima Athenae* [...] *Opimae & gloriosae inclytae Athenae Graeciae propugnaculum, inquit Pindarus; cui propterea à Thebanis gravissima fuit multa irrogata. Verùm Athenienses hanc pro Pindaro multam exsolverunt. Inter Sunium & Eleusinem sitae sunt Athenae, totius Graeciae receptaculum, insularum choro redimitae, brachium protendentes accedentibus, in Phalerum portum eos excepturae* [...]"

[69] Lauremberg 1660, p. 1: "[...] *haec in extremam imbecillitatem et infirmitatem redacta, et a fato membratim lacerate, pristinum imperiul amisit* [...]," and p. xiv (*Introductoria dissertatio*, p. 5): "*Fuit quondam Graecia, fuerunt Athenae: nunc neque in Graecia Athenae, neque in ipsa Graecia, Graecia est.*"

Figure 6. Johannes Lauremberg, "Achaia quae et Hellas" [Achaia which is Hellas]. Lauremberg 1660. American School of Classical Studies at Athens, Gennadius Library.

Figure 7. Johannes Lauremberg, "Attica." Lauremberg 1660. American School of Classical Studies at Athens, Gennadius Library.

Impact and Closing Remarks

The works of humanist geography published between the late 15th century and the early 17th familiarized the early modern educated elite with the image of Greece as an antique sovereign state, with Athens as its principal city. Editions of cosmographies and the atlas of Ortelius all enjoyed extraordinary publishing success. Sophianos's map went through dozens of editions up to the beginning of the 18th century; the introduction of Gerbel that accompanied the map, which had been re-edited and enlarged in 1550, was included in volume 4 of Jakob Gronovius's *Thesaurus Graecarum antiquitatum* (1699) together with Lauremberg's atlas of ancient Greece and the Greek works by Meursius. Roberto Weiss noted that Meursius's description of the monuments of Athens remained the indispensable guide of every cultivated traveler to Athens for over a century.[70] Likewise, Cluverius's introduction to universal comparative geography went through dozens of editions, many of them enhanced with maps; successive generations of students at the Jesuit colleges learned about the world through this teaching handbook, as François de Dainville observed.[71] The *Parallela geographiae* of Briet, despite appearing in one sole edition, also reached a large audience. So many French libraries own a copy of this work that Mireille Pastoureau regarded it as the most widely circulated atlas in 17th-century France.[72] Lauremberg's atlas of ancient Greece was widely disseminated not only through its inclusion in the lavish Dutch atlases published by Johannes Janssonius,[73] but also as a teaching handbook, in cheaper, smaller-format editions addressed to a clientele of students; it was frequently reprinted in Leiden and Amsterdam until the mid-18th century.

These works, with the powerful cartographic images they often contained, endowed ancient Greece with a sovereign territorial status, imprinting that notion in the memories of generations of students. It should therefore not come as a surprise that the fresh, first-hand descriptions of Athens and its monuments were produced not by scholars, but by clerics educated at Jesuit colleges. Indeed, it was an itinerant French Jesuit father, Jacques-Paul Babin, who visited and described the city as the ancient capital of Greece; and the French Capuchin missionaries established in Athens were the ones to conduct empirical topographical surveys of the Athenian monuments, the first based on in situ observations, two centuries after Cyriac of Ancona.

Babin's book was published in 1674 in Lyon by the antiquarian scholar Jacob Spon, with the title *Relation de l'état présent de la ville d'Athènes, ancienne capitale de la Grèce, bâtie depuis 3400 ans. Avec un abrégé de son Histoire et de ses Antiquités*.[74] This work, together with the topographical plan of Athens made by the Capuchins, most probably a collective work from around the same time, inaugurated the study of the topography of Athens and its monuments and opened the way to the 18th-century wave of antiquarian explorers. In representing the city, the Capuchins' plan emphasizes the presence of the ancient material remains. The ruins of Athens are the main subject of the survey, while the urban fabric of the modern city fades around them like a watermark (Fig. 8).[75]

---

[70] Weiss 1969, p. 131.
[71] Dainville [1940] 1969, p. 181. Van der Heijden (2002) calculated that Cluverius's work appeared in over 60 re-editions.
[72] Pastoureau 1984, p. 90.
[73] See Zacharakis 2009, no. 1906/1277.
[74] Babin 1674.
[75] Laborde discovered and published a document in the Bibliothèque nationale de France (1854a, vol. 1, pp. 78–80) entitled "Explication de la nouvelle Athènes." It contains a list of 17 locations marked on the map, 14 of which were ruins of monuments.

Figure 8. Plan of Athens drawn by the French Capuchin monks in Athens ca. 1670, after a manuscript preserved in the Bibliothèque nationale de France (Département des manuscrits, supplément français, 19). Laborde 1854a. American School of Classical Studies at Athens, Gennadius Library.

✳✳✳

This survey of the place of Athens in the humanists' construct of ancient Greece reveals that the early modern geographical conceptions of the sovereign state extended their scope to the past[76] and that the rediscovery of Athens during the Enlightenment had deep roots. Between the late 15th century and the late 17th, humanists regarded Athens as the capital of a Greece long-lost in the past. It was a ruined city, and this constituted its very identity.

    The ruins of Athens were silent. Archaeology was taking its first steps, and doubts were expressed about grasping the past by studying the remains of its monuments. Among the skeptics of the day, let us recall Michel de Montaigne's reticence in front of the ruins of Rome:

---

[76] See n. 6 above.

> We can see nothing more of Rome than the sky under which it lay, the area, and the diagram of its site. All the knowledge we possess thereof is of an abstract and contemplative nature, in no way submitted to the senses. Those who affirm that they might at least behold the ruins of Rome, affirm too much. The ruins of a mechanism of such terrible power should suggest more reverence and respect to its memory. What we see is naught but a grave.[77]

The materials for the recovery of the ancient city lay thus not in its remote and silent ruins, but in the ancient texts; the written word was the domain of exploration, the ancient texts and their commentaries the main resource, philology the sole means of investigation. In their effort to extract from the ancient sources testimonies on the central position of Athens in shaping the origins and the definition of Greece, humanist geographers turned to ancient geographical descriptions, especially Pliny, Strabo, Pomponius Mela, Ptolemy, and Pausanias, all authors of the Roman imperial era, and enhanced their findings with material extracted from Greek, Roman, and Late Antique authors, such as Pindar, Euripides, Thucydides, Cicero, Aelius Aristides, Ausonius, and Isidore of Seville. They borrowed from Pliny and Isidore the Athenian etymology of the geographical term "Greece," which they understood as the founding myth of the country; from Strabo, notions on the process of Hellenization, which they understood as the gradual expansion of Greece; and from Ptolemy, the list of provinces forming Roman Achaia, which they understood as representing Greece's provincial structure. They combined these elements with excerpts from rhetorical or poetic tributes to Athens, extracted from classical authors, but mainly from authors of the Second Sophistic, especially Aelius Aristides, whose Athenocentrism served their purpose well. Their eclectic compilations intermingled successive layers of meaning, merging reminiscences of the city's classical potency, Roman philhellenic nostalgia, notions of early modern universalism, and the modern idea of an antique sovereign state.

The gradual recognition of Athens as a metropolis or national center of the ancient Greek world testifies to the transition from the ethnocultural notion of Hellenism to the historical spatial concept of Greece. By adopting a perspective based on modern criteria, the humanists defined ancient Greece as a state and Athens as its metropolitan center. The territorialization of Hellenism was a precarious undertaking, however, since the notion of Greece and of Hellenism did not have the same weight in their meaning. It is not always clear to which of the two our sources were referring when proposing descriptions of Greece. Furthermore, within this general scheme, we can detect variations that can be charted according to the cultural areas of Humanism and the value attributed to Greece and Greek studies. The Italian and French perspectives inclined toward a resilience of Hellenism, and therefore of Greece, in the Eastern Roman Empire and beyond, as did Nikolaos Sophianos, while the Reformed German perspective advocated the utter collapse of Greece and claimed Hellenism as Germany's heritage.

In either case, the venture appears as a convoluted process of modernization and antiquation, through which Athens was retrieved as a relic of the past. The plethora of early modern descriptions of the ancient city contrasts to the scarcity of its visual representations. This appears as a stance at once intentional and emblematic. Athens was not an eternal city like Rome, nor holy like Jerusalem, nor was it a city with successive changes of power and culture like Constantinople. It belonged to a

---

[77] January 26, 1581. Rat and Thibaudet 1962, p. 1212. Peiresc also favored the study of antique objects over the study of ruins. See Schnapp 1993, p. 165.

deeper layer of history, on the foundations of which the Christianized Roman world was erected. It was a cultural remnant and a historical fossil, ravaged by the Turks like a second Troy. The more forcefully the significance of the ancient city was stressed, the stronger the image of its present-day desolation became. Thence, the exaggeration of the injurious barbarism of the Turks, an argument which also served well the political agenda of the day: after its erosion over many centuries, the enemy had brought upon Athens the decisive finishing blow.

Reconsidering Documents about Athens under Ottoman Rule: The Vienna Anonymous and the Bassano Drawing*

Tasos Tanoulas

Since time immemorial, some people have felt that they could afford to leave their homes, not for war or material gain, but for the sake of learning about other places and different cultures.[1] Athens is one of the locations that, already in Antiquity, had become a popular destination for travelers. They visited the city for its celebrated monuments and for the education cultivated in its famous schools of philosophy.[2]

The material vestiges of Athens' ancient magnificence continued to attract visitors even after the end of Antiquity, when the city had shrunk in size and political significance. They often reported their experiences in writings and drawings—documents rich in information that, if used cautiously, allow us to restore, albeit very fragmentarily, the condition of Athens and its monuments at the time of their visits. A few additional documents that refer to the monuments of Athens, almost all of them anonymous, are thought to have been written by local people, addressed to other locals or visitors.

In order to avoid misinterpreting the data, these documents have to be studied systematically in combination with other relevant documents that may be contemporary or of earlier or later date; archaeological data must also be taken into account in this process. In my studies of the history of the Propylaea and the western end of the Athenian Acropolis from Late Antiquity to the present day, I took virtually all of the existing evidence from written sources and drawings (dating from 1385 to the late 19th century) into account in relation to the archaeological evidence, published and archival, and closely examined the traces that survive in situ.[3] The present study draws on material from my earlier research pertaining to Athens in the medieval and the Ottoman periods. It focuses on two separate documents of the Ottoman period, a written account and a drawing, re-evaluating the information they provide for the topography of the Acropolis and highlighting the methodological care necessary to interpret the data correctly.

---

* To the memory of my dear friend, Luigi Beschi, "... *miglior fabbro* ..."
[1] Casson [1974] 1994; Starkey and El Daly 2000.
[2] Watts 2006, pp. 24–142; Kaldellis 2009, pp. 19–22.
[3] Tanoulas 1987, 1997a, 1997b, 2005, 2011, 2012.

Interpreting the Data

The main problems of interpretation arise from the fact that Athens emerged into the modern world enveloped in the aura of a legend that had been woven in the Middle Ages.[4] During a period of more than a millennium, the city was modified in complex ways that created a composite image with surprising and often confusing manifestations. Parallel transitions transformed the city's social structure and institutions, as well as the spatial distribution of the population throughout the long span of the Roman Empire in its prime.[5]

The form and content of the cosmopolitan cities of the Greco-Roman world changed radically. Even in cities such as Athens, which never experienced any interruption of habitation, public spaces became fragmented, and their original functions disintegrated. In this altered urban landscape, the Classical monuments that survived destruction lost their initial context and were deprived of their original identity. This phenomenon is evident in a mid-18th-century view of Athens depicting the Horologion of Andronikos (the so-called "Tower of the Winds") in a townscape completely irrelevant to the monument (Fig. 1).[6] Forced to coexist with these monuments, the modern inhabitants of ancient

Figure 1. View of the Horologion of Andronikos (the "Tower of the Winds"). Stuart and Revett 1762, ch. 3, pl. 1.

---

[4] Tanoulas 1997b, especially pp. 11–17 and n. 33; Tanoulas 2011; Kaldellis 2009.
[5] Mango 1980, pp. 60–87; Ousterhout 2008, pp. 7–9; Tanoulas 2011.
[6] Stuart and Revett 1762, ch. 3, pl. 1; Travlos 1971, pp. 281–288.

cities viewed them as remnants of an alien past; superstition made it imperative to exorcise these mysteries by explaining the form and reason for their presence among citizens. This procedure was necessary in order to integrate these relics into the everyday life of the community.[7]

Already in Late Antiquity, there seems to have been a conscious effort to interpret the monuments and the actual topography of Athens in a manner that would present an idealized image of the ancient city's glory.[8] This custom continued uninterrupted throughout the Middle Ages, as the writings of Michael Choniates in the 13th century make evident: in order to identify the surviving monuments of Athens, he had to rely on local tradition.[9]

The Vienna Anonymous

Before the Ottomans established their rule in Athens, two visitors left valuable accounts of the city. The first of them was Niccolò da Martoni, a notary from Capua who visited in 1395. His diaries, published at the end of the 19th century, provide valuable information on Athenian topography.[10] The second visitor was the eminent Cyriac of Ancona, who visited Athens twice, in 1436 and 1444. The impact his texts and drawings made on artistic and intellectual life in Italy was significant, not only during his lifetime but also throughout the Quattrocento and the High Renaissance. Many of his accounts have come down to us in copies.[11]

The Ottomans captured the city of Athens in 1456 and the Acropolis in 1458.[12] Dated shortly after the Ottoman conquest, to around 1460, a Greek account by an unknown author entitled Τὰ θέατρα καὶ τὰ διδασκαλεῖα τῶν Ἀθηνῶν [The theatres and the schools of Athens] has been interpreted as a guide addressed to foreign visitors to Athens. Usually referred to as the Vienna Anonymous, it is considered to be the earliest surviving document of its kind from the Ottoman era.[13] In spite of the fact that all surviving manuscripts of this text date to about 1460, the Italian scholar Marco Di Branco has claimed that the text itself should be dated much earlier, to the 11th or 12th century.[14] Based on this suggestion, Antonio Corso goes further, asserting that the text undoubtedly dates to the 11th or 12th century. In the following pages I will demonstrate why this is not the case.

The argument Di Branco used for redating the Vienna Anonymous is based on a section of the document that refers to an official, the duke [δοὺξ]:

> [...] there is a very big and beautiful arch bearing the names of Hadrian and Theseus.
> Inside [...] was a royal residence supported from below by very many columns [...]

---

[7] For an enlightening discussion of the phenomenon, see Dagron 1984, pp. 13–19. On references to Antiquity used by the medieval rhetoric of building and shaping townscapes, see Tanoulas 2004, especially pp. 313–328, with references to previous literature. For more recent bibliography, see especially Saradi 2011 and Kinney 2011.
[8] Pausanias 1; Casson [1974] 1994, pp. 229–237, 262–265, 294–299.
[9] Kaldellis 2009, pp. 178–195, especially pp. 181–184.
[10] Legrand 1895; Judeich 1897; Paton 1951, pp. 30–36. See also Rubio y Lluch 1908, pp. 33–34; Miller 1908, vol. 2, pp. 35–37; Setton [1948] 1975, pp. 227–232; Tanoulas 1997a, vol. 1, pp. 39–40, 42; Tanoulas 2011, pp. 337–341.
[11] Bodnar 1960, 1970; Bodnar and Foss 2003, especially pp. 15–21. See also Gregorovius 1889, especially pp. 336–364; Paton 1951, pp. 174–177; Setton [1948] 1975, pp. 232–235; Colin 1981; Tanoulas 1997a, vol. 1, pp. 40–42; Tanoulas 1997b, passim; Beschi 1998, pp. 89–102.
[12] Tanoulas 1997a 1, pp. 24–25.
[13] Ross 1855; Tanoulas 1997a, vol. 1, pp. 43–44, 58 n. 1, with complete bibliography of the previous publications of the text.
[14] Di Branco 2005, pp. 101–123; Di Branco 2006, pp. 232–239; Corso 2011.

Figure 2. Top: View of the Arch of Hadrian from the north-west, with the columns of the Temple of Olympian Zeus in the background. Between the gate and the columns on the left, the Temple of Artemis Agrotera. Stuart and Revett 1827, ch. 2, pl. 16.
Bottom: View of the Temple of Olympian Zeus as seen from the Temple of Artemis Agrotera by the Ilissos River; to the right, the south-west corner of the temple. Stuart and Revett 1827, ch. 3, pl. 19.

Figure 3. View of the Temple of Artemis Agrotera by the Ilissos River from the south-west. Stuart and Revett 1762, ch. 2, pl. 1.

> To the south is a very beautiful royal residence where the duke went to be amused. The Kallirhoe spring is there and [the duke], after bathing in it, went up to a temple said to be [the temple] of Hera and [there] he prayed. By now this [temple] has been converted by the faithful into a church of the Holy Mother of God.[15]

There is no question that the royal residence behind the gate bearing the names of Hadrian and Theseus was considered to have been standing on the columns of the Temple of Olympian Zeus. The duke would have bathed in the Ilissos River and would have prayed in the little Temple of Artemis Agrotera, which, by the time our document was written, had been turned into a church (Figs. 2–3).[16]

The fact that the duke prayed to a pagan goddess led Di Branco to conclude that the term "duke" should not be connected with the Latin dukes of Athens, as had been suggested by older commentators on the Vienna Anonymous, but to a pagan military commander of the Roman administration. He therefore believes that the text originated in the 11th or 12th century, before the Latins ruled Athens. To explain the clustering of all the surviving manuscript copies of this text around 1460, Di Branco argues that even if the text had been composed then for a particular occasion, as proposed by William Miller,[17] it could not have been composed *ex nihilo*. No one would ever suggest that a text such as the Vienna Anonymous could have been composed *ex nihilo*; compilation from existing sources was common practice in the Middle Ages and, rather than inventing information, the Vienna

---

[15] Di Branco 2005, pp. 114–115; Di Branco 2006, p. 237.
[16] Travlos 1971, pp. 112–120.
[17] Miller (1908, p. 441) suggested that the text was written expressly for the visit of Sultan Mehmed II to Athens in 1458.

Anonymous author would have had recourse to the available written and/or oral tradition(s).[18] In fact, I believe that the author of the new account would have felt obliged to update his sources to make them correspond to the existing material evidence. By necessity, this would bind the new text to the time of its composition.

If we compare all available documents relating to the monuments referred to in this text, various problems arise from Di Branco's proposed redating of the Vienna Anonymous. Dated to about 16 years after Cyriac of Ancona's second visit, the text is absolutely compatible with the information provided by him. On the other hand, the testimony of the Vienna Anonymous is totally incompatible with the state of the Propylaea and its environs before the period of the Latin dukes of Athens (Fig. 4).

The Vienna Anonymous says:

> Upon entering into the Acropolis, we find a small teaching school that was of the musicians; this very one was established by Pythagoras of Samos; on the opposite side is a very big palace and below it numerous [columns] are standing, very rich in white marble, along with the ceiling and the walls; next to the north side were all high administrative offices [καγγελαρία] made of white marble and columns. To the south of this [that is, of the high administrative offices] was the stoa in variegated beauty [ἐν ποικίλῃ ὡραιότητι], gilded all around the inside and on the outside, also adorned with precious stones; it was after this [stoa] that the philosophers who had been educated in it were called Stoics; across from this, the school of the Epicureans was thriving [Figs. 5, 7].[19]

No scholar has ever doubted that the school of the musicians established by Pythagoras should be identified with the Temple of Athena Nike (Figs. 5A, 7A), nor that the palace across from the school is the central building of the Propylaea (Figs. 5B, 6B, 7B), nor that the chancery, that is, the administrative offices, was located in the northern wing of the Propylaea (Figs. 5C, 6C, 7C).[20]

The palace is described as situated above the columns and the marble ceiling of the building of the Classical period; the Vienna Anonymous clearly uses the term "palace" only for the private apartments in the upper story added above the ceilings and entablature by the Acciaiuoli in the first half of the 15th century (Fig. 6B).[21] All evidence supports the view that in the Middle Ages, independently of whether the rulers were Byzantines or Latins, the ground floor of the north wing (including the so-called "Pinakotheke") housed the chancery (Figs. 5C, 6C, 7C). The Vienna Anonymous refers to the administrative offices in the northern wing, using a Byzantine term [καγγελαρία] originating from Latin [cancellaria], in the past tense, which means that they were no longer there.[22] This information corroborates the view that the Vienna Anonymous was written after the Acropolis was ceded to the Ottomans.

The close reading of the Vienna Anonymous in juxtaposition with other relevant accounts provides more evidence for the buildings on the Acropolis at the time of the Ottoman conquest. As I have argued previously, I believe that the stoa in which the Stoics were supposed to have been trained

---

[18] The dependence of documents of this kind on older texts and/or oral tradition is discussed by Dagron (1984, pp. 21–60); Mercati (1964) related the Vienna Anonymous to an older document, but accepted that it should be dated about 1460; Di Branco 2006, pp. 233–234.
[19] Tanoulas 1997a, vol. 1, pp. 43–44; Ross 1855, p. 253.
[20] Tanoulas 1997a, vol. 1, pp. 310–323, vol. 2, drawings 63–73, pp. 311–313. Di Branco (2005, p. 122) also accepts these identifications, whereas Corso (2011, p. 80) avoids dealing with this part of the text.
[21] Tanoulas 1997a, vol. 1, p. 43, p. 58 nn. 3–5.
[22] Tanoulas 1997a, vol. 1, p. 43, p. 58 n. 6.

should not be identified with the Erechtheion, as Ross had suggested (Fig. 7F),[23] nor with the east portico of the Propylaea (Figs. 5E, 6E, 7E), as Wachsmuth believed,[24] but with the spacious west hall of the central building (Figs. 5D, 6D, 7D). According to the Vienna Anonymous, the "stoa" that I identify with the west hall was located immediately to the south of the north wing. Both earlier identifications of the stoa with the east portico (Figs. 5E, 6E, 7E) and the Erechtheion (Fig. 7F) are to the east (not to the south), but are also too distant to have anything to do with what the Anonymous says.

When the Vienna Anonymous author mentions the palace for the first time, he is indisputably referring only to the story added by the Acciaiuoli on top of the central building (Fig. 6B). Although he mentions the marble columns, ceiling, and walls of the Ionic Hall, he does not consider this hall (Figs. 5D, 6D, 7D) as part of the palace. He must have entered it immediately after visiting the north wing (Figs. 5C, 6C, 7C): he focuses on the considerable remains of the original gilding and bright colors that must still have been visible at that time, describing the space as "in variegated beauty [...] gilded all around [...] also adorned with precious stones."

If we read the text of the Vienna Anonymous taking the chancery (that is, the north wing of the Propylaea; Figs. 5C, 6C, 7C)[25] as a common reference point for the topography of the philosophical schools, then we would also identify the school of the Epicureans referred to by the Vienna Anonymous with the south wing of the Propylaea (Figs. 5G, 7G), as I have suggested elsewhere.[26] The stoa of the Stoics is said to be "to the south of this" [κατὰ νότον δὲ ταύτης], while the school of the Epicureans is "across from this" [ἀντικρὺς δὲ ταύτης]. In any case, the school of the Epicureans must be closely related to the stoa of the Stoics, that is, to the Ionic Hall of the central building. The fact that the Vienna Anonymous does not describe any visible features of the school of the Epicureans can be explained by the fact that the south wing of the Propylaea was, by then, covered by the tower built over it during the rule of the Acciaiuoli.[27]

New research into the topography of the Acropolis in the Late Middle Ages has fortunately allowed us to assemble a solid body of information about the history and topography of the Acropolis under Byzantine, Latin, and Ottoman rule. This material has also enabled erroneous identifications of monuments in the area to be corrected. For example, without this new information, Wachsmuth identified the school of the Epicureans with the Erechtheion (Fig. 7F), instead of the south wing of the Propylaea (Figs. 5G, 7G), as being opposite the east portico of the Propylaea (Figs. 5E, 6E, 7E), while Ross suggested the Temple of Rome and Augustus (Fig. 7H) as a possible candidate for the school of the Epicureans, as being located across from the Erechtheion (Fig. 7F).[28]

The identification of the Propylaea, or of some parts of it, as buildings originally housing schools appears for the first time in the Vienna Anonymous and reappears in later accounts. Reinhold Lubenau in the late 16th century and Evliya Çelebi in 1667[29] also identified the Propylaea as an ancient school. This suggests that the author of the Vienna Anonymous used a "learned" tradition that was current at the time of its composition and which remained popular among the locals for at least two more centuries.

---

[23] Tanoulas 1997a, vol. 1, pp. 43–44; Tanoulas 2005, p. 93; Ross 1855, p. 272.
[24] Wachsmuth (1874, p. 739 n. 1) identified the school of the Stoics with the east portico of the Propylaea; he is followed by Di Branco (2005, p. 122 n. 44).
[25] Ross 1855, p. 272; Wachsmuth 1874, p. 739 n. 4. Di Branco (2005, p. 122 n. 45) follows Wachsmuth.
[26] Tanoulas 1997a, vol. 1, pp. 43–44; Tanoulas 2005, pp. 90, 93.
[27] Tanoulas 1997a, vol. 1, pp. 317–319, vol. 2, drawings 63–68, pp. 311–313. Setton ([1948] 1975, pp. 237–238) interestingly identifies the west portico of the central building with the stoa where the Stoic philosophers taught, adding "and nearby, appropriately enough, he [the Vienna Anonymous] puts the school of Epicurus." Although he presents no arguments, his view is almost identical to mine.
[28] See n. 25.
[29] Paton 1951, pp. 48–49; Tanoulas 1997a, vol. 1, pp. 44–45.

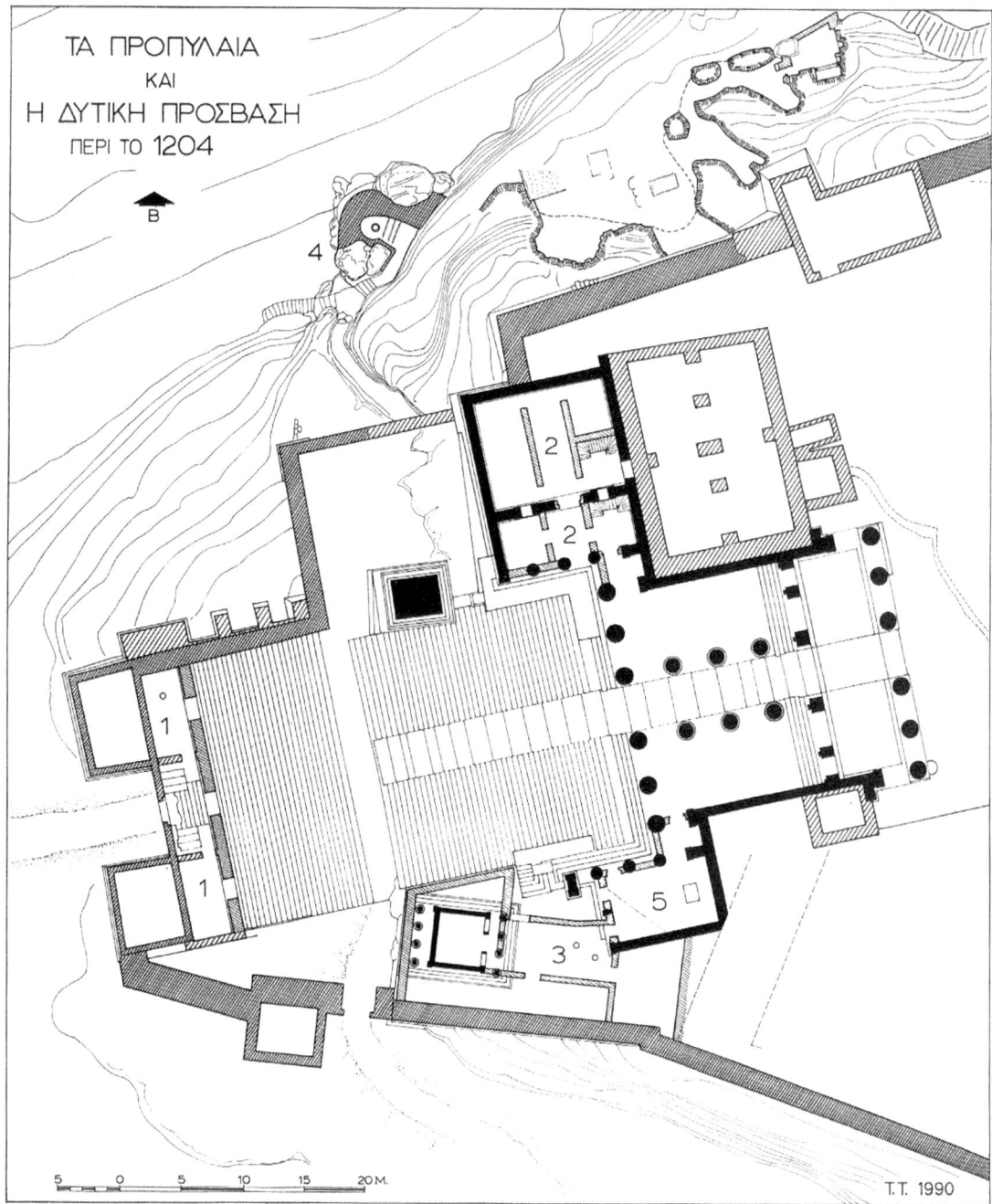

Figure 4. The Propylaea and the western access of the Acropolis, ca. 1204. 1) Byzantine additions along the east side of the Beulé Gate; 2) Ground floor of the bishop's residence; 3) Court with cisterns in the Athena Nike bastion; 4) Chapel with holy water at the Klepsydra; 5) Chapel in the Propylaea south wing. Drawing T. Tanoulas.

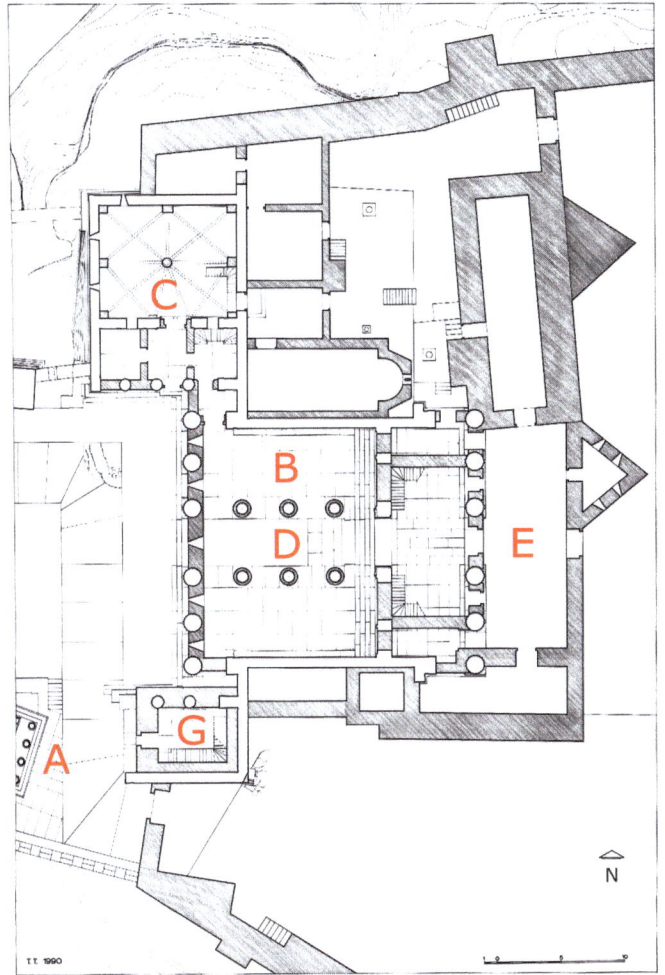

Figure 5. Ground plan of the duke's residence in the Propylaea in 1458. A) "School of the Musicians" (Athena Nike); B) "Palace" (Florentine addition on top of the central building of the Propylaea); C) "High Administrative Offices / Chancery" (*Καγγελαρία*, that is, the Propylaea north wing); D) "Stoa of the Stoics" (west hall of the Propylaea central building); E) The east portico of the Propylaea, proposed by Wachsmuth as the Vienna Anonymous' "Stoa of the Stoics;" G) "School of the Epicureans" (Propylaea south wing). Drawing T. Tanoulas.

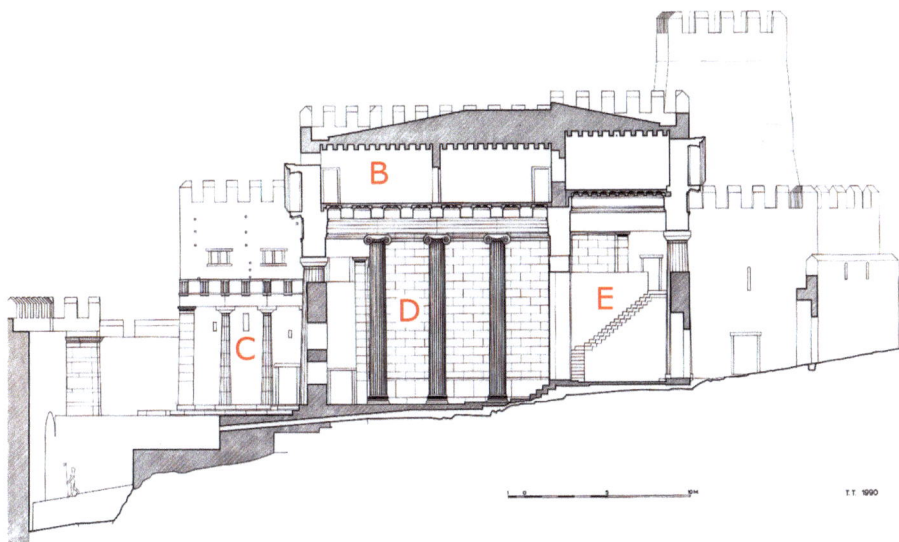

Figure 6. Cross-section of the duke's residence along the central passageway of the Propylaea central building in 1458, looking north; B) "Palace" (Florentine addition on top of the central building of the Propylaea); C) "High Administrative Offices / Chancery" (*Καγγελαρία*, that is, the Propylaea north wing); D) "Stoa of the Stoics" (west hall of the Propylaea); E) The east portico of the Propylaea, proposed by Wachsmuth as the Vienna Anonymous' "Stoa of the Stoics." Drawing T. Tanoulas.

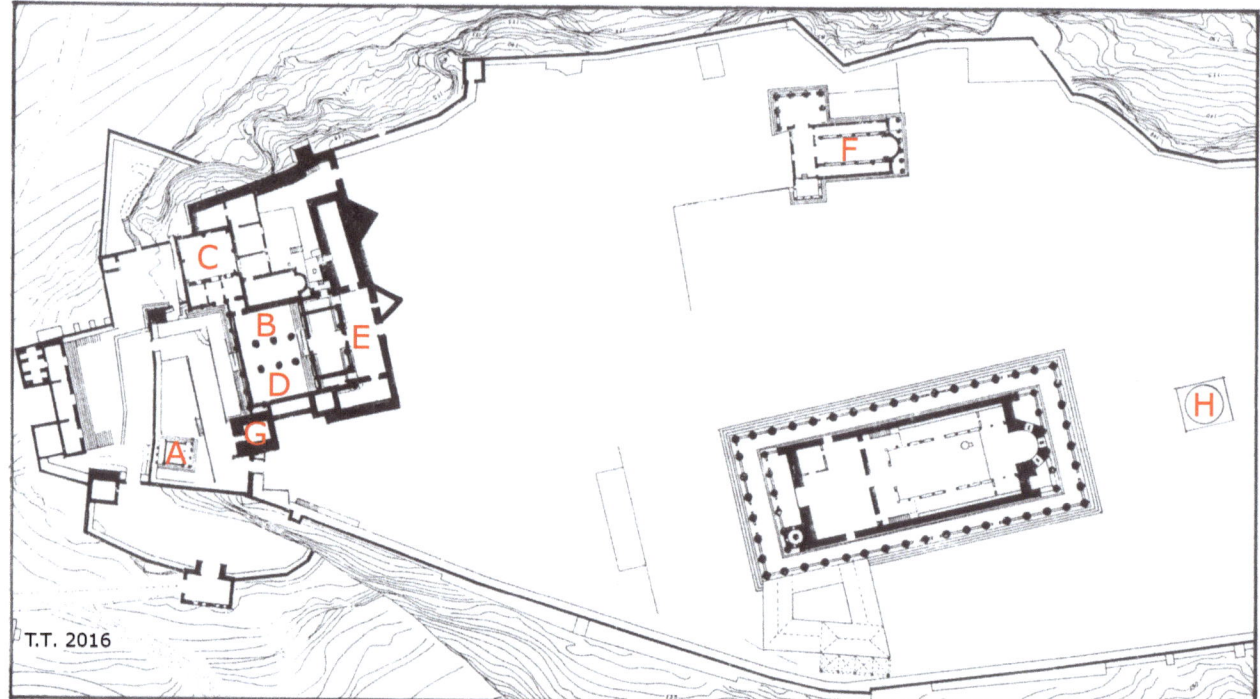

Figure 7. Plan of the Acropolis in 1458: A) "School of the Musicians" (Athena Nike); B) "Palace" (Florentine addition on top of the central building of the Propylaea); C) "High Administrative Offices / Chancery" (*Καγγελαρία*, that is, the Propylaea north wing); D) "Stoa of the Stoics" (west hall of the Propylaea); E) East portico of the Propylaea, proposed by Wachsmuth as the Vienna Anonymous' "Stoa of the Stoics;" F) the Erechtheion, proposed by Ross as the Vienna Anonymous' "Stoa of the Stoics" and as the "School of the Epicureans" by Wachsmuth; G) "School of the Epicureans" (Propylaea south wing); H) Temple of Rome and Augustus, proposed by Ross as the Vienna Anonymous' "School of the Epicureans." Drawing T. Tanoulas.

Patterns of Identity Modification over Time

My study of similar documents has made me realize that the creation of such identifications and their modification over time follow some common, simple patterns.[30] To be more specific, the current function of a building is never believed to be identical to its original one; the author of an account feels that he has to look for the "true," the "historic," or the "legendary" identity of the building, in other words, he must resort to written sources or to oral tradition. Once the building's use changes, the recently abandoned practical use can replace what had been held to be the "original" identity until that moment, but the proposed identity is always projected ultimately onto a remote past.

The Vienna Anonymous, for example, identifies the palace of the Propylaea with the private residence added by the Acciaiuoli on top of the central building, which was a recent structure at the time. The north wing, encumbered with the Frankish additions on top of and to the east and north of the Classical structure, is identified with its more recent use as well, as the chancery. The Classical

---

[30] Tanoulas 2011.

parts of the central building and of the south wing of the Propylaea are identified with the stoa of the Stoics and with the school of the Epicureans respectively; both identities refer to a remote past.

A few years later, Urbano Bolzanio identified the Propylaea as a palace, adding the modifier *a la Romana*, "in the Roman style," to the structure's definition.[31] This adds a first layer on top of the past. More than two centuries later, at the end of 1699, the anonymous writer of the logbook of the ship *L'Assuré* identified the Propylaea as the Palace of Theseus, linking the palace to the remote mythological past.[32]

As already mentioned, Evliya Çelebi described the Propylaea as an ancient school in his account of Athens, which means that the local tradition evidenced by the Vienna Anonymous was still popular in 1667. He then added a piece of information from the recent past: this school had been turned into a magazine by the Ottomans, before it was destroyed by an explosion of gunpowder, an incident that, as we know from historical sources, happened in 1640.[33]

A mere 36 years after the explosion in the Propylaea and nine years after Evliya Çelebi's account of it, this information had taken on a new spin. In 1676 Jacob Spon recorded that, according to local tradition, the Propylaea was the "Arsenal of Lycurgus."[34] Less than a decade after Evliya Çelebi's description, the function of the Propylaea as a storeroom for weapons had been projected onto Classical Antiquity, assigning a new identity to the structure. Local belief that the Propylaea was the "Arsenal of Lycurgus" still flourished a century after the explosion, during the visits of John Montagu, 4th Earl of Sandwich, in 1738 and Richard Pococke in 1740.[35]

Looking at these accounts today from the perspective of our modern knowledge of history, topography, and archaeology and by examining the context of these documents, we understand that this pattern can be applied not only to the identities of monuments, but to identities of a different sort as well. Let us take, for example, the identity of the duke of Athens: when the Vienna Anonymous was composed, the lords of Athens had held the official title of duke for more than two centuries. It would be natural for the local inhabitants in the 15th century to apply this title to the bygone lords of Athens as well. That in *A Midsummer Night's Dream* William Shakespeare identifies Theseus not as the king, but as the duke of Athens is not without significance. William Miller commented on the title of the duke of Athens:

> The title [...] has become famous in literature, as well as in history, from its bestowal, by a pardonable anacronism [*sic*], upon Theseus by Dante, Boccaccio, Chaucer, and Shakespeare, and upon Menelaos by the Catalan chronicler, Ramón Muntaner. All of these authors, except Shakespeare, were the contemporaries, one of them—Muntaner—the friend, of Athenian dukes. Accordingly, they transferred to the legendary founder of Athens the style of its mediaeval rulers, whose names were well known in Italy, and thence passed to England.[36]

---

[31] Ziebarth 1899, pp. 73–74; Beschi 1984, pp. 17–18; Tanoulas 1997a, vol. 1, p. 44. Bolzanio, it seems, did not gain access to the Acropolis.
[32] Paton 1951, pp. 165–166; Tanoulas 1997a, vol. 1, pp. 65–66.
[33] Tanoulas 1987, p. 420; Tanoulas 1997a, vol. 1, pp. 45–46.
[34] Spon 1678, vol. 2, pp. 136–142; Tanoulas 1997a, vol. 1, p. 50.
[35] Sandwich 1799, pp. 61–62; Pococke 1745, pp. 161–162; Tanoulas 1997a, vol. 1, pp. 67–69.
[36] Miller 1908, pp. 107–108. Shakespeare (Alexander [1951] 1968, p. 198) depended on the Knight's Tale, the first of *The Canterbury Tales* by Geoffrey Chaucer (Hutchins 1952, pp. 174–211). Theseus was identified as the duke of Athens by Dante Alighieri in the *Inferno* 12.16–18 (see Vandelli and Polacco 1974, p. 90) and by Giovanni Boccaccio (see Agostinelli and Coleman 2015). I am indebted to Professor Ioannis Theodorakopoulos, who is working on the Vienna Anonymous from a different point of view, for drawing my attention to the references that antedate that document.

In this context, Di Branco's contention—that the Vienna Anonymous's vague reference to a potentially pagan duke of Athens should be taken as a hint to assign a much earlier date to the composition of the text—becomes completely groundless.

However, the Vienna Anonymous contains more that corresponds to late medieval and/or early modern conceptions of antique monuments. The section referring to Hadrian's Gate and the Temple of Olympian Zeus, "[...] there is a very big and beautiful arch bearing the names of Hadrian and Theseus. Inside [...] was a royal residence supported from below by very many columns," has already been cited above. The same pattern, almost a topos, of a lofty palace on the second story of an ancient colonnaded structure is used to describe the palace at the Propylaea. Niccolò da Martoni in 1395 and Cyriac of Ancona in 1436 also referred to the columns of Olympian Zeus as bearing the Palace of Hadrian on top.[37] Not until after the middle of the 18th century was this belief challenged by James Stuart.[38] In this conception of a magnificent residence built on higher levels, we might recognize a reflection of the Italian *palazzi* of the Late Middle Ages and the Early Renaissance, which were situated in the upper stories of buildings. In the 16th century, Palladio, following Vitruvius, still placed the *piano nobile* on a colonnaded facade.[39]

The various lines of reasoning of the preceding discussion make it clear after all that, at least as far as the Acropolis is concerned, the testimony of the Vienna Anonymous would be completely out of context if a date in the 11th or 12th centuries were accepted.

The Bassano Drawing

Let us now turn to the discussion of a pictorial representation of the Athenian Acropolis from the Ottoman period. It is the so-called "Bassano drawing," a well-known view of the Acropolis from the top of Philopappou Hill, dated to 1670 and kept in the Museo Civico of Bassano del Grappa in Italy (Fig. 8, top). This drawing, discovered, fully documented, and discussed by the late Luigi Beschi in 1956,[40] was analyzed further in my 1997 book on the structural history of the Propylaea in the Middle Ages.[41] This drawing is of exceptional importance, since it is the first depiction of Athens that aimed to provide a realistic and objective view of the city, so to speak. This realism and objectivity are, however, deceptive to a certain degree, for they seem to have lured Jordan Dimakopoulos into discussing the Bassano drawing in an article that appeared in 2001 without consulting any literature relevant to the topography and history of Athens during the Ottoman era.[42] Dimakopoulos declared that he happened to see the Bassano drawing in a book on his bookshelves[43] and that he did not consult Beschi's article, because he could not find it.[44] His discussion leaves no doubt that he knew nothing of the analysis of the Bassano drawing published in my book.[45] This ignorance of fundamental data led Dimakopoulos to several arbitrary conclusions. In 2003, Luigi Beschi and I published an article

---

[37] Paton 1951, p. 33; Setton [1948] 1975, 233; Zorzi 1959, pp. 117–118; Tanoulas 1997a, vol. 1, p. 58 n. 5.
[38] Stuart and Revett 1827, pp. 77–84.
[39] See n. 37.
[40] Beschi 1956.
[41] Tanoulas 1997a, vol. 1, pp. 46–47; vol. 2, p. 287, fig. 2.
[42] Dimakopoulos 2001, pp. 60–70.
[43] Dimakopoulos 2001, p. 62, referring to Perocco and Salvadori 1976.
[44] Dimakopoulos 2001, p. 60.
[45] Dimakopoulos (2001, pp. 78–79) discusses the evidence of the Bassano view for access from the west side and for the Propylaea.

Figure 8. Top: View of the Acropolis from the south-west in 1670, unknown artist, pen and ink on white paper, 30 x 45 cm. Bassano del Grappa, Museo Civico, Collezione RIVA, 11599. Photo Museo Civico di Bassano del Grappa.
Bottom: Model representing the Acropolis, ca. 1500, view from the south-west. Reconstruction T. Tanoulas, model made by P. Dimitriadis, 1985.

intended to reaffirm reality in regard to the information provided by the drawing.[46] It will be useful here to discuss the main issues in that article, using it as a model of the methodology appropriate for interpreting documents of this sort.

Dimakopoulos's approach was to look at individual details in the drawing and to take them for granted, as if they were the only indisputable evidence in existence. In response, Beschi suggested that the information provided by the picture should not be taken for granted, because it distorts reality in many cases, as can easily be shown. He referred to the following key points.[47] The Parthenon is depicted with six columns on the west front instead of eight, while the long side is shown to have twelve columns instead of seventeen. The east pediment is shown smaller but complete, rather than being broken in the middle. The Thrasyllos Monument is depicted as a three-dimensional structure instead of as the flat facade that it really was. The flat columnar facade in front of Hadrian's aqueduct on the west slope of Lycabettus is shown as a three-dimensional building as well. The ruins of the Temple of Olympian Zeus are missing completely, while the flat Hadrian's Arch (or Gate) is depicted as a three-dimensional domed structure.

I will limit myself here to discussing Dimakopoulos's remarks concerning Athenian topography, especially the monuments on the Acropolis. As mentioned, the east pediment of the Parthenon is depicted smaller than the west one, but its top appears to be intact. Dimakopoulos considers this as proof that the east pediment was complete at the time the drawing was made.[48] By extension, this would mean that its center was destroyed between 1670, when the Bassano drawing was made, and 1674, when Jacques Carrey produced the detailed drawings that depict a clear break in the middle.[49] No historical event justifies such a conclusion.

A view of a model of the Acropolis from a vantage point that corresponds to that of the Bassano drawing (Fig. 8, bottom) explains why the east pediment in the drawing appears smaller than the west: the middle of the east pediment was already broken, as represented in the model, and, thus, the peak of the southern part of the pediment was lower. The unknown draftsman of the Bassano drawing had obviously not been on the Acropolis and could therefore not understand the situation in the middle of the east pediment. In the end, he made the peak of the pediment low, by representing the east pediment complete, but smaller in scale.[50]

The second discrepancy between Dimakopoulos's interpretation and the contextual evidence centers on the fact that the minaret of the mosque in the Parthenon is shown as emerging from behind the northern side of the Parthenon.[51] Dimakopoulos sees this as proof that the minaret was standing to the north of the Parthenon. At least two other drawings confirm the position of the minaret at the south end of the Opisthonaos and show that it was built upon the Byzantine or, rather, Frankish tower, the lower part of which is still standing there (Figs. 9-10). A view of the Acropolis (1687) from Lycabettus Hill in Francesco Fanelli's book (1707) shows the minaret emerging above the south end of the west pediment (Fig. 9, bottom). In Fanelli's contemporary view from the south-west, the minaret rises above the outline of the Parthenon (Fig. 9, top), in the same way as in the Bassano drawing.

This can be explained by the fact that the minaret was built within the main body of the Parthenon. From a distance, only the upper part of the minaret, which rose above the outline of

---

[46] Beschi and Tanoulas 2002–2003.
[47] Beschi and Tanoulas 2002–2003, pp. 384–385.
[48] Dimakopoulos 2001, pp. 75–76.
[49] Beschi and Tanoulas 2002–2003, pl. 93; Bowie and Thimme 1971, pls. 3–4.
[50] Beschi and Tanoulas 2002–2003, pp. 388–389.
[51] Dimakopoulos 2001, p. 77.

Figure 9. Top: View of the Acropolis from the south-west after the 1687 explosion in the Parthenon, Francesco Fanelli, after a drawing by G. M. Verneda. Fanelli 1707.
Bottom: View of the Acropolis from the north-east during the 1687 explosion in the Parthenon, Francesco Fanelli, after a drawing by G. M. Verneda. Fanelli 1707.

the building, could be seen; and this is how it was drawn. A free-standing minaret built on the rock to the north of the mosque, however, would have been a massive structure, the remains of which would be visible to and noticed by visitors to the Acropolis after the Parthenon was destroyed in 1687. The traces of such an imaginary minaret would certainly be observable even today.[52]

Another conspicuous inaccuracy in the Bassano drawing's view of the Acropolis is that the upper stories added on top of the northern wing and the central building, as well as the tower built on the southern wing of the Propylaea, are crowned by machicolations, in other words crenellations projecting above corbels bearing arches. There is no evidence that machicolations ever existed on these buildings, and the view of the Acropolis dated 1674 (Fig. 10), only four years after the Bassano view, leaves practically no doubt about that. Significantly, the bastion that the Franks had built in the 13th century

Figure 10. View of the Acropolis from the south-west in 1674, unknown artist, probably pen and ink on paper, 20 x 30 cm. Bowie and Thimme 1971, fig. 8. Paris, Bibliothèque nationale de France.

[52] Beschi and Tanoulas 2002–2003, pp. 389–390.

between the Athena Nike bastion and the base of the Monument of Agrippa was mistakenly omitted in the Bassano drawing. This exclusion makes the three sections of the Propylaea appear very tall, as if rising directly from the much lower level of the first bastion, which had enveloped the Beulé Gate by that time. This erroneous detail caused Dimakopoulos to identify the tower added by the Acciaiuoli on the Propylaea south wing with the tower on the west side of the gate below the Athena Nike bastion; he argues that it was built by the Ottomans in order to enable a complete view over the plain of Athens.[53] However, no tower of this height appears in any textual or pictorial source before the Bassano drawing. In addition, it could not have reached a level higher than the top of the tower built on the south wing of the Propylaea; no need for such a tall tower therefore existed. Last, but not least, such a tower would be over 50 m high and would need a thick substructure that could not have disappeared completely in the four years that elapsed between 1670 and 1674, when Charles-Marie-François Olier, Marquis de Nointel, visited Athens with an entourage that left many documents of value concerning Athens and its monuments.[54]

Conclusion

To find inaccuracies in documents of the sort discussed above is natural. Such texts were typically not written on the spot, but from memory after the author had returned to his or her room. They could even be revised after the travelers had returned to their home countries in order to improve the style or to make the descriptions conform to some prestigious source of information. The same was true of the pictorial documents. Sketches were normally made on the spot and used later for a final drawing or painting. Much of the work was done when the landscape or object depicted was no longer visible to the artist. Some inaccuracies are due to misunderstandings of details seen from a distance or to the misinterpretation of notes or sketches done on the spot.

A modern scholar's task is to establish as much of the reality contained in these documents as possible; this can be done only by means of a careful study of the context. As observed at the beginning of this essay, the interpretation of early travelers' accounts demands systematic study that ought to examine each individual account in relation to other relevant documents that may be contemporary, anterior, or posterior to it. In the course of this examination, archaeological data must also be taken into account. The scholar has to discover the key, in other words, to apply the most appropriate method to decode documents that reflect conceptions different from those now current.

---

[53] Dimakopoulos 2001, p. 78.
[54] Tanoulas 1997a, vol. 2, drawings 4–5; Beschi and Tanoulas 2002–2003, pp. 390–393, with a detailed analysis of the data. See also the essay by Fowden herein, pp. 67–95. On the west side of the gate below the Athena Nike bastion's south-west corner, the foundations of a rectangular tower survive; they were built as a part of the Post-Herulian fortifications of the Acropolis, which must have been in use throughout the Middle Ages. See Tanoulas 1997a, vol. 1, pp. 265–267, 286–288, 303–304, vol. 2, figs. 8, 10, 15–16, 30–32, 47, 53–55, 369, drawings 47–50, 55–56, 60–68. The tower must have been in a ruined condition before 1687, but it was restored or rebuilt by the Ottomans while they were awaiting the attack of the Venetian troops under Morosini. See Tanoulas 1987, p. 436. However, the surviving evidence leaves no doubt that it was of a moderate size and never exceeded the height of the neighboring crenellations by more than a few meters.

The Parthenon Mosque, King Solomon, and the Greek Sages

Elizabeth Key Fowden

Reflecting on changes in intellectual perspectives, the historian Arnaldo Momigliano commented in the late 1970s, "Nowadays few people would take for granted what my teacher Gaetano de Sanctis and his teacher, Julius Beloch—the one a Catholic and the other a materialist—both took for granted, namely that the Parthenon was more beautiful than Hagia Sophia and that Plato or even Cicero wrote better than St Augustine."[1] Tastes change, along with our intellectual preoccupations. Almost a half-century later, we are now fascinated by cultural transfers and architectural reuse. We are also more alert to the ambiguities of such catch-all concepts as "European," "Islamic," "Western," and "Eastern" and are wary of simplistic binary juxtapositions of these terms.[2]

The "Parthenon mosque" is not a binary construct, nor is it a contradiction in terms. It is a historical reality that has been sidelined for interconnected political and ideological reasons, and also a stimulus to rethink how the Classical Greek past has been variously inherited and reworked not only by Christians, but also by Muslims. Part of my goal in this essay, and in the monograph on the Parthenon mosque that will follow, is to loosen the grip of a single valuation of the building that we have inherited from the west European antiquarians who began to arrive in the Ottoman period, when the Athenian Acropolis barely resembled the stripped-down space we see there today.[3] What

---

* It is a pleasure to express my gratitude to the Gerda Henkel Stiftung for their generous support (including funding translations by Thomas Sinclair, whom I warmly thank for his collaboration) and to James Montgomery at the Faculty of Asian and Middle Eastern Studies at the University of Cambridge. The germ of this project can be found in Fowden 2010, a review of Kaldellis, *The Christian Parthenon: Classicism and Pilgrimage in Byzantine Athens* (2009). I thank Garth Fowden and Anthony Kaldellis for their comments on this essay. Subsequent to presenting a preliminary version of it in Athens, I have benefited from invitations to speak to audiences in Oxford, Cambridge, Edinburgh, and Kavala about diverse facets of this project. More recently, I have benefitted from discussions in Cambridge with Suna Çağaptay, whom I also thank. Final discussion and writing was within the framework of the "Impact of the Ancient City Project" led by Professor Andrew Wallace-Hadrill (Faculty of Classics, University of Cambridge). This project has received funding from the European Research Council [ERC] under the European Union's Horizon 2020 research and innovation programme (grant agreement no. 693418).

[1] Momigliano [1978] 1980, p. 275. I owe the reference to Garth Fowden.
[2] For a clear statement of the problem, see https://www.the guardian.com/world/2016/nov/09/western-civilisation-apriah-reith-lecture?CMP=share_btn_link.
[3] On the destruction of post-Periclean material, see the comments of Charalambos Bouras, architect and architectural historian, who, together with Manolis Korres, was the linchpin of the current Acropolis Restoration Project that began in 1975: "During the nineteenth and twentieth centuries, the infinite admiration for ancient Greece and art in the age of Pericles became the cause for the systematic destruction of all medieval and modern-day edifices on the Acropolis. As a result, a significant archaeological site was deprived of all evidence relating to its modern history. This generated the fallacy that, all along, some lifeless ruins have been standing there on their own. In other words, 'diachronic stratification' on the Acropolis has

they would have seen instead was architecture from different periods, including pagan, Christian, and Muslim elements, that mirrored the many meanings those who lived there over time would have given the buildings, expressed through the stories they told and the adaptations they made to the structures. This organic accumulation of forms and functions, along with the almost endless variety of seemingly incompatible interpretive angles from which the Parthenon can be viewed, is what provides the greatest stimulus for studying the building in its early Ottoman phase.

One of the relatively few scholars to have concentrated on Athens during the early modern period (in contrast with the Classical period, or even the 18th century onwards) was Léon de Laborde. His two-volume *Athènes aux XVe, XVIe et XVIIe siècles*, published in Paris in 1854, is a collection of sources linked by his comments to form a narrative.[4] The intention of his ironical dedication in the second volume, "*Aux vandales, mutilateurs, spoliateurs, restaurateurs de tous les pays, hommage d'une profonde indignation*," would have been self-evident at the time, referring to all those who spoiled the original appearance of the ancient city's monuments. To most if not all scholars today, the meaning of vandalism, mutilation, spoliation, and reworking (here the best translation of "*restauration*") is no longer so clear-cut.

Despite the demolition of the material evidence for the post-Classical Parthenon, today we are more aware of the ever-evolving life of monuments and focus less exclusively on "original" structures and meanings. The post-Classical Parthenon has recently been the focus of important studies of Byzantine, post-revolutionary Greek, and 20th-century Surrealist interpretations.[5] The Ottoman phase, especially in the first 250 years before the arrival of many European visitors, has not attracted sufficient study in terms either of the architectural fabric of the two Parthenon mosques, before and after the Venetian bombardment in 1687, or of the Parthenon's cultural significance for the Ottoman viewer. Long before Europeans expressed their disappointment in the "sad relic" of ancient Hellas that they found in contemporary Greece, and identified themselves as the true heirs of ancient Greek wisdom, Muslims had been in dialogue with Greek writings thanks to the Greco-Arabic translation movement begun in 8th-century Baghdad and later inherited, through both diffusive infiltration and more conscious development, by the Ottomans. The impact of this inheritance on Ottoman views of Athens, and the Parthenon, is a dimension of the city's history open to further exploration.

The many views of Athens discussed in this essay include, of course, my own: that of a long-time resident of Greece and a Late Antique historian trained in the study of early Islamic inheritance and reformulation of pagan and Christian architectural and cultural forms in west Asia. My attempt to understand the early Ottoman Parthenon draws on many specializations, and I am the beneficiary of important new studies of that extraordinary viewer of cities Evliya Çelebi, in particular, and more generally of work on Athens by Ottomanists, Hellenists, and early modern Europeanists, each approaching the city from different disciplinary angles. It is my hope that each will discern his or her own role in my attempt here to focus on the more neglected, composite imaginary that synchronized

---

been lost with the exception of the Byzantine staircase of the Parthenon belfry" (in Bouras, Ioannidou, and Jenkins 2012, p. 8, with fig. 18, a drawing of the spiral staircase). I will return to the staircase below. See also the excellent McNeal 1991 and the rarely cited Moutsopoulos 1986.

[4] Laborde's work, combining texts (some in facsimile) with contemporary illustrations, is still fundamental. Curt Wachsmuth followed 20 years later with an appendix to his *Die Stadt Athen im Altertum* entitled "Die aeltesten Berichte ueber die antiken Reste in Athen," which contained original texts on Athens from Cyriac of Ancona, the Vienna Anonymous, the Paris Anonymous (not in Laborde), and Jacques-Paul Babin, with incisive notes (Wachsmuth 1874, pp. 727–763).

[5] Respectively, Kaldellis 2009, Hamilakis 2007, and Yatromanolakis 2012, pp. 67–112.

monotheist myth, Qur'anic legend, Arabic historiography, Athenian lore, and Greek history to explain the city's architecture.

I am especially interested in how, in the early Ottoman tradition, the ancient monuments of Athens were peopled with Greek wise men—but also with Qur'anic prophets. Athens, the "City of the Sages" [*Medinetü'l-Hukema*] was the stage on which prophetic legend, philosophical biography, and public architecture met. I have chosen to focus my attention here particularly on the idea of the accretive collage as a mode of interpreting Athenian monuments. This is a mode of interpretation that can accommodate what Gottfried Hagen has termed a "multilayered simultaneity,"[6] in contrast to the more linear mode of reconstruction that has come to predominate. I suggest that the late 17th century and the early 18th was a time when topography and buildings were still susceptible to both widely varying and sometimes intersecting interpretations. Ottoman, local Greek, and European observers of Athenian monuments described them in a way that mirrors the composite nature of the physical fabric.[7] I discuss three Ottoman viewers—Sultan Mehmed II, who visited Athens in 1458, Evliya Çelebi, who visited in 1667,[8] and Mahmud Efendi, a little-known early 18th-century historian of Athens[9]—and sideline the more familiar early European visitors. I also bring into the discussion a description of the building in the 1590s made by the Spanish captive Diego Galán, who claims to have visited Athens as an Ottoman galley slave. His description deserves to be known outside Hispanophone scholarship, as it provides our only detailed account of the Parthenon, both its figural decoration and its interior appearance, from the time between the building's conversion into a mosque and the handful of descriptions from the late 17th century.[10]

While my discussion spans the 15th to the 18th centuries, I concentrate mainly on two decades, the 1660s and 1670s, because it is from this time that we possess the better-known descriptions in Ottoman Turkish, French, and English, and a few visual depictions. We find these observers trying to make sense of their various sources of information, both oral and written, in their encounter with ancient monuments in continuing use. Awareness of their various "sources"—from Greek and Latin historians to the Qur'an, early Arabic biography of the Prophet Muhammad, costume albums, and local legends—gives us a finer appreciation of the variety within and between European and Ottoman encounters with monuments from the past. Yet I am increasingly wary not only of the handy terms European and Ottoman, Christian and Muslim, but also of the sort of source-critical reading that tends to isolate the parts of the whole, especially when applied to the Ottoman viewers.

---

[6] Hagen 2004, p. 241.

[7] Contrasts, stimulating if overly schematic, between 17th-century European and Ottoman modes of thought have been highlighted by Hagen (2006, pp. 532–535), who discusses the two geographical conceptions applied in the two versions of the *Cihannüma* [Cosmography] by the great scholar Katip Çelebi. He characterizes the Arabic geographical tradition as "synthetic" geographical thinking, "in which a vision of geographical space is obtained by adding up numerous individual descriptions of small units, such as cities, while the elements which these have in common, and which ultimately help to constitute the larger units, such as regions, are not addressed directly," contrasting this with the more "analytical" approach of contemporary European descriptive geography. On Katip Çelebi's accommodation of European geographical description, see also Hagen 1998, esp. pp. 104–107, on cosmography and on the influence of Mercator's atlas and other European books on Katip Çelebi.

[8] For a compelling investigation of Evliya Çelebi's compositional technique which supports the widely held view that he did indeed visit Athens, however multiple were the sources (actual and imaginary) that he added to his eye-witness experience in order to describe the city, see MacKay 2011. My argument below concerns the very complex nature of Evliya Çelebi's encounter with the ancient city in continued use.

[9] For discussion of this text, see Tunalı 2013a, 2013b, and herein, pp. 97–121.

[10] I thank Cecilia Tarruell for drawing my attention to Diego Galán, whose description of Athens and its wider environs includes not only the Parthenon, the pine forests between Athens and Megara, and a reference to the Hexamilion, but also ethnographic observations, especially on Christian habits.

King Solomon, Talismans, and Sages

Let me begin with Evliya Çelebi. Guided by his maxim, "travel, trade, and pilgrimage" [*seyahat, ticaret,* and *ziyaret*], he visited Athens in 1667 and included a description of the city in his immense *Seyahatname* [Book of travels].[11] When Evliya Çelebi was not marveling at King Solomon's architectural interventions in Athens or describing the lingering scent of sulfur in the caves on the Acropolis slope, where the ancient sages had performed their alchemical experiments, he was wondering at the workmanship of Plato's marble throne inside the Parthenon, which he praises as the most resplendent mosque in the world.[12] Part of what makes Evliya Çelebi such good company is his boyish enthusiasm about the world he observes, and his patent enjoyment of the playfully paradoxical and baroquely allusive connections he makes. Evliya Çelebi's usual approach to a city is to start with its foundation myth, mixing history, the Qur'an, and legend. These myths (including those of Athens) are populated with famous pre-Islamic founders, such as the ubiquitous Alexander, who appears in the Qur'an as Dhu'l Qarnayn, "he of the two horns."[13] Evliya Çelebi then describes the city's prominent buildings, markets, and goods, its people, celebrated events, and its language—all of this held together by his personal observations and imaginative yet often learned associations. His account of Athens is distinctive because the city he sees is so crowded with ancient wise men. The reason for this is that Athens is known in "the chronicles of all nations," as Evliya Çelebi explains, as the "City of the Sages".[14] Here he does not exaggerate, as the memory of Athens had indeed survived in the Islamic world, thanks to its philosophers.

Evliya Çelebi's wise or learned men do not belong to an ossified world of philosophical handbooks, but remind us of the Late Antique sages who do things. People expected the philosopher to use his wisdom to practical effect. Knowledge and action were made to work together in a multi-sensory engagement with the world to which the philosopher belonged. Though he does not know him by name, Evliya Çelebi would have felt at home with the hierophant Nestorius, who in A.D. 375 set up a statue of Achilles in the Parthenon to save Athens from an earthquake.[15] Late Antique philosophical biography is notoriously alive with philosophers who had attracted to their persons superhuman powers

---

[11] Evliya Çelebi studies are flourishing: see Tezcan, Tezcan, and Dankoff 2012 (recent bibliography and especially Açik 2012) and Dankoff 2004 (biography and cultural context). For an important study of Evliya Çelebi's intellectual and imaginative heritage, see Hagen 2004, esp. pp. 233–243, on the historiographical tradition Evliya Çelebi inherited and adapted, and pp. 220–221, on the mixture in early modern Ottoman writing of what Hagen calls theological and philosophical traditions of making sense of the world. It is this mixture that I am interested to highlight in Ottoman views of Athens.

[12] Evliya Çelebi's Parthenon description is found in the *Seyahatname*, vol. 8, pp. 114–116 (translated by Dankoff and Kim, henceforth Evliya Çelebi 2010, pp. 281–286). In addition to Thomas Sinclair, I would like to thank Dimitris Loupis for discussions relating to Evliya Çelebi. All adjustments to the Dankoff and Kim translation (Evliya Çelebi 2010) are by Sinclair. For a sympathetic assessment of travel accounts as an essential complement to archival documentation, see Lowry 2003, pp. 99–102. I thank Felipe Rojas for sending a pre-publication version of Rojas and Sergueenkova (2017, pp. 148–150) on ancient monuments and olfactory associations, including the alchemists' caves below the citadel.

[13] Evliya Çelebi's onomastic approach to history, in which emblematic names and peoples become interlinked, belongs to a wider Arabic tradition—what Arrigoni (1989, p. 69) calls the *via genealogica*—and is also repeated in Antoine Galland's short article "Athiniah" in d'Herbelot's *Bibliothèque orientale* (1697), which relied heavily on Katip Çelebi (see below). The debt is obvious from the fact that the *Bibliothèque* not only calls Athens "Medinat al Hokama" but continues, "Il y a aussi quelques Autheurs qui veulent que Jounan pere des anciens Grecs ou Ioniens, fût originaire de cette ville: cependent cet Jounan n'est autre qu'Iavan fils de Japhet, dont les Juifs font descendre les Grecs qu'ils appellent dans leur langue Javanim" (d'Herbelot 1697, p. 145). The habit of associating Greek and Qur'anic figures common in later Arabic geographers is found as early as Hisham b. al-Kalbi in the 8th century: see Rosenthal 2002, pp. 343–344.

[14] *Seyahatname*, vol. 8, p. 113 (Evliya Çelebi 2010, p. 278).

[15] Zos. 4.18.

that enabled them to act as miracle-working protectors of cities, a tradition with a long life in Arabic and Ottoman writing. This tradition is also found in Evliya Çelebi's account of the talismans planted by sages to protect Athens. "In those days," he explains, "each of the learned men in the city devised for it a different sort of wonderful talisman and marvelous charm. And so this city never had plagues, snakes, centipedes, scorpions, storks, crows, fleas, lice, bedbugs, mosquitoes, or houseflies."[16]

Evliya Çelebi brings with him to Athens a mythosynthetic mode of seeing and writing that allows him to pick up and elaborate on what he sees and hears, casually Islamizing along the way, easily joining philosophers and monotheist prophets in the aetiological myths and legends that animated the city's topography and buildings. The most striking—and original—example of this is his comment,

> In those days, the sages who came to this city took up residence in these caves [around the base of the Acropolis], where they taught classes and held learned discussions. They knew all the occult sciences and perfected all branches of knowledge [...] There were sages then who day and night were in wordless communication with the sages of Baghdad. It is quite a mystery how scholars in Baghdad and Athens could commune with each other, the two cities being a five-month's journey apart; it is a miracle on the level of Jesus's life-giving breath.[17]

However strange the philosophers have come to seem through the transformative magic of the master storyteller, Evliya Çelebi could imagine the sages of Classical Athens and Golden-Age Baghdad in conversation only because all of them were conceived of as the educated Ottoman's intellectual ancestors. Then again, for Evliya Çelebi one deft trans-historical pairing is never enough. He augments it with a flourish, almost an aside, in which he alludes to the miracle described in Sura 3:9, in which Jesus breathes life into a clay bird, an evocative Qur'anic vignette that would naturally come to mind when confronted with a city as full of life-like statues as 17th-century Athens.

I would not for a moment try to present Evliya Çelebi as a philosopher. He is an educated viewer—heir to what Emilio Arrigoni calls a "vera e propria *koinè* culturale panislamica"[18]—who entertainingly demonstrates how Greek philosophers had insinuated themselves into a composite Ottoman frame of reference. In order to make clear my point about the role of the philosopher in Evliya Çelebi's Athenian mythoplasty, I offer a very schematic overview of the naturalization of Greek philosophy into Islamic culture. My overview is shaped by two main currents in pre-modern Islamic culture: first, a facility for thinking and writing across what we would see as genre lines, such as history, biography, geography, and literature; and second, the fact that in Islamic tradition biography and philosophy were closely intertwined, since it was understood that philosophy (like theology) was communicated through individuals, not institutions. The figures of Aristotle, Galen, Pythagoras, and Plato peopled Arabic philosophical discourse well into the Ottoman period. Part of the reason for this was that the Greco-Arabic translation movement that stimulated so much creative debate and

---

[16] *Seyahatname*, vol. 8, p. 119 (Evliya Çelebi 2010, p. 289).
[17] *Seyahatname*, vol. 8, p. 119 (Evliya Çelebi 2010, p. 290). Evliya Çelebi's seeming obliviousness to chronology causes Dankoff and Kim to "correct" the text's "Baghdad" by inserting "(i.e., Babylon)" into their translation. Arrigoni (1989, p. 71, n. 31) shares my understanding that there is no need to substitute Babylon. In Evliya Çelebi's mind, their common philosophical interests are what join the sages of "Golden Age" Athens and Baghdad across time.
[18] Arrigoni 1989, p. 69, n. 27.

writing in 8th- to 10th-century Baghdad was originally inspired by a very practical need to create a universal empire drawn from all the cultural traditions the Abbasid Empire had inherited.[19] I am concentrating on the Greek dimension, but the incorporation of Iranian and Indian knowledge was also part of the process. The earliest translations commissioned were chosen for their practical importance: medical, astrological, alchemical, gnomological, and philosophical texts.

From my first point about a facility for thinking and writing across what we would see as genre lines, I should draw out the place of mythical thinking, especially in the urban biographies laced with wonders that served to heighten the city's prestige as well as to encourage pilgrims and other visitors. In Evliya Çelebi's account of Athens, we see the convergence of these two cultural trends, in which mythologically charged geography and topography meet philosophical biography. So well-knit into his description are Qur'anic prophets and figures from the Greek past that it may be more reasonable to assume that local Muslims, like the Christians before them, had already begun the process of making ancient Athenian history and monuments their own, and that Evliya Çelebi embellished what he heard in Athens to create his own account.[20] For example, it is a commonplace in Arabic and Ottoman literary, geographical, and historical writings for outstandingly impressive ancient buildings or ruins to become associated with King Solomon—sage, prophet, and architect.[21] Making sure to cite his sources (even if they bemuse us today), Evliya Çelebi records, "All the Christian and Coptic chroniclers agree that the original builder of Athens was Solomon, peace be on him!"[22] He goes on to explain that after Solomon's marriage to Belkis, the Queen of Sheba, who for his sake embraced Islam, Solomon commanded the jinn to build a palace for his bride at a place called Temaşalık, comparing it with the "garden of the many-columned Iram," an elliptical allusion to the Qur'an 89:7 that Evliya Çelebi commonly employs in his urban descriptions.[23] The palace was a soaring structure with "variegated columns and vaults of Chosroes and lofty domes,"[24] what older Athenians know today as the "Στύ-λες" or "Columns," the Temple of Olympian Zeus, which made an impact on all the visitors who left visual records. We have no drawings to accompany Evliya Çelebi's description, but one of the earliest sketches of this structure was made by an artist who visited Athens with the Marquis de Nointel, only seven years after Evliya Çelebi (Fig. 1).[25] Evliya Çelebi's written account is mirrored in the earliest European drawings, for example, in the gigantic proportions of the columns and arched gate.

---

[19] For seminal work on this topic, see Gutas 1994 (on gnomologia and philosophical compilations); Gutas 1998; Gutas 2015, esp. p. 330 (on the accommodation of mythological and philosophical views of reality) and pp. 347–348 (on the importance of the Greco-Arabic translation movement in the early Ottoman period).

[20] Kaldellis (2009, pp. 182–185) argues that Michael Choniates was responding to such local identifications and legends in his inaugural homily at Athens.

[21] Iafrate 2016, pp. 160–214, esp. 197–200 with n. 90, on Belkis's throne and Solomon's palace (Qur'anic *sarh*) and on the Persian as well as monotheist scriptural strands in Muslim elaborations of Solomon; Borrut 2011, pp. 217–228; Borrut 2003; Gonzalez 2002, pp. 26–32, 36–41; Soucek 1993; Yerasimos 1990. Muslims were not alone in reworking the Queen of Sheba story for particular purposes: Anagnostakis and Kaldellis (2014, pp. 118–123 and n. 45) offer a delightful discussion of a 10th-century Greek recasting in the Peloponnese.

[22] *Seyahatname*, vol. 8, p. 113 (Evliya Çelebi 2010, pp. 278–279, with adjustments). Evliya Çelebi delights in multiple chronologies, e.g., the start of his description of the Castle of Medina: "All the Ottoman and Arab chronicles still follow the calendar of the Hijra or migration of the Prophet. The Greeks, on the other hand, begin their history with Alexander; the Jews with Noah, the second Adam; the Copts with Idris [Enoch]. These various calendars are still in force in their chronicles:" *Seyahatname*, vol. 9, 279a (7) – (9), in Evliya Çelebi 2012, pp. 33–34 (text/trans. Gemici/Dankoff).

[23] Arrigoni (1989, pp. 62–63 with notes) provides a fascinating, if digressive, discussion of Evliya Çelebi's Attica, including the Throne of Belkis. Evliya Çelebi compares another Solomonic palace, the Temple of Poseidon at Sounion, with the legendary pre-Islamic *qasr* of Khawarnaq near the Euphrates that became the metonym for a luxurious palace in Arabic, Persian, and Ottoman literature: Arrigoni 1989, pp. 85–86 and n. 52.

[24] *Seyahatname*, vol. 8, p. 118 (Evliya Çelebi 2010, p. 288).

[25] Reprinted in Omont 1898, vol. 2, pl. XXIII, and in Bowie and Thimme 1971, pl. 41. The note at the bottom of the manuscript page reads, in the original orthography, "*No. 10. Veue d'une partie de la ville d'Athenes, d'une porte et un Edifice, bastis par l'Empereur Hadrien, et d'une partie des environs de la mesme ville.*"

Figure 1. Throne of Belkis / Palace of Hadrian and walled town, by an unknown artist in the Nointel suite, 1674, red and black pencil, 26.6 x 45 cm. Paris, Bibliothèque nationale de France, Cabinet des Estampes, album Fc 3a (Réserve), no. 10, fol. 27.

Evliya Çelebi describes the monumental structure as having "variegated columns and vaults of Chosroes and lofty domes," even though there were no vaults or domes in the temple. That is beside the point: by alluding to the vaults of the Persian king Chosroes, Evliya Çelebi was not describing what he saw, but drawing Athens into a long-lived Arabic and Ottoman literary mode of summoning up past architectural grandeur either to lament its ruin or, as here, to enhance present appearances by association. It may not be unrelated that, long before Evliya Çelebi, an anonymous Ottoman chronicle of 1491 concerned mainly with legends of Istanbul described a Solomonic palace, constructed for another bride, called Şemsiye, the princess of a rival king, at a place called Temaşalık in a city in Greece, where the ancient building was still standing.[26] Legends are as malleable and quixotic as jinn: what they leave is a residue of associations that once breathed life into a space. Evliya Çelebi draws on a broad interpretive repertoire, local and imported, to create a description that is a complex and allusive response to ancient structures in continued use. The fact that the temple was known at least in the Post-Byzantine period, if not earlier, as the Royal Palace and the Arch of Hadrian as the

---

[26] For the text and thematic commentary, see Yerasimos 1990; this passage is translated on p. 6.

Princess's Gate[27] suggests that Evliya Çelebi was not simply imposing identifications from the Ottoman tradition, but fitting them creatively to stories he heard from local people: the princess elides naturally into Belkis, the daughter of the King of Sheba, and Solomon's queen.[28] Evliya Çelebi's association of the Temple of Olympian Zeus and related structures with Belkis was not simply the ephemeral fancy of an Ottoman tourist: roughly 50 years later, Mahmud Efendi also identified the structure as the Throne of Belkis, as we will see below.

In a similar manner, we see Evliya Çelebi fitting the citadel mosque—*kale cami*, as he knows the Parthenon (Fig. 2)—into an Islamized history when he tells a story about its dome (which also never existed). Elaborating on the 8th-century writer Ibn Ishaq, Muhammad's earliest surviving biographer, Evliya Çelebi recounts how, on the night of the Prophet's birth, the Arch of Chosroes at Ctesiphon and the fire temple of Nimrod collapsed, as did the domes not only of the Parthenon cathedral, but also of the churches of Hagia Sophia, in both Constantinople and in Thessaloniki.[29] This was not the first time that the Parthenon had been incorporated into symbolic moments of monotheist history. The Italian pilgrim Niccolò da Martoni in 1395 had been shown the column on which Dionysius the Areopagite had carved a cross at the moment when he became aware of Christ's Passion in Jerusalem because the earth shook.[30] In this case, we might see Evliya Çelebi linking up local legend heard from an informant with the Islamic tradition of associating the collapse of proud buildings with Muhammad's birth. The crosses and inscriptions carved on many of the Parthenon columns, in particular one column that had attracted over 30 Greek votive and liturgical inscriptions, would naturally have stimulated Niccolò and Evliya Çelebi to speculate.[31]

Evliya Çelebi sees the statues and the other figural works of art preserved in Athens as living beings that interact with him: they smile or gaze threateningly. This, together with his special interest in the ancient sages, and his conviction that they were able to manipulate secret powers that continued to be active, especially in statues, is reminiscent of the *Patria* of Constantinople, a collection of stories about the city's buildings. The compilation as we have it today is thought to date to the late 10th

---

[27] Royal residence [εἰς ἥν οἶκος βασιλικὸς ὑπῆρχε πλείστοις κιόσιν ὑποκάτωθεν στηριζομένη] is the identification given in the 15th-century catalogue of Athenian monuments known as the Vienna Anonymous, entitled Τὰ θέατρα καὶ τὰ διδασκαλεῖα τῶν Ἀθηνῶν [The theaters and the schools of Athens], para. 6; for facsimile and text, see Laborde 1854a, vol. 1, pp. 15–20, at p. 19. In the introduction and notes to his Greek translation of Evliya Çelebi on Attica, Biris (1959) promotes Evliya Çelebi as a passive recipient of local Athenian legend and is not concerned with the Islamic tradition of animating great architecture that Evliya Çelebi brings with him to Athens and which forms the matrix in which he recasts what he hears. His comments on this passage are typical (Biris 1959, p. 23, n. 8): through the "medieval confusion," the original Greek mythology surrounding the Temple of Olympian Zeus survives, "faded and distorted." For lively criticism of Biris, see Arrigoni 1989, pp. 53–59 and 68, n. 26.

[28] Our literary evidence does not reveal when the gate came to be called the Princess's Gate [Πόρτα Βασιλοπούλας], a name simply reported without documentation by Kominis (2008, p. 19, n. 65), Travlos ([1960] 1993, pp. 198–199), Biris (1959, p. 14), and Philadelpheus (1902, vol. 2, pp. 133–134); the last explains the association with a princess as an allusion to the medieval Erotokritos myth, again with no evidence to suggest how old such an association might be. Did the inscription with Hadrian's name spawn the association with a king from which the princess identification grew? Until further evidence is discovered, it is important to remember how undefined the pathways of encounter are. For example, if it was not a Byzantine appellation, Πόρτα Βασιλοπούλας could even have been an instance of Greek adaptation of the Muslim identification with Belkis.

[29] For the commonplace, see Savant (2013, p. 180, nn. 32–33) on the collapse of Chosroes' *iwan* and the extinguishing of the fire temple at Persepolis on the occasion of the Prophet's birth, noted in Qur'an commentaries as early as Muqatil b. Sulayman in the 8th century. See also Chabbi 1994 on Islamic mytho-historical representation of the past with special reference to the Zoroastrian past.

[30] "*Intus quas columpnas est una columpna signata, in qua sanctus Dyonisius, tempore passionis Domini nostri Yhesu Christi, stabat adhesus, et cum tremuerunt omni predicta hedificia propter terre motum factum in toto mundo, sanctus Dyonisius tunc dixit hec verba: 'Aut machina mundi destruetur, aut Filius Dei aliquid patietur'; et signavit sua manu dictam columpnam quadam cruce sua manu. Que crux adhuc permanet in illa columpna.*" The text: Legrand 1895, p. 651; Kaldellis 2009, p. 169.

[31] This interior column stood at the south-west corner of the church/mosque, behind which rose the medieval, spolia-built tower/belfry/minaret. On the tower, see nn. 49–50 below. Alexopoulos (2015, esp. pp. 166–174) hazards no such imaginative leap, but his discussion of the columnar inscriptions contains important comments on the liturgical use and architectural adaptation of the Christian Parthenon.

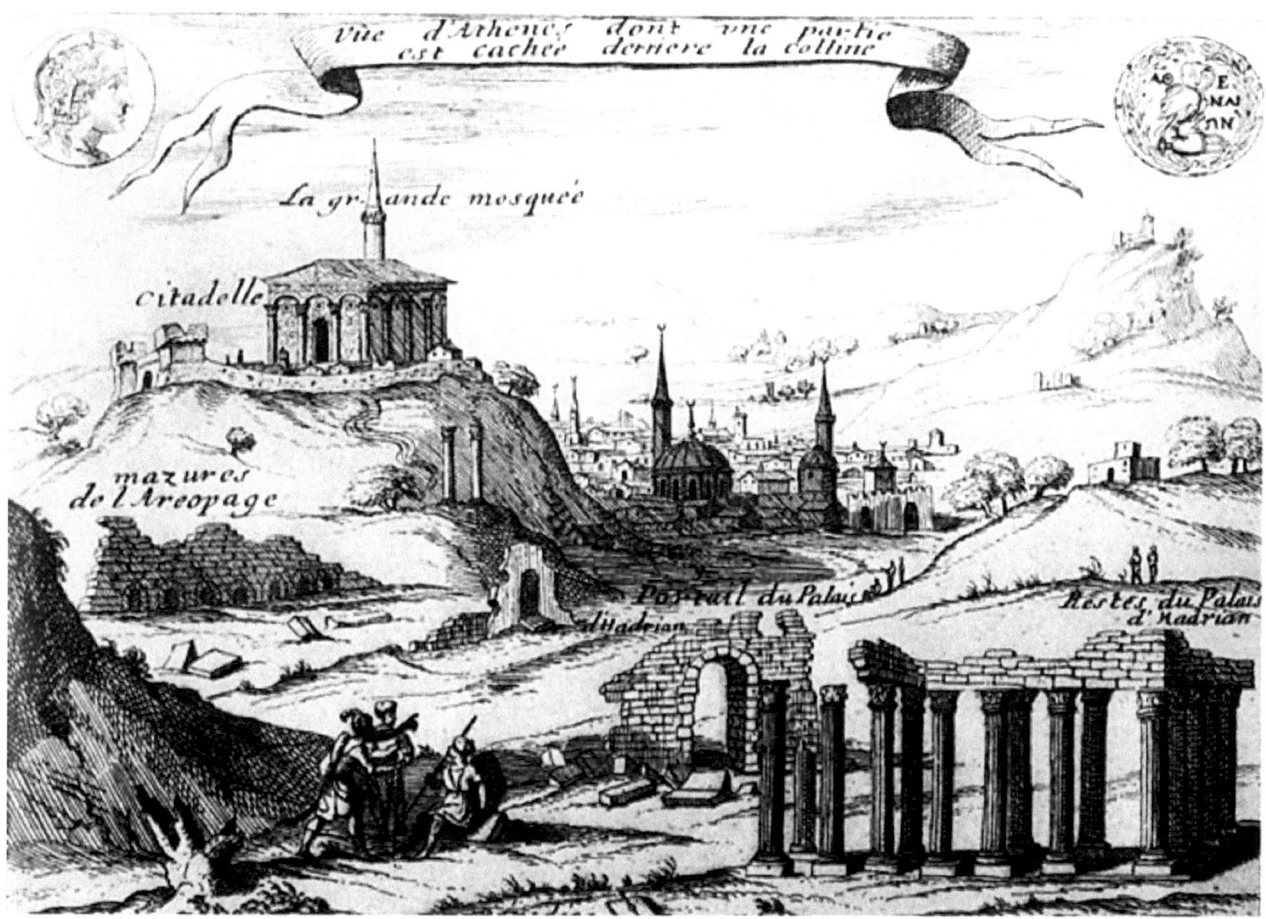

Figure 2. "Vue d'Athènes dont une partie est cachée derrière la colline," engraving showing the columns and gate of Hadrian's Palace, the citadel mosque with adjacent houses, and the walled city below. Babin 1674. American School of Classical Studies at Athens, Gennadius Library.

century, but the material reaches back to the 6th–9th centuries. One of these texts, the Διήγησις [Narration], about the construction of Hagia Sophia, is known to have been read and used by contemporaries of Mehmed II in the development of the Ayasofya legends.[32] By this time, the inhabitants of Istanbul had more or less lost contact with their city's earlier historical strata, whose physical remnants nevertheless confronted and provoked them on every street corner. Evliya Çelebi, a native of the city, resembles the authors of the *Patria*, except that he brings the whole spectrum of Islamic culture to his interpretive effort as well. Evliya Çelebi lacked the exact historical knowledge already available to European scholars of his day; but his own interpretive tools, honed in a long tradition that merged pre-Islamic and Islamic history, geography, and "Praises of Cities," served him well as he stood in front of a monument as complex as the Parthenon mosque. For Evliya Çelebi, it was not enough simply to describe the extraordinary technical achievement of the entire temple, its pagan

---

[32] The *Patria*: Berger 2013; see also Cameron and Herrin 1984; Necipoğlu 1992, p. 199 and n. 7 (bibliography on the Διήγησις and its Ottoman development).

sculpture, Christian mosaic, and painted decoration still largely preserved; it was the building in use that attested the architect's skill:

> The shiny marble slabs on the walls of this mosque are each the size of an elephant. The strange thing is that even a master architect cannot detect the places where these slabs are joined—it is as though the entire wall, 40 cubits high, were a single slab. And the wall is so shiny that the slightest speck of dust is visible. In particular, the faces and kneelings and prostrations of the worshippers—God save them!—are all reflected in the surrounding walls as though in a mirror.[33]

Evliya Çelebi's portrayal of the sights and wonders of Athens is inseparable from the effect they all have on him: the visitor's "[...] eyes are dazzled at its marvelous paintings and statues, in the Frankish manner. The figures in the paintings seem to be alive, and the statues smile or frown or look askance."[34] Inside the Parthenon, Evliya Çelebi tells us about the rare colored materials and techniques: highly polished green and red marble columns, gold and painted decoration surpassing that by Mani, the paradigmatic artist in Islamic tradition, or the impossibly thin white marble ceiling, which he associates with the celebrated skill of Fahri of Bursa.[35] He chooses to focus on the colors and brilliance of the pieces of varicolored marble and precious stone in the "qibla dome," which reminds him of the mosaic in the Dome of the Rock in Jerusalem, rather than describe the figure of the Virgin and Christ Child, which we know from near-contemporary travelers still adorned the eastern apse.[36] This choice has nothing to do with Muslim sensitivity to figural images, since Evliya Çelebi delights in the other painted or carved figures in the Parthenon. Instead, it reflects his imaginative engagement with a different ecphrastic tradition that is sparked by linking the building's adornment to other wonders, such as the Dome of the Rock (another building he also calls the most beautiful mosque in the world), and the legendary artistic feats of Mani and Fahri of Bursa.

In his awestruck description of the Parthenon's interior light, Evliya Çelebi adds, "[...] above the aforementioned vault and pure column is a night-lamp [şebçerağ]. In the darkness of night all the priests, patriarchs, and monks would read the Gospel and sections from other texts by the night-lamp, which threw out such vivid light with its blaze."[37] Rather than assuming this is a fanciful cliché,

---

[33] *Seyahatname*, vol. 8, p. 116 (Evliya Çelebi 2010, p. 284).
[34] *Seyahatname*, vol. 8, p. 113 (Evliya Çelebi 2010, p. 279). I discuss Evliya Çelebi's attitude to "Frankish" artistic representation in Athens at greater length in my monograph, but the suggestion that Evliya Çelebi might here be using the expression specifically to describe painting in the Florentine houses on the Acropolis is worth mentioning; see MacKay 2011. In the late 1590s Diego Galán had a similar reaction to life-like statues. Arriving at the harbor of Athens, he comments that on the way up to the city "among the vineyards and olive groves I saw many life-like [*tan al vivo*] statues of men and animals, made of finest marble, for which many would have paid a lot of money in other regions, but the Turks do not appreciate them at all since they have no use for figures whatsoever" [*entre las viñas y olivares vi muchas estatuas de mármoles finísimos de hombres y animales tan al vivo que en otras partes dieran por ellos mucho dinero, pero los turcos no los estiman en nada porque no usan de figuras en ningún modo*]: Diego Galán 2011, ch. 19, pp. 130–131 (the earlier version, MS E); cf. Diego Galán 2001, ch. 20, p. 231 with n. 2222 (for both manuscript versions and variations).
[35] Mani also appears, e.g., in Medina: *Seyahatname*, vol. 9, 281b.29 (Evliya Çelebi 2010, p. 49). On Fahri of Bursa, see Çağman 2013. On the Ottoman architectural ecphrastic tradition as it emerged from the 15th century, see, e.g., Kafescioğlu 1999.
[36] Three nearly contemporary descriptions, by Babin (1674, pp. 32–33), Guillet (1675, pp. 192–193), and Wheler (1682, pp. 364; he visited Athens in 1676), recount a dramatic event that was said to have transpired inside the Parthenon when a Muslim fired on an image of the Virgin only to be killed by the ricocheting bullet. That variations of this tale appear across the Mediterranean world in stories of iconoclasm and punishment from Late Antiquity onward does not preclude its telling in the Parthenon as well. In fact, it would be surprising had the story not been told in such an exuberantly figured setting. These same passages also mention an Ottoman tale of plague-filled marble cupboards inside the mosque, left over from the Christian period (see below).
[37] *Seyahatname*, vol. 8, p. 115 (Evliya Çelebi 2010, p. 283, with adjustments).

might we not hear in his comment local memories—Christian and also Muslim? The remark resembles other stories that circulated in Arabic writing to breathe life into the conversion of churches into mosques. Retaining and recasting the Christian history of buildings had a long pedigree that fortified rather than detracted from the Muslim presence. Evliya Çelebi remarks that the divine Plato used to hang a night-lamp in the qibla dome, and explains how such a lamp worked as the naphtha-soaked wicks were heated by the sun and ignited.[38] He deploys this scientific explanation, common also in late 17th-century European attempts to take the measure of the world, to scoff at the gullible Christians, who, he says, "revered this mechanism as a talisman, calling it the Lamp of Divine Light."[39] His comment about the Christian tradition sounds like a scholium on what Evliya Çelebi was told by a local informant, which he merges with his own observations. Miraculous light exuding from thin marble blocks or from a lamp, or both, appears in many descriptions of the Parthenon interior from the 12th century onwards.[40] Evliya Çelebi speaks of the night-lamps in the past tense, since he reports that they were taken away by "Sultan Mansur" along with other spoils, including "chains of jewels and thousands of idols and candlesticks and jewel-encrusted crosses."[41] Yet Evliya Çelebi is still awed by the interior luminosity he attributes to "fire-stones" in the east wall. Some 70 years before him, a Spanish visitor to the Parthenon mosque, the Christian slave Diego Galán, had been struck by the same effect at the east end, where he saw a stone that was, as he vividly recalls, "transparent as a crystal, and when the sun shines on it, the whole temple gleams."[42]

Galán continues with a description of the centrally placed, raised ambo (Christian pulpit), supported on columns.[43] Here we glimpse the native of Toledo in the process of trying to take apart and identify the accumulated layers of the building's use by pagans, Christians, and Muslims on the basis of his own expectations of church and mosque interiors: "[It] has a high choir like that of the Christians, and in the middle of the temple there is something like an octagonal monstrance [*custodia*] made of marbles and fine jaspers, with a roof of gilded bronze supported by eight columns of fine jasper. This seemed to me to be the setting for some idol left over from the time of the pagan Athenians, since the Turks do not use this kind of decoration in their mosques."[44] This elaborate fixture caught Evliya Çelebi's eye too, especially on account of its rich marbles and "magical" decoration, and he identified it as Plato's throne, from which the divine sage taught.[45] While Evliya Çelebi does not mention pagans

---

[38] On the use of naphtha in lamps instead of oil, see McKenzie 2007, p. 384, n. 71.

[39] *Seyahatname*, vol. 8, p. 114 (Evliya Çelebi 2010, p. 281).

[40] Kaldellis 2009, pp. 196–206, gives some examples.

[41] See Anderson 2017b, pp. 255–258, for discussion of the Arab rulers conflated in Evliya Çelebi's report. I thank Ben Anderson for sending a proof copy of this article.

[42] Diego Galán 2011, ch. 19, pp. 130–131: "*tan transparente como un cristal, que cuando da el sol en ella resplandece todo el templo;*" cf. the later elaboration in Diego Galán 2001, ch. 20, pp. 233–234. I thank Isabel Toral Niehoff, Javier Martínez Jiménez, and especially Alessandra Russo for discussions about the translation. In the previous paragraph, Galán describes the exterior decoration of the "*mezquita*," both the frieze and the pedimental sculptures. This is not the place for a full discussion of Galán's previously neglected description. A full treatment of both versions of the description will appear in my monograph.

[43] Norre (1966, pp. 29–32) and Korres (1994, p. 148) discuss the pre-modern descriptions of the ambo and the difficulties of relating them to what cuttings still appear in the floor. Galán's description, not included in these discussions, confirms the identification of the ambo as raised on columns.

[44] Diego Galán 2011, ch. 19, p. 131: "*En medio del templo hay una como custodia de mármoles y finos jaspes en forma ochavada con un techo de bronce dorado que sustentan ocho colunas de finos jaspes. Esto me pareció a mí que sería puesto de algún ídolo en tiempo de los gentiles atenienses, porque los turcos no usan de este adorno en sus mezquitas;*" cf. Diego Galán 2001, ch. 20, p. 234 with notes for notable manuscript variations. For example, in Diego Galán's later revision he writes "*ocho columnas de mármol tan blanco como la leche*" instead of "*finos jaspes*," and clarifies his original "*puesto*," which I have translated as "setting," by calling it a "*capilla*," by which I imagine he means "shrine" rather than "chapel." Clearly, the Orthodox ambo struck him as exotic, and his later clarification shows him struggling to make it intelligible to his audience and more elegant.

[45] My conjecture that both Galán and Evliya Çelebi are describing the same fixture, most likely the ambo, is based on the fact that they both devote more

or refer explicitly to the building as a former pagan temple, his awareness of the mosque's Christian past slips through when he retells the story of Gospel-reading by priests and monks, and also in the jibe about the Christian lamp talisman, the lamp which he himself attributes to Plato in accordance with his characteristic preference for the city's philosophical rather than Christian identity.

A Brief History of Conversions

I have deliberately started with Evliya Çelebi's way of encountering the building in use, which is quite different from our usual diachronic sorting-out of layers and accumulations.[46] With his allusions to the Parthenon's Christian past, when the Divine Light was indeed one of the church's most celebrated attributes, I will now step back very briefly to the Parthenon's many conversions.[47] Begun by Pericles in 447 B.C. as a temple to Athena, the building suffered dramatic fire damage in the later Roman period, when it was repaired with generous quantities of mortar.[48] In the late 5th century or the 6th century the temple was converted into a church: only the two-chambered core of the building was roofed, using ceramic tiles rather than the original marble ones; a surrounding colonnade remained open to the sky; an apse was created at the east end, the former temple entrance, so that the church (and later mosque) was entered at the west end, through the west chamber, which came to serve as a narthex, where traces of painting were visible still in living memory. The narthex was linked to the east chamber, now a three-aisled nave, by three doors that were opened into the wall that had once separated the two chambers. After the original conversion into a church dedicated to the Panagia Atheniotissa, further adaptations were made in the 12th century, including the expansion of the eastern apse, the addition of galleries elevated on stone supports alongside the inner colonnade of the eastern chamber, and the piercing of three windows into the north and south walls in order to bring more light into the interior at the level of the sculpted frieze that ran around the outside of the original cella and west chamber of the Periclean temple. A final important new feature was the stone tower with an internal spiral staircase of brick and stone in the south-west corner, probably a Frankish construction that once served as an observation tower.[49] It is widely assumed that the tower should be identified with the

---

than usual attention to its marbles and jaspers, multiple supporting columns (Galán recalls eight columns of jasper in the earlier version, which he corrects to milk-white marble in the more elaborated version; Evliya Çelebi, six of white marble), and what must have been the visible, raised underside of the pulpit that was decorated with a striking design that encouraged Galán to link it with the pagan past and Evliya Çelebi with a "head of cheese […] carved out of white marble resembling a belly." MacKay (2011) associated Evliya Çelebi's odd phrase with a conjectured guide's explanation of the rounded knob at the central focal point of the decorative pattern as an omphalos, which in ancient Greece assumed a rounded shape; see his comment in Dankoff and Kim 2010, p. 282, n. 63. Mahmud Efendi's description of the interior, to be treated in detail elsewhere, is an intriguing mix of written accounts and oral history mingled with his own observations about the present day, but includes no comments on liturgical furniture.

[46] For fascinating studies of "multi-sensory engagement" with buildings and objects from the Hellenic past in the 4th–15th centuries and in the late 18th and 19th centuries, see Papalexandrou 2003 and Hamilakis 2011, respectively. For an approach closer to my own, though concerned mainly with the later Ottoman period, see Anderson 2015.

[47] Kaldellis 2009, pp. 196–205 (on the Divine Light). For the building's physical conversion, see Alexopoulos 2015, esp. pp. 160–164 (overview with bibliography); Lambrinou 2012; Bouras [2010] 2017, pp. 146–154; Kaldellis 2009, pp. 23–31; Ousterhout 2005; Korres 1996. I warmly thank Lena Lambrinou for discussing the Parthenon conversions on site, commenting on my discussion of the Parthenon's material conversions, and making available to me the text and illustrations of her unpublished lecture to the Association of the Friends of the Historical Archive of the Archaeological Service in January 2015, on structural information about the Parthenon derived from travelers' accounts and drawings.

[48] Lambrinou 2015, pp. 136–159 and 184–254.

[49] This identification was made by Manolis Korres (1994, esp. p. 40, fig. 19); recently discussed by Lambrinou and Papavasileiou (2013, pp. 30–34); Tanoulas 2012, pp. 34–35, with bibliography. I warmly thank Tasos Tanoulas for his learned guidance on site at the west end of the Acropolis and for his generosity in sharing work both published and unpublished.

Figure 3. The minaret rises at the south-west corner of the Parthenon, which is shown surrounded by houses constructed within the citadel walls (detail of Fig. 4).

base of the church's belfry and later the mosque's minaret (Fig. 3), though some scholars have questioned this assumption and sought the minaret elsewhere.[50]

For the appearance of the church as well as of the mosque, which would have required only minor modifications to the Christianized structure, we have to piece together the descriptions by Evliya Çelebi and the handful of medieval and early modern west European visitors who saw and commented on the building's interior before its destruction. The Venetian bombardment in 1687 toppled the minaret and gutted the building, destroying the roof, the east wall with its apse, the inner colonnades of the nave, the dividing wall between the nave and narthex, much of the north and south walls of the prayer hall, the central columns of the north and south colonnades, and the upper masonry courses of the west end, which was nonetheless the better preserved of the two facades.[51] What was lost had been the result of gradual, largely undocumented adaptations of the original temple structure for Christian

[50] Lambrinou and Papavasileiou (2013, pp. 30–40, with bibliography) provide a painstaking new discussion of the tower, surveying the various theories that have been advanced and offering new insights from study of travelers' drawings. For the proposition that the tower served as the minaret, see the discussions held in 1898 concerning which of the later accretions to the Parthenon should be preserved, and which demolished: Mallouchou-Tufano 1998, pp. 93–94, n. 310. The view that the tower served as the minaret was held by Balanos and later by Korres; see also Tanoulas in Beschi and Tanoulas 2000–2003, pp. 389–390. In the first years of the 20th century, the archaeologist Kavvadias wrote in favor of preserving the spiral staircase/minaret as a memento of the Ottoman impact and the west portal as a reminder of the building's transformation into a Byzantine church: Mallouchou-Tufano 1998, pp. 101–102 and n. 338. Xyngopoulos, another archaeologist involved with the restoration, raised doubts about the identification of the tower with the minaret, suggesting that the latter could have been located elsewhere (Xyngopoulos 1960).
[51] For a collection of early drawings, with discussion, see Hadjiaslani 1987; Bowie and Thimme 1971, pp. 30–36.

and Muslim use over the course of almost 1,200 years. To look more closely at the problems surrounding the conversion from church to mosque, I now turn to the first reported visit to the Parthenon by a Muslim admirer of the City of the Sages, the learned Sultan Mehmed II, in 1458.

Sultan Mehmed II in Athens

The historian Kritoboulos of Imbros (1410–1470) mentions that Sultan Mehmed the Conqueror made a four-day visit to Athens in late August 1458, just after the city had been newly incorporated into his empire.[52] Before he became Mehmed's historian, Kritoboulos served as governor of his native island of Imbros. Kritoboulos had many ambitions and prided himself on his network of politically influential, and also learned, associates, such as Cyriac of Ancona, whom he had guided around the antiquities of his native island in 1444. We might have expected more information about what the sultan would have seen in Athens from the younger, Athenian-born Laonikos Chalkokondyles (ca. 1420–1490).[53]

It was a small world with a center of gravity that pulled educated men to Edirne and the Ottoman court, where Mehmed commissioned them to serve his intertwined political and intellectual interests. The sultan's taste for Greek learning is well-known, and the conjecture that on his visit to Athens he had his tents pitched near the place known as Plato's school comes as no surprise.[54] Mehmed's campaign to capture Constantinople as the crown of his empire was not based only on the best military knowledge available at that time. The prince's wide-ranging curiosity mirrored the enormous embrace of his empire. His library and scriptorium included Greek philosophy and geography, Constantinopolitan legend, Arabic philosophical biography, and Persian astrology, for he was an energetic heir to the Greco-Arabic translation movement that had taken off at a similar universalizing moment, in Abbasid Baghdad.[55] Mehmed's adoption of Hagia Sophia, the great church saturated in Solomonic symbolism, as his new royal mosque on the occasion of his conquest of Constantinople is perhaps the most important parallel for the almost wholly undocumented conversion of the Parthenon. We should expect that his ecumenical approach to annexing the past in order to validate his own rule would have been foremost in his mind on his visit to Athens.

What do Laonikos and Kritoboulos tell us about the visit? Thanks to a reconsideration by Anthony Kaldellis of the date when Laonikos was writing his account of the fall of Byzantium and the rise of the Ottoman Empire, we now see that the younger historian was writing in the 1450s

---

[52] Kritoboulos, *Histories* 3.9.4–7 (Kritoboulos 1954, 3.51–53, trans. Riggs). On Kritoboulos, see Mavroudi 2014, esp. pp. 202–204.
[53] On Kritoboulos, Laonikos, and Cyriac, see Kaldellis 2014, pp. 15–16. Attention has been drawn to many more interconnections between Greek and Latin intellectuals associated with Mehmed's court. One example is the aforementioned Gemistos Plethon, two of whose works were translated (one in excerpts) from Greek into Arabic in Mehmed's reign: Mavroudi 2013, p. 195; Raby 1983, p. 23.
[54] Babinger (1978, p. 161) notes that Mehmed "seems to have preferred to pitch his tents in the olive grove near the Academy or by the banks of the Ilissus." While citing no source, Babinger's conjecture is reasonable in light of contemporary maps that show "Plato's school in the garden" [τὸ τοῦ πλάτωνος διδασκαλεῖον εἰς τὸ παραδείσιον], as in the first paragraph of the 15th-century Τὰ θέατρα καὶ τὰ διδασκαλεῖα τῶν Ἀθηνῶν, reprinted in Laborde 1854a, vol. 1, p. 17; see n. 27 above. Compare the drawing of Athens in 1670, now in Bonn, where the "*Schola di Platone*" is marked in an open space to the east of the city (Omont 1898, 1, pp. 8–9, and 2, pl. 29; see also Bowie and Thimme 1971, p. 23), and the description of the gardens and "*l'École et l'Académie de Platon*" in the environs of Athens (Babin 1674, pp. 49–52).
[55] Interest in Greek learning at the court of Mehmed II has been the focus of important work, most recently by Mavroudi (2013, 2014) and Akasoy (2013). Necipoğlu (1992, 2010, 2012) and Raby (1982, 1983) have produced seminal research on the intersections of art, architecture, literature, philosophy, and political culture, as well as an exemplary study (Necipoğlu 2008) of architecture, space and accretive narratives. While palimpsest is not a useful term to describe the Parthenon with its various organically overlapping associations, Necipoğlu's description of the Dome of the Rock as a "nexus of intertwined narrative threads" (Necipoğlu 2008, p. 32) could aptly describe the Parthenon too. The Cordoban caliph al-Hakam II's appropriation of Greek wisdom and Roman spolia, especially the figures of philosophers reused in the Umayyad palace at Madinat al-Zahara, has recently been studied by Calvo Capilla (2014).

and ended abruptly in the mid-1460s.⁵⁶ As a result of this correction, Laonikos should no longer be considered the last but the first of the four historians who recorded these events in Greek, which opens up the possibility that Kritoboulos had access to Laonikos's *Histories*. Both portray the sultan as "amazed" by the Acropolis, although neither historian mentions particular buildings.⁵⁷ In Laonikos's *Histories*, the only other sight that evokes the sultan's wonderment is a mass impalement by the Wallachian King Vlad III Țepeș.⁵⁸ In keeping with the sultan's military concerns, Laonikos chooses to frame Mehmed's admiration of Athens and Piraeus harbor with the sultan's praise for his general Ömer, son of Turahan, who took the city peacefully and preserved it. "I have heard that the sultan thought more highly of this city and its Acropolis than any other in his territory," Laonikos remarks, "and he greatly admired its ancient magnificence and its buildings."⁵⁹ Laonikos returns to Athens briefly at the end of Book 9, where he inadvertently provides confirmation that the Acropolis was in use by the janissaries left in control by Ömer.⁶⁰

In the Imbriote's panegyric of Mehmed's reign, the sultan's impressions of Athens are not presented as hearsay. Instead, consonant with his portrayal of Mehmed as a cultured ruler, Kritoboulos boldly presents Mehmed as a "wise man"⁶¹ marveling at the buildings of Athens and the "ruins and remains" on the Acropolis.⁶² It is a pity that neither Laonikos nor Kritoboulos makes any mention of the Parthenon or, in particular, its conversion into a mosque on the occasion of the sultan's visit, something Ottomanists assume must have happened, though we possess no archival or epigraphical evidence to prove it.⁶³ It is reasonable to imagine Mehmed, the New Alexander, as his Greek admirers (such as Kritoboulos) liked to call him,⁶⁴ inclining in prayer within the Parthenon as a seal of the town's conquest. Such an action would have been in accord with the time-honored habit of understanding prayer as the seal of conversion—known from the caliph Umar's refusal to pray in Jerusalem's Church of the Holy Sepulchre in favor of Mt. Moriah, and also from Mehmed himself in Hagia Sophia.⁶⁵ For the conversion of the Parthenon church into a mosque we lack a narrator, such as Mehmed's court historian Tursun Beg, who described the new ruler's adoption of Hagia Sophia and the Islamization of its architecture and its legends. Rather than such a formally orchestrated description

---

⁵⁶ Kaldellis (2012) offers a convincing redating of Laonikos's composition and its relationship to later accounts of Mehmed's reign, including that by Kritoboulos.

⁵⁷ Chalkokondyles, *Histories* 9.18; Kritoboulos, *Histories* 3.9.6.

⁵⁸ Chalkokondyles, *Histories* 9.104: "The sultan was seized with amazement and said that it was not possible to deprive of his country a man who had done such great deeds." Cf. 9.102 (Chalkokondyles 2014).

⁵⁹ Chalkokondyles, *Histories* 9.14 (Chalkokondyles 2014).

⁶⁰ Chalkokondyles, *Histories* 9.59.

⁶¹ Kritoboulos, *Histories* 3.9.5–6 on Athens. The marginalium "and a Philhellene" is found at 3.9.6, lines 27–28. The manuscript was dedicated to the sultan and kept in his private library. Chalkokondyles's *Histories*, by contrast, circulated among contemporaries (possibly with additions made by Georgios Amiroutzes) and was translated into many languages: see Kaldellis 2014, pp. 238–239.

⁶² Kritoboulos, *Histories* 3.9.6.

⁶³ The ideal archival proof of the Parthenon's conversion would consist of the mosque's appearance in the cadastral tax surveys [*tahrir defters*] for the sanjak of Eğriboz, which included Athens. Unfortunately, the earliest surviving register dates to 1506, followed by 1521, when the citadel mosque [*cami-i kale-i Atina*] is indeed mentioned: Kiel (2002, pp. 115–117) comments that it was usual for "small sultanic foundations in the provinces" to be funded not through an endowment [*waqf*], but by local taxes [*jizya*], which was in fact the arrangement for the Parthenon mosque, and baptizes it the Sultan Mehmed Fatih mosque. Necipoğlu (2014, p. 355) and Kiel (2008, pp. 138–141) express the reasonable assumption that the Parthenon was converted into a mosque on the occasion of Mehmed's visit.

⁶⁴ Necipoğlu 2012, pp. 6–15; see G. Fowden in Fowden and Fowden 2008, pp. 160–162, at p. 160, on Mehmed playing Alexander to the Aristotle of any of "the three Greek Christian Georges who either belonged or aspired to belong to his circle: Trapezuntios who submitted to Rome and made his career in Italy, Scholarios who flirted with Union but later turned against Rome and accepted the patriarchal throne, and Amiroutzes who perhaps became Muslim."

⁶⁵ The topic of variations in the conversion of holy sites in west Asia has received much-warranted attention in recent scholarship; see, e.g., Guidetti 2016. The richest collection of examples is still Hasluck 1929; see especially vol. 1, pp. 6–19, on the "Transference of Urban Sanctuaries," discussing both Hagia Sophia and the Parthenon with brevity and perceptiveness. The Ottoman inheritance: Yerasimos 1990; Necipoğlu 1992, 2010, 2012. For accounts by Oruç Bey and Mustafa Ali concerning Mehmed's acquisition of knowledge about Hagia Sophia, its history and legends, see Tunalı 2013a, pp. 296–297.

of Islamization, Evliya Çelebi's account, just under 200 years later, can be understood to reflect a process of accumulative and ongoing reinterpretation of the Parthenon. To our disappointment, in his description of the Parthenon, Evliya Çelebi does not ascribe the conversion to Mehmed; in an unnoticed passage from his description of Skopje, however, he does compare the impressive craftsmanship of that city's citadel with what he saw in the "mosque of the Conqueror" in Athens.[66] This confirms, at the very least, that by the 1660s the Parthenon's conversion was assumed to have coincided with Mehmed's visit to Athens.

That both Evliya Çelebi and, as we shall see below, Mahmud Efendi associated the Parthenon mosque with Mehmed II, and that conversion was a standard feature of peaceful conquest, are strong reasons to agree that the conversion coincided with Mehmed's first visit in 1458, or less likely in 1460 on his return from the successful Morea campaign. To have allowed Christians free use of the city's most symbolically and strategically potent topographical feature, on which janissaries were quartered, would have been an unlikely scenario. The Ottoman forces were there to stay; they deflected a Venetian attempt to take the citadel in 1466. A late 15th-century Italian *Itinerario* mentions that "*è nel detto castello una chiessia che già fu tiempo antique,*" which has tempted a few scholars to conjecture a sort of transitional period when the Parthenon still remained a church after Mehmed's visit.[67] Yet the mention of a "*chiessia*" cannot, in any case, bear much weight, since European visitors not unusually referred to mosques as churches in this period. A more serious problem is that the author did not ascend the Acropolis, but viewed it from afar, an exclusion that again points toward Ottoman control of the citadel. To fill the gap, the author used information about the buildings on the citadel from what sources he could, local and written. In 1984 Luigi Beschi persuasively argued that the Italian visitor was in fact the learned friar Urbano Bolziano, who was known to have written an *Itinerario* of his eastern Mediterranean travels that was later lost.[68] Like those of Cyriac of Ancona before him, Urbano's interests lay in antiquities, not in current circumstances, and he certainly cannot be taken as a source of knowledge that the building was not a mosque in the decade between 1475 and 1485 when Urbano must have visited. Perhaps modern scholars have expected a minaret as a sign of conversion. Yet a minaret does not make a mosque, use for Muslim prayer does, and there is no serious reason to doubt that the citadel mosque could have served the community of Muslims quartered there.

Local Legends and Local Residents

I have tried to convey the various registers of Islamic engagement with the Greek philosophical tradition that enabled Mehmed II and Evliya Çelebi to feel themselves heirs to the Hellenic world. At the same time, I have also underlined the complex mode of thought Evliya Çelebi brought to all the cities he

---

[66] *Seyahatname*, vol. 5, 169b, p. 296 (Demetriades 1978, pp. 100–101).
[67] For the text, formerly known as the Ambrosiana Anonymous, or Milan Anonymous, see Ziebarth 1899, pp. 72–88. Delayed conversion has been a topic of speculation since the mid-19th century, with some scholars suggesting 1460, as a response to the conspiracy to reinstall Franco Acciaiuoli that Mehmed discovered on his return from the Morea, and others preferring 1466, after the Venetian attack. For bibliography, see Setton [1948] 1975, p. 238, and Nikoloudis 2017, who both favor the longer delay, while the latter judges the evidence insufficient to decide whether the Parthenon church was in use by the Orthodox or Latin community during this short period. Norre concludes that the conversion must have happened early, with Mehmed's first visit, on military grounds (1966, pp. 54–55, 57–58), and also citing the short lines "τὸ κάστρο εἶναι ἡ ἀκρόπολις· τὸ ἰσμαΐδι, εἶναι ὁ ναὸς τῆς ἀθηνᾶς τῆς παλλάδος" [the citadel is the Acropolis; the mosque is the temple of Pallas Athena], from a brief description of Athenian monuments known as the Paris Anonymous (Par.gr. 1631 A fol.158b), a 15th- or 16th-century copy of an earlier text similar in character to the better known Vienna Anonymous: for the text and brief discussion see, respectively, Wachsmuth 1874, pp. 742–744, and Foerster 1883, pp. 30–32.
[68] Beschi, 1984; see also the essay by Tanoulas herein, pp. 59–65.

described and his application of this mode to the distinctive stories he heard in Athens. Yet what can we know about the pre-existing legends in the absence of written local accounts from this period? The underlying problem propelling the argument of Anthony Kaldellis's book *The Christian Parthenon* (2009) is the discomfort Christians felt about their inheritance of pagan Athens. The situation was different for our educated Ottoman visitors, because such incongruities had been made Qur'an-compatible through the translation and gradual recasting of Greek philosophy, and the subsuming of the Greek philosophers into the roll-call of ecumenical sages, who were reshaped according to evolving needs across the Islamic cultural commonwealth. Kaldellis argues that alongside efforts to Christianize the pagan past, we also find culturally Christian writers preserving and reweaving legends that associated monuments of Athens with celebrated Athenian historical figures.[69] Kaldellis does not extend his work into the Frankish or Ottoman periods, but is aware of the name-dropping habits that appear, for example, in the 15th-century catalogue of Athenian monuments known as the Vienna Anonymous.[70] Frequently cited sources of such local identifications for European visitors were the Capuchins and Jesuits who had been resident in Athens, and later Chalkis, since the late 1650s.[71]

The Jesuit priest Jacques-Paul Babin wrote a description of Athens that he sent to a fellow Jesuit in Istanbul, who, in turn, made it available to the antiquarian Jacob Spon, who published it with commentary in 1674, before his own visit to Athens. The identifications in the engraving that accompanied the text deserve note. Consistent with the book's title, *Relation de l'état présent de la ville d'Athènes*, Babin's labels present the city as it was known in the 1670s, with the Parthenon described not with the aphaeretic eye that sees only the ancient temple, but as "*La grande mosquée*," the Acropolis as "*citadelle*," and the Temple of Olympian Zeus as "*Restes du Palais d'Hadrien*" (Fig. 2). Frequently spoken of in the same breath as the Capuchins of Athens as a source of local information is the French and later English consul Jean Giraud, who lived in Athens from 1658 until after 1688 and had married into a prominent Athenian family. These figures represent a middle ground between local traditions and enquiring early west European travelers, as well as between the world of mirabilia and source-driven antiquarianism.

European Visitors

Charles-Marie-François Olier, Marquis de Nointel, ambassador of Louis XIV to the Sublime Porte, has already been mentioned above, thanks to his greatest benefaction to us today—the remarkable drawings made in Athens by the commissioned artists who accompanied him in late 1674, the same year in which Spon published Babin's description of Athens with its drawing of the contemporary city.[72] Nointel knew that his orchestration of detailed drawings, not only of the Parthenon sculptures but also of other Athenian monuments, was inspired and completely exceptional. This emerges clearly

---

[69] Kaldellis 2009, pp. 182–191; Yakovaki 2006, pp. 247–253.
[70] See n. 27 above.
[71] The most important discussion of European visitors to Athens in the 17th century and the early 18th is Yakovaki 2006. With scholarly fervor and literary style, she traces the shift in the European view of Athens from one that belonged to the traditions of mirabilia stories to one characterized by an incipient scientific approach in which buildings are understood as monuments and archaeological artifacts. She identifies the 1670s and 1680s, when Nointel, Spon, Wheler and Vernon visited, as the turning point. It is a loss that her work has not been translated into English to reach a wider audience, although she is not concerned with Ottoman views. For brief comparisons of spatial and social perceptions recorded by Evliya Çelebi and contemporary European visitors, see Pitsos 2013; Apostolou 2009; and, most recently, on travelers to Athens, Lagogianni-Georgakarakou and Koutsogiannis 2015 (with extensive bibliography). Accessible to the strictly Anglophone reader is the useful first chapter of Constantine 1984 [2011].
[72] The Nointel album is kept in the Bibliothèque nationale de France, Paris [http://gallica.bnf.fr/ark:/12148/btv1b7200482m]. Reproductions of the drawings: Omont 1898; Bowie and Thimme 1971. Omont (1898, vol. 1, pp. 8–20; vol. 2, pls. 29–45) performed a great service by assembling and pub-

in the letter he dispatched from Athens to the Marquis de Pomponne, the French secretary of state for foreign affairs.[73] What he could not have known, of course, was that only 13 years later, the Parthenon and its sculptures would be devastated by the Venetian bombardment. Nointel's ambassadorial mission and personal interests were entangled and complex, including the delicate negotiation of the Capitulations, which involved both trading privileges for French merchants in the Ottoman Empire and French protection of the Empire's Christians. It was in connection with that mission that he had been commissioned in France to acquire Greek and Arabic manuscripts; in 1673, he began an extended tour of the Christian parts of the Empire, where he also collected antiquities in large numbers. In his suite was the young Orientalist Antoine Galland (1646–1715), whose knowledge of the Greek language was also an asset. Galland later contributed to d'Herbelot's influential *Bibliothèque orientale*, published in 1697 and based partly on the work of the great Ottoman scholar Katip Çelebi, who flourished in the first half of the 17th century. Galland secured his fame as the first translator of *Les mille et une nuits*, published in 1704,[74] but an important part of his intellectual training had taken place in Istanbul 30 years earlier, when he and Nointel belonged to circles that included leading intellectuals concerned to use culturally varied sources for the writing of history and philosophy, such as Demetrios Cantemir and the Ottoman universal historian Hezarfen, a native of Cos.[75] Given such company, we might ask whether Galland and Nointel would have approached a visit to Athens as an opportunity to explore the intersection of Classical, Christian, and Muslim history.

To commemorate his visit to Athens, Nointel had an oil painting made that is thought to be the earliest surviving realistic depiction of the city. The enormous canvas, measuring 2.60 x 5.20 m, hangs today in the Museum of the City of Athens–Vouros-Eutaxias Foundation (Fig. 4).[76] The ambitious painting's composition is best-described as a 17th-century compilation of scenes rather than an integrated whole. Made up of discrete scenes brought together by the artist, the painting is an eloquent visual expression of the composite and agglutinative nature found also in the written descriptions of contemporary Athens and its monuments compiled in the same period. A slim minaret rises from a Parthenon that dominates the Acropolis rock. The building is not represented in isolation, but rather as part of a densely inhabited citadel with well-delineated houses, Frankish tower, and the Propylaea (Fig. 3). The citadel dwarfs the tile-roofed houses, churches, and mosques, rendered with striking detail in and around the walled town below. In the foreground we see Nointel, dressed in an Ottoman kaftan, posing with his suite on the lower slopes of Mt. Lycabettus. On the right, we see groups of stereotyped Ottoman figures that belong more to the world of costume albums than individuals Nointel might have met on the streets of Athens.[77] On the left side of the canvas, the soaring columns outside

---

lishing the earliest depictions of Athens. Note especially the fine drawing of Athens in 1670, Omont 1898, vol. 1, pp. 8–9; vol. 2, pl. XXIX (Kunstmuseum, Bonn). For discussion and bibliography of the very similar drawing in the Museo Civico in Bassano, probably deriving from the same source, most likely Venetian, as the Bonn drawing, see Beschi and Tanoulas 2000–2003 and the essay by Tanoulas herein, pp. 59–65.

[73] Omont (1898, vol. 1, p. 5) quotes part of the letter, written in December 1674, almost 13 years before the Venetian bombardment of September 1687, in which Nointel suggests the Parthenon sculptures deserve to be sheltered in the safety of His Majesty's galleries: "*Tout ce que l'on peut dire de eslevé de ces originaux, c'est qu'ils mériteroient d'estre placés dans les cabinets ou galleries de Sa Majesté, où ils jouiroient de la protection que ce grand monarque donne aux art et aux sciences qui les ont produits. Ils y seroient mis à l'abry de l'injure du temps et des affronts qui leurs sont faits par les Turcs, qui, pour éviter une idolâtrie imaginaire, croyent faire une œuvre méritoire en leur arrachant le nés ou quelque autre partie.*" In the same year, Babin (1674, p. 28) compared the Parthenon sculptures with "*les figures et statues du Château de Richelieu.*"

[74] Galland's lost Qur'an translation: Larzul 2009, pp. 153–157.

[75] For a brief and insightful portrait of this world and its relevance to Evliya Çelebi, see Hagen 2004, pp. 248–256. See also Tunalı 2013a, pp. 29–32 and 166–167 with further bibliography in the notes.

[76] For a detailed discussion of the ongoing controversy over Nointel's artists and the authorship of the drawings and paintings commissioned by him, see Meyer 2017.

[77] William Kynan-Wilson (pers. comm. 2014).

the city walls are the same columns Evliya Çelebi had described just seven years earlier as a palace built by King Solomon for the Queen of Sheba.

So close is the resemblance between the configuration of the columns, arched gate and city walls in the Nointel artist's drawing reproduced above (Fig. 1) and in the Nointel canvas that we can only assume that the painter used the former as a preparatory sketch for the painting. One detail has been changed: the painter moved the domed church from north of the walls to the east, near the gate

Figure 4. Charles-Marie-François Olier, Marquis de Nointel, with his suite in Athens in 1674, unknown artist, oil on canvas, 2.60 x 5.20 m. Chartres, Musée des Beaux-Arts, on permanent loan to the Museum of the City of Athens–Vouros-Eutaxias Foundation.

and columns, while retaining the oversized proportions of the extramural monuments.[78] The sketch can be found today in the Nointel album, famous for the aforementioned drawings of the Parthenon sculptures.[79] It is one of three lesser-known drawings, all labeled by Galland and all unique depictions of the late 17th-century city, bound at the back of the album.[80] While the arched gate and columns would become standard landmarks in European drawings of Athens, a second sketch by one of Nointel's artists (Fig. 5) clearly depicts an open-air mosque with a fused mihrab/minbar and low

---

[78] For Homolle (1894, p. 524), this church, presumably the Soteira Lykodemou, and its placement represented *"une des plus bizarres déviations"* of the Nointel painting. The fascinating topic of wandering extramural churches in the early European drawings of Athens cannot be broached here.
[79] Reprinted in Omont 1898, vol. 2, pl. XXII; Bowie and Thimme 1971, pl. 42.
[80] In addition to the two discussed here, drawing no. 9 in the Nointel Album (Omont 1898, vol. 2, pl. XX), which Galland labeled "Ruine d'un Édifice Antique d'Athènes," shows the colonnaded west facade of the Library of Hadrian against which the church of the Aghioi Asomatoi sta Skalia was built, with the Acropolis hastily sketched in the background as a few houses and a minaret. See Bowie and Thimme 1971, pp. 82–84; cf. Simone Pomardi's sepia drawing made in 1805: Camp 2013, cat. no. 62, opposite p. 184.

enclosure wall in the north-east corner of the ancient peribolos.[81] This place of open-air prayer is pictured, still in use, in Louis Dupré's drawing (Fig. 6) made over a century later.[82]

The inclusion of the open-air mosque in drawings by the Nointel artist and later by Dupré converges exactly with Evliya Çelebi's description of the "open-air prayer ground with soaring columns in praise of which the tongue falls short."[83] Evliya Çelebi also provides the extraordinary detail that it was the site to which all Athenians went to pray for rain.[84] More than through the description of buildings confined by different ecphrastic traditions, it is thanks to the observation of contemporary practice, preserved in drawing and in writing, that the overlap between the European and Ottoman visitors becomes palpable to us and we can imagine our viewers in situ.

Figure 5. Throne of Belkis / Palace of Hadrian with the mihrab/minbar and low enclosure wall of the open-air mosque, by an unknown artist in the Nointel suite, 1674, red and black pencil, 26.6 x 45 cm. Paris, Bibliothèque nationale de France, Cabinet des Estampes, album Fc 3a (Réserve), unnumbered, fol. 28.

---

[81] Antoine Galland's note at the bottom of the page reads, in the original orthography, "*Veue d'une porte et d'un Édifice Antique d'Athènes bastis par l'Empereur Hadrien, avec une partie de la ville d'Athènes.*" The manuscript title page of this album reads, "*Temple de Minerve à Athènes bâti par Adrien* ['*bâti par Adrien*' crossed out by a later hand]. *Dessiné par ordre de M^r. Nointel, ambassadeur à la Porte, avant que ce temple ne fut renversé par une bombe des Vénetiens.*"
[82] Destruction of post-Classical evidence in this region by 19th-century Greek archaeologists: Bouras 2010, pp. 96–98.
[83] *Seyahatname*, vol. 8, p. 118 (Evliya Çelebi 2010, p. 288).
[84] It was a tenacious practice: Hasluck (1929, vol. 1, p. 324, n. 7) identifies four works, one late 17th- and three early 19th-century (when Dupré made his drawing), that mention the Temple of Olympian Zeus as the site where the population converged to pray for rain. See the stimulating discussions by Cohen 2018 and Anderson 2017a.

Figure 6. "Le Temple de Jupiter Olympien et l'Acropolis d'Athènes," showing the columns of the Throne of Belkis and the mihrab/minbar of the open-air mosque in 1819, by Louis Dupré. Dupré 1825, pl. 22. American School of Classical Studies at Athens, Gennadius Library.

In 1676, more European travelers visited Athens and provided descriptions—most notably the Frenchman Jacob Spon and the Englishmen George Wheler and Francis Vernon. Spon and Wheler had traveled first to Istanbul, where they discussed Athens with Nointel and Galland, then continued on to Athens, where they overlapped with Vernon, who had arrived in 1675. Comparison of Evliya Çelebi's account of Athens with those by Spon, Wheler, and especially Vernon reveals striking differences in their methods of making sense of what they saw. Generally speaking, we find a tendency among the west European visitors, in contrast with Evliya Çelebi and the European residents of Athens, to attempt to cut through the accumulated layers of local legend and associated toponyms, like digging an archaeological trench to find the "original" level. The building that Evliya Çelebi knows as "Plato's Pavilion," west Europeans from the 1670s onward label as the "Tower of the Winds" and the "Horologion of Andronikos," based on Vitruvius and Varro, since Pausanias, their preferred guide, did not happen to mention this monument in his 2nd-century A.D. *Description of Greece*.[85] We should not, though, imagine that these early west European visitors inaugurated a dramatic shift from legendary identifications to those based on ancient sources. What is fascinating about this period is precisely

---

[85] Also the "Temple of the Eight Winds" and the "Tower of Andronikos Cirrhestes." Hasluck (1929, vol. 1, p. 13, n. 1) brings together the multiple associations and functions of this "ambiguous" building. In a delightful note Hamilakis (2011, p. 68, n. 32) mentions Evliya Çelebi as a recorder of "indigenous archaeology," including legends surrounding the Tower of the Winds, citing Biris (1959, p. 47).

the mixture of ancient and later, more legendary, identifications through which the Athenian landscape was understood, for example, the 1698 inventory of drawings by Nointel's artists in which the Tower of the Winds is identified as the "Tomb of Socrates."[86] Impressive buildings attracted multiple stories. Evliya Çelebi had reported the Tower as both Plato's Pavilion and Philip the Greek's tomb, commemorated, he says, by the Christians who visited it on feast days.[87] European renderings of the city also range widely from maps of varying precision to schematic, often somewhat fantastical, drawings that still show a mix of legend and history, especially those by Wheler.

Wheler's account was designed to complement that of his fellow traveler Spon, whose book appeared first. To some degree, this accounts for his greater attention to and commentary on the contemporary world he sees around him. Spon and, above all, Vernon are much stricter in their scientific exercise. However, neither Spon nor Wheler can resist including in their checklist verification of Pausanias's text a few other details that we would today classify as mirabilia and curiosities, most notably a monstrous hybrid child born to an Ottoman woman in the citadel of Athens.[88] Such details sound like stories told by locals. Wheler relates a tale, also told by Galland (and Guillet), about certain mysterious marble cupboards inside the Parthenon from the Christian period: once upon a time, a Muslim opened one of them, and the town was immediately afflicted by plague.[89] They all mention certain colored stones that emitted a wonder-working light, most likely the "fire-stones" Plato had placed in the eastern wall, according to Evliya Çelebi's telling.

Spon, Wheler, and Vernon shared a mania for cross-checking, against the evidence on the ground and in their ancient sources, the contemporary, highly successful book about Athens by Georges Guillet de Saint-George (1625?–1705), written under the pen name Guilletière. Guillet's work belongs more to the composite mode, an inventive mix of legend, ancient sources, knowledge of present-day circumstances, and sensory responses to ancient spaces in contemporary use. Interspersed amidst fact and fantasy (and laced with mockery of the earnest Protestant antiquarian fever) is fascinating information about Orthodox–Catholic relations, just the sort of information Antoine Galland was commissioned to gather on his travels with Nointel. Guillet's indulgence in a good story, combined with his false claims of autopsy and his factual errors, is precisely what pushed Spon, Wheler, and Vernon over the edge into moral and scientific outrage.[90] Guillet's main local source was the Capuchins, which was perhaps another reason his book cut too close to the bone, since all "real" visitors also relied on them, at least as a supplement to their ancient authors. The plan of Athens included in the 1675 Paris publication is thought to have been based on a plan drawn up by the Capuchins and is provided with a key listing no less than 151 sites in Athens, and a striking mix of ancient and contemporary identifications.[91] For Spon, Wheler and Vernon, it was bad enough that Guillet spiced up his architectural de-

---

[86] The inventory of the drawings made by the collector Michel Bégon in 1698 is reprinted by Bowie and Thimme (1971, p. 17).
[87] *Seyahatname*, vol. 8, pp. 118–119 (Evliya Çelebi 2010, pp. 288–290).
[88] Spon (1678, vol. 2, pp. 134–135) relates the incident. Wheler (1682, p. 419) reports the story on Spon's authority, noting that a French surgeon who was resident in Athens had attempted to have the creature embalmed and shipped to France (for a cabinet of curiosities?), but the Ottoman officials refused; they had the monster sentenced to death and buried as a devil. Presumably the anatomical anomalies had captured Spon's attention, as the other medical doctor's, and justified the story's inclusion in the antiquarian's description of Athens.
[89] Guillet 1675, p. 198; also Wheler 1682, p. 364. Spon (1678, vol. 2, p. 91) mentions that the Ottomans refused to open the cupboard for Nointel, but omits the local legend. Galland (1881, vol. 1, pp. 38–39) recalls a slightly different punishment, writing in his journal entry for January 27, 1672, that he heard from Nointel, who heard from a Capuchin monk, who had heard at second hand from a janissary who had been in Athens, that the Ottoman feared blindness as retribution for opening the cupboard.
[90] See Vernon 1676, p. 579.
[91] In the original French publication, the plan was included as a fold-out insert between the front matter and Book One (University Library, Cambridge) or at the back (Gennadius Library, Athens), while the key to the plan was printed at the end of Book Three (Guillet 1675, pp. 339–347). The

scriptions with local color, for instance, in his intriguingly realistic report that until recently the Parthenon interior had been crammed with Muslim votives, having become a focus of dervish pilgrimage.[92] Guillet even went so far as to describe to his readers how the wind sounded as it howled through the windows and rattled the multitude of hanging lamps, or the sight and sound of the muezzin performing the call to prayer from the mosque's highest point. Such evocation of the sensory experience reminds us more of Evliya Çelebi's description of the Parthenon interior than that of any other contemporary European visitor. Guillet also had an eye for continuities at the Parthenon, remarking that, "The same star which once made Athens so superstitious in the time of idolatry, so pious amidst the fervor of Christianity, makes it still religious, in the manner of the Turks."[93]

Mahmud Efendi and the City of the Sages

None of these contrasting epistemic modes of encountering and interpreting material remains of the past changed overnight, but through multiple processes of experiment and conflict. The story continues on much more familiar classicizing ground with the west European visitors of the 18th century. I will conclude by briefly discussing a lesser-known and under-studied Ottoman description of Athens from the first decades of the 18th century. The manuscript, which survives in the Tokapı Palace Library in Istanbul, was noted by Cengiz Orhonlu in the early 1970s and became the subject of an ambitious dissertation by Gülçin Tunalı in 2013; her transcription of folios 1b – 240a and translations of short sections are extremely useful and tantalizing.[94] The title is *Tarih-i Medinetü'l-Hukema* [The history of the city of the sages], written by Mahmud Efendi, a Muslim whose family lived in Chalkis, Thebes, and Athens. He tells us he began writing in 1715.[95] His work is a complex history of Athens, integrating ancient Greek and medieval Arabic writers, eyewitness observation, and conversation with locals, plus the Arabic and Ottoman tradition of geographical description that interlaces places with prophetic and pre-Islamic figures.[96] For their help in translating Greek, Latin, Modern Greek, and

---

copies of the English translation (Guillet 1676) I consulted include neither map nor key. Bowie and Thimme (1971, pp. 26–28) reprint the engraving from the original French publication and include a translation of the key as the "Explanation of the Numbers that Designate Remarkable Sites in Old and New Athens." See also p. 45, Fig. 8.

[92] Guillet 1675, pp. 193–194. Modern scholarship has sided with Spon and Vernon, writing Guillet off as a fraud (e.g., Pollard 2015, p. 100: "indeed entirely fanciful") without engaging with his book on its own terms, or possibly without reading it. (Beard [2002, p. 76] breaks the mold by parenthetically acknowledging his "correct observations and interpretations.") For a discussion of "authenticity," see Constantine 1989; Walker (2013) represents a significant advance in our knowledge and understanding of Francis Vernon and receives due attention in my monograph, but his interest in Guillet is only tangential. The regular disregard of Guillet is largely because most readers of these late 17th-century accounts are interested in scientifically verifiable archaeological detail. Hasluck had other interests, and the seriousness with which he reads Guillet's account of the dervishes is worth noticing: he links Guillet's comment that the dervishes were from Konya with the well-attested cult of Plato among the Christians and Muslims of Konya, home to the Mevlevi dervishes, where Plato was deeply woven into the cultic and topographic tradition (Hasluck 1929, vol. 1, pp. 14–15; vol. 2, pp. 363–378). See also Nixon 2004, pp. 433–439.

[93] Guillet (1675, p. 195): "*La mesme Etoille qui a rendu autrefois Athenes si superstitieuse pendant l'Idolatrie, si pieuse pendant la ferveur du Christianisme, la rend encore religieuse à la maniere des Turcs.*"

[94] Topkapı Sarayı Emanet Hazinesi, no. 1411. Orhonlu 1972, 1973–1974; Arrigoni (1989, pp. 75–77, n. 37) discusses the text in an extensive footnote. I want to thank Gülçun Tunalı for her generosity in providing a copy of her dissertation (Tunalı 2013a), Dimitris Loupis for a photograph of the entire manuscript, and both Seyyed Mohammad Shariat-Panahi and Thomas Sinclair for translating passages of the text.

[95] On Mahmud, see Tunalı 2013a, pp. 1–2, pp. 32–43 (biography and the history of his composition), and pp. 27–32 (broadly describing his "intellectual horizons"); Tunalı 2013b.

[96] Tunalı (2013a, pp. 124–126) suggests ways in which Mahmud "Ottomanizes" ancient Greek history, closely examining his treatments of Theseus (pp. 126–143), Alexander (pp. 143–160), and Constantine (pp. 160–172) as case studies of what she calls Mahmud's "Ottomanization" of "foreign cultural units" (p. 124). On Theseus and Ottoman "Hellenism," see Tunalı 2013b.

"Frankish" sources for him, he thanks two learned Greek contemporaries, Papa Kolari and Papa Sotori, reasonably identified by Tunalı as the well-known abbots of Kaisariani monastery, Theophanes Kavallares and Gregorios Soteres.[97] Tunalı has also traced close correspondences between Mahmud's history and Georgios Kontares's history of ancient Athens, published in Venice in 1675, coinciding with the visit by Spon, Wheler, and Vernon to Athens.[98]

Mahmud had gone to Istanbul for his madrasa education and returned to Greece as the mufti of Athens, but would not have had the opportunity to preach a sermon in the same Parthenon mosque that had been visited only half a century earlier by our travelers. After the Venetian bombardment in 1687 that left the building filled with rubble, a Parthenon mosque was eventually rebuilt inside the roofless remains, reduced in size and with its orientation shifted towards Mecca. As a harbinger of what lay ahead, the new house of prayer was confined to a free-standing structure within the shell that had once embraced the organic historical procession of use. This second mosque is shown in John Travlos's section drawing and plan (Fig. 7) and in a rare aquatint copy of a daguerreotype (Fig. 8)[99] by Pierre-Gustave Joly de Lotbinière of 1839, made only four years before the mosque's destruction.[100]

Finally, Mahmud offers us an opportunity to compare Evliya Çelebi with another Muslim viewer who also described Athens in writing. Such comparison makes it possible to tease out a few Islamizing local stories heard by both and relayed by each for his own purposes. Like Evliya Çelebi, Mahmud integrates Athens into monotheist history from the start, opening his account of Athens with Adam. Solomon and Belkis make their appearance, again linked to the Temple of Olympian Zeus. Both Evliya Çelebi and Mahmud refer to the Tower of the Winds as a tent, Mahmud qualifying it as a janissary tent; and while Evliya Çelebi associates it with Plato, Mahmud's philosopher of choice is Socrates.[101] Like Evliya Çelebi, Mahmud links sages closely with buildings and other urban features.

As noted earlier, Kritoboulos's account of the visit to Athens by Mehmed the Conqueror does not explicitly mention the conversion of the Parthenon church into a mosque. Mahmud, however, writes the following:

> In the same manner that [the sultan] had commanded the reanimation [*ihya*] of the other mosques [*cami*] and prayer halls [*mescit*] in conquered territory, he ordered that this ancient temple too be reanimated by inclusion in an imperial charitable foundation. He arranged for two imams, four muezzins, a caretaker to light the

[97] *Tarih-i Medinetü'l-Hukema* 2a.
[98] See Tunalı 2013a, pp. 67–77 (Athenian abbots), pp. 77–82 (historian and priest Georgios Kontares, who took the name Gregorios when he was elevated to the metropolitan throne of Servia and Kozani), and pp. 89–102 (Kontares's Ἱστορίαι [1675] as a source for Mahmud's own history of Athens).
[99] Joly de Lotbinière identifies the building in his notes as "*Le Parthénon ou temple de Minerve.*" Publisher N.-M.-P. Lerebours commissioned the daguerreotypes, which appeared in his *Excursions daguerriennes. Vues et monuments les plus remarquables du globe* (Lerebours 1842) with the caption "*Le Parthénon à Athènes.*" [http://www.getty.edu/art/collection/objects/200938/noel-marie-paymal-lerebours-grece-le-parthenon-a-athens-french-1842/?dz=0.3426,0.3470,1.46.].
[100] Desautels (2010) reprints and discusses Joly de Lotbinière's comments on each of his Athenian daguerreotypes (for the Parthenon, see pp. 338–341 and p. 381, which mentions "*cette mosquée sert maintenant de musée pour les débris que l'on veut conserver*"). On Joly de Lotbinière, the first to "photograph" the Parthenon, see Tsirigialou 2015, pp. 78–80. For different interpretations of what the "true illusion" of Athenian monuments was, as seen through the lens of two late 19th-century photographers, see Szegedy-Maszak 1987, pp. 128–129 and passim. Bohrer (2015, pp. 96–97) briefly discusses the Parthenon daguerreotype, whose subject he describes as the "remnant of an Ottoman mosque, which had stood for decades [*sic*] in the site of the ancient sanctuary." Joly de Lotbinière's notes do not suggest the 21st-century interpretation that Bohrer projects onto the Parthenon daguerreotype: "It [the image] juxtaposes, indeed makes a single whole of, the products of a variety of intermingled cultures, marks of temporalities both ancient and modern, pagan, Christian and Islamic." Hamilakis and Ifantidis (2015) offer a stimulating 21st-century exploration of "multi-temporality" on the Acropolis.
[101] *Tarih-i Medinetü'l-Hukema* 140a – 140b (Tunalı 2013a, p. 63).

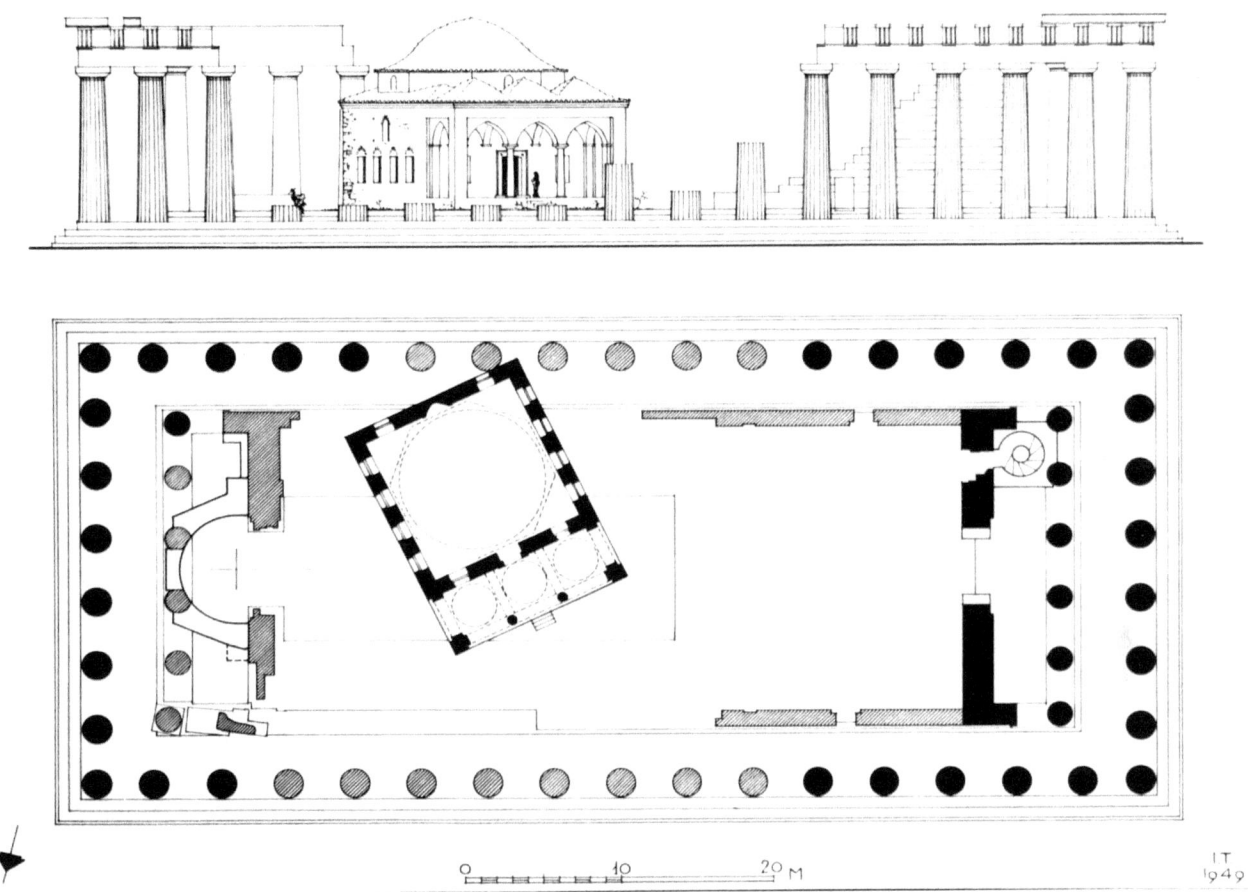

Figure 7. Section drawing from the north and plan of the second Parthenon mosque, after the 1687 explosion. Drawing John Travlos. Travlos [1960] 1993, p. 203, fig. 137.

lamps, a cleaner, doorkeepers, [and] a *vaiz*-cum-instructor to be appointed; each of these was allocated appropriate duties, while the remainder of the mosque's expenses was covered. The mosque's presence [in the citadel] led to [the decision] to send all the unbelievers out of the citadel, while a citadel commandant was appointed with an adequate number of ordinary soldiers at his command. To these were added a caravan official, a *cebeci* captain, and an artillery commander. In short, a full garrison was appointed.

[The sultan] surveyed the strange ancient buildings inside the citadel. The pavilion built of pure white marble, and standing on pillars in the form of four [*sic*] maidens, became a matchless imperial seat. The decision, motivated by personal attraction, to direct the imperial gaze at the wonders and curiosities of Athens, subjected at the above-mentioned date to the detailed taxation survey, was the occasion and cause of the sultan's remaining in Athens a few days. He examined and perused the ancient monuments, whether inside the citadel, in the area around the citadel [*varoş*], or in the environs of the city.[102]

This is what we would expect—a sultanic foundation created on the occasion of Mehmed's visit; and it is what Ottomanists assume was the case.[103] The matter-of-fact style in which Mahmud reports the conversion and the details he offers concerning the provision made for the mosque's care could suggest that he had access to documentation now lost, or simply to local traditions handed down from the time of the conversion. He might, of course, have invented the Parthenon story along the lines of what was more or less routine procedure, but that would be the extreme skeptic's view. Mahmud does not simply record the logistics of the conversion, but brings the scene to life by evoking both the city's exotic architecture and the sultan's distinctive curiosity. Mahmud's striking description of a marble pavilion [*köşk*] on pillars in the form of four maidens is the unique account of the Erechtheion by a Muslim viewer, since Evliya Çelebi does not mention the building. In addition to this, the sultan's desire to linger in Athens a few days to "gaze at the wonders and curiosities" and explore the "ancient monuments" corresponds not only to Mehmed's well-known reputation for learning, but more specifically to the brief reports by Laonikos and Kritoboulos that depict the sultan marveling at the ancient citadel's buildings.[104] Of course, Mahmud's description of the Parthenon's conversion into a mosque is a not an archival record, but part of a highly synthetic history of Athens by one of the city's Muslim officials. The style and specificity of the report nevertheless present the firmest known evidence for dating the conversion to Mehmed's visit. Our study of Mahmud's history has only begun, but promises new perspectives on early Ottoman and local Athenian encounters with pre-Islamic Antiquity before the later 18th century and the 19th, which have attracted so much attention.[105]

Conclusion

I will close with an extraordinary example of Muslim creative engagement with the Hellenic past. The passage comes in Mahmud's account of Pericles and his attempts to justify the construction of a new temple to the Athenian taxpayers. The statesman is depicted in consultation with the assembled "right-thinking learned men in a council,"[106] before whom he argues that in Jerusalem Solomon constructed a peerless temple, but it was too far away for would-be pilgrims in Greece (Mahmud's Rumeli) to reach. The new temple in Athens would be as great as Solomon's and, like it, would attract admiration

---

[102] *Tarih-i Medinetü'l-Hukema* 240a – 241a (beginning) (trans. Sinclair; see also Tunalı 2013a, p. 45); note that only four Caryatids are mentioned.

[103] Guillet (1675, pp. 196–198) describes being told by the imam of the Parthenon that the mysterious luminosity of the Parthenon interior was a sign from the Prophet Muhammad given to Mehmed II on the day when the church was converted into a mosque. He also reports (p. 157) that when he asked the leading Greeks of Athens why their prosperous city was not "*la Residence d'un Sangiac, ou d'un Bey*," he was told that out of kindness towards the Athenians Mehmed II had saved them from that onerous fate. This information (without the confusion of a sanjak for a title rather than an administrative division) is also found in other accounts, including those of Mahmud Efendi and Kritoboulos, who says that Mehmed "noted with pleasure the respect of the inhabitants of the city for their ancestors, and he rewarded them in many ways. They received from him whatever they asked for." (Kritoboulos, *Histories* 3.9.6 [Kritoboulos 1954, p. 136]). The time has come to reread Guillet as one more link (with its own distinctive difficulties) in the preservation of local memory of these events.

[104] See Chalkokondyles, *Histories* 9.18 and 102–104; Kritoboulos, *Histories*, 3.9.6.

[105] See also the article by Tunalı herein, pp. 97–121.

[106] *Tarih-i Medinetü'l-Hukema* 124a (trans. Sinclair).

Figure 8. "Grèce. Le Parthénon à Athènes," showing the second Parthenon mosque in September 1839, before its demolition in 1843, aquatint copy, 1842, of a daguerreotype by Pierre-Gustave Joly de Lotbinière, 15.1 x 20.3 cm. Digital image courtesy of the Getty's Open Content Program.

and pilgrimage. Note especially how Mahmud pulls the Classical Parthenon into Islamic sacred history and practice by using current Ottoman terminology and the expectation that the foundation of a place of worship could serve a salvific purpose for the "whole community's place in the Afterlife:"[107]

> In noble Jerusalem the sainted Solomon (greetings be to him) has built a rare, valuable temple, and all, high and low, are desirous of going to worship in it. However, the Greek population of Rumeli, which is extremely far away, has formidable difficulties in reaching [Jerusalem] to worship in the temple. But we must construct an out-

[107] *Tarih-i Medinetü'l-Hukema* 125ba (trans. Sinclair). Tunalı (2013a, p. 126) observes, "Mahmud Efendi mentions Pericles in the section on the building of the Parthenon with terminology belonging specifically to Ottoman culture. If some charitable building such as a fountain or mosque was built, a verse specifying the date of the building and the name of the person who funded the charity were written at the entry gate." The Pericles section has otherwise not been previously discussed. Thomas Sinclair and I discussed the passage in separate papers at the 22nd Symposium of the Comité international des études pré-ottomanes et ottomanes (Trabzon 2016).

standing and magnificent temple, unsurpassed in quality. Its walls should be of pure white marble. The roof that will rest on the walls should be supported on beams of white marble too, and indeed so should its ceilings and substructures be constructed of white marble. Our region will acquire learning and religious knowledge; most of its population [already] has a pious insistence on asceticism and on worship.[108]

What we have here is an unusual example of the fusion of Classical and monotheist history, viewed from an Ottoman perspective, to explain a building. On a first hearing, we may think of the many surrogate pilgrimage shrines that from the early Islamic period have sprung up all over the Muslim world for those who cannot make the Meccan hajj. Of course, we also find this notion of surrogacy in replicas of the Holy Sepulchre found across Europe. More than this, Mahmud, who had studied in Istanbul, is bringing the Parthenon into the charmed world of other great monotheist buildings, such as the Haram al-Sharif complex in Jerusalem and, above all, Hagia Sophia, which had become venues of association, but also competition for rulers who would emulate and try even to surpass Solomon, the greatest monotheist king, sage, prophet, and builder. Elsewhere in his history, Mahmud goes so far as to compare the Parthenon mosque with Hagia Sophia: referring to the citadel mosque at the time of its bombardment by the Venetians, he notes that "The temple [*mabed*], the noble, richly decorated mosque [*cami*], resembled Ayasofya."[109]

Solomon had a habit of appearing at times when a strong authority was needed to bolster political claims in regions over which the presence of the past still hung heavily. The Umayyad dynasty in Syria, for instance, reinforced its political claims and architectural reformulations with overt Solomonic associations.[110] The Umayyad architectural legacy has been understood as a process of absorbing, rejecting, and reformulating artistic and architectural language and forms inherited from the Greco-Roman tradition as it had evolved in Christian Greater Syria. The material process was accompanied by recast legends and a Qur'anization of space, in which the prophet-king Solomon was given a leading role. In terms of size and political importance, Mahmud's early 18th-century Athens cannot be compared with 7th-century Damascus, one of the most important cities in Late Antique west Asia, which became the Umayyad caliphal capital. Istanbul, not Athens, was of course the necessary showcase of power where the Ottomans played the Umayyads, so to speak, in their quest to reformulate and rival the culture they supplanted. Yet Athens retained its hazy prestige, as it was, after all, the City of the Sages. We should not underestimate the power of this reputation when combined with the omnipresent monumental past in a city where ancient buildings had been constantly adapted in the living urban fabric. This space, so enlivened by great historical figures and wondrous structures, was precisely where competition with the past was most intense, and where Solomon's magical powers were required to

---

[108] *Tarih-i Medinetü'l-Hukema* 124b (trans. Sinclair). Tunalı (2013b, p. 491, text in n. 18) translates Mahmud's description of the Parthenon figures depicting Theseus and the centaurs.

[109] *Tarih-i Medinetü'l-Hukema* 133a (trans. Sinclair; cf. Tunalı 2013a, p. 59).

[110] I thank Nasser Rabbat for his comments at the stimulating conference organized by the MOHA Research Center in Kavala in April 2016. Rabbat emphasizes the contrast between early Islamic use of Solomon, most prominently in Jerusalem and at Palmyra, and later medieval geographers and historians, who no longer required the added support of Solomonic claims once Islamic hegemony was established. See also Borrut 2011, pp. 217–228.

impress Islamic tradition more deeply into the Athenian landscape. This process is what we find in Evliya Çelebi's and Mahmud's synthesizing descriptions of the Athenian built environment.

Given the richness of the mythoplastic rapport with the past in the Ottoman present that we are only beginning to glimpse in Athens, it is difficult not to lament the destruction of nearly all traces of the post-Classical Parthenon. Our responses to the evolving life of buildings are, of course, indicators of our own cultural priorities. The architectural contraction represented by the second Parthenon mosque was mirrored by an intellectual and imaginative shrinkage that has left us ignorant of the building's Ottoman past, even while knowledge about the Classical (and Archaic) phase grew. The physical detachment of the new prayer hall from the cella walls and the surrounding stoa made it easier to take away the building's sculptures, which were no longer an organic part of the experience of visiting the mosque with its "statues made of white marble," so vividly depicted by Evliya Çelebi. The physically but also conceptually detached marble figures—both in Athens and in foreign collections—could now become objects of scholarly attempts to recover their "original" meaning and a single interpretation.[111] The single-mindedness of this new European mythology of the Greek past cut through the layers of Christian and Muslim experience of living with, interpreting, and reinterpreting the buildings of Athens. The new European approach, driven to isolate the "Classical" moment—and to label buildings according to their "correct" identifications—was very different from the mode of viewing articulated by Evliya Çelebi and Mahmud Efendi, which shows them snatching up elements from the pagan and Christian past, seen through a Qur'anic imaginary and an inherited Arabic geographical and historiographical tradition; and, in the case of Mahmud Efendi, even infusing his history with ancient Greek and Roman sources at second hand. While Evliya Çelebi and Mahmud Efendi are the only two voices representing this synthetic mode of engaging with Athens that can be heard today, they give us a sense of what was possible. This is enough to help us begin to recall from oblivion a more capacious mode of responding to the ancient buildings of Athens, above all the Parthenon, that ran against the narrowing and subtraction dominating our imagination, and actions, in more recent centuries.

---

[111] The volume edited by Damaskos and Plantzos (2008) explores the problem of monopolizing views in many periods of Greek history, but omits discussion of the Islamic imaginary in Greece. I thank Liz Cohen for the reference.

An 18th-century Take on Ancient Greece: Mahmud Efendi and the Creation of the *Tarih-i Medinetü'l-Hukema*

Gülçin Tunalı

In 1974, Cengiz Orhonlu published an article entitled "Bir Türk Kadısının Yazdığı Atina Tarihi" [The history of Athens by a Turkish judge] to introduce a manuscript, *Tarih-i Medinetü'l-Hukema* [The history of the city of the sages], the single copy of which is preserved in the Topkapı Palace Library in Istanbul.[1] Since Orhonlu, no historian has focused on the *Tarih-i Medinetü'l-Hukema*, although there are some scarce references to it.[2] This might be attributed firstly to the text's difficulty: the manuscript's narrative is hard to comprehend because it concerns the ancient history of Athens combined with Islamic perceptions, requiring a reader specialized in both fields to decipher it. Second, as late 18th- and early 19th-century Ottoman intellectual history has received scant attention, the manuscript itself has aroused little interest. Third, and perhaps most importantly, as traditional Greek and Turkish historiography has been based on nationalist paradigms focusing on conflicts and wars, a history of Athens written by an Ottoman mufti (a jurist) may be considered bizarre. In this essay, I introduce the author and sources of this text and present its contents.

The Author of the *Tarih-i Medinetü'l-Hukema*

The *Tarih-i Medinetü'l-Hukema*, the compilation of a mufti of Athens,[3] was based among other things on anecdotes told during the friendly gatherings of Muhsinzade Mehmed Pasha, at the time of his

---

* This essay is based on my dissertation (Tunalı 2013a). I want to thank Vera Andriopoulou for her translations from Greek; Gregory Stournaras, Evangelia Balta, Marinos Sariyannis, and Antonis Liakos for their moral and academic support; and Dimitris Drakoulis and the Ioannis Trikoglou Collection in the Rare Books Collection of the Central Library of Aristotle University of Thessaloniki for the photos of the text of Kontares 1675. I dedicate this essay to my beloved daughters, who grew up with my thesis; as the essay was finished in the month of Muharram, I also dedicate my humble efforts to *Penç Âl-i Abâ*.

[1] Orhonlu 1973–1974. Mahmud Efendi, *Tarih-i Medinetü'l-Hukema*, Topkapı Sarayı Emanet Hazinesi, Istanbul, no. 1411 [hereafter *TMH*].

[2] Strauss 2002; Kiel 1991; Vryonis 2002, p. 54; Göyünç 1976.

[3] The name of the author is not mentioned anywhere in the manuscript. Orhonlu found the name Mahmud Efendi in a document in the Başbakanlık Devlet Arşivi Genel Müdürlüğü [General Directorate of State Archives of the Prime Ministry of the Republic of Turkey], Istanbul, no. 7393. Göyünç (1976, p. 477) rejected this claim and argued that the author's name must be Hüseyin, on the basis of another document in the Archive (Maliye Defter-

guardianship of the fortress of Nauplion in 1738.[4] Mahmud Efendi was originally from south-central Greece; his relatives lived in Thebes and Athens, and on Euboea.[5] He states that he left his homeland in 1682/3 for the sake of his education. After staying for 16 years in Istanbul, where he married, he was appointed as mufti of Athens in 1698/9. In 1710/11, he translated two books from Arabic into Ottoman Turkish, one on jurisprudence (*Tuhfetü't-Tüccar*) and another on the value of holy war (*Tuhfetü'l- Guzat*). Mahmud Efendi notes that he began to compile the *Tarih-i Medinetü'l-Hukema* in 1715, which took years to complete, with the help of two "very profound" Greek abbots: Theophanes Kavallares and Gregorios Soteres. Their main source of inspiration was Georgios Kontares's Ἱστορίαι παλαιαὶ καὶ πάνυ ὠφέλιμοι τῆς περιφήμου πόλεως Ἀθήνης [Ancient and useful stories of the famous city of Athens].

On July 14, 1715,[6] Mahmud Efendi met Damad Ali Pasha, a patron of scholars and a book collector,[7] while preaching the Friday sermon to the Ottoman army stationed in Thebes. News of the conquest of the island of Tinos reached the soldiers while they were listening to Mahmud's prayers in the mosque, and, according to tradition, he was rewarded with many gold coins. He informs us that, "The sultan ordered this humble person [Mahmud Efendi] to follow him [the Pasha] to the Peloponnese."[8] After reconquering Corinth, the army reached Nauplion, where Damad Ali Pasha appointed Mahmud Efendi as a preacher in the mosque that he had endowed, as a professor at the madrasa of his chamberlain, Ibrahim Aga, and as an overseer of these two charitable endowments with a daily wage of 120 *akçe*. Mahmud Efendi also retained his duties in Athens as mufti and professor, thus holding several positions at the same time.[9]

The Contents and Sources of the *Tarih-i Medinetü'l-Hukema*

The *Tarih-i Medinetü'l-Hukema* is a small manuscript, 195 x 122 mm, with 19 lines on each page, written in the Naskh calligraphic style. Of its 291 folios, the first 240 (fols. 1b – 240a) cover many centuries, starting with the foundation of the city of Athens in ancient times and ending with the expedition of the Ottomans to the Morea at the beginning of the 18th century. The manuscript does not have a conclusion and therefore appears to end abruptly.

One of the most notable aspects of the manuscript has to do with its sources. In the Ottoman tradition, authors very rarely informed their audience about the sources they employed, unless they were commissioned to translate a certain book, or considered certain treatises, especially of west European origin, pertinent to the intellectual concerns of the Ottomans. Extensive bibliographies

---

leri, no. 1360, p. 18), but the date of that document is 50 years later than the date of the *Tarih-i Medinetü'l-Hukema*. Thus, I concur with Orhonlu on the name of the author. I also found a small, late 17th-century tract in the Süleymaniye Library, Istanbul (Ali Nihat Tarlan Collection, no. 144, between fols. 57b and 60a), that was translated by Atinalı Mahmud b. Hasan, in other words, Mahmud of Athens. Orhonlu wrongly characterized Mahmud Efendi as a judge [*kadi*], whereas Mahmud Efendi himself states that he was appointed as a mufti of Athens.

[4] *TMH*, 2b. Here Mahmud Efendi calls Muhsinzade Mehmed Pasha a vizier; thus, it can be understood that he also witnessed Muhsinzade Mehmed Pasha later becoming a vizier, between 1765–1768 or 1771–1774.
[5] *TMH*, 267a.
[6] Ertaş 2007, p. 26.
[7] In addition to reconquering the Morea, Damad Ali Pasha was widely known as a bibliophile. He prohibited the export of books from Istanbul and founded a library that bears his name. His books were confiscated after his death: see Erünsal 1987.
[8] *TMH*, 273b.
[9] *TMH*, 285b.

are missing, and the information is rare. Several compilations exist, for which the sources have not been identified. Although reasons related to authorship might be at play here, the lack of a bibliography was common practice. The *Tarih-i Medinetü'l-Hukema* is of course no exception. Besides "Herodotus of Halicarnassus [...], Thucydides of Athens, Plutarch from the ruined castle of Chaironeia near Livadeia, and Diodorus from the island of Sicily," Mahmud Efendi does not refer to any other source.[10] However, he informs us that Theophanes Kavallares and Gregorios Soteres translated passages for him from French (the sources of which are unknown), and the "dead languages" (ancient Greek and Latin), which Mahmud Efendi then translated into Ottoman Turkish (sometimes with the intermediary help of another translator).[11]

A closer look at the text suggests that Mahmud Efendi made extensive use of Georgios Kontares's Ἱστορίαι παλαιαὶ καὶ πάνυ ὠφέλιμοι τῆς περιφήμου πόλεως Ἀθήνης, published in Venice in 1675.[12] Although a line-by-line comparison of Kontares's book with the *Tarih-i Medinetü'l-Hukema* would be a commendable project, for the purposes of this essay the detailed tables of contents of the two books (see Appendix 1 and 2) are sufficient to establish the relationship between the two texts. A question that immediately arises is how Mahmud Efendi got hold of this book. He may have obtained it through his connection with Damad Ali Pasha or via a different network. Unfortunately, the information known about intellectual networks as well as book gifting and trading in the Ottoman Empire is limited, as there has been no extensive research on this topic. We could safely argue, however, that Mahmud Efendi, Theophanes Kavallares, and Gregorios Soteres belonged to such networks.

Theophanes Kavallares and Gregorios Soteres

Theophanes Kavallares was an eminent teacher of grammar, literature, and science. Like Gregorios Soteres, he was abbot of the monastery of Kaisariani, considered one of Attica's most significant religious foundations. Kavallares came from a well-known Athenian aristocratic family,[13] which in the late 16th century or early 17th had founded the church of St. Dimitrios in Athens.[14] According to the historian Dimitrios Kambouroglou, Kavallares was one of the most highly educated abbots at Kaisariani[15] and a prominent Athenian scholar.[16] Kavallares taught in Athens from 1709. A year later, the metropolitan of Athens, Meletios, appointed him as a teacher (in the decree he is referred to as the wisest and most pious among monks, as well as a schoolmaster) paid from the bequest of Abbot Epiphanios in Venice. On September 18, 1712, Kavallares was elected by the Council of Forty of the Greek community of Venice as a schoolteacher in Athens under the guardianship of the abbot's office.[17] He was one of the first teachers recruited by Soteres at his Seminary of Greek Studies in Athens and continued lecturing until late 1728, when he was appointed as abbot of Kaisariani.[18]

---

[10] *TMH*, 4a.
[11] At the end of the book, he identifies himself as "this humble translator" [*bu fakir mütercim*]: *TMH*, 285b.
[12] I would like to thank Nikolas Pissis for directing me to Kontares and his work. Without his guidance and information about Kontares, I would not have realized the parallels that exist between the Ἱστορίαι and the *Tarih-i Medinetü'l-Hukema*.
[13] Kambouroglou 1889–1892, vol. 1, p. 81.
[14] Orlandos 1923, p. 145.
[15] Kambouroglou 1889–1892, vol. 2, p. 202.
[16] Kambouroglou 1889–1892, vol. 3, p. 197.
[17] Hellenic Institute in Venice, Proceedings of the Council of Forty, September 18, 1712, ΑΕΙΒ, Α'. Οργάνωση – λειτουργία, 3. Πρακτικά Συνεδριάσεων, Κατάστιχο 8, fols. 191v–196r, from their digitized archive: http://eib.xanthi.ilsp.gr/gr/boundmaterials.asp?cursort=boundCategory&selectFieldValue=&vpage=7.
[18] Sicilianos 1960, p. 195.

Gregorios Soteres, or Soterianos, a monk from Athens, studied ancient Greek and Latin in Italy.[19] Prompted by requests made by Athenians, he returned to his hometown in order to establish the first permanent school of the city. Around 1717, he bought an old house in the center of Athens, near the church of the Great Panagia, inside Hadrian's Library; there he constructed a significant, large school, called the Seminary of Greek Studies, where he offered his services as a teacher free of charge, and endowed it with a library of 600 volumes. When the number of students increased, he recruited other teachers, including Theophanes Kavallares (1722). Due to the great expense of the construction and furnishings of the school, no endowment was left to maintain the Seminary. The main revenue of the school was a mere 50 ducats per year, the proceeds of the bequest of Abbot Epiphanios from Venice. This amount was insufficient to cover even the salary of one teacher, which amounted to 200 ducats. Subsequently, the property of the school was seized, and eventually it merged with the school established in 1750 by Ioannis Dekas. Soteres was later appointed metropolitan of Monemvasia and Kalamata in the Peloponnese.

Georgios Kontares

Little is known about the life of Georgios Kontares. In his brief account of Kontares's life and work, Christos Patrinelis notes his importance for Kozani.[20] The earliest and fullest biographical notice of Kontares was written by Charisios Meidanis, a scholar and teacher from Kozani: in his book of 1820 about the school of Kozani, he devoted an extensive paragraph to Kontares, its first teacher:[21]

> Kontares was born and raised in Servia [near Kozani] [... He] descended from illustrious ancestors who served as public officials during the reign of the Greco-Romans and who are mentioned in Byzantine history. They were dispersed in many places with political tasks both before and after the conquest of Constantinople. There were branches of this family in Kastoria, the Peloponnese, in Servia, and in Venice, where they served in the ministries of the [local] aristocracy. In 1540, as administrator of the Venetians in Nauplion, Alexandros Kontares handed the town over to the Turks following the peace treaty. Georgios went to Venice to his relatives there and was an expert in the Latin and Italian dialects. We do not have accurate information about his education in Greek, nor about his teachers. The one thing we do know is that he was an Aristotelian and was persuasive in speech, dignified in manner, had a venerable character, and preferred unmarried life. He taught in the school of Kozani for three years and then he went to Servia, his native town, to practice his profession. After the death of Dionysius, Bishop of Servia, he was ordained priest at the demand of the people of the province, and took the name Gregorios. He served as bishop in the see for four years. He still used the name Georgios when he wrote a History of Athens in our vernacular language, which was also published in Venice at the time. Because of the history that he wrote, the Athenians took action when their arch-

---

[19] Vryonis 2002, p. 65.
[20] Patrinelis 1997; see also Legrand 1894, pp. 318–321.
[21] Patrinelis 1997, p. 459.

bishop died, and he was transferred and became the archbishop of Athens. He was a very skillful embroiderer of sacred vestments with gold thread, and the Epitaphios of Christ the Lord which hangs opposite the archiepiscopal throne in the katholikon [church] of Kozani is a work of his hands, and shows his exceptional adroitness.[22]

Teacher, writer, translator, collaborator at a publishing house in Venice, bibliophile, embroiderer, priest, and finally bishop of Servia and metropolitan of Smyrna,[23] Georgios Kontares was born in Servia, near Kozani, probably shortly before 1638. He is first attested in 1668 as a priest in Venice, where he had family. After losing his wife, he became a monk, assuming the name Gregorios. From 1668 to 1675 and again from 1683 to 1684, he served as supervisor at the Flanginian School in Venice.[24] During the period from 1675 to 1683 he probably taught in Kozani and Thessaloniki. According to a handwritten note he made on his personal copy of a work by Symeon of Thessaloniki, he was teaching in Thessaloniki in 1682.[25] Among the subjects that Kontares taught, Aristotle took first place.[26]

In 1684 Kontares was ordained bishop of Servia. Some years later, he is thought to have been elected metropolitan of Athens, but his name does not appear on the lists of metropolitans of Athens for this period. The only explanation would be that he served for only a short time, around 1688, just after the Venetian occupation of Athens and the destruction of the Parthenon in 1687, when the Athenians had deserted the city. Indeed, a chronological gap in the records would warrant this theory.[27] In any event, in 1690, he was appointed bishop of Smyrna, where he died in 1698. His personal library, which he donated to the Evangelical School of Smyrna, formed the nucleus of the school's library.[28]

Kontares's History

Almost a century later, the Swedish traveler J. J. Björnstahl found Kontares's book in the monastery of Dousikou. He noted that, "On 24 May [1779] I read the history of Athens, written in *koine* [Modern Greek] by Georgios Kontares from Servia and published in Venice in 1675. It is remarkable. However, it is ridiculous to read about the wonders of ancient Athens in simple language, barbaric words in the mouth of Demosthenes, and about the great navy of Xerxes."[29] Dimitris Apostolopoulos has located copies of the book in Athens and Thessaloniki, and on Mt. Athos, as well as in libraries in Paris, Moscow, and Sofia.[30]

Kontares dedicated his book to Petros Gaspari and Giannoulis Poulimenos. Gaspari was of Athenian origin; a merchant who resided in Venice, he was an especially prominent member of the city's Greek community, since he was elected governor of the Brotherhood of St. Nicholas on April 6,

---

[22] Meidanis 1820, pp. 45–46.
[23] Patrinelis 1997, p. 460.
[24] Patrinelis 1997, pp. 462 and 464.
[25] "This book was written by me, the monk Georgios Kontares, [humble] teacher, in Thessaloniki, in the holy monastery of the Kamariotissa, on [3 February 1682]."
[26] Patrinelis 1997, p. 464.
[27] Patrinelis 1997, p. 465
[28] Karanasios and Petsios 2004, pp. 103–104; Patrinelis 1997, p. 466.
[29] Patrinelis 1997, p. 469.
[30] Apostolopoulos 2005, p. 87.

1674.[31] Gaspari helped the Venetians in the war for the Morea. During the Venetian interlude between 1687 and 1688, the Athenians had abandoned their city. While some went to Venetian-held Zakynthos and others to Nauplion or Salamis, most of them fled to Aegina under the leadership of Gaspari.[32] Sicilianos says that some, led by Demetrios Gaspari, fled to Aegina, and others under the leadership of Petros Gaspari to Salamis.[33] He also states that Petros Gaspari had married the daughter of the Astrakaris family, one of the twelve archons of Athens.[34] Gaspari, leader of the Athenian volunteers, died from fever.[35] Significantly, Kontares drew a parallel between Theseus and Gaspari that fits into the Athenian "founder-hero" character of Theseus. In his prologue, Kontares wrote the following:

> The ancient Greeks and our ancestors were never so eager for any other project as they were in rewarding greatly those who wanted to excel for their country. As was their custom, they sometimes dedicated great temples to them, for others they built bronze and marble statues, artfully made. And for others they displayed their images in public, as a way of rewarding their bravery. As we can see clearly in their stories, they dedicated many temples in the name of Theseus, they painted Themistocles, Aristeides, Miltiades, and all the other generals in the public palace, they built statues in honor of Demetrios Phalireus in the agora and in public places, where people spent their day. And they also had this other habit, that they would honor those who did well for the country, not only with monetary honors, but also by praising them. This they did all together, even little children. This is what they did in the time of Theseus, who rebuilt Athens with his own money, that is what they did at the time of Konon, who rebuilt his city's walls that had been destroyed by the Spartans, and the same they did for many others. Therefore, if they paid so many honors to those at these times, how many honors should we give to your excellency, Sir Petros Gaspari, you who showed similar love for your country. You have spared no expense, but have spent lavishly in order to help your country. Thus you have received honors from all, and I have wanted first to dedicate to you this History that I have begun. Your Grace resembles Theseus and, like him, you wanted to help your country and rebuild, like Theseus did, as is evident in the History, where his name and actions will be remembered forever. I have decided to give to you the same honor and to write this History also for your dear friend Giannoulis Poulimenos. Because Theseus went through all the labors alone, but shared the wealth and glory with his beloved friend Peirithous, for whom he endangered his life many times. Similarly, you gave your wealth alone, but received glory and eternal fame together with him. This is why I dedicate this book and give it to both your hands, and let me be pardoned for that. I have not met the honorable Giannoulis with my own eyes, but many truthful and honest people have told me that he is such a worthy man that even if I sought another with Diogenes' lamp, I would not find someone better. Because the love and

---

[31] Apostolopoulos 2005, p. 94.
[32] Miller 1921, p. 413.
[33] Sicilianos 1960, p. 113.
[34] Sicilianos 1960, p. 226
[35] Sicilianos 1960, p. 414.

concord that exists between you shows clearly that there is no difference between you, but you are of one mind and soul in two bodies. So the family of Giannoulis should also accept this gift of his best and most beloved friend.

It is a work sanctioned by God (with the help of Petrakis Gaspari) to labor for the common good of our brothers in faith, especially at the present time since they do not have their freedom or what is necessary for education, to work in order to give them a helping hand, not only through advice, the lives of the saints, and holy scripture, but also through ancient history. Because the wisdom of God wished to bring light through truth and knowledge to people who lacked not only His word and advice, but also knowledge of ancient and useful history from the beginning of the world [...] The Holy Scripture teaches us that it is God's will to try and save what of the old stories is worthy of narration, that is, the lives of famous men and cities. So we will begin writing the history of Athens, not by using rhetorical praise or excessive words (because that should be avoided, according to Lucian), because it is not the work of a historian to mix narrative with poetry and rhetoric. Thus, we will narrate the facts simply, without exaggeration, how I found them in old Greek and Italian books, which I translated into the common language. And we have not left anything out, nor added our own words.[36]

As Apostolopoulos notes, it would have been natural for the two Greeks, Petros Gaspari and Kontares, to meet in Venice, but "If we want to find the deeper reason for this cooperation, we must look at the purpose that the book meant to serve and explain why the sponsor was persuaded to undertake the expense of its publication."[37] By narrating the history of ancient Athens from the time of Cecrops to the arrival of the Apostle Paul in Athens, Kontares wanted to highlight and stimulate historical memory among the "New Greeks." Additionally, by presenting infidels and merciless tyrants, he forced young Greeks to realize their origin and their history, and to imitate their ancestors in learning, wisdom, and bravery.[38] Apostolopoulos concludes that the strong anti-Turkish (pro-Venetian) tone, which dominates Kontares's book, reflects the sponsor's ideology rather than that of the author.[39]

Preliminary Observations

More than a century after the completion of the *Tarih-i Medinetü'l-Hukema*, Kambouroglou stated,

> [...] the voice of the muezzin, coming from the Acropolis and heard around it, in the place where the most sacred memories of ancient and Christian Athens are to be found, marked for the Athenians the beginning of a new phase in their life. But in the areas around the Acropolis, where the voices of Pericles, of Demosthenes, of

---

[36] Kontares 1675 (translation by Dr. Vera Andriopoulou and Dr. Stefanie Kennell). It is difficult to assign page numbers for Kontares's Ἰστορίαι (see the note in Appendix 2). This passage is located in the "prologue," after the index, which is at the beginning of the book.
[37] Apostolopoulos 2005, pp. 94–95.
[38] Apostolopoulos 2005, p. 96.
[39] Apostolopoulos 2005, p. 98.

> Plato, and of St Paul were once heard, there is no place for the voice of the imam, which represents the negation of the political, patriotic and moral principles advocated by them. Shadows of the creators of the great feats of humanity, do not be sad; the Koran's principles cannot grow roots in the soil of Attica. The kind of dust of the people who are buried in it would resist them, since, even if barbarism absorbs every strength, one day the breath of freedom will uproot it [...][40]

Mahmud Efendi's manuscript has the important historiographical distinction of being the only work completely devoted to the history of Athens written in Ottoman Turkish. As the *Tarih-i Medinetü'l-Hukema* stands against such segregationist approaches, his narrative about Athens raises many questions, most of which are outside the scope of this essay. To address them would require delving deeper into its contents. What I would like to stress here, however, is what this text suggests about "the Greek connection"[41] of Ottoman intellectual life, and intellectual realities in general.

Among its various features, the *Tarih-i Medinetü'l-Hukema* attests to the "shared world" Molly Greene has eloquently described in her book on trade in the 16th-century eastern Mediterranean. To quote her, "[...] from the time of the Fourth Crusade in 1204 onward, the eastern Mediterranean was the point of intersection for not two but three enduring civilizations—namely, Latin Christianity, Eastern Orthodoxy, and Islam."[42] Although it is a common place today to make sense of the eastern Mediterranean as a shared world, the fields of intellectual and cultural history remain bound to those particularities that entertain the existence of strict barriers between ethnic and religious groups. This is not to say that particularities play no role; it is to challenge formations that ascribe culture a strict essence. A quick look at Greek and Turkish history textbooks makes it evident that they assume no interaction or communication between the two "cultures," as if the Greek and Turkish spheres had somehow survived without any contact in the past.[43] Such textbooks offer a stable and homogeneous understanding of culture rather than of the reciprocal cultural influences that lead to hybridization.[44] Mahmud Efendi's text, on the contrary, demonstrates the existence of cultural cooperation: that he wrote his text by collaborating with two Greek abbots is conclusive proof of this interaction. Although they helped him with translations of books on the history of Athens, it should be borne in mind that the Hellenism of Mahmud Efendi and that of the three Greek intellectuals differed from each other. The mufti appears to have internalized the story of Athens, but his images of ancient Athens and those on the mental maps of Kavallares, Soteres, and Kontares are quite different.

Every book is a product of its time, of course. The manner in which Mahmud Efendi reads the city as a "signifier" and composes a history for 18th-century Ottomans allows me to argue that his cultural context served as a meaning-generating framework. The perception and the understanding of the relatively unknown have always been formed by the projection of the well-known, whereby the unknown becomes familiar to us. Every understanding of the unknown occurs through its integration into the already known, in other words through its domestication into the known culture. So,

---

[40] Translated and quoted by Hamilakis (2009, p. 61).
[41] For a detailed study on the issue, see Strauss 2003.
[42] Greene 2000, p. 4.
[43] Soysal and Antoniou 2002, 2004.
[44] Welsch 1999, p. 198. For the problematics of different terminology concerning cultural interactions, such as "hybridization," "borrowing," "melting pot," "creolization," "glocalization," and "interculturality," see Stockhammer 2012, p. 46.

An 18th-century Take on Ancient Greece

appropriation occurs.[45] As Burke remarks, "If the past is a foreign country, it follows that even the most monoglot of historians is a translator. Historians mediate between the past and the present and face the same dilemmas as other translators, serving two masters and attempting to reconcile fidelity to the original with intelligibility to their readers."[46]

This statement is true for Mahmud Efendi, who was also a translator. Being both a translator and a historian, he mediated between the ancient past and the Ottoman present. Even by looking at the tables of contents of the two books, the original and its "translation," what Mahmud Efendi did when he confronted the "foreign country" in question is very important to understanding the strategies he followed, such as the Ottomanization of Theseus;[47] when he provides information about the ancient rulers, he employs Ottoman terminology for titles such as padishah, sultan, and bey anachronistically. In addition, he retrojects such concepts as poll tax [*cizye*], traditional agricultural tax [*öşür*], and excise and special taxes [*rusumat*] as if they had existed in ancient Athens, even though they belonged to the Ottoman administrative system. In the same vein, he also uses terms that are connected with the Ottoman political system—preserve public order [*nizam-ı memleket*], justice [*adalet*], and tyranny [*zulm*]—at various points in the *Tarih-i Medinetü'l-Hukema*. Along the same lines, he refers to Solon as Süleyman Hakim. The word "Süleyman" is used here as an attribute meaning "lawmaker."[48] What is also interesting is that in the depiction of this King Süleyman—Solon—entering the city, the components of the welcoming ceremony are predominantly Ottoman; they are called New Year's celebrations [*nevruz*].[49] In a different description, an incident of misbehavior is explained in terms borrowed from the Qur'an and widely used by the Sufi tradition as the soul that incites evil [*nefs-i emare*].[50] Moreover, for the Spartans at the Battle of Thermopylae (480 B.C.), by using the term *serdengeçti*,[51] meaning a soldier who, in the Ottoman context, puts himself in the front line and so becomes a martyr, he attempts a transcultural comparison. He also compares the Boeotians led by the Thebans at the Battle of Leuctra against the Spartans to Rustam, a famous Persian hero from the *Shahnamah* of Firdawsi.[52] When he describes Aristotle and Plato, he mentions their views on faith in one god.[53] He identifies Socrates as one "enlightened with the light of the Unity of God" [*nur-ı tevhid ile mücella*].[54] Furthermore, in explaining some events, he enriches the story with short Qur'anic verses, hadiths, and Ottoman idioms.[55] While writing about philosophers, he mentions the three, the seven, and the forty saints [*üçler, yediler,* and *kırklar*] as they appear in various forms in Alevi, Bektashi, and Sufi literature.[56] In another example, while describing the time of Pericles, Mahmud Efendi devotes 20 pages to the Parthenon. He mentions

---

[45] On the appropriation of ancient Athens by Mahmud Efendi, the definition by Willem Frijhoff (quoted from Marcel Barnard's translation [Barnard 2009, p. 11]) is worth noting: "[…] appropriation is a process of giving meaning, in which groups or individuals attribute their own meaning to the object presented, imposed or prescribed by others, and thus make it acceptable, liveable, bearable or humane to themselves. It is cultural recreation."
[46] Burke 2007, p.7.
[47] Tunalı 2013b. Mahmud Efendi also narrates the story of Cleobis and Biton in the same way as he treats Theseus: see *TMH*, 64a – 65a.
[48] As Darling (2008, p. 515) put it, "Suleyman acquired the epithet 'lawgiver' because he presided over the harmonization of dynastic law and Islamic law, and because his courts exercised a justice like that of the biblical Solomon."
[49] *TMH*, 54a. For the celebration of the New Year in the Ottoman context, see And 1982.
[50] *TMH*, 32a, 33a, 36b, 67b, 68b, 136a. For the stages of the soul according to Imam Ali b. Abi Talib, the summit of all of the chains of Islamic spirituality, see Kazemi 2007.
[51] *TMH*, 85b.
[52] *TMH*, 183b.
[53] *TMH*, 149a – 150b. Similar trends may be seen in early translations of Aristotle and Plato from Greek into Arabic. For a detailed discussion of the translation of names of Greek deities into Arabic, see Walbridge 1998, p. 389.
[54] *TMH*, 116b
[55] *TMH*, 61b, 17b.
[56] *TMH*, 132a, 133b. For an explanation, see Schimmel 1975, pp. 200–203.

Pericles in the section on the building of the Parthenon with terminology specific to Ottoman culture and narrates the story of the Parthenon as if it had been built not in ancient Athens but in any Ottoman city, starting with Pericles' words to the Athenian assembly explaining the reason for building an endowment [*hayrat*].[57]

Mahmud Efendi's curiosity about Antiquity differs from the later Tanzimat interest in Hellenism, which was woven into the Westernization process of all spheres of life, including mythological elements from the ancient world.[58] Thus, although his *Tarih-i Medinetü'l-Hukema* has many pioneering and distinctive features, Mahmud Efendi's style of "reading" the ancient world had almost no effect on the intellectual world of the Ottomans and no repercussions among the Ottoman literati. Perhaps if all the right socio-economic and cultural circumstances had been present in the 19th century, as Dimitri Gutas has shown so well for the Greco-Arabic translation movement in the early Middle Ages, it would be possible to discuss some kind of Greco-Ottoman translation movement at that time.[59] The Tulip Era (1718-1730) did not produce such a movement, however, so Mahmud Efendi stands alone, as does the scholar Esad Efendi from Ioannina (d. 1731).[60] Over a century later, in the Tanzimat period, the Ottomans seemed to accept that to be European and civilized, people had to know ancient history and literature, create museums and preserve ruins to show the ancient glory of their land.[61] Nevertheless, Mahmud Efendi tried to dress up in Ottoman and Islamic garments what he had learnt from his Greek contacts about the history of Athens. To succeed in his attempt to "Ottomanize" foreign cultural units, first Ottoman institutions, customs, traditions, and titles were projected onto the elements of ancient Greece, then the phrasing was set up by a particular process of Ottomanization, using local linguistic elements, such as proverbs and idioms. In these aspects his approach diverges from his contemporary Greek connections, but also from Tanzimat-period intellectuals, making him appear absolutely *sui generis*.

---

[57] *TMH*, 124b – 126a. See also the essay by Fowden herein, pp. 67–95.
[58] See Strauss 1992, 2003.
[59] Gutas 1998.
[60] Küçük 2013.
[61] Considering the symbolic role of antiquities in Europe and in Greece, Shaw (2003) questions the Ottoman Empire's interest and profits from the Hellenistic collections and antiquities within its own territory.

Appendix 1

Detailed Table of Contents of Mahmud Efendi's *Tarih-i Medinetü'l-Hukema**

1b – 2a: Arabic invocations (*basmala, hamdala, salwala*) and the reason for compiling and translating the manuscript
2a – 2b: Two Greek abbots presented as sources; the date the task was started
2b – 3a: The role of Muhsinzade Mehmed Pasha in composing the text
3a – 4a: The difficulty that was experienced; appeal to the readers to forgive potential faults
4a – 4b: The names of the historians of the written sources
4b – 6a: The topography of Athens
6a – 6b: The government of Athens
6b – 7a: The areas under Athenian rule
7a – 7b: The rulers of Athens
7b – 8a: Sultan Mehmed II
8a – 8b: Athens under Ottoman rule
8b – 9a: Athens from Adam to Cecrops I
9a – 9b: Athens after Noah
9b–10a: The people of Athens; their hair adorned with riveted cicadas of gold, silver, and copper
10a – 10b: The question of Athens' name
10b – 11a: Athena
11a – 11b: The stratum system in Athens and the reigns of Cranaus and Amphictyon
11b – 12a: The reigns of Erichthonius and Pandion
12a – 12b: The reigns of Thrace, Erechtheus, and Cecrops II
12b – 13a: The king of Crete
13a – 13b: The Minotaur and Aegeus
13b – 14a: Aegeus, his wife, and Theseus
14b – 15a: Theseus slays Periphetes
15a – 15b: Theseus slays the robber Sinis at the Isthmus of Corinth
15b –16a: Theseus kills the Pinebender, destroys the sow of Crommyon, and hurls Sciron into the sea
16a – 16b: Theseus defeats Cercyon in wrestling, slays Procrustes, and arrives in Athens
16b – 17a: His stepmother, Medea, wants to poison him
17a – 17b: Theseus recognized by Aegeus while eating
18a – 20a: Medea warns Theseus' rivals, nephews of Aegeus, of the danger to the throne; they fight with Theseus
20a – 20b: Theseus wins and asks to go to Crete with the third delegation of tribute to the Minotaur
20b – 21b: Aegeus demurs, but Theseus persuades him
21b – 23a: Theseus wrestles with the Minotaur and overcomes him
23a – 23b: Theseus asks that the tribute of seven girls and seven boys be abolished
23b – 24a: The king of Crete wants his daughter to marry Theseus; they marry
24a – 25a: Theseus and his bride depart from Crete, but the captain forgets to hoist white sails in place of black ones on the Athenians' return from Crete
25a – 25b: Aegeus throws himself into the sea believing that Theseus is dead; Theseus laments his father for 40 days
25b – 26a: Theseus succeeds to the sovereignty of Athens
26a – 29a: Theseus accompanies Hercules on his campaign against the women warriors (Amazons)
29a – 29b: Theseus wins battles against the Amazons and takes Hippolyte away as his concubine
29b – 30a: Theseus' friendship with Pirithous
30a – 32a: Theseus fights with the "soldiers of

* Translated and arranged by Gülçin Tunalı.

Candavro" (the Centaurs) at the wedding of Pirithous, then returns to Athens with Helen

32a – 33a: Theseus' fame increases; he builds a palace and begins to live in luxury. His character changes; he demands the daughters of the rulers of other city-states, sometimes by force

33a – 34a: Theseus demands the daughter of the king of Sparta; the king refuses. With the assistance of Pirithous, he carries Helen off to Aphidnae, where his mother Aethra lives; because Helen is so young, he leaves her with Aethra for safekeeping

34a – 34b: Theseus wants the daughter of the king of the Molossians

34b – 35a: Theseus and Pirithous are held prisoner

35a – 35b: Pirithous is killed in prison by the dog Cerberus

35b – 36a: Theseus is rescued by Hercules

36a – 36b: The soldiers of Helen's father, the king of Sparta, loot the city of Athens

36b – 37b: The notables of Athens gather to talk about Theseus' deeds

37b – 38a: Menestheus is appointed ruler by the notables of Athens

38a – 38b: Theseus goes to Euboea with his family and slaves

39b – 40a: Theseus is killed by Lycomedes while hunting a bird; his bones are brought back from Skyros to Athens by Cimon

40a – 41a: The Sanctuary of Theseus

41a – 45a: Helen's affair (with Paris); the war against Troy

45a – 48a: People come from Troy to Padua by ship

48a – 49a: Foundation of the city of Venice

49a – 49b: The reign of Menestheus

49b – 50a: The reigns of Demophon, Oxynthes, Apheidas, and Thymoites

50a – 51a: The reign of Codrus

51a – 51b: The age of rulers for life begins

51b – 52a: The reigns of Medon, Akastos, Arkhippos, Thersippos, Phorbas, Megacles, Diognetos, Pherekles, Ariphron, Thespius, Agamestor, Aischylos, and Alkmaion

52a – 52b: Decision to limit the term of rule to ten years

52b – 53a: Drakon

53a – 62b: Solon

62b – 65b: Solon's visit to Cyprus; Croesus in the Golden Age

67b – 68a: The sons of Solon

68a – 68b: The murder of Hipparchus

68b – 69a: The overthrow of Hippias

69a – 69b: Hippias flees to Sardis (Anatolia) to the court of the Persian Artaphernes and promises the Persians control of Athens if they help restore him

69b – 70a: The victories of Miltiades

70a – 71a: Persian victories in the Aegean Islands

71a – 71b: The Persians arrive on Euboea in midsummer; they march to the coast of Attica en route to completing the final objective of their campaign, the punishment of Athens

71b – 72a: Battle of Marathon; Themistocles, Callimachus, Miltiades, and Aristides

72a – 72b: The Persian soldiers, unable to find food and water, flee to the sea. After three days, the battle ends when the Persian center breaks; they flee in panic towards their ships, pursued by the Greeks

72b – 73a: The heroism of the Athenian commanders; Callimachus murdered during the battle

73a – 73b: Herodotus records that 6,400 Persian bodies were counted on the battlefield and the Athenians lost 192 men

73b – 74a: The Persian naval forces are too exhausted to invade again

74a – 74b: The Persians return home

75b – 76a: Miltiades leads an Athenian expedition of 70 ships against Greek-inhabited islands deemed to have supported the Persians; he attacks the Cyclades, which the Persians had recently added to their empire

76a – 76b: Charged with treason, Miltiades is sentenced to death, but the sentence is converted to a fine of 50 talents

76b – 77a: Miltiades is sent to prison and dies there
77a – 77b: Miltiades' debt is later paid by his son, Metiochos
77b – 78a: Darius' death; his son, Xerxes [Darius b. Behmen], kills Darius b. Darab
78a – 78b: The Persian army crosses the Hellespont and marches through Thrace, Mt. Athos, Macedonia, and Thessaly
79a – 79b: The Persian king demands earth and water in Thessaly. Darius sends emissaries to all the Greek city-states, demanding gifts of earth and water in token of their submission to him
79b – 80a: The Athenians believe their only way out is death
80a – 80b: The Athenians kill the Persian envoy; the king is furious
82a – 82b: A massive fleet is created under the leadership of the politician Themistocles to fight the Persians
83b – 84a: Inhabitants of the Peloponnesian cities make backup plans for the defense of the Isthmus of Corinth
84b – 85a: Ephialtes, a Greek from the route of the Persians' march, betrays the Greeks by showing the Persians a small path leading behind Greek lines
85a – 85b: General Demophilos refuses to leave and commits himself to fight with 700 Thespians
85b – 86a: The Greeks fight with spears until all are shattered, then switch to short swords; the death of the Spartan king Leonidas at Thermopylae
86a – 86b: Recovery of Leonidas' body by the Persians; Xerxes orders his head to be cut off and his body crucified
86b – 91b: Greco-Persian wars
92a – 92b: The Persians indicate that they lack food
92b – 93a: The Persian king returns home due to the political situation in India; a small number of soldiers remains in Athens and the Peloponnese
93a – 93b: Famine in Athens
93b – 94a: The Persian soldiers complain about Athens; after the soldiers withdraw, Athens progresses
94a – 94b: Spartan envy of the Athenians; Themistocles is sent as envoy to the Peloponnese
94b – 95a: The Spartans threaten Themistocles and Athens
95a – 95b: Themistocles excites pity for the conditions in Athens and tells the Spartans that they should send an envoy to Athens to see for himself
96a – 96b: Spartan envoys observe that Themistocles is right; this dispels the Spartans' envy and hostility
96b – 97a: Spartans and Athenians cooperate to reconquer the islands that had been taken by the Persian king
97a – 97b: Themistocles wins over the islands with soft words, the Spartans by force
97b – 98a: Aristides
98a – 98b: Athens prospers because war and sickness are absent
98b – 99a: The Spartan commander is not courteous or smooth-talking; the Athenians want to teach him a lesson
99a – 99b: The Athenians ask the Spartans to build a tower on the island of Mykonos and to institute tithes and cleruchs
99b – 100a: The Spartans accept the Athenian offer and erect buildings
100a – 100b: They appoint a garrison and cleruchs to the island and accumulate property for ten years
100b – 101a: The Panathenaic Stadium in Athens
101a – 101b: The buildings of Athens
101b – 102a: Athens becomes a place of pilgrimage; the eastern part has barracks for soldiers
102a – 102b: The artisans' workshops around the barracks
102b – 103a: Shops associated with the navy around the port of Piraeus and the military
103a – 103b: Schools in the southern section of Athens; the shops associated with them, such as bookbinders; courts also present there
106a – 106b: The Persian king fights for 15 years

around India and Transoxiana, but Athens and Sparta are always in his thoughts

106b – 107b: The king sends gifts and letters to the military commanders of Athens and Sparta in order to bring them over to his side; the Spartan Pausanias' letters to Xerxes

107b – 108a: Pausanias' death

108a – 108b: Themistocles leaves Athens for Argos

108b – 109a: Themistocles cuts down trees in the Black Sea region and builds ships; a huge navy is created

109a – 110a: Themistocles' death by poison; Athenians grieve deeply as they read his letter

110a – 110b: The navy sails from the Black Sea to the Mediterranean and conquers Cyprus and Rhodes

110b – 111a: The Athenians take the treasure from Cyprus because the Persians will come and take it; the Spartans claim that if Pausanias had been alive, the Athenians would not have dared to do it

111a – 111b: The Persian navy encounters Athenian ships off the coast of Rhodes; since the Athenian ships are smaller, they escape easily to Egyptian waters

111b – 112a: Running continues, and the Persian navy progresses slowly

112a – 112b: The Persian ships are split off into a rocky area by a storm; Athenian forces enslave the Persian soldiers

116a – 116b: They return to Athens and organize celebrations; birth of Socrates

116b – 117a: Socrates gives lectures on wisdom and philosophy; he owns four schools, each with 7,000 students

117a – 117b: At this time, nine wise philosophers rule Athens

117b – 118a: There are 500 philosophers divided into ten sections; they choose seven, seven choose three, and three choose the one

118a – 118b: There is also a Board of Forty, and the Areopagus court has a place on it

121a – 122a: Miltiades is killed; Cimon takes his place

122a: Pericles

124a – 129b: Physical description of the Acropolis

129b – 132b: The sculpture and cult of Athena

132b – 134a: The mosque inside the Parthenon; its bombardment

134a – 138b: The operation of the law courts

138b – 143a: The Tower of the Winds described in detail

143a – 147a: The debts of Pericles due to the building of the Parthenon

147a – 148b: Socrates and the philosophers

148b – 150a: How the Athenians worshipped deities

150a – 151a: The philosophers' faith in one god; Socrates tries to hide their beliefs from the Athenians

151a – 155a: Alcibiades

155b – 157b: Pericles and Nicias

157a – 157b: An oracle

157b – 158a: Ravens at Delphi peck at the golden head of an idol in the form of a girl, a bad omen for the mission to Sicily; Alcibiades nevertheless insists on the expedition and kisses Socrates' hand before they march away; Socrates advises him not to display belief in one god

158a – 158b: Alcibiades conquers Sicily and displays his belief in one god

158b – 159a: Due to his belief in one god, Alcibiades is discharged from office by the Athenians; the Spartans help the Sicilians and they defeat the Athenian navy

159a – 159b: Accordingly they know of Socrates' belief in one god and plan to kill him

159b – 160a: The Athenians ask Socrates how he wishes to be killed; he replies with poison; Plato tries to prevent his death

160a – 163a: Socrates' death; his funeral and tomb

163a – 163b: Alcibiades' life at the Spartan court; his relationship with Timaia, wife of King Agis II

163b – 164a: Other women complain to Agis II

164a – 164b: Agis II wants to punish his wife, Timaia

164b – 165a: Timaia's relatives tell Agis II that he

should protect his wife and other women; he decides to remove Alcibiades from his territories

165a – 165b: Alcibiades escapes from Sparta and takes refuge with the Persian satrap Tissaphernes

165b – 166a: The Spartans learn that Alcibiades has taken refuge at the court of Tissaphernes; they become sad and send letters inviting him back

166a – 167a: Alcibiades is recalled by the Athenians

167a – 168a: The Athenians capture the Persians' horses near Istanbul and bring them to Athens

168a – 168b: Alcibiades returns to Athens, deeply resentful of the Athenians' killing of Socrates, and is welcomed by a large crowd

168b – 169a: The Athenians try their best to smooth Alcibiades' way

169a – 169b: The Spartans become envious of his situation; the women, in particular, force their husbands and men to mount an expedition against Athens since "the fire of envy burned their livers too much"

169b – 170a: The Battle of Abydos; the Athenians ask Alcibiades to be their commander

170b – 171a: He appoints Thrasyboulos to the Athenian fleet

171a – 171b: Spartan victory; Alcibiades flees to the Persian king

171b – 172a: The soldiers complain that Alcibiades ordered them not to attack; the Athenians' love for Alcibiades turns to hate

172a – 172b: They ask the Persian king for Alcibiades to submit to them

172b – 174a: The Athenian envoys explain Alcibiades' actions in detail

174a – 174b: They corner Alcibiades and fire on the castle in which he has taken shelter

175a – 175b: The Athenians cooperate with Thebes against the Spartans

175b – 176a: The Spartans pay tribute to the Athenians

176a – 176b: Demosthenes and his fortification of Athens

176b – 179b: About the wall; the Spartans ask Demosthenes why he built the wall and arrest him, then envoys come; ultimately Demosthenes is freed

179b – 180a: The Spartans try to contravene the treaty between Thebes and Athens

180a – 180b: They start preparing to attack Thebes

180b – 183a: War between Thebes and the Spartans; the Battle of Leuctra

183a – 184a: Praise of the Thebans' courage

184a – 185a: The Spartans return home wounded; their fear of the Thebans; the Athenians find ease thanks to the people of Thebes

188b – 189b: Iphikrates

189b – 190a: The Thebans and the Athenians live in pride, hedonism, and arrogance because of their conquests; the Theban hegemony consequently ends early

190a – 192b: Philip the Macedonian emerges and makes an expedition towards Thebes; a bloody war takes place; the Third Sacred War

192b – 195b: Alexander advises his father about the Thebans and tries to convince him to make peace with them; Philip finds the Thebans excessively brave and audacious

195b – 196a: The Athenians invite Aristotle to Athens

196b – 197a: The Athenians host Alexander the Great and his tutors

197a – 197b: Alexander stays 40 days in Athens, then returns to Philip

197b – 198b: Philip's expeditions

198b – 199a: Darius wins the battle and rapes Philip's wife; peace agreement held concerning 300 golden eggs

199a – 199b: Alexander is born; Philip's wife does not tell him the true identity of the child's father

199b – 200a: Philip dies; Darius demands 900 eggs from Alexander for the previous three years

200a – 200b: In response, Alexander sends two symbolic military vessels

201a – 202a: The main difference between Alexander and Darius: Alexander treats his soldiers well

202a – 202b: Darius is killed

202b – 203b: Darius' last demand from Alexander; his advice
203b – 204a: Alexander's Eastern campaigns
204a – 204b: The difference between Alexander the Great and Dhu'l-Qarnain, the prophet who is mentioned in the Qur'an (Sura 18:83–101)
204b – 207b: Dhu'l-Qarnain according to Islamic scholars; confusion regarding his identity
207b: Alexander and Dhu'l-Qarnain not the same person
207b – 208a: Alexander's death
208b – 214b: Antipater; Demosthenes; Cassander; Phokion; Antigonus Gonatas; Demetrios
214b – 217a: Battle of Pydna
217b – 218a: The Roman Emperor Augustus
218a – 220a: The Apostle Paul comes to Athens and tries to teach Christianity
220a – 222a: Hadrian and his deeds in Athens
222b – 225a: Constantine the Great
225a – 231a: The legends of Hagia Sophia
232a – 233b: Hercules in the time of the Prophet Muhammad
233b – 234a: Julian II
234a: Venice and Mehmed II
234a – 240a: Mehmed II's expedition to the Morea and visit to Athens

[The final 51 folios are not listed here, because they concern Ottoman expeditions held in the Morea and are outside the scope of this essay.]

Appendix 2

Detailed Table of Contents of Georgios Kontares's *Ἱστορίαι παλαιαὶ καὶ πάνυ ὠφέλιμοι τῆς περιφήμου πόλεως Ἀθήνης*

It should be noted that the contents section of Kontares's book appears to be in alphabetical order, rather than in page-number order, more like an index than a table of contents. Dr. Vera Andriopoulou has tried to decipher the Greek page numbers, and I have arranged them in a "modern" order. The contents page in fact begins with A and page number 175 [*ροε'*].

p. 3: How Athens obtained its power
p. 3: The first king of Athens
p. 4: Origin of the names Athena (Athens) and Atthis (Attica)
p. 4: Cecrops, the first king of Athens; his death
p. 5: The Athenians began to sow grain for the first time
p. 6: The birth of Theseus
p. 8: The death of Theseus
p. 10: The first money in Athens
p. 11: Who were the Pallantides
p. 11: Theseus draws his bow against the Pallantides
p. 12: Theseus kills the Pallantides
p. 12: Theseus tames the bull of Marathon
p. 13: Gifts for the Minotaur
p. 14: Request of Minos to the Athenians
p. 14: Mass kidnapping of children in Athens
p. 14: Youth of Athens on Crete as gifts to the Minotaur
p. 15: Goodwill of Theseus
p. 16: Theseus defeats the Minotaur
p. 16: The labyrinth on Crete in which Theseus was put
p. 17: The captain's mistake
p. 17: Aegeus' death
p. 18: The ship
p. 19: Athens is rebuilt by Theseus
p. 19: The prytaneion is founded by Theseus
p. 19: Theseus institutes democracy, the prytaneis, and the festivals; he divides the people into tribes
p. 19: The democracy of Theseus; festivals in Athens
p. 20: The Amazons attack Greece
p. 20: Theseus expands Attica's borders; he defeats the Amazons
p. 21: The wisdom of Hippolytos
p. 21: The deceit of Phaedra
p. 22: Phaedra's death
p. 22: Hippolytos is accused of adultery
p. 22: Hippolytos' death
p. 23: The friendship of Pirithoos and Theseus
p. 23: The wedding of Pirithoos
p. 24: Theseus tames the hippocentaurs
p. 24: Theseus abducts Helen
p. 24: The nature of hippocentaurs; how Theseus tamed them
p. 25: Cerberus; what it was
p. 25: Theseus hated by Menestheus
p. 25: The cruelty of the Centaurs to Theseus and Pirithous
p. 26: Menestheus' shrewdness
p. 26: The brothers of Helen in Athens
p. 27: Lycomedes deceives Theseus
p. 29: The destruction of the democracy
p. 31: Menestheus' death
p. 32: How an eagle indicated Theseus' remains and they were brought to Athens
p. 32: Codrus, king of Athens
p. 34: The rule of Solon
p. 35: The Athenians fight the Megarians
p. 35: Solon's prudence; his laws

p. 35: The Megarians fight the Athenians and lose
p. 35: The Athenian reply to Darius
p. 36: Solon pretends to be impudent
p. 37: Salamis taken by the Athenians
p. 39: The cruel manner of the wealthy Athenians
p. 39: Solon elected ruler by the Athenians
p. 40: Solon makes laws
p. 40: Strict laws of Drakon
p. 41: Solon divides up the land of Attica
p. 42: Solon makes different laws
p. 45: Solon leaves Athens
p. 45: His answer
p. 46: Solon's disagreement with Aesop
pp. 46–47: Peisistratos' eloquence; how he became sole ruler
p. 48: Peisistratos' payment to Solon
p. 48: The Megarians are captured by the Athenians
p. 49: The Megarians are defeated again
p. 49: The first library appears in Athens
p. 50: The place of Peisistratos' birth
p. 51: Peisistratos' virtues
p. 52: Hippias, tyrant of Athens
p. 53: Democracy is restored in Athens
p. 53: Hippias exiled from Athens
p. 54: Hippias defeats the Spartans
p. 55: Hippias defeated by the Spartans
p. 55: Fight between Kleisthenes and Isagoras
p. 55: Exile of Kleisthenes
p. 56: Death of Isagoras and Philo
p. 56: Cleomenes disturbs Athens
p. 56: Kleisthenes' return from exile
p. 57: Hippias marches on Athens
p. 57: Hippias defeated by the Athenians
p. 58: Chalkis defeated by Athens
p. 58: Chalkis asks the Athenians for the olive tree's wood
p. 58: The Boeotians and the people of Chalkis are defeated by the Athenians
p. 61: Darius' answer to Hippias means a declaration of war
p. 61: Darius' mission to Athens
p. 62: Darius' resentment towards the Athenians

p. 62: The union of the Athenians and the Ionians
p. 62: The Athenians burn Sardis
p. 64: Darius' campaign against Greece
p. 66: Address of Panas to the Athenians
p. 66: The Athenians leave for the Battle of Marathon
p. 68: The Athenians defeat the Persians
p. 73: The Athenians' envy
p. 76: The Athenians' praise
p. 77: The Athenians take over all the Greek lands
p. 79: Darius' glorious death
p. 64: Destruction of Eretria by the Persians
p. 65: Differences between the Persians and the Athenians
p. 65: The Athenian generals
p. 65: Vote of the ten generals
p. 65: Advice of the ten generals
p. 65: The Persians advance on Athens
p. 67: The Battle of Marathon
p. 68: The Athenians defeat the Persians
p. 69: Magnanimity of the Athenians
p. 70: Fame of the ten Athenian generals
p. 70: Bravery of Callimachus
p. 72: Concord of the Athenians
p. 72: The death of Hippias
p. 73: The flight of the Persians
p. 73: Miltiades captures the Cyclades
p. 73: The Athenians' envy of Miltiades
p. 74: Decision against Miltiades
p. 74: Xanthippos' envy of Miltiades
p. 75: Plutarch criticizes the Athenian procedure of ostracism
p. 75: Resentment of judges and the Athenian people towards Miltiades
p. 75: The Athenians' ingratitude toward Miltiades
p. 75: The reproach of Plutarch and Tarkaniotes against the Athenians concerning ostracism
p. 76: Praise of the Athenians
p. 78: Study on Greece
p. 78: The sciences and arts first developed in Athens

p. 79: The wars of the Persian kings
p. 80: The wars of the sons of Darius
p. 80: Artaphernes' advice to Xerxes
p. 80: Xerxes' plan for his Greek campaign
p. 81: Xerxes' anger toward Artaphernes
p. 81: Demaratos' letter to Athens
p. 81: The killing of Xerxes' ambassadors by the Athenians
p. 82: Xerxes' pride
p. 85: The letter of Xerxes to Athens
p. 85: How Xerxes decorated the plane tree
p. 86: Themistocles explains the oracle
p. 87: The Athenians take their possessions to other cities
p. 87: The monsters in Xerxes' army
p. 88: How Xerxes' army crossed the sea with a bridge
p. 88: Another monster in Xerxes' army
p. 89: Xerxes' fear and cowardice
p. 90: First victory of Themistocles
p. 90: Destruction of the Persians' fleet
p. 90: The magnanimity of Leonidas
p. 91: The spies sent by Xerxes to Leonidas; their death
p. 92: Other spies and their deaths
p. 92: The Persians cross the mountains
p. 93: The bravery of Leonidas; his words to his soldiers
p. 93: Leonidas' battle at Thermopylae and his death
p. 94: Xerxes' question to Demaratos
p. 95: The Persian fleet nears the Greek fleet
p. 96: The Athenians defeat the Persians at sea
p. 96: The defeat and destruction of the Persian fleet
p. 97: Battle of the Greeks and the Persians at Artemision
p. 98: Xerxes' anger at the Athenians
p. 99: How Xerxes sent troops to attack the Temple of Apollo
p. 99: Phokis is abandoned because of Xerxes
p. 99: Leonidas' death

p. 100: Xerxes takes Athens
p. 100: Temple of Apollo attacked by Persians
p. 101: The Greeks fear the Persians
p. 101: Themistocles advises the Greeks
p. 102: Themistocles' pride towards the Alcmeonids
p. 102: The general councils of the Greeks
p. 105: Themistocles' letter to Xerxes
p. 106: Xerxes' fleet attacks the Greek fleet
p. 106: The justness of Aristeides
p. 107: Aristeides sends news to the Greeks
p. 107: Victory of the Athenians over the Persians
p. 108: Flight of the Persians
p. 109: Aristeides kills the Persians
p. 110: Flight of Xerxes
p. 110: Bravery and death of Masistas
p. 111: How Xerxes' soldiers also fled
p. 113: Athens freed again
p. 114: Olynthos captured by Mardonius
p. 114: Themistocles receives honors from the Greeks
p. 114: Mardonius captures Olynthos
p. 115: Mardonius sends Alexander Amyntas against the Athenians
p. 116: Alexander Amyntas sent against Boeotia
p. 117: The Boeotians taken by Mardonius
p. 117: Cruelty of the Athenians
p. 117: Mardonius takes Athens
p. 117: The letter that Mardonius sends to Athens
p. 118: Mardonius burns Athens
p. 118: The Athenians' houses and temples burned down by Mardonius
p. 119: The Lacedaemonians march with the Athenians against Mardonius
p. 119: Another sea battle between the Greeks and the Persians
p. 121: The ranks and divisions of the Greek army
p. 122: Battle of Plataea
p. 123: Pausanias' letter to the Athenians
p. 123: The death of Kallikrates
p. 123: The death of Kallimachos
p. 123: Socrates the philosopher
p. 123: Flight of the other nations in the war

p. 124: Death of Mardonius
p. 124: Athenian victory over the Persians at Plataea
p. 124: Leotychides' defeat at Plataea
p. 124: Alliance of the Greeks and the Persians
p. 125: Alliance among Thebes, Boeotia, and Athens
p. 125: The tripod dedicated at the Temple of Apollo
p. 125: How many people died at Plataea
p. 126: The great sacrifice of the Greeks
p. 127: Cimon defeats the Persians at sea
p. 127: Two Greek victories in one day
p. 129: The Athenians wage war against Thebes
p. 129: Death of Artaklos and Eubazos
p. 129: Happiness of the Athenians
p. 130: Four battles between the Athenians and the Persians
p. 130: Thebes brought to justice
p. 130: Aristeides' just judgement
p. 133: The Athenians take over the Thebans' land
p. 134: The Lacedaemonians' envy of the Athenians
p. 135: Themistocles' reply to the Spartans
p. 135: Themistocles' cunning
p. 136: Themistocles builds the fortifications of Piraeus
p. 137: Themistocles' exile
p. 137: Exile a usual practice in Athens
p. 138: Aristeides' exile
p. 138: The just judgment of Aristeides
p. 139: Aristeides returns once again to Athens
p. 139: Aeschylus the poet
p. 139: The Athenians give the ten generals their reward
p. 140: Exile of Damon
p. 140: Accusations against Themistocles
p. 141: Themistocles betrayed by Pausanias
p. 141: Themistocles flees to Persia
p. 142: Themistocles' excellent reply to the dragomans [interpreters]
p. 143: Themistocles learns Persian in one year
p. 143: Themistocles is pardoned and receives favors from Xerxes

p. 144: Themistocles' death
p. 145: The pride of Pausanias
p. 146: Pausanias is convicted by his compatriots
p. 146: Cimon is voted general by the Athenians
p. 148: Cimon defeats the Phoenicians
p. 148: Leonidas again defeated
p. 148: The Athenians defeat the Persians and take their spoils
p. 149: What Cimon built in Athens
p. 150: Cimon again defeats the Persians
p. 150: Cimon hated by many
p. 151: Cimon's exile
p. 151: Beginning of hostilities between the Spartans and the Athenians
p. 152: The clemency of Cimon
p. 153: The dream of Cimon
p. 154: The beautiful sculptures of Pheidias
p. 154: Cimon's philanthropy and hospitality
p. 156: The poet Tyrtaeus
p. 156: Tyrtaeus' poem for the victorious soldiers
p. 157: The victory of the Lacedaemonians
p. 158: The Lacedaemonians defeated by the Athenians
p. 158: The bravery of Pericles
p. 159: The Athenians again in distress
p. 161: The fervor of the Athenians and the Lacedaemonians
p. 161: The Corinthians oppose the Athenians
p. 162: The victory of the Athenians
p. 163: The Athenians are defeated and killed by the Corinthians
p. 163: The distress of the Spartans
p. 163: The flight of the Corinthians
p. 163: The people of Phokis governed by the Spartans
p. 164: The Athenians defeat the Boeotians
p. 164: The Athenians burn down the Spartan arsenal
p. 164: The Spartans again defeated by the Athenians
p. 165: The Sicyonians are defeated by the Athenians
p. 165: Pericles against the Peloponnesians
p. 166: Pericles elected general by the Athenians for a second time
p. 166: The Athenians defeat the Samians

p. 166: The Megarians revolt against Athens
p. 167: Pericles takes Samos
p. 169: Pericles takes Byzantium
p. 169: Pericles takes 50 children from Samos
p. 169: The Athenians blockade Samos and destroy it
p. 170: Pericles praises those who were killed in the war
p. 170: Phormion, Athenian general
p. 171: Pericles' charity
p. 172: Konon the Athenian is voted general
p. 172: Pericles' kind character
p. 173: Pericles accused of abuse of funds by Thucydides
p. 173: Pericles' response
p. 173: How Konon the Athenian sent two ships to Athens
p. 173: The exile of Thucydides
p. 174: Pheidias the sculptor; his drawings
p. 174: Pericles' prudence
p. 175: The sculptor Agorakritos
p. 175: The sculptor Alkimenes
p. 175: Other excellent sculptors
p. 176: A dispute between Alkistides and Euripides
p. 176: Gorgias the philosopher
p. 176: Euripides
p. 176: Excellent poets
p. 176: Sophocles the poet
p. 177: Sophocles' prudence
p. 177: Euripides' death
p. 177: The unbearable distress of the Athenians
p. 178: Battle between the Athenians and the Lacedaemonians
p. 179: Archestratos the general in Athens
p. 179: The Potidaeans revolt against Athens
p. 180: Potidaea defeated by the Athenians
p. 180: Counsels of the Corinthians against the Athenians
p. 182: Speeches of Sthenelaidas and Archidamos at Sparta
p. 183: Gelon asks to become ruler of Athens
p. 183: The Spartans make strange demands on the Athenians
p. 184: Pericles speaks about issues regarding the Spartans
p. 186: Treachery of the Thebans against the Plataeans
p. 186: The Plataeans' reply to the Thebans
p. 187: The Lacedaemonians prepare for war
p. 189: The letter that Konon sent to Athens
p. 189: Konon the Athenian goes to Artaxerxes
p. 190: The Plataeans' land burned by the Thebans
p. 190: War between Athens and Sparta
p. 190: Konon the Athenian defeats the Spartan fleet and receives honors in Athens
p. 190: The Lacedaemonians march against the Athenians
p. 190: Pericles' foreknowledge of the war
p. 192: The Lacedaemonians withdraw
p. 192: The Athenians are defeated
p. 192: Damage to the Peloponnese caused by the Athenians
p. 193: Klinias, Athenian general
p. 193: Konon the Athenian burns the lands of the Spartans
p. 194: The Lacedaemonians again attack Athens
p. 195: Athenians suffer death, hunger, and war in their own land
p. 196: The Athenians storm the Peloponnese
p. 196: The Athenians complain about Pericles
p. 197: The Athenians destroy Epidauros
p. 199: Death of Pericles
p. 199: Hippocrates
p. 200: The death of Alkamenes
p. 200: Death of Melissandros
p. 200: Lacedaemonian envoys killed in Athens
p. 200: Phormion elected general
p. 201: The Potidaians surrender to Athens
p. 202: The Lacedaemonians' cruelty towards the Plataeans
p. 202: The Plataeans' trust in Athens
p. 203: Phormion goes to Chania with his fleet
p. 205: Defeat and destruction of the Peloponnesian fleet
p. 206: The magnanimity of Thrasyllos

p. 206: Mytilene blockaded by the Athenians
p. 208: Athenian cruelty against Lesbos
p. 209: The Athenians send an army to Sicily
p. 210: Demosthenes and Prokles travel with the fleet to the Peloponnese
p. 210: Nicias the Athenian in Melos
p. 210: Prokles the Athenian with the fleet in the Peloponnese
p. 210: The Tanagrans defeated by the Athenians
p. 211: Aitolians defeated by the Athenians
p. 212: Eurymedon the Athenian in Sicily
p. 212: The Lacedaemonians defeated by the Athenians
p. 212: An admiral leads the fleet to Sicily
p. 213: The Lacedaemonian fleet is blocked in Plemmyrion
p. 214: Kleon's victory over the Spartans
p. 214: War between Athens and Syracuse
p. 215: Brasidas of Lacedaemon
p. 215: Nicias the Athenian destroys much territory in the Peloponnese
p. 216: Hippocrates, Athenian general, attacks Boeotia
p. 216: The Lacedaemonians march against Athens
p. 216: Flight of the Athenians
p. 217: Sicyon revolts against Athens
p. 218: Nicias the Athenian destroys Mende
p. 219: Sicyon captured by the Athenians
p. 220: Nicias the Athenian marches against Chalkis
p. 221: Cleon captures Torone
p. 222: Cleon's death
p. 222: The Athenians defeated at Amphipolis
p. 222: Alliance between the Athenians and the Lacedaemonians
p. 223: Aristophanes the comic poet
p. 223: Timon the misanthrope
p. 224: Alcibiades attacks Argos
p. 228: Guards imprisoned
p. 229: Alcibiades accused in Athens
p. 232: Alcibiades flees from the ship
p. 233: Lais brought to Athens

p. 233: Nicias the Athenian's treachery against the Syracusans
p. 234: Syracuse defeated
p. 236: Lamachos defeats the Syracusans; death
p. 237: Gylippos of Lacedaemon in Syracuse
p. 237: The port of Plemmyrion taken by the Athenians
p. 238: Demosthenes in Sicily
p. 239: The port of Plemmyrion retaken by the Syracusans
p. 241: Demosthenes fights against Syracuse
p. 241: Distress of the Athenians
p. 242: Syracuse defeats Athens
p. 243: Nicias the Athenian's magnanimity
p. 243: Another battle between Athens and Syracuse
p. 244: Another naval battle between Athens and Syracuse
p. 244: The Syracusans set a trap for the Athenians
p. 244: Syracuse's deceit toward Athens
p. 244: The Syracusans burn the Athenian fleet
p. 245: Leonidas defeated by the Athenians
p. 245: Alliance between Athens and Sparta
p. 247: Xenokrates pleads successfully with Gylippos to spare his life
p. 247: The Athenians surrender to the Syracusans
p. 247: Demosthenes surrenders to the people of Syracuse
p. 248: Honors that Syracuse gave Gylippos
p. 248: Gelon's desperate address to Demosthenes and Nicias
p. 249: Demosthenes' death
p. 249: Xenokrates' death
p. 249: Death of Nicias and Demosthenes
p. 250: At this time, Alcibiades becomes the cause of Athens' destruction
p. 253: The Spartans name Alcibiades general
p. 254: Alcibiades' love for Timaia
p. 255: Alcibiades flees from the Spartans
p. 256: The poet Tyrtaeus
p. 257: Good things that Alcibiades did for his country
p. 257: The Athenians destroy the democracy

p. 257: Death of Phrynichos
p. 258: The Athenians restore the democracy
p. 258: The Lacedaemonians are defeated by the Athenians
p. 259: Honors received by Alcibiades at the court of Tissaphernes
p. 260: Menelaos the Lacedaemonianp.
p. 260: Sea battles between Athens and Sparta
p. 261: The Athenians pursue Tissaphernes
p. 261: The Athenians defeat the Spartans
p. 262: Alcibiades imprisoned by the Persian satrap; then he escapes
p. 263: Alcibiades joins the Athenian army against the Persians
p. 263: The death of Medaors the Lacedaemonian
p. 263: Pharnabazos defeated by the Athenians
p. 264: The people of Kyzikos enslaved
p. 264: Trophies constructed by the Athenians
p. 265: Alcibiades conquers Selymbria
p. 265: Pharnabazos defeated by the Athenians
p. 266: The Lacedaemonians defeated by the Athenians
p. 266: Selymbria captured by Athens
p. 266: Chalkedon enslaved by the Athenians
p. 267: Pharnabazos defeated by the Athenians again
p. 267: The Athenians conquer Byzantium
p. 267: Syracuse captured by Thrasyboulos
p. 268: Celebrations in Athens for the return of Alcibiades
p. 269: King Cyrus, the beloved friend of Lysander
p. 269: Lysander, the Lacedaemonians' general
p. 270: What Lysander requested from Cyrus
p. 272: Alcibiades flees to Thrace
p. 272: Methymna destroyed by Kallikratidas
p. 273: The Spartan blockade of the Athenian fleet
p. 273: The Athenians send a new fleet
p. 275: Lysander the Spartan
p. 275: Lysander captures Lamachos
p. 275: Celebrations of the Athenian fleet
p. 275: The oracle given by Delphi to Athens
p. 276: The Athenian blockade of the Spartan fleet
p. 276: The Spartans capture the Athenian fleet
p. 276: The Athenian fleet reaches Sicily
p. 276: New law in Athens; the amnesty
p. 277: Lysander takes all the lands in Asia and the islands from the Athenians
p. 277: Lysander fights against Athens
p. 278: The Corinthians defeated by the Athenians; Corinthian cruelty to the Athenians
p. 278: The Lacedaemonians blockade Athens
p. 278: Distress of the Athenians
p. 278: Spartan goodwill toward the Athenians
p. 279: Second alliance between the Athenians and the Lacedaemonians
p. 279: Kallias, Athenian general
p. 280: Kallias' death
p. 280: The Thirty Tyrants in Athens
p. 281: Alcibiades flees to Persia again, for fear of the tyrants
p. 282: Alcibiades' death
p. 282: Cruelty of the Thirty Tyrants
p. 282: Plato in Sicily
p. 283: The Sicilians defeated by the Athenians; their goodwill toward the Athenians
p. 284: Thrasyboulos' nature and conduct
p. 285: Thrasyboulos defeats the Thirty Tyrants
p. 285: The Thirty Tyrants take away the Athenians' weapons
p. 286: The Thirty Tyrants exiled by Thrasyboulos
p. 286: The death of the Thirty Tyrants
p. 286: Thrasyboulos sends the Thirty Tyrants into exile and frees Athens
p. 287: Thrasyboulos receives a laurel crown from the Athenians
p. 287: Origins of the philosophers
p. 289: Agesilaos defeated by Konon
p. 290: Rebuilding of the city of Athens
p. 291: The Athenians defeat all the lands
p. 292: Iphikrates the Athenian defeats the Spartans
p. 295: Thrasyboulos becomes captain of his homeland; his death
p. 295: Tribon the Spartan defeated by the Athenians

p. 296: Envoys of Artaxerxes in Athens
p. 296: Iphikrates the Athenian again defeats the Spartans at sea
p. 297: Athenian alliance with the Spartans
p. 297: Wars between Thebes and Sparta
p. 297: Timotheos, Athenian captain; his victory over the Spartans
p. 298: Menasippos the Lacedaemonian defeated by the Athenian Stesikles
p. 299: The historians Herodotos and Thucydides
p. 299: Gifts that Iphikrates the Athenian received from Artaxerxes
p. 300: Alexander of Pherae conquers Larissa; his death
p. 300: Larissa taken by Alexandros of Pherae
p. 300: Pelopidas defeats Alexander of Pherae
p. 300: Pherae wages war against the Greeks
p. 301: Civil wars among the Greeks
p. 302: Chabrias the Athenian surrounded by the Lacedaemonians
p. 302: Death of Epaminondas
p. 303: Chabrias the Athenian; his courage and death
p. 304: Kings of Macedonia
p. 305: Larissa taken by Philip
p. 305: Philip the Great rules Macedonia
p. 305: Philip the Great takes Athens and Thessaly
p. 306: Philip the Great loses an eye
p. 306: The Greeks lose their freedom
p. 306: Lesbos revolts against Athens
p. 307: Philip the Great elected captain by the Thebans
p. 307: The Phokians loot the Temple of Apollo
p. 308: Philip the Great's schemes
p. 308: Mytilene captured by the Athenians
p. 308: Democrates the Athenian's rude answer to Philip
p. 309: Philip the Great's cruelty
p. 309: All the Phokians killed by Philip
p. 309: Phokion, general of Athens
p. 310: Phokion defeats Philip's army
p. 311: Menestheus, captain of the Athenians

p. 312: The Athenians go to Byzantium
p. 312: Alexander the Great
p. 312: Alexander the Great's love of learning
p. 313: Phokion takes the Megarid
p. 313: The other Demosthenes (the rhetor)
p. 313: The eloquence of Demosthenes the rhetor
p. 314: Demosthenes the rhetor's first speech
p. 316: Alexander the Great's alliance with the Athenians
p. 316: Philip the Great sends envoys to Athens; his goodwill toward Athens and cruelty to Thebes
p. 317: Alexander the Great campaigns against the Athenians
p. 317: Alexander the Great enslaves Thebes
p. 318: Alexander the Great defeats Darius, king of the Persians
p. 318: Advice that Phokion sends Alexander
p. 318: Gifts that Alexander the Great sends Phokion not accepted
p. 319: Harpalos in Athens
p. 320: How Demosthenes the rhetor accepted money from Harpalos
p. 320: Demosthenes the rhetor flees Athens
p. 321: Demosthenes the rhetor pardoned; he returns to his homeland
p. 321: Aeschines the rhetor
p. 321: Demades the rhetor
p. 321: Isokrates the rhetor
p. 322: Hypereides the rhetor
p. 323: Blockade of Antipaxos
p. 324: The Athenians defeat Antipaxos
p. 324: Leosthenes, commander of the Athenians; his death
p. 325: Melos captured by the Athenians
p. 325: Phokion elected captain again
p. 325: Lamachos, Nicias, and Alcibiades
p. 326: Leonnatos the Macedonian defeated by the Athenians
p. 327: Antipaxos attacks Athens
p. 327: Hypereides' unjust death
p. 328: Demosthenes the rhetor's death
p. 329: Antipaxos' cruelty and amoral behavior

p. 329: War among the successors of Alexander
p. 331: Nikanor, general of Cassander
p. 331: Phokion's death
p. 332: Demetrios, son of Antigonus, moves against the Athenians
p. 332: Demetrios of Phaleron in Athens
p. 332: Battle between Antigonus and Cassander
p. 333: Demetrios of Phaleron flees Athens
p. 334: Liberties that Demetrios, son of Antigonus, gave the Athenians
p. 334: Stratocles the Athenian ambassador
p. 335: Theophrastos the philosopher
p. 335: A young man teases Xenokrates
p. 336: Demetrios, son of Antigonus, defeats Cassander
p. 336: Tutors in the Academy
p. 337: Demetrios, son of Antigonus, besieges Athens
p. 337: Lachares, ruler of Athens
p. 338: The Athenians revolt against Demetrios
p. 339: Demetrios, son of Antigonus, is captured
p. 339: Demetrios, son of Antigonus; alliance with Athens
p. 340: Demetrios, son of Antigonus, regains his freedom
p. 340: Antigonus II
p. 341: The Macedonians plunder the lands of the Athenians
p. 342: Philip marches on Athens
p. 342: Mithridates in Greece
p. 344: Alliance made by Mithridates with the Athenians
p. 344: Silas the Roman in Greece
p. 345: Silas the Roman fights against Athens
p. 345: Famine in Athens
p. 346: Silas the Roman enters Athens
p. 346: Children sent from Rome to Athens to study
p. 347: Mark Antony in Athens; his favors to the Athenians
p. 348: Dionysius the Areopagite; how he became a Christian
p. 348: The Apostle Paul in Athens

The Neighborhood of Karykes and the Fountain of the Exechoron

Dimitris N. Karidis

Contrary to common beliefs, Athens expanded exponentially from the earliest years of Ottoman rule. As little-studied Ottoman archival sources indicate, the city's population rose sharply. Long before visitors inspired by Enlightenment ideas considered Athens as an intricate metonym for something even more intricate, the topography of the town was already well-structured; and so was its corresponding urban form. In fact, as this essay argues, Ottoman topography can be said to have enveloped the first official plan implemented in the city (1834). This may be a paradox confounding the clarity of urban discourse: the plan of the new capital city was meant to interrupt tradition by obliterating the urban fabric in which history was embedded, and the alteration in the physical fabric of society did not keep pace with the plan's new intentions.

The Topography of Athens under Ottoman Rule

In accordance with the conditions favorable for urban development that prevailed in Athens after the mid-15th century, Ottoman archival sources attest that some 10,000 people were living in this town by 1506.[1] In 1570, almost a century after the Ottoman conquest, the population had risen to almost 15,000 inhabitants, corresponding to the highest population figures throughout the time of Ottoman rule. In the middle of the 16th century, the built-up area was approximately 70 ha, and the average population density 250 people per ha, roughly speaking. Specialists in Athenian history have claimed that for some years after the conquest the built-up area did not extend beyond the limits set by the Late Roman fortification wall, built in A.D. 267.[2] If this had been the case, the town would have had a density of between 1,000 and 1,200 people per ha. Yet urban history teaches us that in all European towns between the 13th and the 16th century the density never exceeded 100–170 people per ha.

We have additional written proof that the town of Athens expanded early in the Ottoman period. This is clear, for instance, in two 16th-century documents, both referring to the area of the town outside

---

[1] For further documentation of the demographic conditions of Ottoman Athens based on archival sources, see Karidis 2014, ch. 1, pp. 23–54.
[2] Travlos 1960, p. 74

the Late Roman fortification wall.[3] The first document, dated July 6, 1548, is the official attestation of a Greek Athenian issued on the occasion of his purchase of a house in the quarter [*mahalla*] of "Karyki." Thanks to the church known by this name, this urban quarter is understood to have been located on the north-east side of the city, quite far away from the medieval town boundaries. The second document, dated to 1506, is related to the construction of a fountain in Athens and to the improvement made at that time to the system of water supply from Hadrian's aqueduct. The fountain in question was built in the area known then as "Exechoron:" a fountain by this name is known to have existed close to the present-day Syntagma Square, thus much further from the limits of the A.D. 267 fortification wall. In other words, by 1570 the greater part of Ottoman Athens was already in place. On the basis of what Pierre Lavedan has defined as "Le Loi de l'Insistance du Plan,"[4] the much later, very accurately drawn 18th- and 19th-century plans of Athens allow a sound understanding of the structure of the town during the early years of Ottoman rule (Fig. 1).

Figure 1. The street layout in Ottoman Athens, topographical survey by Stamatios Kleanthes and Gustav Eduard Schaubert, 1832. Redrawing D. N. Karidis.

[3] Kambouroglou 1889, pp. 90, 179.
[4] Lavedan 1926, p. 91.

After 1456, the first residential areas developed close to the market, that is, to the north of the Frankish-period town. In 1570, Athens experienced a second phase of urban growth, this time towards the north-east. It was mainly Albanian families who settled here. There is little evidence of when the western part—the area between the Theseion and the Stoa of Attalos—developed. The area had long been uninhabited, as it was less healthy and attractive to settle in. Nevertheless, by the middle of the 16th century, some building activity must have taken place in this sector as well, although resulting in much lower density. Until a few years before the War of Independence broke out, Athens was thinly populated. Its built-up area had hardly changed since the early period of Ottoman rule, but its population had diminished considerably, at least in relation to the mid-16th century. This is clearly evidenced in the exquisite early 19th-century pencil drawing by Georg Gropius showing a panoramic view of the town from the north-east corner of the Acropolis hill (Fig. 2).

Figure 2. Detail of Georg Gropius's panoramic view of Athens, ca. 1810, pencil drawing, 0.41 x 2.22 m. London, British Library, Department of Manuscripts. Photo © Trustees of the British Museum.

We shall now turn our attention to specific issues of housing conditions. According to an Ottoman archival source of 1530, the smallest urban quarter in Athens had 16 households [*hane*] and the largest 107 households.[5] There were 23 quarters with 60–70 households, corresponding to almost 70% of the total households. Almost three centuries later, the town had moved beyond those early demographic conditions: now 70% of the city's quarters corresponded to residential areas containing 15 (mainly) to 65 households, instead of 60 to 70 as was the case earlier.

The northern part of Athens, stretching north from the east–west axis of Hadrian Street (Odos Adrianou), schematically divided the town into the "Chora" and the "Exechoron." It included higher-density housing areas with small, low-income dwellings, some of which, close to the bazaar area, integrated artisans' workshops. The part of the town that stretched south of the aforementioned main east–west axis comprised mostly larger, wealthier housing units, most of them at some distance from workshops. These dwellings, located on the gentle slopes of the Acropolis, commanded a splendid view towards the extensive olive groves to the north-west, Mt. Hymettus on the east, and the hills and mountains far beyond—a truly idyllic natural environment.

---

[5] TD 367: I thank Dr. M. Kiel for introducing me to this document and providing relevant information.

The pattern of social division of space that prevailed in Athens during the Ottoman period produced no great social discrepancies among the residential areas in ethnic or religious terms. Indeed, the conditions of economic and social development throughout the period of Ottoman rule were such that the town did not manifest any strong patterns of segregation. Since the Muslim population was strongly outnumbered by the Greek Orthodox and Albanian populations, ethnic/religious factors did not appear to play an important role in establishing strict dividing lines.

As for land use, even within the limitations of a small-scale provincial town, Athens' structure can be said to have followed the Ottoman urban model, with the central market area strictly distinguished from the rest of the town. Yet, within the bounds of the residential areas, a certain mingling of evenly distributed activities did occur in Athens.

It can be argued that climatic and topographical factors had little bearing in determining which locations within the urban structure counted as prestigious; most probably, such factors had no serious effect on sale prices. Of course, in pre-capitalist towns land values were determined by competition to acquire prestigious sites. However, in a society that used space and architectural expression to represent its power symbolically, such sites were to be found strictly and solely in the marketplace, the center of commerce and administration. In Athens, the boundaries between urban space and social structure were not based on a dichotomy between Muslim and non-Muslim citizens' residential districts. Instead, one might expect to encounter a "natural," enforced segregation between groups vested with political and military power on the one side, and the majority of the population, subject to political rule and fiscal exaction, on the other. Alternatively, these boundaries might be defined by differences between Christian and Muslim artisans and small tenant farmers on the one hand, and large landowners, Christian and Muslim, on the other.

An interesting peculiarity arises at this point. For a place such as 19th-century Athens, visited by so many foreigners in search of the city's glorious past, that a prestigious focal point was apparently centered on the Frankish community might be considered a logical consequence. Indeed, since the end of the 17th century, the small Capuchin monastery located in the south-eastern part of the town, diametrically opposite the bazaar, seems to have become such a focal point, adjoining as it did the picturesque 4th-century B.C. Choragic Monument of Lysicrates (Fig. 3). The monks used the monument as a library and reading room. Apart from a few mansions of the

Figure 3. "The French Capuchin Monastery at Athens" by W. Page, also showing the Monument of Lysicrates, copper engraving, 9.3 x 6.5 cm. *Forget Me Not: A Christmas and New Year's Present for 1826*, London 1826, p. 293. Private collection.

wealthy and certain important churches nearby, the Capuchin monastery, a subject beloved by visiting artists, was structurally integrated into the town plan, understood and experienced by the inhabitants as a reference point, retaining its own inherent beauty and striking appearance. Thus, we might argue that this part of Athens provided a second prestigious focal point. That was not the case, however; the monastery was always second in importance to the bazaar, an urban entity too powerful to be overshadowed by other areas or buildings, even if the latter incorporated significant landmarks. It was the bazaar area, containing the key administrative and cultural functions, and not the Capuchin monastery, where the ruling class needed to demonstrate its power symbolically (Fig. 4).

Figure 4. "Mercato d'Atene," colored copper engraving, 11.5 x 17 cm, from Giulio Ferrario, *Il costume antico e moderno* ..., Florence 1828. Private collection.

It was therefore no accident that the great and the strong chose to reside there, close to the bazaar, whether they were powerful Christian-Orthodox, Muslim officials, or even west European consuls. For instance, the house of the French artist and consul Louis-François-Sébastien Fauvel was located close to the market area, not at the other end of the town. In the early 19th century, when

Fauvel found himself in need of a larger house (apparently because his collection of antiquities had grown too large), his new premises (see p. 234, Fig. 2) were located south-east of the Odeion complex in the Ancient Agora, just a stone's throw from the market.[6]

The First Plan of Athens

The first official plan of Athens as the capital city of the independent Greek state, drafted by Stamatios Kleanthes and Gustav Eduard Schaubert and approved in 1833, partly overlapped with the existing town, and the keystone of its composition was epitomized by an isosceles triangle that provided the backbone for future development. A closer reading of the plan reveals that public space was structured on the basis of a network of securely interrelated linear elements and radial-concentric squares. Orthogonal planning was a common feature of this period, with the plan of Philadelphia (John Reed, 1774) and the plan for the expansion of Berlin (Peter J. Lenné, 1820) among the most prominent.

Until recently, no explanation has been given of the relationship established by the new plan between the street layout and the Acropolis itself. Of course, the ideological assumptions inherent in the juxtaposition of the Royal Palace and the Acropolis are repeatedly mentioned. Yet the exact orientation of the axis linking the two (that is, Athinas Street and the two streets parallel to it), according to the plan, which deviates from the direction of the astronomical north, needs to be clarified.

In fact, the orientation given to Aiolou Street (Fig. 5) on the map is justified by the fact that it forms a direct link between the octagonal Tower of the Winds (the Horologion of Andronikos) and the Erechtheion. As pedestrians followed this street from north to south, moving from the old town

Figure 5. The Tower of the Winds and the newly opened Aiolou Street (in the background), unknown artist, 1843, lithograph, 10 x 18 cm. Private collection.

---

[6] Thompson 1962, p. 31.

towards the Acropolis, the northern facade of the Erechtheion became fully inscribed within the geometric features of this newly designed street. The outcome of this design initiative was to provide an impressive view, with the octagonal tower functioning as a significant landmark for the lower town, and the Erechtheion crowning the vista at the summit of the Acropolis, framing the whole dramatic scene. It is as if the two architects presented the late 5th-century B.C. temple on the Acropolis as a theatrical backdrop, meant to be seen from afar, in the exact manner defined by Edmund Bacon as a "shaft of space," a design thrust that "provides the generating force of much of the finest 18th-century northern European civic development."[7]

Further scrutiny of the new plan reveals that the length of the long side of the great rectangular structure of the Library of Hadrian is the spatial element that must have determined the distance between the two parallel streets Athinas and Aiolou: 115 meters. Consequently, the two new streets that cut through the fabric of the old town bounded Hadrian's Library on its eastern and western sides. Another issue that in some way links the topography of the old town with the topography of the about-to-be-built capital city is the surface area of Hadrian's Library, which corresponds in size to almost 70% of the building plots featured in the new city plan by Kleanthes and Schaubert. In this way, the new Athens plan came full circle, combining the intentions of symbolic representation with principles of urban design (Fig. 6). The two architects had studied under Karl Friedrich Schinkel at the Bauakademie in Berlin. If we examine the details of the urban design procedure, we can see more clearly how they took advantage of the topography of the old town.

Once the alignments of Athinas and Aiolou Streets were determined on the map, the base of the isosceles triangle was fixed in an east–west direction, incorporating the picturesque Middle Byzantine church of the Kapnikarea. A free urban space was created around this celebrated cross-in-square construction, the church jutting upward as a free-standing landmark in the center of this space. In the original version of the new Athens plan, this east–west axis (Ermou Street) is strangely not quite perpendicular to Athinas and Aiolou Streets, which run in a north–south direction, but diverges slightly from the right angle. This cannot be mere error, not least because all other streets parallel to Ermou are in fact perpendicular to Aiolou Street.

I propose the following explanation. Had the east–west axis of Ermou Street been designed to run perpendicular to Aiolou Street, the former street would have led westward right onto another Middle Byzantine church, Agioi Asomatoi. The convergence of Ermou Street with this church would have obliged the two architects to develop a planning arrangement on the west similar to the one proposed for the Kapnikarea church. Yet it seems their intention was to avoid formalistic rigidity and to dispense with a quasi-Baroque repetition and symmetry induced by the doubling of the same urbanistic effect. Choosing to align Ermou Street so that it met with Aiolou Street, but not at a right angle, they succeeded in leading Ermou westwards at a certain distance from the church of Agioi Asomatoi, so that the space around the church now appeared as a semicircle, not as a circular area encompassing the entire building (as was the case with the Kapnikarea). A closer look at the Kleanthes–Schaubert plan shows that the same awareness of "contained" space was the creative drive for at least ten other Middle Byzantine churches that the two architects had decided to integrate into their planning proposal for the contiguous unities implied by each component in the plan's composition (Fig. 7). The aim may have been for specific monumental buildings from the past not merely to serve as free-standing landmarks, but also to become nodes of reference within a tightly woven urban fabric. By exemplifying

---

[7] Bacon 1967, p. 171.

such an approach, the two architects showed their adherence to the view that all existing monuments within the traditional topography should merge Antiquity with the Middle Ages. That view approximated the Romantic-classicizing approach to urban design, a style that the two architects had no reason to disregard. By adopting this method, they tried to restore the significance and meaning of ever-evolving forms caught in the flow of time for the community's collective memory, thus showing true respect for tradition.

In addition to the previous "geometric" analysis of the urban design principles essential to the first Athens plan, factors relating to living conditions in early 19th-century Athens and to the character of the traditional built-up area should also be examined. The first factor is related to the market area, the bazaar. The way the isosceles triangle lay on this area, the precise center of economic life during the period of Ottoman rule, proves that the busy core of the old town was meant to give life to the new city as well, right at the place where two of the most important thoroughfares of the new capital city, Ermou and Aiolou Streets, intersected. This traditional market area remained a vibrant hub of local life throughout the 19th century. The second factor is related to the adaptation of the new plan to the

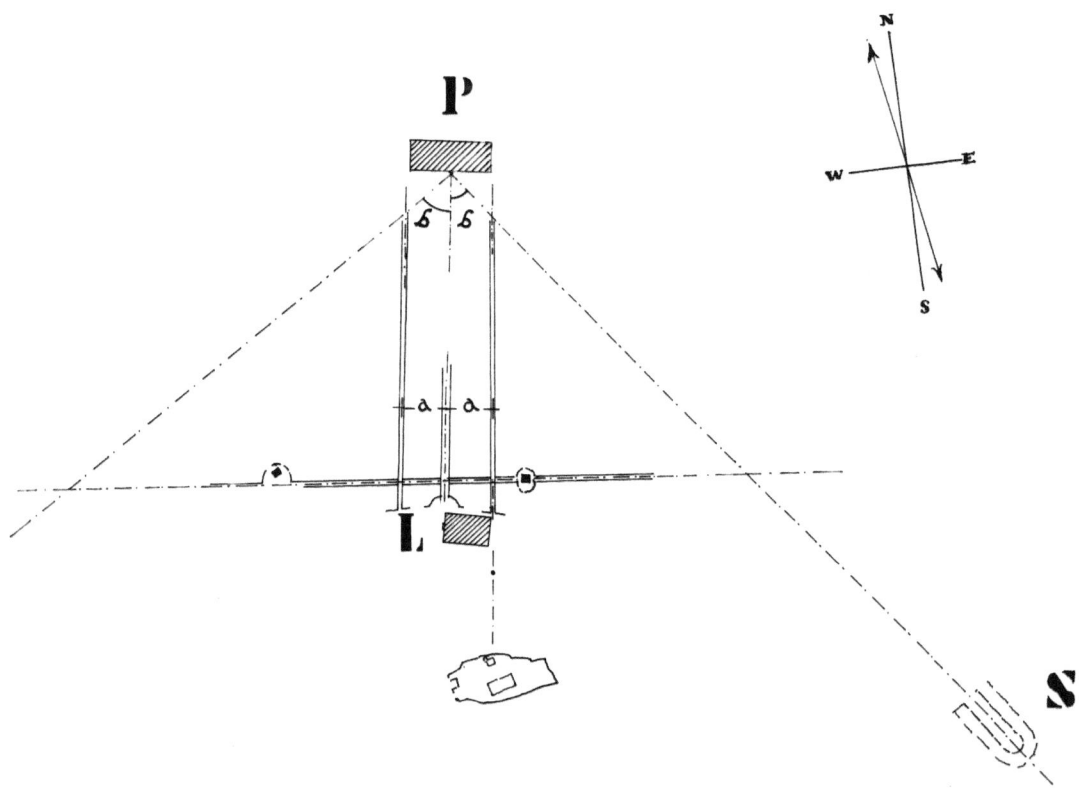

Figure 6. Decoding urban design principles in the first Athens plan: the longitudinal dimension of Hadrian's Library (L) determines the distance (a) set between Aiolou Street and Athinas Street (the bisector of the top corner). The third parallel line to the west, set at equal distance 'a' defines the longitudinal dimension of the Royal Palace (P). The whole synthesis starts from Aiolou Street, set on the map so as to link the Erechtheion and the Tower of the Winds. Karidis 2014, p. 105, fig. III.3.

existing street network: the two circular spaces to the east and north, corresponding to the present Syntagma and Omonia Squares, coincide with the two most important traffic nodes of the city's Ottoman-period topography. The one on the east was located at the point where the major rural roads branched off to the fertile plain of the Mesogeia; from the other, on the north, rural roads led to Thebes and the northern hinterland.

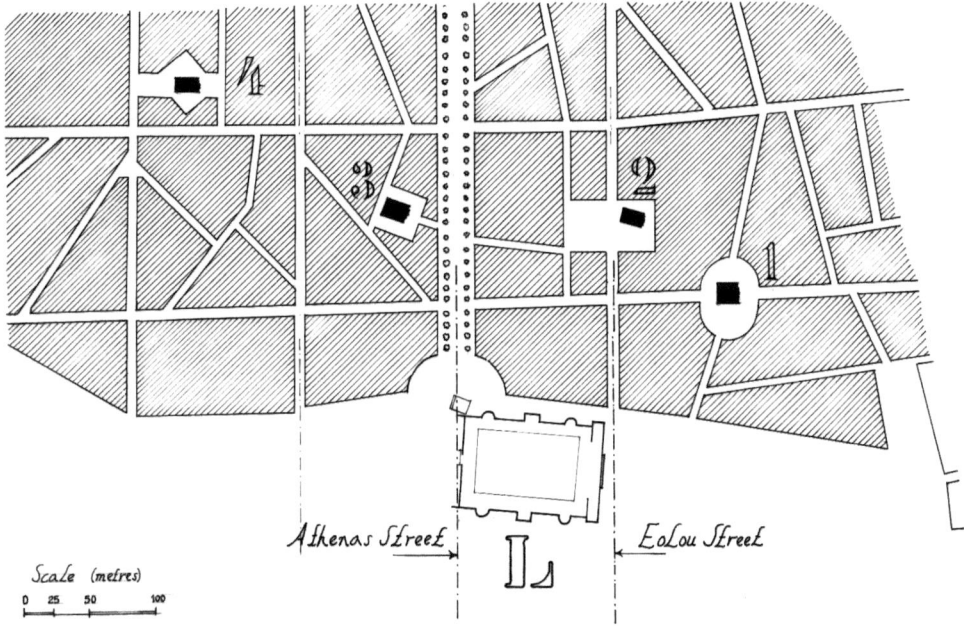

Figure 7. A closer look at the lower part of the Stamatios Kleanthes and Gustav Eduard Schaubert plan of Athens: their masterful ability to create public space around the Byzantine monuments, each time with its own inherent identity. Karidis 2014, p. 107, fig. III.4.

A Violent Break with the Past?

Let us now proceed to possible relationships between the new plan of Athens and traditional topography on the basis of other factors related to social structure, which was about to change, and to elements of customary law. Though the urban restructuring proposed by Kleanthes and Schaubert has been assumed to have triggered virulent dissent by those landowners who sensed an obvious threat to their vested interests, focusing on this dissent seems short-sighted if it is considered to be the sole reason why the planning proposal was rejected.[8]

---
[8] Bastéa 2000, p. 131.

The transition from the pre-capitalist period to modern times was intimately related to the concept of public space acquiring more open features than those of previous periods. In the new planning arrangement, the emphasis lay heavily on formal composition as a whole, precluding any diverting details. The sequence of spatial units, with wide, straight streets linking geometrically elegant squares, was meant to emphasize the importance of the building facades lining the new boulevards. Whereas the amorphous masses of the medieval quarters had developed over time so that unity in variety prevailed, as each individual architectural entity retained its meaning only insofar as it was experienced as part of the entire fabric of the city, the new urbanistic architectural vocabulary of the early 19th-century planning environment was conceived as a more or less theatrical, Baroque "grand style," an autonomous architectural entity intended to be understood only within a specific urban complex that straightforwardly related buildings to streets and carefully designed squares. This violent break with the past was necessary in order that new stratagems might be implemented. Continuity of facades along the street fronts implied an altogether new urban aesthetic awareness. The insertion of modern avenues offering inherently dramatic perspectives and long-distance views followed a new principle of geometric design that was a novelty in itself. New commercial areas were meant to be accessible from the promenades, but not in the same way that the small shops and dwellings of the old town had opened onto the winding streets. The antithesis between traditional and modern urban environments was a fact, yet all traditional hierarchies had to be explicitly repudiated. Thorny fields of transgression had to be taken into account by the two Bauakademie-trained architects, as was the case with the traditional layout of Athens.

Athens' narrow streets had hitherto retained a purely functional role in the hierarchy of a network based on pedestrian movement and the transportation of goods. The traditional layout allowed each part of the built environment to come together in a unity expressive of the town's modest scale; but under the conditions of a modern city, within the new interplay of space and volume, some of the streets would become arteries and thoroughfares fulfilling new ceremonial and aesthetic demands. It was only logical that in the capital city's early years, the sphere of private life would gradually turn inward, becoming almost encapsulated, with private interests subsuming public ones. The assignment of more rigid social roles in the modern city demanded an equally strict definition of space, a strict definition of the private and public spheres. The transition from one state of affairs to the other would not be easy. The passage from a phase where the basic social unit was the small parish community to one where the independent family or household might prevail, even the emergence of individuals no longer constrained by communal life, was not necessarily an automatic process. That the vast majority of the population should experience some sort of sudden enlightenment putting an end to its supposedly age-old lethargy was definitely not the case! In 1833, modern Athenians were commanded to abandon their long-established pre-modern social and mental attitudes (Fig. 8).

If we imply that the transition from one stage to the other had no traumatic social effects, the transition from pre-capitalist traditional town to modern European city would certainly have entailed the breakdown of an organic social solidarity forged over the centuries. In the very early years of Athens' life as the capital of the nation, the members of a family living in a traditional house would have found it difficult to grasp from one moment to the next that the space in front of their dwelling would be managed not according to their ancestral ethos, but on the basis of inexplicable decisions taken on their behalf by a group of educated citizens whom they ignored, and that moving from their own homes to new parts of the town would no longer coincide with their own spontaneous decisions.

Figure 8. "Modern Athenians," artist and date unknown, lithograph, 25 x 18 cm. Private collection.

Conclusion

Even under unpropitious conditions people can adapt to changes in their urban environment, perhaps even ones that afford proper neighborhood sources of income, but this process of adaptation needs time. Demographers posit 25 to 30 years as the minimum length of a single generation. If this is so, to what extent could we maintain that the first plan envisioning Athens as a modern capital city had any chance of being welcome only a year after the demise of the Ottoman medieval town? Furthermore, how justified can it be to misunderstand why the plan was considered so woefully inadequate that it could not be implemented?

We should recall that in 1833, the old system of local government by the "elders" [δημογέροντες], which had been in operation during the long Ottoman period, was still functioning. The new Greek government, or rather the Bavarian regency, eager to institute an imported administrative system shaped by the French Revolution of July 1830, was obviously completely ignorant of local conditions and failed to recognize that it was precisely that local system of communal administration that shaped public opinion and conferred power on the popular will. To quote George Finlay, those long-established social and political structures formed the context where "public opinion was called into operation as a practical check on official conduct [and] a high degree of local information was kept alive amongst the people, and feelings of public interest were created."[9] How could these conditions change so quickly? To believe that hastily introduced government legislative enactments might have had any effect, or that edicts issued by high-ranking officers of the police or the municipality had any serious chance of being taken into account, is to believe in a political and social mirage, an oxymoron as regards the implementation of the first Athens plan and its successor of 1834. The 1843 revolutionary movement in Athens, usually analyzed on strictly political grounds, may very well be considered a social and psychological reaction by Athens' modest population to the ten years' worth of peremptory demands that had been inflicted on it (Fig. 9).

Figure 9. "The Prince of Wales Leaving Athens." *The Illustrated London News* (November 13, 1875, special supplement). One of the principal axes in the layout of the first Athens plan was Ermou Street, running in an east–west direction through Kapnikarea church (seen here in the middle), approaching another Byzantine church, Agioi Asomatoi, to the west.

[9] Finlay 1836, p. 38.

The Restoration of the Benizelos Mansion: The Sole Preserved Athenian Residence of the Ottoman Era

Yannis Kizis

Until the first decades of the 19th century, the Ottoman mansion model was shaped by elements that assigned unity of tone, mostly independent of local, religious, and ethnic particularities. A unique supranational mansion model was transferred even to the remotest places of the Ottoman realm and grafted onto local traditions, whether in the eastern or western provinces. The two major components were the *oda*, the main central room, and the *hayati*, a transitional space that lay partly outdoors.[1]

Based on several pictorial representations of Athens from the 17th century onward, we may discern the existence of at least 25 large, two-story mansions, with wide facades, arcaded porticos, and open wooden galleries that were often crowned by projecting eaves supported by posts. Strikingly, all mansions faced toward the north and not toward the Acropolis. Today, the only surviving mansion is that of the prominent Benizelos family, built in the first half of the 18th century. Although long neglected, this mansion has recently been restored, so that the visitor may understand the character, quality, and details of urban architecture before the rise of Neoclassicism, which came to dominate the Athenian cityscape after the Greek War of Independence (1821). The Benizelos mansion provides us with hints of how the northern slope of the Acropolis looked before Athens became the capital of the newly formed state.

The Bourgeois Architecture of the Ottoman Era

In the provincial centers of the Ottoman Empire, large, rich residences [*konakia*][2] attest to the economic growth and urban development of each region.[3] Symbolic of social prestige, they were accompanied

---

[1] Turkish *oda* or *hane*; Turkish *hayat*; for the relevant local terminology, see Kizis 1994, pp. 65, 69–70. Since most of the pertinent Turkish terminology has entered Greek vocabulary, I have opted to provide the transliterated Greek form with an explanation in English for the major components of the mansion (for example, *oda*, *hayati*, and *orta-sofa*). Contrary to traditional historiography, which has the tendency to be exclusive and to understand pre-War of Independence trends as foreign to Greek culture, my intention is to make sense of such currents within their context, both local and supranational.
[2] Urban mansion: Turkish *konak*; Greek κονάκι.
[3] Kizis 1988, pp. 269–270.

by outbuildings and auxiliary structures inside a walled courtyard, offering ostentation and security to the household. The *oda* and the *hayati* on the upper story constituted the basic components of the floor plan. Other sections, mainly those connected with support functions, had little or no influence on how the floor plan was configured, since they were usually not located on the main floor or were in outbuildings in the courtyard.

The *oda* was used for all the activities of daily life—eating, sleeping, domestic handicrafts, and social gatherings—with the appropriate equipment kept in cabinets [*mousandra*][4] adjacent to the room. In affluent households, a guest room was set apart for visitors.[5] The interior of a typical *oda* was arranged in a severely rectangular outline, with the center of the composition emphasized by the ceiling decoration. The entrance was on one side, and there was zigzagging access to a lower level through a notional anteroom parallel to the cabinets; the fireplace was set on the axis of symmetry, flanked by windows, niches, or cupboards.

The *hayati*, an open gallery–passage fronting the rooms, which assumed, in the course of its development, a variety of forms, was decisive for the arrangement of the whole space. Its remote areas were used for seating, either as an *orta-sofa*, a recess between the rooms,[6] or like a pavilion, projecting toward the most impressive view.[7]

It was not only the *hayati* and the projecting oriel windows [*xepetachta*][8] that connected the house with the outdoor space. In bourgeois houses, this contact began at the ground-floor level, which was essentially a pillared extension of the courtyard. A large residence with all its subsidiary buildings was thus a labyrinthine walled complex, closed to strangers, but open in its interior, open-air life.

Until the early 19th century, residential architecture in the Balkan Peninsula, as well as in Asia Minor, projected a unity of appearance and function aside from local customs, religion, and ethnic particularities, which did play a role, although not a significant one. Inspired by the Ottoman imperial edifices in Istanbul, the same basic model of a mansion was used by the provincial aristocracy throughout the Ottoman Empire. This developing architectural model provided the rising local elites with a social framework, which, in turn, reinforced their place in local societies. Examples include the residences of the Londos and Petmezas families in the Peloponnese, the mansions of the Phanariots in Istanbul, the school established by Anthimos Gazis in Milies, and the Benizelos family mansion in Athens. For this reason, this architectural structure, with its long-standing historical tradition (showing an osmosis in some cases, but only marginally, with the local vernacular traditions and the creativity of traveling groups of itinerant builders), is perhaps the most authentic element of modern Greek traditional architecture.[9]

Ludwig Lange and Leo von Klenze, the eminent German architects who contributed to the planning of Athens after the Greek War of Independence, recorded the characteristics of this architecture in their sketches of the palace [*saray*] and houses in Nauplion.[10] From this series of images,

---

[4] Wooden storage spaces for linen on the entrance side of the room; two-storied in their complete form with their facade on the upper floor latticed, overlooking the room space. Kizis 1994, p. 302. See also Kuban 1995, p. 117.

[5] Turkish *baş oda* or *misafir-odası*; Greek μουσαφίροντας or καλός οντάς.

[6] Kizis 1994, pp. 69–70: in other words, an intervening seating area, a loose translation of the Turkish term (the *eyvan* of Anatolia) for platforms with cushions, known in Thessaly as racks or beds [κρεβάτα].

[7] Turkish *köşk*; Greek κιόσκι. It was a sort of gazebo or pavilion: Kizis 1988, p. 282.

[8] Enclosed balconies: Turkish *çikma*; Greek ξεπεταχτά, also εξώστεγα, σαχνισιά, or τσικμάδες, according to the region.

[9] Kizis 1988, p. 286.

[10] Kizis 1988, p. 271, fig. 4.

we can understand what Athens must have looked like before 1821 and what was eventually destroyed in order for the city to take on its Neoclassical appearance. We recognize the well-known lineaments of what is today called, in local historiography, the "North Greek" traditional settlement, which actually typifies the idiom of Ottoman times: buttresses supporting timber-framed stories with *hayatia* and belvederes that jut out from the upper floors; walls pierced by arrays of windows and fanlights, with the typical wooden shelf running between them; and roofs with wide eaves crowning the protruding volumes of the oriel windows and the supporting sturdy stone walls.

The Urban Scenery of Athens before the War of Independence

Disregarded during the Middle Ages, Athens had re-emerged in the imagination of west Europeans by the last quarter of the 17th century, as evidenced by the large painting of Athens of 1674 by an unknown artist who accompanied Charles-Marie-François Olier, Marquis de Nointel, on his diplomatic mission to the East for Louis XIV (see p. 85, Fig. 4).[11] For the first time in a painting, the city was rendered with care and precision, shown as densely built-up, with many large two-story buildings in a cohesive urban tissue amid gardens and single-story auxiliary constructions.[12] We can see a fair number of large houses with open *hayatia* on their upper floor, oriented toward the north, away from the Acropolis. Furthermore, we can notice double rows of windows and fanlights, which were typical of the Ottoman architectural style of the period (Fig. 1).

Figure 1. Details from the painting of Charles-Marie-François Olier, Marquis de Nointel, with his entourage in Athens in 1674, unknown artist, oil on canvas, 2.60 x 5.20 m. The enlargements show the Benizelos mansion and its neighbors. Chartres, Musée des Beaux-Arts, on permanent loan to the Museum of the City of Athens–Vouros-Eutaxias Foundation.

---

[11] See Tsigakou 2000, pp. 284–287, 306.

[12] In this period, 2,053 houses were recorded: 1,300 owned by Greeks, 600 by Turks, 150 by Albanians, and 3 by various foreigners. See Travlos [1960] 1993, p. 180.

Another drawing of Athens from the same angle, depicting the explosion in the Parthenon in 1687, was made by the Venetian officer Giacomo Verneda (Fig. 2).[13] It shows at least 25 large two-story mansions with wide facades and arcaded porticos on the ground floor and open wooden *hayatia* on the upper floor, with projecting eaves supported by posts, all facing toward the north or, in a few cases, the west, with wings perpendicular to the building's main facade.

Figure 2. View of the Acropolis during the 1687 explosion in the Parthenon, details of a drawing by Giacomo Verneda. It includes depictions of at least 25 Ottoman-period mansions. Tsigakou 2000, p. 288.

A typical image of an Athenian mansion, the bishop's residence, was sketched by the Russian monk Vasilij Grigorovich Barskij in 1745 (Fig. 3). The mansion was to the north of the Byzantine church of the Panagia Gorgoepikoos, in the location where the Metropolitan Cathedral of Athens was built in the following century.[14] The bishop of Athens received his visitors in the garden, between a chapel and a wooden gazebo. One side of the garden was bounded by a one-story building, probably a guest house, with a double row of windows and fanlights. Enclosed staircases at the back of the courtyard led to

---

[13] Tsigakou 2000, pp. 288, 295–296, 306. See also Tsigakou 2007, pp. 24–25.
[14] Gennadius–Benaki 1979, p. 39.

two two-story wings. The one that looked toward the north had an arched portico surmounted by an open wooden *hayati*. Smaller subsidiary buildings were attached to the complex, which was surrounded by a high courtyard wall.

Figure 3. The residence of the Bishop of Athens and its grounds, just north of the church of the Panagia Gorgoepikoos, drawing by Vasilij Grigorovich Barskij, 1745. Gennadius–Benaki 1979, p. 39.

Barskij's detailed depiction sheds light on the elements of 18th-century Ottoman domestic architecture. A few years later, James Stuart and Nicholas Revett would render the construction details of the architectural vernacular of this building design with greater accuracy: the timber frame, the eaves, the open galleries, the chimneys, the latticework, the shutters—all offer a lesson in the construction methods of the period, particularly as regards the details that, even today, one can find in surviving parts of buildings, both in Athens and in other provinces.[15]

Of similar quality are the depictions by Simone Pomardi, who accompanied Edward Dodwell on his travels in 1805–1806.[16] His drawings of the Ottoman constructions on the Acropolis demonstrate the typical look of the period's buildings. The large, long, narrow two-story residence between the Erechtheion and the Parthenon, with the fanlights above the windows on its west side, has the proportions and appearance of the south facade of the Benizelos mansion, which we will discuss in detail below. Of Pomardi's drawings, the most revealing one, in terms of everyday life, is that of the open *hayati* at Chriso (near Delphi), where the bishop of Salona, sitting cross-legged, has set out a meal for his guests around a brass cooking/serving pan [*sini*].[17]

A standard Athenian *hayati* was depicted by Louis Dupré, in 1819, in the house of Louis-François-Sébastien Fauvel (see p. 234, Fig. 2).[18] Created a little later, his painting entitled *Athenian Woman* illustrates oriel windows.[19] In another picture, the Turkish governor of the city of Athens (voivode) is seen sitting on low sofas with the monuments of the Roman Agora in the background.[20]

---

[15] E.g., before its recent plastering, Richard Church's tower in Plaka preserved the marks of its original windows, with corresponding fanlights above them, the brick cornice with serrated band, and a typical tall, slender chimney. See Kizis 1994, p. 259, fig. 360, and p. 278, figs. 417–418.
[16] Dodwell 1819, 1821.
[17] Kizis 1988, p. 273, fig. 6.
[18] In 1975, John Travlos undertook to recreate it as a model that graphically renders the open-air operation of a typical Athenian house with an arcaded portico on the ground floor and open wooden *hayati* on the upper story. Kokkou 1977, p. 21. See also Gerogiorgi and Katselaki 2005, fig. 38.
[19] See Velmos and Doukas 1931, p. 101.
[20] Dupré 1825.

In 1811 William Gell created a detailed view of Madame Masson's room,[21] showing the step and the low sofas that framed the sharply tapering chimney breast above the fireplace, the series of windows topped by a shelf and plaster-framed fanlights, and the wooden ceiling with its coffered margins.[22] This typical Anatolian room and the house were also sketched by Carl Haller von Hallerstein in 1814,[23] with the lady of the house and her children sitting cross-legged around her on low sofas, as the maid serves coffee. The sketches of Madame Masson's house demonstrate the organization of the entire ground-floor household: the oven, the toilet, the washbasin, the cistern, and the well, all around the courtyard, with the typical Athenian arcaded portico opposite the courtyard gate, and the storerooms and the quarters for the staff in the rear. On the side and a little bit lower down is the garden with its fruit trees, while a grapevine covers half of the courtyard. The outside stairs with a landing lead to a veranda on the upper floor,[24] which is enlarged into a T-shape by a crosswise *orta-sofa*, identical to that found in the Benizelos mansion, the lone survivor of the 25 mansions depicted by Verneda.[25] On the left is the reception room for guests, sketched by William Gell and later by Haller von Hallerstein, and on the right the bedroom, with its door through the cabinets. The latter also drew—and fully annotated—the plans of the house and outbuilding in which he stayed with Charles Robert Cockerell.[26]

In 1816 Haller von Hallerstein made a plan of the Mertrud mansion in Plaka, which was much larger than the Masson house.[27] This complex spread out around an open-air area with a fountain as its centerpiece. Two external staircases ascended to the corresponding wings of the upper floor, situated at right angles to the central structure. The east wing had a veranda, while the west was occupied by a covered wooden *hayati*. The plan of the latter is similar to that of the upper story of the Benizelos mansion: an identical *orta-sofa* projected in a west-facing oriel window, along with two rooms, one on either side, with low sofas and a fireplace in one of them, accessed via a small anteroom through the cabinets. There was a hammam on the ground floor in the north-west corner of the complex, with a kitchen on the upper floor. A small church, which could also be accessed directly from the street, was embedded between the hammam and the residential spaces. The notations reveal exceptional details, such as the garden with bitter orange trees, the grapevine, the stable, the installation for heating water for the bath, and the storage jars for oil in the porticos, as well as the special access points to the church and the stairway for the staff to serve dinner on tables in the upper floor. The rich and multifaceted complex of structures would also be sketched later by Otto Magnus von Stackelberg (reproduced in an engraving of 1834).[28] This rendering depicts the main courtyard with the fountain and the slightly pointed arcades of the ground-floor porticos, with marble capitals typical of the period and comparable

---

[21] She came from an Athenian family, possibly of French origin: Kambouroglou 1889–1892, vol. 1, p. 218, in which "Andreas Masson, Athenian" is listed among the subscribers to the Philomousos Etaireia [Society of the Friends of the Arts] in 1814.
[22] See Knithakis, Mallouchou, and Tigginagka 1986, p. 121.
[23] Bankel 1986, pp. 167–202. The subject seems to have been especially attractive, so that others also copied (?) it; see the engraving attributed to Otto Magnus von Stackelberg: Koumarianou 2005, p. 139.
[24] "Gallerie ouverte" in Haller's notes. See also Biris and Kardamitsi-Adami 2001, p. 74.
[25] See Kizis 2014.
[26] See Bankel 1986, pp. 202–203.
[27] The Mertruds were an Athenian family, possibly of French origin. See Kambouroglou 1889–1892, vol. 3, Π (appendix), p. 51 [να], in which Vasileios Mertrud appears in 1827 as making an attestation about the services of Angelos Gerontas as a citizen, "a native of this city of Athens," and p. 56 [νστ], where in 1833 he signs a certification about the services of D. Zografou. Manolis Korres has produced illustrative restorations of the mansion: Korres 2010b, pp. 125–127. See also Biris 2010, p. 133.
[28] See Gerogiorgi and Katselaki 2005, fig. 16. The house is described as the luxurious residence of Spiros Logothetis, an official interpreter of the British consulate, where Lord Elgin and his family were guests during their stay in the city.

to those in the Benizelos mansion. The strongly projecting eaves protect the open *hayati*, while columns (probably of steel) and beams on the veranda were intended to support cloth awnings. Fanlights with the usual curvilinear frames and tracery accompanied the window openings of the sunroom.

In depictions of 1819,[29] the same architectural form is discerned in other Athenian mansions near the Tower of the Winds, as well as at the voivode's residence, a short way up the hill from the Library of Hadrian. Nevertheless, we can discern a steady shift in style with the addition of Neoclassical features. More specifically, on the west front of the voivode's residence, a parapet was erected, and the facade assumed a new look, with windows of Neoclassical proportions. In later depictions, one can discern the mixture of styles, with Neoclassicism ultimately dominant, in the extensive modifications to the facades of older buildings.[30]

Much later, sash windows would be added to the open wooden *hayatia* to transform these open spaces into closed sunrooms. A sketch made by Yannis Tsarouchis in 1930 depicts a house in the Vlassarou quarter (western section of the Plaka) that was expropriated on account of the excavations of the Ancient Agora, in which glazed windows coexisted with open *hayatia*.[31] Shortly after World War II, the architect Aris Konstantinides produced a survey of this last urbanized evolutionary stage of the traditional Ottoman dwelling.[32]

Additional information about Ottoman houses in Athens may be gleaned from the notary acts of the period, in which the individual spaces are described in detail with their local appellations; for example, "[…] they sold their dwelling […] two rooms, one with a cabinet, and with a *hayati* and *orta-sofa* and veranda on the side, a stone staircase and two cellars below, and outside a wine press with its basin and an arcaded portico below the *hayati*, with an oven and privy and cistern, and a bitter orange orchard in the courtyard, and two grapevines, a stone trough, and a conduit for the water of the fountain, and a courtyard and two entrances."[33]

The Benizelos Mansion and Its Restoration

Of similar structure, yet significantly larger and more opulent than the houses discussed above, is the mansion at 96 Adrianou Street that once belonged to the prominent Benizelos family. This family of notable intellectuals was part of the ruling class of the Athenian aristocracy from the 16th century to the 19th in the context of the self-administration of the Christian community of Athens during the Ottoman era.[34] The structure is the last extant Ottoman-period residence of the Athenian

---

[29] See Museum of the City of Athens–Vouros-Eutaxias Foundation 2004, p. 65 (Anonymous, *The Horologium of Andronicus Cyrrhestes*) and p. 79 (Joseph Thurmer, *Hadrian's Library and the Bazaar*).

[30] See Museum of the City of Athens–Vouros-Eutaxias Foundation 2004, p. 51 (Joseph Schranz, *Partial View of Athens with the Acropolis in the Center and Piraeus in the Background*, ca. 1842, watercolor) and p. 78 (Andrea Gasparini, *Hadrian's Library*, 1844, colored engraving).

[31] Velmos and Doukas 1931, p. 175.

[32] See Konstantinides 1950.

[33] Philadelpheus 1902, vol. 1, pp. 306–307: "[…] επούλησαν την οσπιτοκάθεσίν τους […] οντάδες δύο, ο είς με μουσάνδραν και με το χαγιάτι και ορτάσοφαν και ταρακίκιαν εις το πλευρόν και με την σκάλαν πέτρινην υποκάτωθεν αυτών κελλάρια δύο και έξωθεν πατητήρι με το πουρλάκι του, με καμάραις υποκάτωθεν του χαγιατίου, με φούρνον και χρείαν και στέρναν, με νεραγκέαν εις την αυλήν μίαν, με κλήματα δύο και γούρναν πέτρινην και με το κουντίτο της βρύσις με το νερόν του, και με την αυλήν και εμβασίας δύο."

[34] Angelos Benizelos (born ca. 1490), whose name declares a rather Frankish origin, was the father of St. Filothei (1522–1589). He participated in the administration of the Greek Confraternity of Venice, representing the Greeks who had settled in Venice from various regions [*terre non nominate*], one of which was Athens. He taught at the School of the Confraternity (1634–1639), and it is likely that he taught in Athens as well. Ioannis Benizelos (born ca. 1625), son of Angelos, was a teacher at the Common School of Athens (1676–1677). Another Ioannis Benizelos (the ancestor of

aristocracy.³⁵ Its open *hayati* over an arcaded portico, its *orta-sofa* with an oriel window jutting toward the south, its side pavilions [*sofades*], the great winter room with the distinctive fireplace with its peaked chimney breast, alongside the walls perforated by double rows of windows and stained-glass, plaster-framed fanlights, the symmetrical summer room to the west, the elaborately fashioned wood construction elements, and all the ornamentation that has survived today give only a glimpse of the glamor that the 18th-century mansions that once filled the northern slopes of the Acropolis rock had (Fig. 4).

Figure 4. The restored Benizelos mansion: *hayati* and south side. Photos Y. Yerolymbos.

The wooden mansion was erected in the mid-18th century on top of two older buildings, with two large *odas*, a long open *hayati* with two side pavilions, one at each end, and an *orta-sofa* in the center, jutting out from the south facade. The model for the urban aristocratic residence of the period was transferred wholesale onto the pre-existing infrastructure in a manner that recalls comparable additions of the period.³⁶ The older structures that were incorporated into the ground floor are, according to tradition, associated with the life of St. Filothei, Revoula Benizelos, who lived in the 16th century and devoted herself to the education and emancipation of women. The mansion's construction and form bear witness to high aspirations and make it particularly significant at the Athenian level and beyond, since it constitutes a typical example of the rich urban architectural

---

Joannes Gennadius), author of the Ιστορία των Αθηνών [History of Athens], was a distinguished member of Athenian society during the 18th century. His work narrates eyewitness accounts of the events of his home town with clarity and objectivity. Descendants of the family distinguished themselves throughout the period of Ottoman rule as elders, notaries, men of letters, teachers, etc. Members of the family also played a significant role in the Greek War of Independence. There is evidence of intermarriage between the Benizelos family and two other important families in Athens: the Palaiologos (considered cousins of the despots of Mystras) and the Acciaiuoli family, the Italian dukes of Athens during Frankish rule. Kambouroglou 1889–1892, vol. 1, p. 29, vol. 3, pp. 251–260. For the Benizelos family, see Benizelos 1986, p. 23 [κγ], n. 1 [earlier bibliography], and pp. 118, 1517.

³⁵ Kambouroglou 1889–1892, vol. 1, p. 30.
³⁶ E.g., the Dervish-Aga (now Karakosta) mansion on Paidon Street in Chalkida (Kizis 1994, pp. 84–85) and the Voulgaris residence on the island of Hydra (Prokopiou 2001, pp. 46–47).

tradition prior to the War of Independence, which has disappeared to a high degree, particularly in southern Greece.

The monument was first studied and summarily published by Anastasios Orlandos in 1940. Interventions of the 19th and early 20th centuries, such as division into two properties, partitioning of individual spaces, enclosure of the *hayati* with sash windows, removal of the jettied oriel window, and modifications to window and door openings, had obscured the original look of the building.[37] The house was also published in the same condition by John Travlos in 1960.[38] Thus, the building's typology and actual construction remained unexplained until recently. In 1979–1980, modern interventions were dismantled, and consolidation work helped to decipher its unique past.[39]

The mansion was restored following a study by the author and a team of experts in 2005–2009 according to two principles: a) the promotion of the great artistic and historical value of the urban mansion; and b) the conservation of the archaeological evidence that was uncovered in the subsoil of the courtyard and the basements (a section of the Late Roman fortification wall, a medieval cistern, a wine press, storage jars, and so on), testifying to habitation through time from Antiquity to the present.[40] Despite the poor state of preservation and practically the complete loss of its ornamentation, the building kept a satisfyingly full range of elements that allowed the work of restoration to be convincing and robust. The building's structure was consolidated, and the elements of its construction were conserved using methods compatible with the original construction. The old members have been preserved to the greatest possible degree, so as to emphasize the authenticity of the monument. The evidence for sporadic interventions has been preserved, in order to keep the building's history comprehensible.

The central mass of the building is a two-story rectangle measuring 9.30 x 23.70 m. Its north side, facing the courtyard, is open, with an arcaded stone portico on the ground floor and a wooden *hayati* on the upper story. The mansion's garden lay to the south, overlooked by an oriel window that protruded from the middle of the house, forming a roofed belvedere with the *orta-sofa*. To the east, a section of the Late Roman fortification wall is preserved to a fair height. The space today extends open, southward of the boundaries of the present property, where there is also a medieval olive oil press, which presumably belonged to the Benizelos family. Here, the University of Athens is conducting excavations at the so-called "Diogeneion" (Gymnasium of Diogenes).[41] The lateral faces of the mansion on the east and west were formerly unencumbered, as can be seen from the windows blocked by more recent constructions, which were built touching them after successive divisions of the original property.

---

[37] In his somewhat synoptic and perhaps rushed study of the monument, that great and usually sharp-eyed scholar did not suspect what was lying hidden behind the remodelings, despite the fact that the marks of the fanlights and the belvedere were clearly visible. He described the "complete absence of overhanging balconies [...] and [...] of small windows for illumination [...] above the downward-looking ones." The authoritative weight of his signature perpetuated erroneous information about the mansion and Athenian pre-revolutionary architecture in general: Orlandos 1939–1940, pp. 198–205.

[38] Travlos [1960] 1993, pp. 227, figs. 152–153. See also Kizis 1988, p. 273, fig. 7.

[39] The project, which included a detailed survey of the building, was spearheaded by architects Yannis Kizis and Constantinos Mylonas and the Hellenic Ministry of Culture, into whose possession the building had come. On the basis of these plans, which accurately documented the mansion's condition before these dismantlings, the civil engineers Eleftheria Tsakanika and Stratis Lazouras made drawings in 1988 of the wooden frame that had been revealed for their thesis at the National Technical University of Athens. This dossier of drawings, supplemented with new measurements and observations, was digitized in order to form the design basis of the study for restoring the monument. For a synoptic report of the results of that investigation, see Kizis 1994, p. 84, fig. 58.

[40] The study (2005–2009) was commissioned by the Holy Archdiocese of Athens, to which the use of the building had been granted, from the architects Yannis Kizis, Klimis Aslanidis, and Christina Pinatsi, the civil engineer Eleftheria Tsakanika, and the mechanical engineer Christos Zompolas.

[41] Travlos 1971, pp. 281, 579, fig. 722; Travlos [1960] 1993, pp. 90, 126.

The stone-built ground floor of the mansion has three rooms, accessed through the portico that features slender, monolithic marble columns with conical impost capitals adorned with acanthus and reedy leaves. As is evident from traces on the walls, the ground-floor spaces correspond to two older, relatively humble dwellings that stood on the site before the mid-18th century with a semi-basement and an upper room with a fireplace. The lower parts of these dwellings were incorporated into the ground floor of the new edifice. In their oblong spaces, cross arches of soft limestone were added to support the new floor beams. One of these vaults is located at the east end of the building, which means that the earlier property extended further to the east, probably in the form of a single-story structure with a rooftop terrace.

The upper floor is reached via masonry stairs on the east side of the courtyard, creating an arched passage underneath (Fig. 5). A basin for hand-washing is integrated into the lateral facade, under the stairs, while the well of the house is preserved in the center of the courtyard; its head, along with the level of the courtyard, were raised in the 19th century. The stairway leads to the open northern *hayati*,[42] which is continued to the middle with a transversal wing, the *orta-sofa*, jettied toward the south. At the beginning of the 20th century, a stone wall closed off the south side of the *orta-sofa* after the jetty had been cut off. The jetty is visible in late 19th-century photographs,[43] with two large Neoclassical windows that had replaced the original triad of shuttered windows crowned by stained-glass fanlights; in that period, the openings between the posts of the *hayati* were also closed up with sash windows.

Figure 5. The Benizelos mansion: views of the stairway on the east side of the courtyard leading up to the *hayati* in 1979 and 2017. Photos Yannis Kizis and Y. Yerolymbos.

[42] The orientation of these open *hayatia*, which varies according to location by reason of the particular circumstances and criteria of their specific period, frequently refutes the efforts of some scholars in our own time, who insistently search for "bioclimatic" or "energy" strengths in houses belonging to the older tradition. To them, in contrast, Periklis Giannopoulos would say "life was outdoors!"

[43] Giakoumis 1997, p. 132. See also Travlos and Manousakis 1967, p. 152.

The *hayati* gave access to two symmetrically arranged *odas*, which were later subdivided into separate spaces with timber-framed lath and plaster walls. The original rooms were configured in the typical 18th-century manner: the entrance was at the end of the long side through two-tier stacked wooden cabinets that occupied the entire short side. Opposite the cabinets, a seating area of low sofas was created along the other three walls, with a fireplace flanked by windows in the middle of the wall facing the cabinets (Fig. 6).[44]

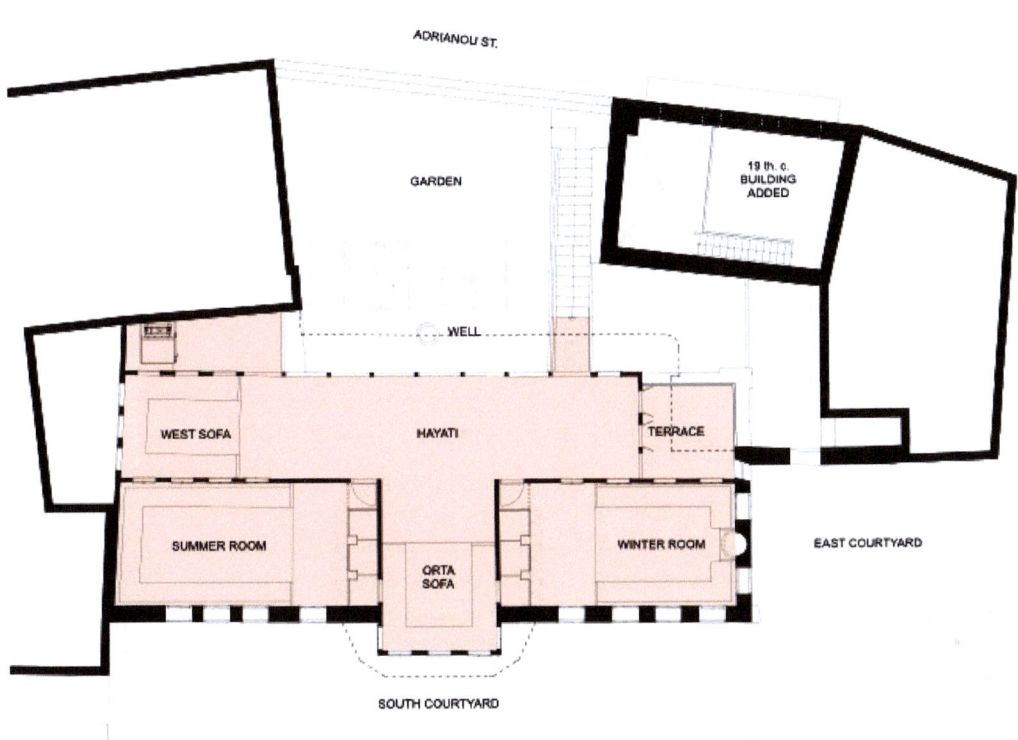

Figure 6. The Benizelos mansion: floor plan of the upper story as restored in 2010. Kizis Studio.

The north and west walls of the upper story were timber-framed, while those on the south and east were made of timber-tied stone. The rooms had rows of relatively small arched windows, topped by either rectangular (north and west) or arched (south and east) fanlights. On the east side, the windows end in slits, like loopholes in fortifications. Their inner face was sealed by ornamental stained glass with plaster moldings.[45] The original windows were all blocked, and some new windows had been opened in the late 19th century. The general shape of the original doors is attested by the preserved door frame of the western room. Above the doorways of the rooms were fanlights with wooden fretwork that permitted visual contact between the level of the cabinets and the *hayati*.

---

[44] Kizis 1988, p. 277, fig. 12.
[45] Fragments of plaster tracery and small pieces of stained glass were found by the writer in 1980 after the unblocking of the fanlight to the right of the fireplace. Unfortunately, it was insufficient to give an idea of the form of the stained-glass window.

The arrangement of the facades is generally simple. The parapet of the *hayati* was arranged in two registers: the lower one was solid, with plastered brick panels painted white, and the upper one was pierced, as shown by the holes for holding the latticework that are preserved in certain places. Broad wooden eaves protruded above the *hayati*, while on the south and east facades the cornices were made of sawtooth brick.

Inconsistencies and differences in construction between the stone walls and the timber-framed ones and the way in which the timber frame was filled in suggest the various building phases as well as a restoration of the 18th-century superstructure. The method of how the timber frame was fastened together elucidated the investigation, particularly the mortise-and-tenon jointing, which obeyed a clear sequence in the erection of the individual parts when they were first assembled.

The floor plan of the upper story follows the typology of dwellings that are typically encountered in a large part of the former Ottoman Empire[46] and are characterized by an open *hayati* running above the facade.[47] As we have seen, this form was usual in Athens. As a rule, stone-built walls defined an L- or U-shaped building with two or three wings. The whole structure was completed with thin wooden walls and rows of wooden posts, exactly as in the case of the Benizelos mansion. The insertion of the *orta-sofa* along the axis of symmetry situates the building in the first stages of the typological development of this dwelling model, in which the semi-outdoor spaces prevailed over enclosed rooms.[48] The simplicity of the forms and the organization of the floor plan, with the spacious *hayati*, are connected with life as it was lived in the 18th century and the early decades of the 19th.[49] The very few remnants of the house's ornamentation do not permit more precise dating.

The restoration has focused on showcasing the 18th-century mansion,[50] presenting the building as an educational exhibit, with the purpose of helping the visitor to become aware of the character and quality of the space, as well as the details of the architecture of this urban residence before the Greek War of Independence and the rise of Neoclassicism. By highlighting "personalities such as Rigoula [Revoula] Benizelos, afterwards Osia [St.] Filothei, Theophilos Corydalleus, Angelos and Dimitrios Benizelos, [and] the Patriarchs Theophanes Karykis and Neophytos II," as well as "institutions such as the Common School [Κοινόν Σχολείον] of 1722 and the Dekas School [Σχολή του Ντέκα] of 1750," the Benizelos residence reinforces the idea that under Ottoman rule Athens was a thriving community and a center of intellectual life with "mindful and well-spoken" citizens.[51]

The Museological Intervention to the Monument

Following the initial practical expression of interest in 1979 by the then Minister of Culture, Dimitris Nianias, 30 years of efforts of the architectural team and the keen interest of the Archbishopric of Athens have finally resulted in the preservation and enhancement of this unique monument. The restored

---

[46] Eldem 1984, pp. 22–23, 44.
[47] Orlandos (1936, pp. 183–194) specifically mentions, "The upper story has its two spaces usually arranged in an [sc. uppercase] pi or gamma shape around a covered space otherwise completely open to the courtyard that is called *krevata* [κρεβάτα, literally beds]." See also Kizis 1994, pp. 59–100.
[48] Eldem 1984, p. 26, regarding type A.7.5.
[49] Kizis 1994, pp. 69–70.
[50] According to the Venice Charter, which permits the removal of phases of lesser value in order to present a composition of high aesthetic quality and historical significance, conditional on the existence of a sufficiently well-documented scientific reconstruction.
[51] Konstantios 2005, pp. 6–7.

building has been handed over to the public as a museum. The intent of the museological concept[52] is to familiarize the public with the character and qualities of a typical aristocratic house of Athens during the late Ottoman period. The sweeping effects of the Greek War of Independence and the reconfiguration of the city as soon as it became the capital of the new Greek state 12 years later completely changed the city's appearance, texture, and structure to a degree that makes this restored mansion now seem like a totally foreign body in Neoclassical Plaka. Its connection with the past, the present, and the future of the city of Athens is the essential museological idea that is realized by interventions relating to exhibit design and installation.

The main idea behind the museographical approach is the coexistence of the restored monument with constructions of modern aesthetics and technology. The exhibit-related intervention is complementary to the restored monument, allowing for a personalized experiential approach; various instructional materials (printed panels, videos, digital projections, and applications), designed for all types of visitors and placed in the comfort of the courtyard and upper-story spaces with ample seating, seek the visitor's active involvement and focus on the various uses that had once been housed in this residence.

The visit starts from the north walled courtyard around the well and continues to the rooms of the ground floor that date back to the 16th century, when St. Filothei lived there, with an abundance of finds related to the organization of the household economy. The visitor then ascends to the wooden upper story, which is composed of two large rooms, one for the summer and one for the winter, and the *hayati*, with its distinctive raised seating. Here, projections of old engravings and vistas of the modern city highlight the history of the monument, while an interactive digital application features "Aspects of Ottoman Athens" (Fig. 7). In the winter room, modeled on the guest room in the nearby Masson house as drawn by von Stackelberg, digital projections and select audio travelers' narratives recreate a typical room of the era (Fig. 8). The south courtyard, in combination with the adjacent archaeological area, which, among other things, contains a section of the Late Roman wall and a large medieval oil press, creates a charming environment with a view of the Acropolis and the slopes of the Plaka and offers the possibility for various outdoor events.

Conclusion

With the restoration finally complete, it is important to close by discussing some of its principles. The view of restoring the mansion to its original mid-18th-century condition prevailed, while later additions and alterations were consciously downplayed, as they are well-documented in archival material and are subtly seen in the monument itself. As this path lies outside of dominant restoration practice, why was it chosen and what was the objective?

The goal was to present the monument as it was before the War of Independence: a typical house of one of the prominent families that dominated the Greek bourgeoisie of Athens in the 18th century, a community of educated middle-class merchants who embraced the vision of a free state. Yet, the ideology of the new Greek state came to be served by Neoclassicism, reflecting the glory of

---

[52] The study (2013–2014) was commissioned by the Holy Archdiocese of Athens from Kizis Studio: the architects Yannis Kizis and Thymis Dougkas studied the museography (exhibit design and installation) on the basis of the museology (collection/heritage management) carried out by the archaeologist Pari Kalamara. The mansion opened to the public in 2017; see http://archontiko-mpenizelon.gr/en/.

Figure 7. The upper floor of the restored Benizelos mansion, showing the central intervening seating area [*orta-sofa*] furnished with modern seating and an interactive digital application. Photo Y. Yerolymbos.

Figure 8. The upper floor of the restored Benizelos mansion: the winter room as a "living painting." Photo Y. Yerolymbos.

ancient Greece; few pre-revolutionary examples of domestic architecture survived, considered to be alien forms within the homogenous "national" style.

With the centuries of Ottoman rule often perceived in Greek history as a "black hole," the Benizelos mansion is destined to help make up for our lack of knowledge of the period. It exhibits pre-revolutionary life and household economy as experienced within an example of the supranational Ottoman mansion type. The culmination of that model was the mature architecture and urban expression of the mid- to late 18th century, an integral part of the history of modern Greece.

If visitors come to know their past through this restored mansion, if they contrast this building to the present Athenian cityscape, then the work done at 96 Adrianou Street will have achieved its purpose. The awareness of the historical continuity of Athens, from Classical Antiquity to the post-industrial era, stimulated through this exceptional building will be the happy conclusion of many years of hard work. We hope that the Archaeological Service will soon proceed to the unification of the outdoor areas with the "Diogeneion," allowing access to the excavation in the wider living space of this important aristocratic house.

Documenting the Ottoman Baths of Athens: A Study on Topography

Eleni I. Kanetaki

Drawing on architectural maps and city plans, alongside travelers' accounts, this essay provides documentation on the Ottoman baths of Athens. As no systematic study of the urban organization of Ottoman Athens has been undertaken to date, including the city's hammams, particular emphasis is given to topography.[1] The ultimate intention of this essay is to shed light on some remnants of the city's Ottoman past, neglected by traditional historiography, and to juxtapose the available historical data to in situ architectural surveys.

Ottoman Athens

Following the typical urban organization of an Ottoman provincial town, Athens was served by mosques, religious schools, convents, soup kitchens for the poor, inns, baths, and a few other structures, such as public fountains and aqueducts, that bear witness to the Ottomanization of the city.[2] The urban core, and thus the Ottoman architectural enterprise, was concentrated mainly in the area of the citadel, that is, the hill of the Acropolis [the *Atina kalesi*, "the castle of Athens"], and in the lower city, the market (Fig. 1).[3] All the known Athenian hammams (existing and no longer extant) were located in the center of the city, close to the main bazaar, and in proximity to the religious and administrative buildings. Although we have no precise information about their dates of construction, the architecture and layout of the steam baths of Athens suggest that they were all operational before the city passed briefly into Venetian hands in 1687–1688.

The surviving historical sources for the city's urban grid and its transformations are incomplete, but the spatial layout of Ottoman Athens can be reconstructed from the numerous descriptions of

---

[1] See, however, Karidis 2014; Travlos [1960] 1993, pp. 172–234.
[2] Kanetaki 2011, p. 221. The topic of the typical organization of Ottoman cities has been covered extensively by Bierman 1991; see also Anastasopoulos, Kolovos, and Sariyannis 2008, pp. 51–55.
[3] The map in Figure 1 is supplemented by John Travlos's "Plan of the City of Athens around 1821 on the Brink of the Hellenic Revolution" (Travlos [1960] 1993, p. 221, fig. 150), also documenting a significant number of Ottoman monuments: among others, the Oula Bey Hammam is marked as "O", the Abid Efendi Hammam is marked as "Π," and the Haçi Ali Hammam is marked as "P." For an intriguing discussion on the *Atina kalesi*, see the essay by Stathi herein, pp. 213–226.

travelers, who, in addition to their accounts, often provided sketches or engravings. Once we project those onto 19th-century topographical plans of the city, we get a clearer view of Ottoman Athens and its monuments. Regarding the hammams, it becomes evident that there are still unidentified remnants.

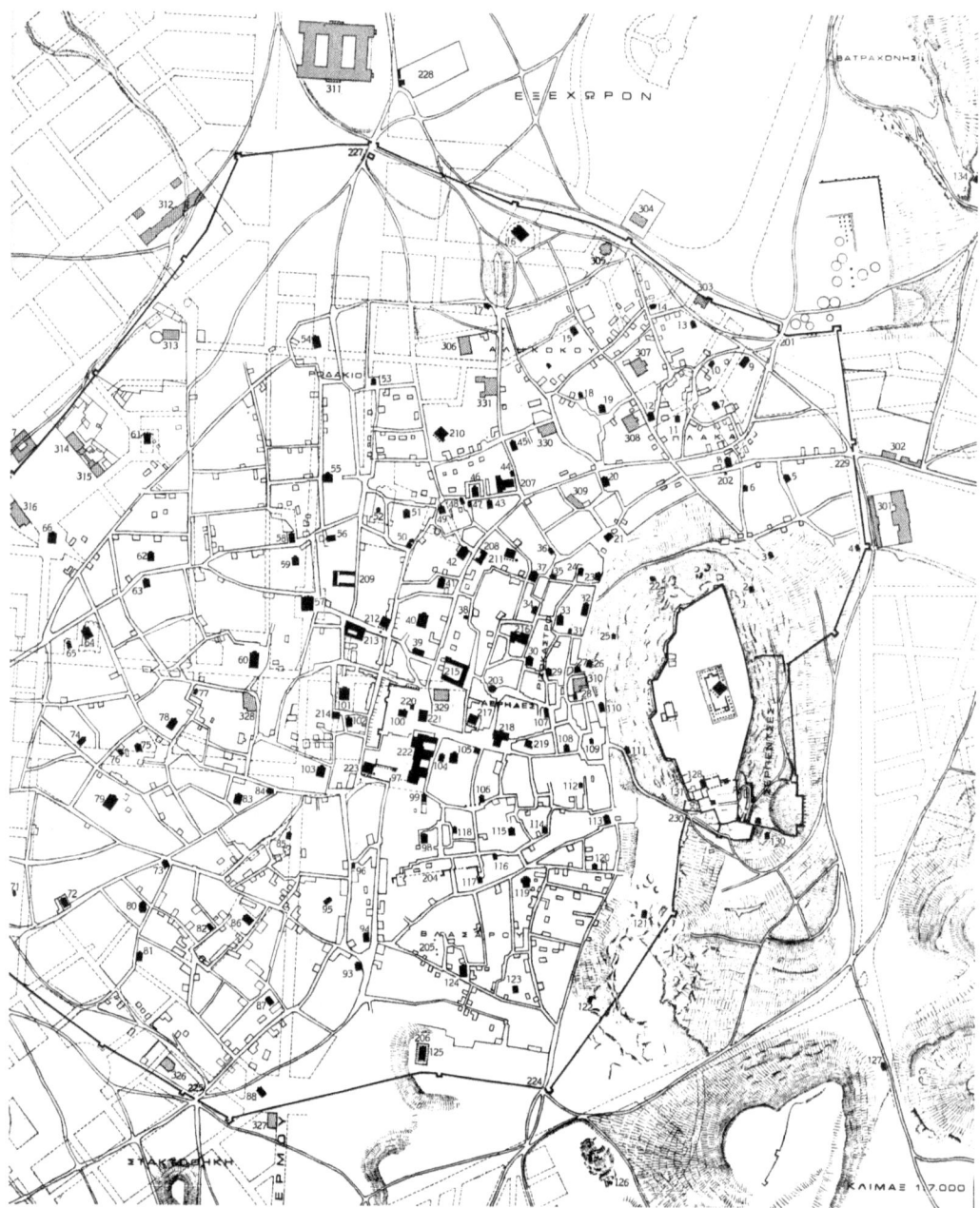

Figure 1. "Map of the Athenian Old City" by Kostas Biris, depicting the buildings which existed during the first decade of the 20th century. Along with other Christian and Muslim monuments, the site of the Ottoman bazaar can be traced, as well as other Ottoman buildings, such as the voivode's mansion (no. 222), the Abid Efendi Hammam (no. 216), the Oula Bey Hammam (no. 218), and the Haçi Ali Hammam (no. 207). Biris 1959, pp. 44–45.

The Travelers' Hammams

From the 17th century onwards, Athens attracted the interest of many west European scholars and travelers, primarily due to its Classical past and monuments. There was a continuous stream of visitors who left numerous accounts, which unfortunately provide little information about the Ottoman (or Byzantine) monuments of the city.[4] The exceptions are descriptions of the steam baths and to a lesser extent the mosques.[5] For one, the care in the construction of the hammams underlined the prosperity of the city. Furthermore, the exotic allure and the important role that hammams played in the maintenance of hygiene impressed European visitors who saw steam baths for the first time. In addition to their sanitary role,[6] baths constituted a public space for various gatherings that provided travelers with much information on everyday life.[7] Religious ablutions in particular played an important role, although we should be careful not to apply excess agency to Islam; the hammams were frequented by non-Muslims as well.[8] John Cam Hobhouse wrote in 1817:

> Yet all the people of the Levant resort frequently to these public baths, and in crowds, the men at one time of the day, the women at another, and not so much for the purposes of cleanliness as of luxury, for I am sure they find a sort of sensual gratification in that state of sleepy languor to which, when stretched upon the couches, they are reduced by the operations of the bathers, and the heat of the surrounding vapour [...] All the women bathe at least once a month, but some much oftener; the men in general once a week. The bath is the coffee-house of the Levant, and, for the females, is the scene of various diversions and ceremonies, as you may have collected from the luxurious, but, as I have heard, not exaggerated, descriptions of my Lady M. W. Montague.[9]

As we learn from the 17th-century *Seyahatname* [Book of travels] by Evliya Çelebi, in the lower part of the city there were "three agreeable hammams" in use that were all "well-constructed."[10] This account was corroborated by George Wheler and Jacob Spon, who contributed greatly to the west European rediscovery of the city with the successful publications of their Athenian visit in 1678: "There are also three or four publick Bagnio's, or Baths, much used here, as in most other eminent Towns in Turkey[...]"[11] These must refer to the three major public baths of Athens: the Oula Bey, the Haçi Ali, and the Abid Efendi hammams. The large number of hammams suggests that Athens was already functioning as a center by then and could also provide hints as to the population of a city, a topic hitherto unstudied. Thorough investigation and in situ architectural surveys of the existing Ottoman hammams by the author have shown that only a few cities in Greece had more than three

---

[4] On these, see Yakovaki 2006.
[5] See the essay by Asvesta and Vingopoulou herein, pp. 167–177.
[6] Ergin 2011, p. 157.
[7] Asvesta and Vingopoulou 2001, pp. 10–15.
[8] Ergin 2011, pp.143–168; Ergin 2009.
[9] Hobhouse 1817, pp. 437–438.
[10] Evliya Çelebi 1994, p. 117.
[11] Wheler 1682, p. 352.

baths.[12] By way of comparison, we should note that a city of the importance of Thessaloniki reportedly had nine steam baths, according to Katip Çelebi, or eleven baths, according to Evliya Çelebi.[13]

The baths continued to attract attention throughout the 18th and 19th centuries. Although travelers' narratives should be used with caution, as they are often enriched with imaginary details in order to provide greater appeal to their audiences, they showcase the importance attributed to the baths. Besides, thanks to some travelers, we learn about some much smaller personal hammams that were constructed in private dwellings, such as the one at the André Mertrud mansion and the small bath incorporated in the house of the Ottoman voivode, Mustafa Aga Tzistarakis.[14]

The Mertrud mansion, one of the richest houses in Ottoman Athens, belonged to a Catholic family probably of French origin and stood on the eastern side of Adrianou Street, possibly at the intersection with Navarchou Nikodemou Street; unfortunately, it has not survived. The floor plans of the two-storied mansion were documented by the architect Carl Haller von Hallerstein, who visited Athens in 1814;[15] in them we can see the layout of a small private bath, as well as its dome with the lighting openings.[16] In his study of the mansion, Manolis Korres published a drawing of the hammam's impressive axonometric section, reconstructing its structure and function.[17]

Mustafa Aga Tzistarakis's house, on the other hand, was at the corner of Areos and Deksippou Streets, close to Hadrian's Library in Monastiraki, the area that comprised the city's upper bazaar at the time. No remains or historical source point to the date of the bath's construction. The Ottoman mansion was abandoned by the beginning of the 1830s, and in 1835 King Otto had the remains of Mustafa Aga Tzistarakis's house demolished in order to construct his infantry and cavalry barracks on the site. Within a century the Ottonian building gradually fell into ruins, and no documentation of its construction has been discovered. An architectural survey of the remains has traced the layout of the Ottoman house and made it possible to reconstruct the design of the bath.[18]

Scant traces of the small private Athenian hammams survive only in engravings and plans, such as the pencil drawing by Charles Robert Cockerell entitled "Little Bath of Athens," which is kept at the Bibliothèque nationale et universitaire de Strasbourg.[19]

The Ottoman Public Baths of Athens

1. The Oula Bey Hammam

The Oula Bey Hammam (*Evvela Beg hammamı*, as Evliya Çelebi calls it, which literally means "In the beginning the hammam of a certain bey") was also known as the Wheat Market Bath [Λουτρό

---

[12] Kanetaki 2004, pp. 9–10. Until quite recently the documentation and preservation of the Ottoman monuments of Greece has been either poor or non-existent, as most of the Islamic buildings have been neglected. Thankfully, numerous Ottoman buildings have been restored lately and have taken their place in the cultural heritage of Greece. Nevertheless, the available documentation on the Athenian hammams that I was able to collect during the research for my Ph.D. dissertation was limited to the plans provided by the architects Kostas Biris and John Travlos, to the architectural survey plans of the Abid Efendi Hammam from the Hellenic Ministry of Culture, and to the travelers' historical accounts.
[13] Demetriades 1983, pp. 415–422, esp. p. 416.
[14] See the essay by Kizis herein, p. 140.
[15] The plans are in the Hallersche Familienstiftung, Nuremberg; see Bankel 1986, pp. 167–168, 202, 242–243.
[16] Bankel 1986, pp. 168, 202–203.
[17] Korres 2010a, pp. 125–127.
[18] Knithakis, Mallouchou, and Tighinaga 1986, pp. 107–124, esp. pp. 119–120.
[19] Bankel 1986, p. 243.

του Σταροπάζαρου] due to its location.[20] Constructed in the south-eastern area of the Roman Agora (Fig. 2), it was frequented by the Muslim population of the city and remained in use until the first decades of the 19th century, when it became a warehouse for the books brought from the royal library of Aegina.[21] Part of the Oula Bey bath house can be seen in the background of Théodore du Moncel's drawing of the "Porte de l'Agora," the Gate of Athena Archegetis (1845), next to the Fethiye Mosque at the west side of the Roman Agora.[22] By 1846 the Greek government ceded the hammam's great hall to the Archaeological Society to store antiquities, including sculptures from the Parthenon and the Temple of Athena Nike, and the Caryatids of the Erechtheion, as well as sculptures from the frieze of the Temple of Apollo Epicurius in Bassae. The western part of the bath was demolished in 1875 in order to open Panos Street towards the Acropolis (Fig. 3).[23] The bath was destroyed by 1890, when the excavation of the site of the Roman Agora began.

Although never carefully documented, a few remnants can still be recovered. A visit to the archaeological site reveals that the existing wall along Epameinondas Street formed part of the bath's masonry; it was probably a retaining wall. The arched openings must have been part of the windows of the bath, while the vertical ceramic tubes that are still visible allowed for the circulation of hot air. It may therefore be proposed that the present wall can be identified with the original external masonry of the bath's hot room (Fig. 4).

Figure 2. To the right, the Oula Bey Hammam in 1870. Photo P. Moraitis © Benaki Museum.

---

[20] Evliya Çelebi 1994, p. 117. I thank Dimitris Loupis for the translation.
[21] Athens, General State Archives [Γ.Α.Κ.], Othonian Ministry of Interior Affairs, dated 20/11/1834 and 22/12/1834, catalogue no. Φ205.
[22] du Moncel 1845.
[23] Kokkou 1977, p. 121.

Figure 3. The Roman Agora from the east in 1877, showing the Tower of the Winds and, to the left, the semi-ruined Oula Bey Hammam. Mallouchou-Tufano 1998, p. 66 (DAI Athens, B.113).

Figure 4. Remains of the Oula Bey Hammam. Photo E. Kanetaki.

2. The Haçi Ali Hammam

The Haçi Ali Hammam, also known as the Rodakio Bath [Λουτρό του Ροδακιού], was situated at the corner of Navarchou Nikodemou and Agias Filotheis Streets. It remained in use for three years after the end of the Greek War of Independence (1831–1833). The bath was razed to the ground in 1890 to make way for the palace of Germanos, Archbishop of Athens. Floor plans from an architectural survey of the building by Johann Gotthelf Fischer von Waldheim (1847) have been published by Wilhelm Schleyer and John Travlos (Fig. 5).[24] The disrobing hall (A) [*camekan*] was equipped with elevated sofas and a fountain [*şadirvan*] for ablutions; the visitors could rest in small wooden cubicles waiting for their turn to enter the hot rooms. Next was the cold room (B) [*soğukluk*], with two smaller auxiliary spaces (Γ, the depilation room, and Δ, the lavatory). The bath's hot room (E) was shaped like an inverted T and was covered by a central semicircular dome, while two smaller private cubicles (Z) were located alongside the bath's furnace (H). Hot air and smoke, produced by the furnace where water was boiled in a cauldron, circulated under the hammam's floor through underground channels, using the traditional hypocaust system; vertical terracotta pipes inserted into the masonry during construction heated both the marble slabs of the floor and the walls of the rooms.

Dimitrios Kambouroglou vividly described a visit made around 1860 to the Haçi Ali Bath, as well as some of the traditional rituals associated with bathing:

> The person entering this room would find himself inside the completely unusual ambience of a tepid environment smelling sweetly of scented soaps and spices used to invigorate and care for hair, sometimes also used to evoke the hair color of the bygone years of youth [...] The ambience of the bath created an ensemble of unimaginable mystery. You would think that some fairytale was about to be spun within which you would live as a listener, as a teller of tales, and simultaneously as the person acting out the plot of the fairytale. The alteration of your own voice by the resonant hum of the domes and by the confusion of the jumbled sounds of the voices of others also added to this otherworldly impression. If the low, trembling note of a mandolin should ever chance to be heard in there at dusk, from an unknown source, you would surely think that you must have been snatched away alive and brought into the magical chambers of an unsolved mystery [...]
>
> During the best period of the bath—in other words, the Tourkokratia—around 2 p.m., the female bath attendants would beat the cymbals for the ladies to leave. The male bath attendants would arrive to tidy up the bath for their male customers. These bath attendants, around 5 p.m., would again beat their cymbals for the male bathers to leave and for them to prepare the bath for their night-time customers.
>
> In the middle of the room, dimly illuminated by the light-emitting glass of the central dome, was a great fountain. The water of this fountain was intentionally scant: from the first basin it fell into the second, the large basin, in melodious drops, the mystical sound of which the bath's other sweet-sounding domes dissolved into

---

[24] Genzmer 1899, p. 30; Schleyer 1909, p. 180; Travlos [1960] 1993, p. 185, fig. 122.

smaller reverberations. These are the sounds—toom, toom—that I still have in my ears [...]

My mother told me in later years that three bathing events in the Tourkokratia were particularly festive: the first for a girl who was passing from childhood to adolescence, the second for the girl about to be married, and the third right after the wedding. And one can imagine the banter aimed at the new bride, as well as the formal wishes, different—to be sure—from those offered during the other two occasions.[25]

The building's only remaining architectural feature was the fountain of the disrobing hall, recorded by Kostas Biris in the courtyard of the archbishop's palace.[26] Unfortunately, during my recent visits to the site, which now belongs to the Holy Archdiocese of Athens, no trace of the bath's fountain was discovered.

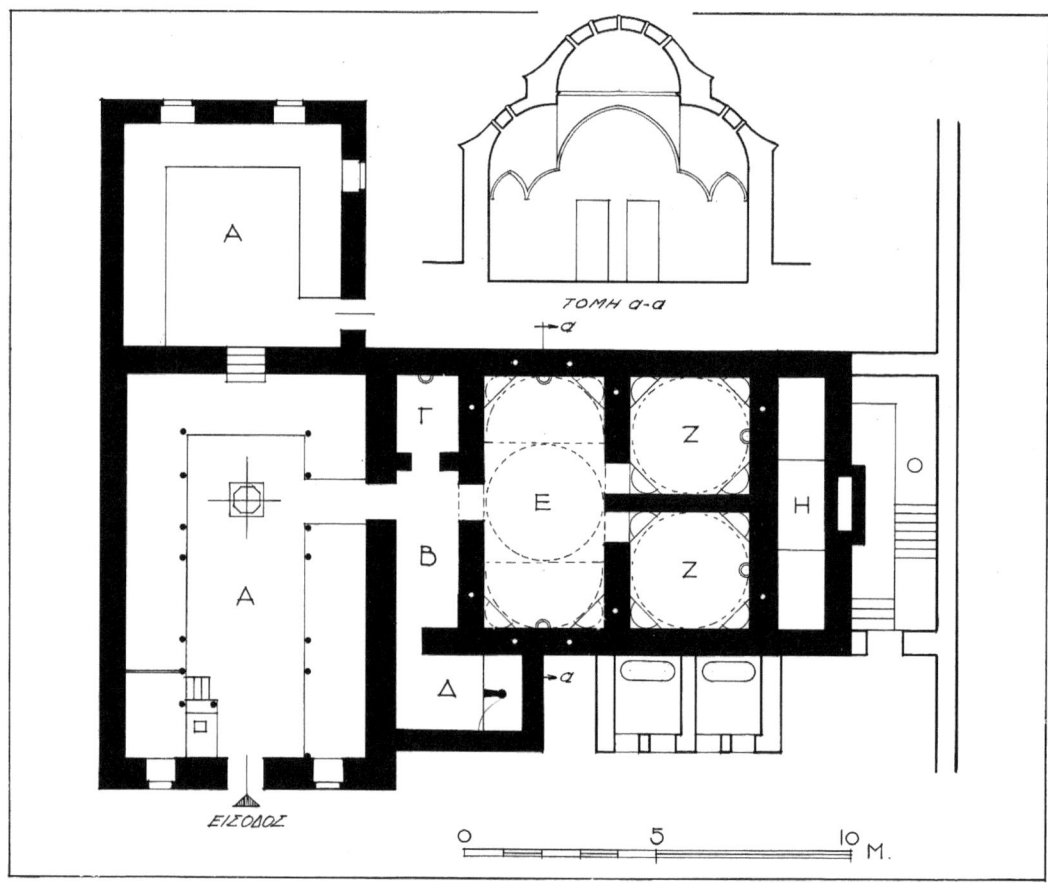

Figure 5. Ground-floor plan of the Haçi Ali Hammam. A) Disrobing hall and waiting area. B) Antechamber and cold room. Γ) Depilation room. Δ) Lavatory. E) Hot room. Z) Warm rooms. H) Furnace. Travlos [1960] 1993, p. 185.

[25] Kambouroglou 1934, pp. 45–48. Author's translation.
[26] Biris 1959, p. 19.

3. The Abid Efendi Hammam

The third public hammam of Athens, the Abid Efendi Hammam, also known as the Bath of the Winds [Λουτρό των Αέρηδων], is situated on Kyrristou Street, close to the Roman Agora and the Tower of the Winds.[27] The bath was most likely initially constructed as a single unit, but was remodeled into a double bath for both sexes in the 1870s. Its ground plan is rather asymmetrical as a result of modifications to the space (Fig. 6). The archaeological record indicates two construction phases, along with early 20th-century additions in the Neoclassical style.[28] The Abid Efendi Hammam continued to function as a bath until 1965. It was relinquished to the Museum of Greek Folk Art in 1984 and has been converted into a museum, which can be accessed from 8 Kyrristou Street.[29]

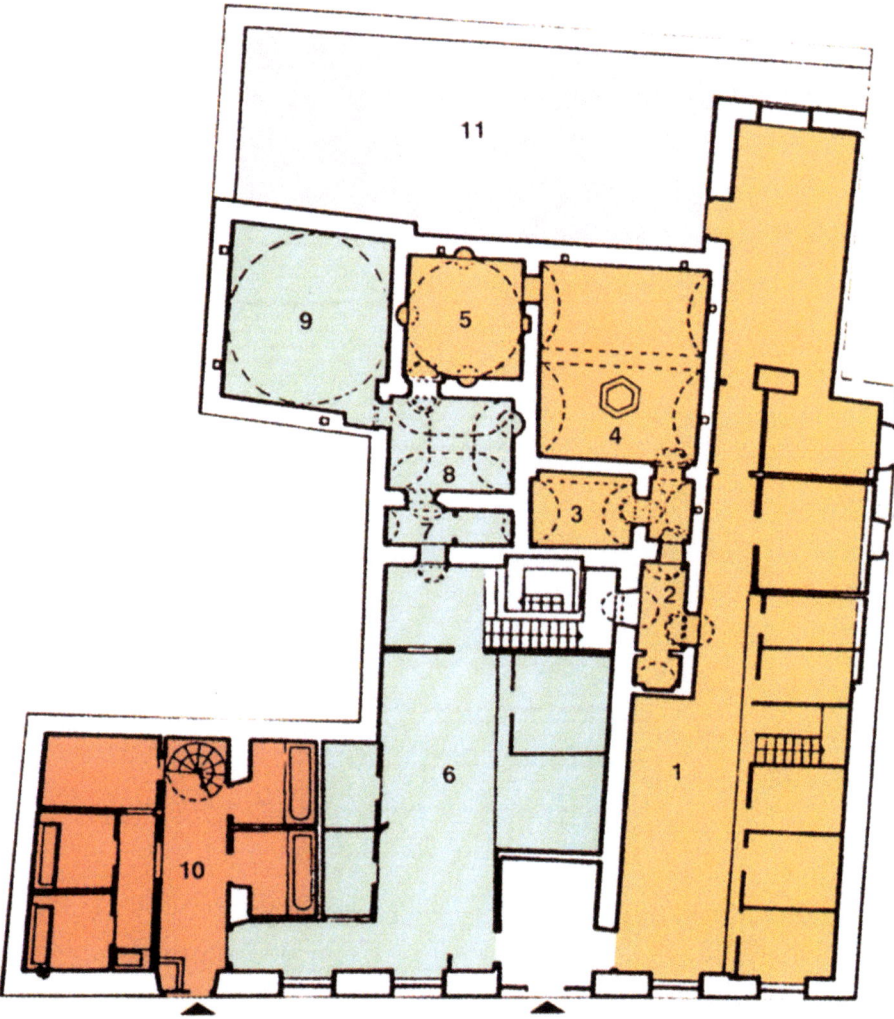

Figure 6. Ground-floor plan of the Abid Efendi Hammam. Kanetaki 2008, p. 81.

[27] Kanetaki 2004, p. 212.
[28] Kanetaki 2008, p. 79.
[29] Kanetaki 2014.

A small foyer leads to the two independent sections: the men's wing on the right and the women's on the left. The men's wing has an oblong ground floor and is equipped with three small cubicles divided by wooden partitions, small rooms for disrobing and storing personal belongings. A wooden staircase leads to a loft that features five small rooms for undressing and relaxation—an area equivalent to a Roman apodyterium—roofed with a system of lowered domes. The men's disrobing room is succeeded by a room with a small lavatory leading to the tepid and hot rooms. The first two rooms are roofed with hemispherical domes, while the roof of the main (warm) room is formed by two barrel vaults separated by an arch. The hot section of the men's wing features a polygonal marble bench for massages, while an opening on the left side of the room leads to a very warm domed private chamber with semicircular niches in the walls.

The women's wing has a similar layout, with four small cells separated by wooden partitions. On the left side of the Ottoman apodyterium, a corridor leads to a modern addition with four private chambers for tub bathing. The disrobing hall connects with two antechambers that lead to the tepid and hot rooms. The warmest area of the women's wing, with a square floor plan, is covered by a hemispherical dome. The hot rooms of the men's and women's wings were constructed adjoining each other to share the same furnace and water tank, located on the south side of the property along Lysiou Street. The rooms of the bath allow light to come in through small round openings in the domed roofs covered by bell-shaped glass fixtures.

The bath, a registered historical monument restored in the 1990s, is used by the Museum of Greek Folk Art as a museum of cleanliness, care and beautification of the body; it also hosts temporary cultural exhibitions of works of art (painting, small sculptures, and photography). A digital exhibition focuses on the architecture and history of the hammam as an institution, a typical component of Ottoman society.[30] As an image of Athens' Ottoman past, the restoration provides a new path for examining and appreciating the city's cohesive multicultural character.

The Ottoman Hammams in the City's Early Topographical Maps

Even after the end of Ottoman rule, the location of the Ottoman hammams continued to be recorded in numerous plans of Athens. The topographical maps by J.-F. Bessan, Stamatios Kleanthes and Gustav Eduard Schaubert, Leo von Klenze, and Friedrich Stauffert, provide enough details about the layout of the Ottoman town in order to identify the baths and testify to the transformation of the urban grid, especially during the second and third quarters of the 19th century.

Athens was designated as the capital of Greece in June 1833. The most significant documents of the city's topography during the early years of the Greek state are two topographical maps of the first quarter of the 19th century depicting the buildings of the time, one by the retired officer Bessan and the other by the architects Kleanthes and Schaubert.

Bessan's "Plan d'Athènes, levé en 1826 par ordre du Général Gourrhas" was commissioned by General Gourrhas, the commander of the garrison of the Acropolis. Its legend details the existing ancient monuments and the new constructions that were built for the defense of the city (Fig. 7). The plan is not always accurate: city blocks are depicted rather vaguely, and it does not give the positions of all monuments known at that time.

[30] Kanetaki 2014.

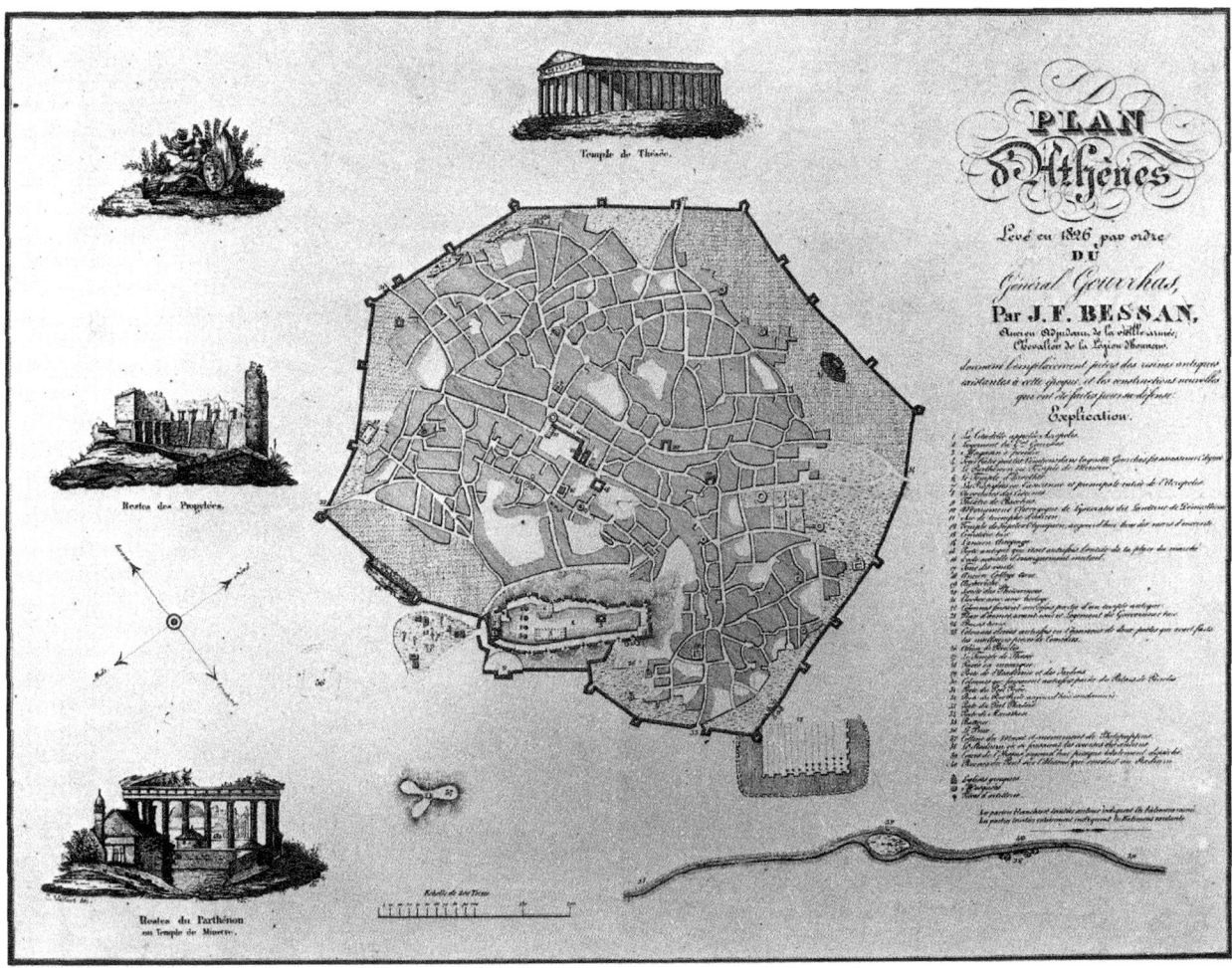

Figure 7. "Plan d'Athènes, levé en 1826 par ordre du Général Gourrhas, par J.-F. Bessan," showing the location of the Oula Bey Hammam as "24. Bains turcs", lithograph, 40.5 x 52 cm. Bessan 1835.

Kleanthes and Schaubert, students of the Prussian architect Karl Friedrich Schinkel, were commissioned in November 1831 to design a plan for the new capital of Athens following a meticulous topographical, architectural and archaeological survey of the city. Their proposal called for a Neoclassical garden city according to the urban planning guidelines of the early 19th century.[31] The Kleanthes and Schaubert plan, which was approved in June 1833, envisioned a monumental character for the capital: wide boulevards run through the city, and large archaeological areas were intended to enhance the ancient buildings and promote their preservation. Its realization, however, demanded large-scale expropriations, which resulted in substantial dissent from landowners, so the plan was abandoned.

Another proposal, from the architect Leo von Klenze, submitted in September 1834, included drastic modifications to the Kleanthes and Schaubert proposal: the area destined for archaeological excavations was reduced, the width of the streets was narrowed, and the surface of the squares was

---

[31] Biris and Kardamitsi-Adami 2001, p. 74; see also the essay by Karidis herein, pp. 123–134.

condensed; neither was this plan adopted full scale (Fig. 8). The legends of von Klenze's "Plan der Neustadt Athen" record the position of ancient monuments (in the upper-left border), as well as Byzantine and Ottoman sites (in the upper-right border), while the legends on the middle-right and lower-right side mention the new buildings that were to be designed.

The exact location of the Oula Bey Hammam is shown in both the 1826 and the 1834 plans: it is marked as "24. Bains turcs" in Bessan's map (Fig. 7) and "5 Θερμά τουρκ [Turkish baths]" in von Klenze's topographical plan (Fig. 8). In a blueprint of the Kleanthes and Schaubert plan of 1833 found in the archives of the British School at Athens,[32] we can decipher the characteristic outline of the Oula Bey and the Haçi Ali hammams, although there is no indication of names or use, as the plan includes references only to churches.

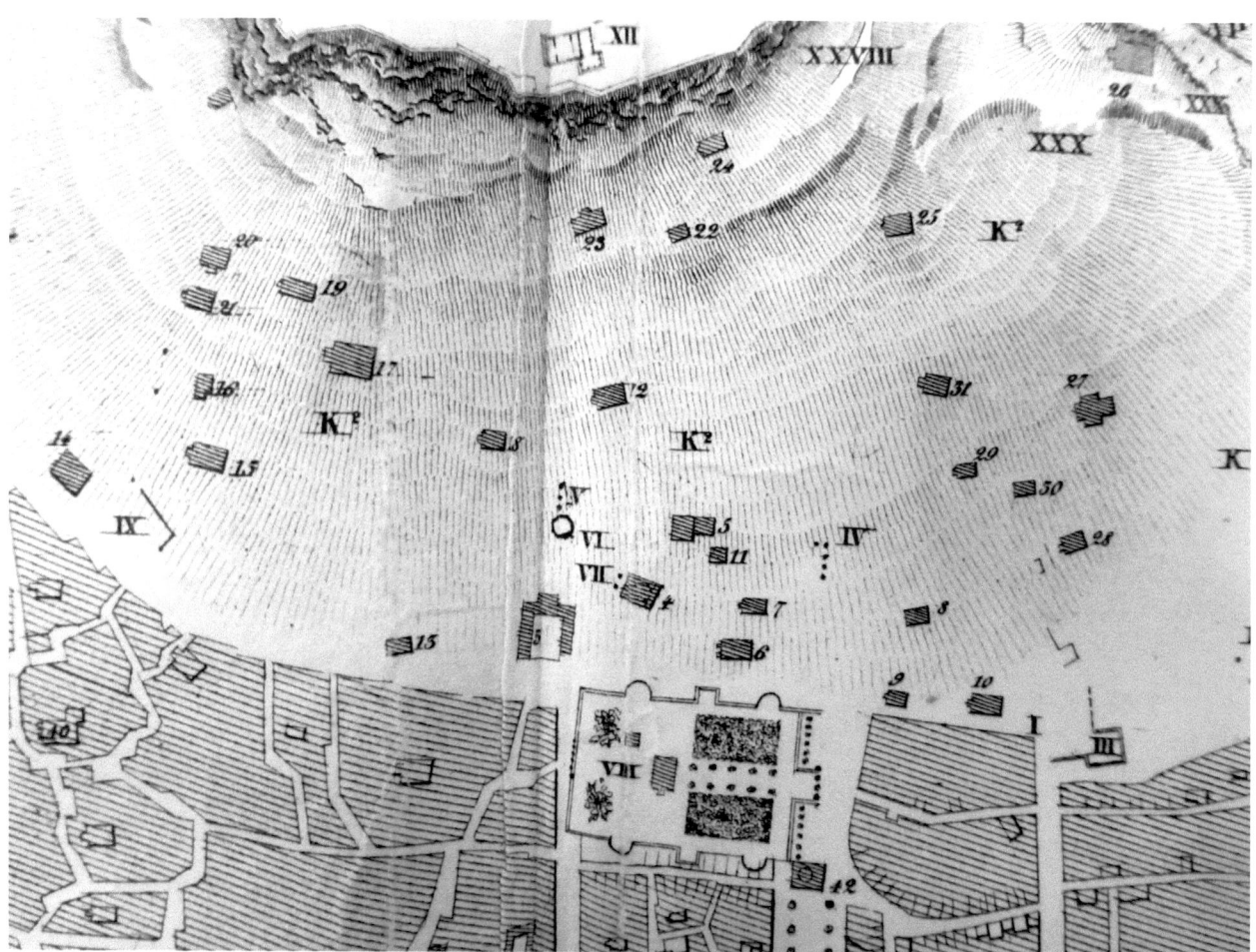

Figure 8. Detail of the "Plan der Neustadt Athen" by Leo von Klenze, 1834, showing the Tower of the Winds (2), the madrasa (3), mosques (11, 14, 42), and a bathhouse [Oula Bey Hammam] (5). Von Klenze 1834.

---

[32] Library of the British School at Athens, maps, blueprint section 17, map 04, 62 x 85 cm.

A lesser-known map is a drawing entitled "Plan d'Athènes en 1820," published in *Athenae Christianae* by August Mommsen, who visited the city in 1866. The plan captures the urban layout of the city in 1820, giving information about 160 numbered sites, including Byzantine and Ottoman monuments (the ground-floor plans of Byzantine churches, Ottoman mosques, baths, etc., are represented with crossed lines). Unfortunately, the relevant appendix is missing; Papageorgiou-Venetas has suggested that it might not have been attached to the map. Only a few sites, as well as the use of certain buildings, are indicated (in French). The lithograph was found in Schaubert's archives, without a signature or date, while Mommsen attributed it to an unknown source.[33] Biris considered the map a printed edition of the architectural survey of Athens that Kleanthes and Schaubert conducted in 1831–1832.[34] The Oula Bey Hammam is marked as no. 84, while no. 601 refers most probably to the Haçi Ali Hammam. Other Ottoman monuments, such as the voivode's mansion (no. 115), the Fethiye Mosque (no. 82), and the tekke (no. 83) close to the Oula Bey Hammam, are marked on the plan, as well as the Tower of the Winds (no. 81).

Wilhelm von Weiler's plan of Athens, designed in August 1834, depicted the area of the Ottoman bazaar in a rather simplified way. While a large number of Christian churches are noted, only a few Ottoman buildings are recorded, such as the Lower Şadirvan Mosque at Monastiraki Square, the madrasa (without denomination, its ground-floor plan represented with a plain contour), and the tekke. Only one bath house is depicted: the Oula Bey Hammam, labeled as the "lower bath."

Although the Athenian town plan proposed by von Klenze had limited the archaeological area zones, the need for future expropriations was evident, so a new topographical map was designed soon after (1836) by Friedrich Stauffert and Schaubert with the help of Christian Hansen. The new plan was accurately drawn, offering thorough information on each city block, as well as the locations of all known buildings. Many of the churches are marked in blue ink, as are some Ottoman buildings, such as the Lower Şadirvan Mosque, the voivode's mansion in the area close to Hadrian's Library, the Fethiye Mosque, the madrasa, the Oula Bey Hammam, and its adjoining tekke at the corner of Epameinondas and Panos Streets (Fig. 9). The other two baths, the Abid Efendi and the Haçi Ali hammams, can also be distinguished on the plan, although they are not marked in blue as are the other Ottoman monuments, but in light grey.

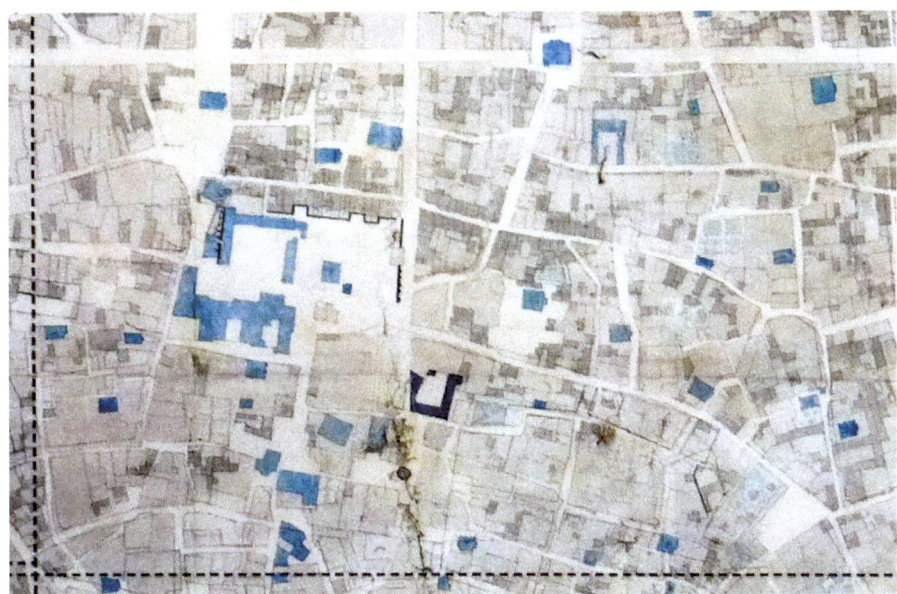

Figure 9. Detail of the plan of Athens by Friedrich Stauffert and Gustav Eduard Schaubert with the help of Christian Hansen, 1836, showing the Oula Bey Hammam. Korres 2010a, p. 222.

[33] Papageorgiou-Venetas 1999, pp. 77, 84; according to whom, the lithograph

In the years that followed, the historic center of Athens underwent significant changes, recorded in numerous plans. In 1875 the archaeologist Ernst Curtius and the topographer–cartographer Johann August Kaupert conducted numerous topographical surveys in Attica and Athens, producing a valuable series of detailed maps, the *Karten von Attica*. The map "Athens mit Umgebung-Karten von Attika, Bild I," drawn by Kaupert in 1875 and published in 1877, shows some of the changes in the wheat market, as the western part of the Oula Bey Hammam had recently been demolished (1875) in order to open up Panos Street, creating a perspective view towards the Acropolis (Fig. 10). Excavations at the archaeological site of the Roman Agora, occupied until then by the bazaar, would start a few years later, in 1890; the area is, therefore, presented by Kaupert as a nucleus with small irregular city blocks.

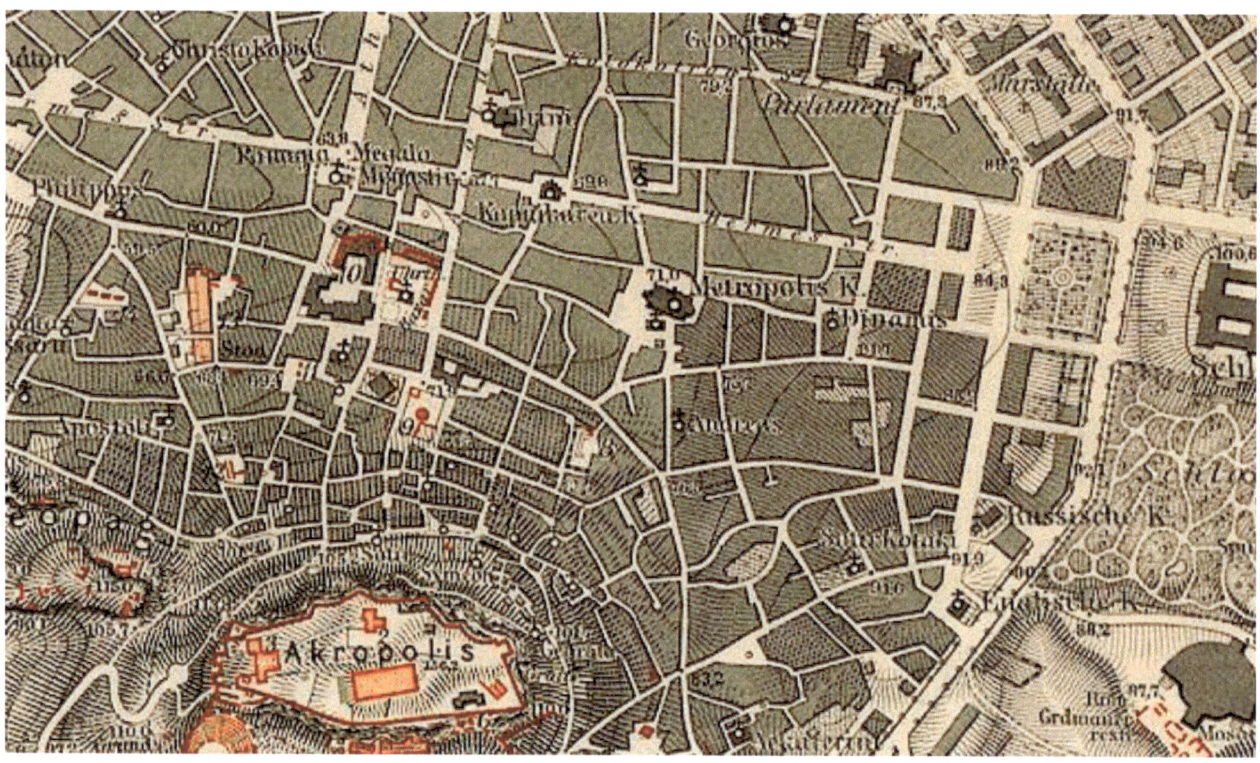

Figure 10. Detail of "Athens mit Umgebung-Karten von Attika, Bild I" by Johann August Kaupert, 1875, as evidence for the demolished Oula Bey Hammam. Curtius and Kaupert 1903.

In addition to the topographical maps, the late 18th-century depictions of the Athenian antiquities drawn by James Stuart and Nicholas Revett (e.g. *The Horologion of Andronikos Kyrristos [Tower of the Winds] in Athens, with the Acropolis in the Background*, 1762) and especially the 19th-century townscapes by Edward Dodwell (e.g. *The Upper Bazaar of Athens*, ca. 1800), Otto Magnus von Stackelberg (e.g. *Athènes. Intérieur d'une maison greque*), Louis Dupré (e.g. *The Ottoman Woman of Athens*, 1820, and *The Voivode of Athens*, 1827), Eugène Peytier (e.g *Athens: The Fethiye Mosque and the Tower of the Winds from the South-west*, 1834), and Baron Jean Antoine Théodore Gudin (e.g. *View of Athens with the Tower of the Winds and the Agora*; Fig. 11) offer significant information. Although the baths do not constitute a central subject matter in these works, their presence was well-noted in the urban scale along with the other Ottoman building types.

Figure 11. Baron Jean Antoine Théodore Gudin, *View of Athens with the Tower of the Winds and the Agora*, oil on card laid on panel, 36.5 x 61.5 cm. France, private collection.

Conclusion

This essay has attempted to document the baths of Ottoman Athens by means of multiple data: historical accounts (memoirs and travelers' accounts), archaeological information (excavation reports), architectural designs (surveys of the buildings and old photographs depicting the monuments), early 19th-century topographical maps (selected city plans depicting the urban grid and its transformations), and artworks (paintings, drawings and engravings), combined with in situ surveys.[35] The Athenian hammams may not have been as luxurious and impressive as those in other cities of the Ottoman Empire, but they testify nonetheless to the size of the city, while they provide sufficient evidence of the continuity of civic space. Because of the lack of systematic studies on the Ottoman architectural enterprise in Athens, partially due to limited access to relevant material, it is difficult to draw safe conclusions and to understand fully the complicated process through which Ottoman Athens was shaped. The field is still expanding; it is evident, however, that what has previously been classified as marginal and foreign has proven to be central. Instead of sharp breaks with the past and a-historical discontinuities, the time has arrived to focus on the available material and to try to make sense of the complexity of the city's landscape as a historical subject in constant dialogue with the changes wrought by modernity.

---

[35] In situ surveys were carried out as possible and where permission was granted, due to the private ownership of certain buildings and as the Roman Agora site is a protected registered area of the Hellenic Ministry of Culture.

Travelers' Narratives Describing the Hammams of Athens

Aliki Asvesta and Ioli Vingopoulou

Two of the most significant accounts of Athens and its inhabitants and monuments on the eve of the Greek War of Independence are those of the well-known travelers Edward Daniel Clarke (1801) and Edward Dodwell (1805–1806).[1] Although they did not mention any personal experiences of visiting hammams in Athens, they did relate numerous scenes, stories, and highlights set against the backdrop of the city's public baths;[2] and many west European travelers visited public hammams in the Ottoman Empire. Before we consider the descriptions of Clarke and Dodwell and those of other travelers, let us first explore the reasons why hammams attracted the attention of west European travelers to the Ottoman realm.

The Appeal of the Ottoman Hammam and Its Rituals

> Arose early, and for the first time went to a Turkish bath. The Turkish baths comprehend three separate chambers, in the first of which the person using the bath [...] undresses himself, and proceeds from thence to a second chamber well heated; here he rests some few minutes in order to try his ability to support the almost suffocating heat of the innermost chamber close adjoining; if he finds himself sufficiently strong he enters it and places himself upon a large circular marble slab in the middle of the chamber raised about two or three feet from the ground. The chamber itself is circular, having a large dome or cupola with small round apertures on the top to allow the heated air to escape. In it [...] is an abundant supply of either hot or cold water. It is in this chamber that the attendants of the bath knead the skin from head to foot of those who present themselves. The skin being thus tempered and the pores so considerably expanded, the attendants pass over the whole body a brush made

---

[1] The dates in parentheses next to each traveler's name indicate the year of his/her visit or of his/her reference to Ottoman baths in Athens.
[2] For their stays in Athens and descriptions of ancient monuments, see Clarke (1814, vol. 3, pp. 462–486 and 784–793) and Dodwell (1819, vol. 1, pp. 288–505). For biographical details on Edward Dodwell and Simone Pomardi, see Camp 2013 (with extensive bibliography). See also the various entries at http://eng.travelogues.gr/.

Figure 1. A relaxing massage in the men's bath. Thévenot 1725, p. 9.

> of the finest mohair, after which operation to make the limbs more supple they place you on your back putting their knee on your breast and snap your joints [Fig. 1]. You now retire [...] and [...] wash away the thick lather of perfumed soap with which you have been covered [...] with no ordinary satisfaction you regain the chamber in which you undressed. You are now supplied with hot towels and a pillow, and repose yourself for some short time, after which you take a cup of coffee and retire [...][3]

This brief statement of J. Oliver Hanson (1814) transports us to Ottoman Athens before the Greek War of Independence. Around the same time, the painter Simone Pomardi (1805–1806) informs us that in Athens the baths were close to the bazaar, and the merchant John Galt (1811) stated that the baths were the Athenians' only public entertainment.[4] About 150 years before Hanson's description, the Englishman George Wheler (1676) and the Ottoman Evliya Çelebi counted three baths in Athens.[5] Evliya Çelebi gave us an abundance of information about hammams, which were numerous and scattered through all the cities and villages of the Ottoman Empire.[6]

During this period west Europeans did not have a good relationship with water and bodily cleanliness, especially when baths were provided in public edifices.[7] In the "East," however, the flow of water for cleansing and the liquidity and fluid socialization of individuals, in ideal public spaces, united clean flesh with the soul's well-being. These spaces drew the attention of travelers as "worthy of curiosity and recollecting." In 1563, the French geographer and traveler Nicolas de Nicolay wrote, with emphasis on the institutional side of the baths, that:

> It must be noted that all nations, of whatever law and religion that they may be, are received and treated without distinction in these baths for their money. But above all others, the Turks, Moors, and universally the Islamized come most often, as much for their voluptuousness and bodily health as mainly for the observance of their law, which commands all Muslims not to enter their mosques without first being well washed and purified.[8]

Regarding the bathing facilities in the Ottoman Empire, Nicolay's compatriot, Guillaume Postel, stated in the mid-16th century that, "Christians, Jews, all the world is welcomed and looked after impartially," and added, "I wish the same opportunity for bathing [were available] for the elderly and the great cities of Christendom as a very healthy thing, which has been an occasion to incite me to want to write at

---

[3] Anghelou 1971, p. 21. Impressions comparable to Hanson's concerning the baths of Athens in 1814 can be drawn from the work that Thomas Robert Joliffe published just over a decade later (Joliffe 1827, p. 237).
[4] Pomardi 1820, p. 131; Galt 1813, p. 119.
[5] Wheler 1682, p. 352: "There are also three or four publick Bagnio's, or Baths, much used here, as in most other eminent Towns in Turkey. The Town is well watered by Chanels under ground, brought from the Ilissus and Eridanus: I mean from Mount Hymettus; and dispersed about the City into several publick Fountains, and Private Houses. That in the Street of the Bazar, is the most eminent, and bears the Name of Ussin." See also Biris 1959, pp. 44, 46. For information about and plans of the locations of the public baths in the city's urban fabric: Travlos [1960] 2005, pp. 184–185, 203, 216; see also the essay by Kanetaki herein, pp. 151–165. On the architecture and organization of the public baths of Ottoman Athens, and also the customs connected with them: Kardamitsi-Adami and Grafakou [1989] 1999, pp. 11–36. A first reference to the baths of Athens (1460) occurs in the work of Laborde (1854b, p. 4).
[6] See Kanetaki 2004, pp. 208–217.
[7] Vigarello 1985.
[8] Nicolay 1577, p. 108. See also Vingopoulou 2004, p. 60.

more length, for the great good that would come of it, which the Ancients knew cured the majority of their illnesses by this means."⁹

West European travelers heartily acknowledged that the bath had therapeutic qualities. They noted that in the East many ailments were rare, and that was owed in large measure to frequent attendance at the public baths. Such writers as Pierre-Augustin Guys (1783) recommended them to the aged, noting from their own experience that sweating, as well as massage with a special sponge, helped to open the pores.¹⁰

The travelers also sketched the multifaceted role the baths had already played in the Greek and Roman world and observed that in all the cities the baths continued a usage that had originated in Antiquity, serving the same needs and customs:¹¹ reasons of health and hygiene, companionship and enjoyment, entertainment, and beauty treatments led all ethnicities in the Ottoman Empire to the bath. According to Guillaume-Joseph Grelot (1671), the Muslims built impressive baths because the incentives for using the baths were officially sealed and determined by Muslim doctrine.¹²

Testimonies of the imposing architecture and ornamentation, evocative atmosphere, and architectural skill were added by Nicolas de Nicolay: "In Constantinople, as equally in all the other Islamized cities in Greece, Asia, and Africa, is found a great number of very beautiful baths, both public and private. These are built in imitation of the ancient Greeks and Romans and constructed with inventiveness, lavishness, and almost admirable expenditure [...]"¹³

The French naturalist Joseph Pitton de Tournefort (1702) provided a detailed description of the different rooms of the bath and the rituals of personal care after he himself was left in the hands of the bath attendants:

> One first enters a beautiful room, in the middle of which is the main fountain, whose basin serves for washing the linens of the house; all around the room runs a divan raised about three feet covered with rushes; one sits on this divan to smoke and to take off one's garments, which are wrapped in a cloth. The atmosphere in this first room is so moderated that one does not realize that one has nothing on one's body except an apron attached to the belt (to cover up in the front and behind). One passes with this outfit into a small room a little warmer, and from there into a larger one where the heat is more perceptible; all these rooms normally end in little domes illuminated by openings, each fitted with a glass bell [...] The paving of this chamber is heated by subterranean furnaces, and one walks about as much as one sees fit. When one wants to be scrubbed off, a bath attendant has you stretch out on your back [...]¹⁴

When the whole ritual of personal care, exercise, cleansing, scrubbing, and exfoliation ends, after stages of difficult breathing and feeling unpleasant, a sensation of complete revitalization and well-

---

⁹ Postel 1560, pp. 28, 30.
¹⁰ Guys 1783, pp. 225–226.
¹¹ Palerne 1606, p. 89.
¹² Grelot 1680, p. 232. For the baths and their relationship to Islam, see *inter alia* Taşçioglu 1998, pp. 34–36; d'Ohsson 1789, vol. 2, pp. 52 and 59–60. For baths in antiquity, see Yegül 2010.
¹³ Nicolay 1577, p. 106.
¹⁴ Pitton de Tournefort 1717, pp. 86–87.

Figure 2. "Cooling Room of a Hammam." Pardoe 1838, opposite p. 15.

being comes over him, and he passes to the lounge area (Fig. 2). There, he continues, "One smokes [...] drinks some coffee, and even has a light meal, for after this exercise one has a wonderful appetite;" these habits were new to him, yet intrinsic to daily life in the Ottoman Empire.[15] From Pitton de Tournefort's reliable text, we also draw information relating to women:

> The ladies are very happy when they are allowed to go to the public baths; most of them, nevertheless, and most of all those whose husbands are wealthy enough to have baths built in their own homes, do not have this freedom [Fig. 3]. In the public baths they converse together without any restriction, and they pass the time more pleasantly than in their own quarters. The husbands who are indulgent to their wives do not deny them these innocent pastimes.[16]

Religious laws, health, personal care, and beauty treatments of course do not have to do only with the male population, but, even more so, are indissoluble elements bound up with the world of

---

[15] Hattox 1985; Galland [1699] 1992. For the introduction of the smoking of tobacco and descriptions of the hookah [*narghile*], see Chandler 1776, pp. 193–194; Woods 1828, p. 278; Bisani 1793, pp. 62–63.
[16] Pitton de Tournefort 1717, p. 88.

Figure 3. "Les Bains," a scene of bathers, serving women, and a small boy inside a public bath. Guys 1783, p. 224.

women. The French naturalist Pierre Belon (1547) associated the baths with natural mineral beauty and hygiene products. He noted that clay and chalk were used by women to rub on their bodies for radiant skin and mainly as shampoo, in combination with henna, for lustrous hair. He added that women remain in the baths for around five hours for personal care and companionship.[17]

The narratives include sundry remarks about the coquetry, social display, and behaviors that developed among women at the baths, given that the venue represented the most important place for beautification and socializing, an ideal space where collective mentalities were on display. When women went to the baths, they were entrusted to the care of their attendants, and the less well-off to the service of the bath women, in a ritual which was repeated with delight. The whole diversion was complemented by sweets, followed by sherbets and coffee. As the French traveler Guillaume-Antoine Olivier (1796) records, the ladies would often watch shadow puppet theater when the baths were closed to the public for the entire day, for the baths constituted one of the very few pretexts for going out of the house.[18]

We may wonder how this whole hidden world of women, with all its details of the inner sanctum of the baths, reached male travelers, given the existence of the most stringent prohibitions on encounters between the two sexes in these spaces. Do their accounts come from women's stories? Do they reveal the travelers' own imagination? Or did rumors and gossip slip out from within the baths? As Grelot (1671) hinted, perhaps it was the young male children who accompanied their mothers to the baths who later on as adults became the source of information for the various details and moments of intense familiarity between women that fed the fantasies of Westerners about this inviolable space.[19]

From the 18th century on, travelers' impressions of the prevailing atmosphere of female camaraderie at the baths are significantly enriched by testimonials from women travelers. Lady Mary Wortley Montagu (1717) gave a detailed description of the last maiden bath of a bride-to-be, though she could not enjoy the complete ritual herself, because she remained tightly bound up in Western-style underclothing.[20]

Narrating the Athenian Hammams

Lady Elizabeth Craven (1786) expressed her vexation at the sight of naked women and flaccid bodies, but at the same time described the adroitness and care which characterized their movements. After she visited a bath in 18th-century Athens, she described it as follows:

> The Baths here are very well contrived to stew the rheumatism out of a person's constitution—but how the women can support the heat of them is perfectly inconceivable—The Consul's wife, Madame Gaspari, and I went into a room which precedes the Bath, which room is the place where the women dress and undress, sitting like tailors upon boards—there were above fifty; some having their hair washed, others dyed, or plaited; some were at the last part of their toilet, putting

---

[17] Belon 1588, pp. 435–437; cf. Sandys 1673, p. 54. On Pierre Belon, see also Vingopoulou 2004, pp. 23–24.
[18] Olivier 1800, p. 190.
[19] Grelot 1680, p. 235.
[20] Montagu 1763, vol. 1, pp. 159–162.

with a fine gold pin the black dye into their eyelids [...]—These Baths are the great amusement of the women, they stay generally five hours in them; that is in the water and at their toilet together [...] We had very pressing solicitations to undress and bathe, but refused [...] the Bath [...] was circular, with niches in it for the bathers to sit in; it was a very fine room with a stone dome—and the light came through small windows at the top—[21]

Clarke presented a picture of intense female companionship comparable to that of Craven, but observed with completely different eyes. Here is his narrative, in the third person, of "a singular adventure:"

About half-way up the steep which leads to the *Propylaea*, he heard a noise of laughter and of many clamorous voices, proceeding from a building [...] which had the appearance of being a public bath. As it is always customary for strangers to mingle with the *Moslems* in such places without molestation, and as it had been the author's practice to bathe frequently for the preservation of his health, he advanced without further consideration towards the entrance, which he found covered with a carpet hanging before it. No human creature was to be seen without the bath, whether *Turk* or *Greek* [...] As the author drew nearer to the door of the building, the voices were heard rather in a shriller tone than usual; but no suspicion entering into his mind, as to the sort of bathers which he would find assembled, he put aside the carpet, and, stepping beneath the main dome of the *bagnio*, suddenly found himself in the midst of the principal women of *Athens*, many of whom were unveiled in every sense of the term, and all of them in utter amazement at the madness of the intrusion. The first impulse of astonishment entirely superseded all thought of the danger of his situation: he remained fixed and mute as a statue. A general shriek soon brought him to his recollection. Several black female slaves ran towards him, interposing before his face napkins, and driving him backwards towards the entrance. He endeavoured, by signs and broken sentences, to convince them that he came there to bathe in the ordinary way; but this awkward attempt at an apology converted their fears into laughter, accompanied by sounds of *Hist! Hist!* and the most eager entreaties to him to abscond quickly, and without observation. As he drew back, he distinctly heard someone say, in *Italian*, that if he were seen he would be shot [...] As the sight of women in *Turkey* is rare, and always obtained with difficulty, the Reader may perhaps wish to know what sort of beings the author saw, during the short interval that his eyes were open within the bagnio; although he can only describe the scene from a confused recollection [...] [Fig. 4].[22]

---

[21] Craven 1789, pp. 263–264. One ear witness of these women's gatherings in Athens was Frederick Sylvester North Douglas (1812), who noted in this connection, "[...] with them ['the Romaic ladies'] the bath is a sort of public assembly; whole days are spent in the enjoyment of it; and the scenes which there take place [...] equal, I am told, the strangest pictures of the Ecclesiazusae and the Lysistrata." (Douglas 1813, pp. 149–150). For the same period in Athens, we also have a description and plan of a house with a private bath that was owned by the merchant Mertrud: Bankel 1986, pp. 167–168.

[22] Clarke 1814, vol. 3, pp. 587–588. The moments, the hours, that the women passed in the baths occupies or sometimes even obsesses the travelers' imagination in their journeys to the great cities of the Ottomans, in Athens as well; this gaze always finds a form of fulfillment, as in Clarke's narrative. The italics in this quotation and the next are Clarke's.

Figure 4. "Bain public des femmes mahométanes." D'Ohsson 1788, vol. 1, pl. 13.

Detailed descriptions of the bathers and their slaves follow, the women reclining on divans, their long hair "hanging dishevelled and straight almost to the ground," their faces rosy from the heat, while the serving women prepare pipes and coffee. Clarke's account continues:

> The cause of this mistake remains now to be explained. This bath was not peculiarly set apart for the use of females: it was frequented also by the male inhabitants; but at stated times the women have the privilege of appropriating it to their use; and this happened to be their time of bathing; consequently the men were absent. Upon such occasions, the *Greek* and *Turkish* women bathe together: owing to this circumstance, the news of the adventure was very speedily circulated over all *Athens*. As we did not return until the evening, the family with whom we resided, hearing of the affair, began to be uneasy [...] well knowing that if any of the *Arnaouts*, or of the *Turkish* guard belonging to the *Citadel*, had seen a man coming from the bath

while the women were there, they, without hesitation or ceremony, would have put him instantly to death [...]²³

The incident of the violation of the inner sanctum of the bath by the garrison commander [*dizdar*] of the Acropolis on the day when the women were bathing violently inverted the relations of power and dependence between the Ottoman officer and Dodwell, an important regular visitor to the fortress. In this case, the adventure-filled action is transferred out of the bath and extends into other spaces of Ottoman Athens and further afield. In trouble, the Muslim garrison commander needed the involvement, mobilization, and generosity of this west European Christian, and this exchange between the two men is illustrated in Dodwell's account of his relations with the commander and his family:

> Of the few indulgences which the jealousy of Turkish husbands allows to their wives, the recreation of the bath is the most highly prized; and hither, as to a public coffee-house, the females eagerly resort, and pass several hours of the day in gossiping and scandal, which constitute their principal amusement, and their highest delight. At these periods, the bath is, of course, accessible only to women; but, though on this point the Turkish manners are so inflexibly severe, the Disdar, or governor of the fortress, had the temerity to venture into that bath, which it was permitted for none but females to use; and like another Actaeon, to feast his unhallowed eyes on the forbidden charms of the young females who were unconsciously exposed to his view, in all their native purity and voluptuous elegance. The rash intruder was soon discovered in this forbidden situation; a scream of terror resounded through the vaulted chamber of the bath; the inexpiable insult was soon known to the infuriated husbands, and the trembling Disdar was compelled to take refuge in the Acropolis! But the Turks threatening to attack him even in that retreat, he soon retired to Aegina, where, not thinking himself secure from the vengeance of his enemies, he was ultimately compelled to conceal himself in the island of Hydrea [*sic*].²⁴

Sometime later, Dodwell, who was residing at the Capuchin monastery,²⁵ obtained permission from the prior to conceal the *dizdar* in his apartments there and he reports that the latter's wife and children would pass in front of the windows of the monastery daily for the aggrieved father to see them. Through the intervention of the prior, the garrison commander was eventually restored to the bosom of his family and to his command. It took some time for everyone to forget the incident, one that likely contained a measure of fiction.

Conclusion

With the bath as their point of reference, these last two narratives permit the description of concrete images of public and private life in Ottoman Athens.²⁶ They show how the rules, laws, customs, and

---

²³ Clarke 1814, vol. 3, pp. 589–590.
²⁴ Dodwell 1819, vol. 2, pp. 26–30.
²⁵ Many foreign travelers stayed at the Capuchin monastery; for the monastery, see Pagonis 1993.
²⁶ For representations of public and private life in Ottoman Athens, see Koumarianou 2005 and Karidis 2014.

behaviors functioned, as well as the relations among power, hospitality, and reconciliation, and the feelings experienced as much between the residents as among the foreign visitors who mingled actively in the life of the city. Athens at that time had a population of approximately 10,000 inhabitants: news spread with great speed, but at the same time was concealed and covered up with collusive effort until it was forgotten and/or forgiven. The factors that encouraged people to attend the baths—health, hygiene, beauty treatments, and companionship—are evident in the descriptions of the hammams of Athens, along with the individual peculiarities of the travelers who were staying in the city. Athens did not cease to attract visitors, mainly because of its ancient past.[27] In the Ottoman capital, conversely, the nebulous world of the baths inspired analogous travelers' texts in which it is the "exotic Eastern" element that is mainly on display, as the twilight of vaporous indolence was deemed suited to the humidity and the rhythms of an Eastern capital. The glory and splendor of Athens did not leave travelers enough time and space for sensual pleasures, which developed and found expression either in fantasy or in some hazardous adventure. These, too, were a part of life in late Ottoman Athens.

---

[27] For more, see Yakovaki 2006.

Broken Pots from Ottoman Athens: A New View from the Agora Excavations

Joanita Vroom

When archaeology was still in its infancy, there was one basic principle all too familiar to most archaeologists working in the eastern Mediterranean. That principle was to dig as fast as you could through the Ottoman and Byzantine layers, remove them, and forget about them. This was considered to be the best, or at least the easiest, way to get directly to the precious treasures of Classical Antiquity in which our predecessors were mainly interested. The practice became known as "digging through the Byz," although it may well have also carried the name "digging through the Ott," as it obliterated the Ottoman-period layers perhaps even more rigorously than those of the Byzantine era.

It took archaeologists several centuries to become wiser, but we have slowly discovered that Mediterranean history did not end with the Sack of Corinth or the Conquest of Constantinople. We gradually realized that the history of habitation of the eastern Mediterranean and adjacent parts of the Near East cannot be understood properly without studying the archaeology of the vast period of time between Antiquity and the modern era, including the archaeology of the Byzantine and the Ottoman periods. Today—let us hope, at least—we are no longer "digging through the Byz," nor "digging through the Ott," but are in fact "digging *for* the Byzantines and the Ottomans."

This essay sets out to demonstrate just how rewarding "digging for Ottoman Athens" can be for archaeology in general,[1] and for our knowledge of the history of daily life in the Mediterranean since Antiquity in particular.[2] It is no coincidence that in recent decades Ottoman archaeology has become one of the most flourishing, fruitful, and exciting new sectors in our field of study internationally. However, Ottoman archaeology is also a rapidly expanding universe, and in order not to get lost in this vast subject, I will limit myself here to the largely untold story of the Athenian Agora during Ottoman

---

[1] This preliminary report draws on finds from the excavations in the Athenian Agora run by the American School of Classical Studies at Athens [ASCSA] from the 1930s onward, with special attention to post-Roman ceramic finds from the older Agora Excavations. The material originates from Ottoman contexts (such as wells) in this part of Athens and can be dated between the 15th and 19th centuries. I would like to thank Professor Jenifer Neils, the current director of ASCSA, Professor Jack Davis and Professor James Wright, former Directors of ASCSA, and Professor John McK. Camp II, Director of the ASCSA's Athenian Agora Excavations, for allowing me to study and publish the later material from the excavations in the Ancient Agora of Athens. Furthermore, I wish to express my gratitude to Dr. Maria Georgopoulou, Sylvie Dumont, and Maria Tziotziou for their help in coordinating the display of some Ottoman-period Agora finds in the Gennadius Library in Spring 2015, and especially to Craig Mauzy for photographing the objects in Figures 7–28.
[2] Vroom 2003, p. 25, and Vroom 2013a, pp. 79–80; see also Frantz 1942 and Rohn, Barnes, and Sanders 2009 for an example of Ottoman archaeology in Corinth.

times. After briefly introducing my research project at Leiden University, of which this subject is an integral part, I will illustrate how finds of the Ottoman period from the Agora Excavations can shed new light on Athenian history.³ We have to keep in mind, of course, that the area of the Agora was initially a western suburb of Athens with a few churches and some industry that started to be developed under Ottoman rule.⁴

For the sake of clarity, the time span under study is divided between the Early Ottoman period (ca. late 15th – 17th century) and the Late Ottoman period (ca. 18th–19th century). Furthermore, the finds from both periods are discussed from a cultural and social perspective, with the focus on eating and drinking manners in Athens under Ottoman rule. Some pottery types are presented here in detail, as their characteristics, production, and distribution make them key to understanding the Ottoman period archaeologically. At the end, a catalogue provides in-depth information for each pottery fragment discussed.

The Athenian Agora

Over the past years I have worked in the Athenian Agora with a small research team on the identification, dating, and documentation of the material culture (specifically ceramic finds) of Byzantine, Latin, and Ottoman times. For this essay, only a few Ottoman examples from the Agora Excavations were chosen, in particular tableware from the older excavations, as most of the time these were simply the pieces that were kept. These excavations took place over the past 85 years, but the majority of the Byzantine, medieval, and Ottoman finds remained unstudied, thus posing greater challenges in their study. Nevertheless, examination of the ceramic finds from the Agora Excavations has much potential for further research. My aim here, therefore, is to present some of our preliminary results concerning the cultural and social conditions of this Athenian material in Ottoman times.

The narrative of Byzantine, Latin, and Ottoman Athens has so far been a succession of brief prosperous periods followed by long times of abandonment, political instability, and poor living conditions, compared to the glorious city of Classical and Roman times. The nearly 400 years of Ottoman Athens are symbolized by two mosques on the Acropolis: the first one inaugurated in place of the church into which the Parthenon was converted in Early Ottoman times, and a second, smaller mosque newly built inside the ruined Parthenon during the Late Ottoman period.

Excavations in the Athenian Agora by the American School of Classical Studies at Athens started in 1931 under the supervision of Professor T. Leslie Shear. The area in question covers some 10 ha and was occupied by 365 modern houses, all of which had to be purchased and demolished. The excavations in the

---

³ This project was awarded a major research grant by the Netherlands Organisation of Scientific Research [NWO] for the years 2010–2015 and currently runs at the Faculty of Archaeology of Leiden University. For this project, I have chosen to study in greater detail the material culture from four urban sites distinguished by their geographical location, long history of occupation, and the variety of socio-economic and political phenomena that they experienced. Two, Athens and Ephesus, are urban centers situated in the core region of the Byzantine and Ottoman Empires, one on the west coast of the Aegean, the other on the east coast. The other two sites are located on the periphery of both empires. Butrint in the western Balkans was affected by its proximity to medieval Italy, while also participating in the economic and political networks that interconnected the western Balkans. Tarsus, on the other hand, became a crossroads of Byzantine, Arab, and Crusader cultures, and the material from the excavations highlights the cross-cultural interaction between the Christian and Islamic worlds. For more information, see https://www.universiteitleiden.nl/en/research/research-projects/archaeology/data-atlas-of-byzantine-and-ottoman-material-culture-archiving-medieval-and-post-medieval-archaeological-fieldwork-data-from-the-eastern-mediterranean-600-2000.

⁴ See Karidis 2014, figs. II.1–3; Camp 2001, pp. 239–244.

Athenian Agora were recorded in three separate sets of notebooks: the field notebooks, the pottery notebooks, and the find notebooks. In addition to these notebooks, a card catalogue system has been used since the beginning of the excavations to record the important information related to inventoried objects—it is good to know that all this has now been digitized. Furthermore, the photographic archive contains over 300,000 images documenting the excavations and catalogued objects.[5]

A plan of the Athenian Agora (divided into sections designated by letters and numbers) shows an overview of all the Ottoman-period wells, pits, cisterns, and cesspools that were excavated by the American team over the previous 80 years (Fig. 1).[6] The upper Post-Byzantine levels of the Agora were largely disturbed and did not yield a clear stratigraphy or context; any remaining buildings present in the Agora were demolished in the 1930s to enable the excavations (as seen above).

In past years my Leiden team and I have focused on the study of the Agora material dating from Byzantine to Ottoman times, a period poorly understood and mostly understudied in Athens. Our research has been carried out in combination with a study of the organization and use of space and the function of buildings by using distribution maps, old photographs, and 3D models.[7] Although our work is still underway, we can already see evidence for different types of activities, including habitation, industry, and public space outside the Late Roman wall. We are also discovering great differences in the type and intensity of occupation in different sections of the Agora in each period. These differences argue against the idea of a uniform pattern of occupation characterizing the entire area of Athens over the course of 13 centuries.

We employ a multidisciplinary approach in our research that combines the examination of archaeological artifacts, written sources, and pictorial evidence as sources of information. Material culture is of course the focal point of our research. In addition, textual sources together with contemporary dining scenes in art can play an important role in understanding the function of excavated material. We would like to construct a conceptual framework for answering questions about Byzantine, Frankish, and Ottoman material culture.[8] Emphasis is placed on the study of ceramics as indicators of production and consumption patterns, of economic conditions, and of social change. Promoting the use of pottery beyond simply being a dating tool, we explore changes in the shape, use, and distribution of ceramics in relation to socio-economic developments.

In order to make sense of thousands of sherds of different fabric, shape, decoration, function, and provenance that come from four different sites and span more than 13 centuries of use, we have systematically recorded everything in our database, which was designed specifically for the needs of this project. The database is also connected to ArcGIS software, which allows us to create distribution maps of ceramics and study the location of pottery in relation to the location of other artifacts.

These spatial distribution maps are not only useful for displaying the location of artifacts, but can also highlight the find spots of pottery with different characteristics in terms of shape, chronology, function, and provenance. This type of analysis helps us to understand changes in the types and locations of activities, and periods of use for the various areas within a site. It also allows us to follow processes of spatial organization, site formation, and site development in the medieval and post-medieval periods.

---

[5] All the excavated material is stored in the Stoa of Attalos. This two-story building with double colonnade, originally built by King Attalos II of Pergamon in the 2nd century B.C., was restored in the 1950s when it was chosen to serve as the museum of the Athenian Agora. Both floors are given over to public display of sculpture, marbles, pottery, and small objects ranging from ca. 3000 B.C. to A.D. 1500. I would like to thank Jan Jordan, Sylvie Dumont, and Pia Kvärnström for their help in the Agora offices and storage rooms.
[6] I wish to thank my post-doctoral researcher, Dr. E. Tzavella, for help with making the maps in Figures 1–2.
[7] Vroom 2013a; Vroom and Boswinkel 2019.
[8] For such a research approach, see Vroom 2000, 2003.

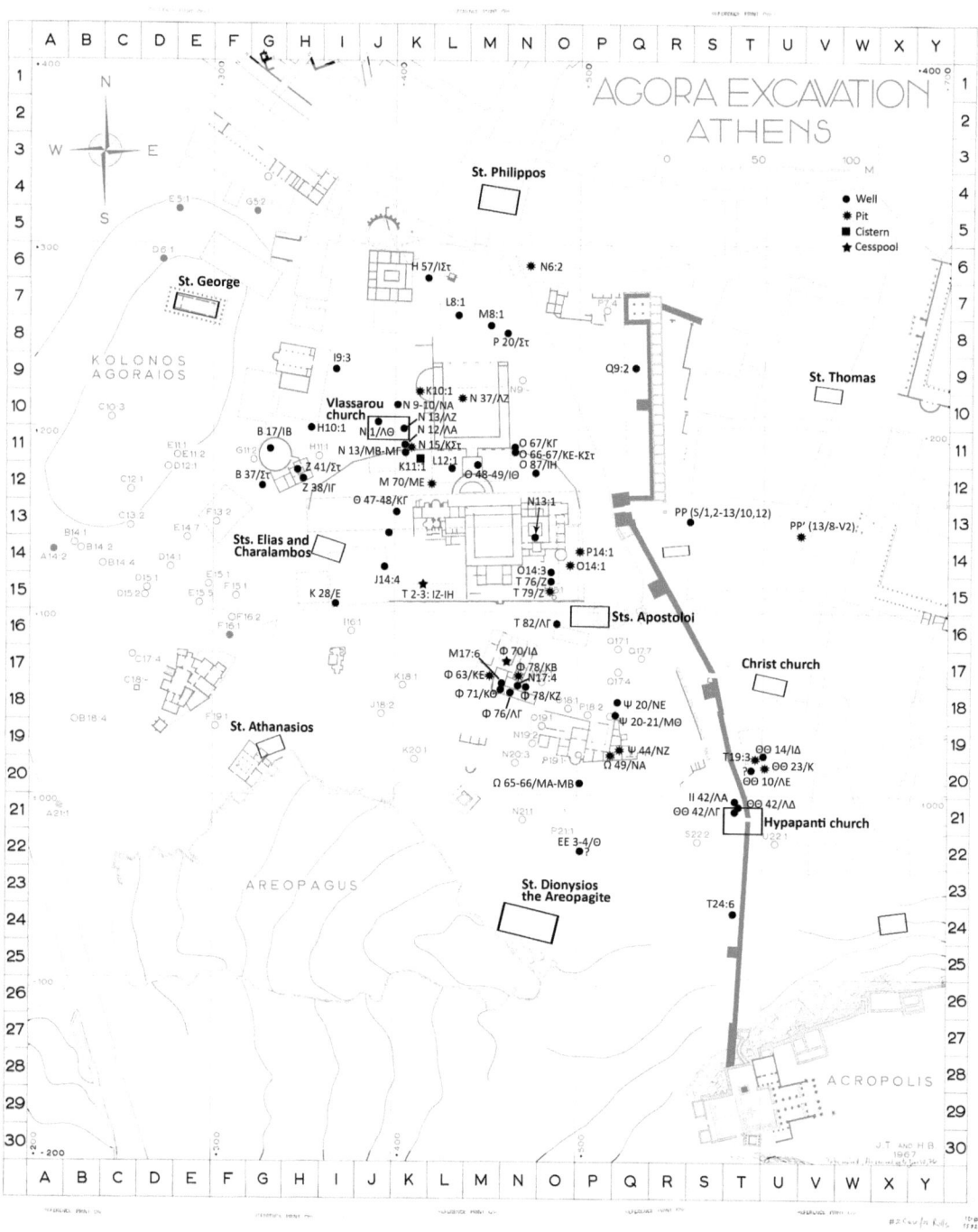

Figure 1. Map of the Athenian Agora with Ottoman contexts. Drawing J. Vroom and E. Tzavella. American School of Classical Studies at Athens, Agora Excavations.

Finds of the Early Ottoman Period (ca. Late 15th – 17th Century)

Although the archaeology of Ottoman-period Athens is still in its infancy, the finds from the Agora Excavations are interesting enough in their own right to merit more detailed study. For example, towards the end of the 15th century and during the 16th, a range of new ceramic products appeared in Athens, of which the most notable are tin-glazed maiolica from Italy and Iznik ware from Turkey (**3, 9**).[9] They were the result of improved pottery technology (using an innovative glaze or fabric, such as fritware) and were apparently designed specifically for meals and for display purposes.

An abundance of these imported glazed wares has been found in various excavated Ottoman contexts in the Agora, as can be seen on the map with only the Ottoman wells (Fig. 2). The wells are labeled in two different ways: either with a deposit number (e.g., N13:1) or, if they lack a deposit number, with the section letter and grid number (e.g., N12–13/MA). In addition, similarly widespread access to these imported upmarket glazed wares, which must have been relatively expensive (because tin was not cheap), can be distinguished at rural Greek sites during this same period.[10]

In the Athenian Agora we have recognized products from western Europe in the Ottoman wells, among them a jug of polychrome painted maiolica from Italy (Figs. 9a–c). Its surface is covered with a tin glaze providing a foundation for the painted designs. Because of its fabric, glaze, and painted colors, the jug shown is clearly an Italian import. This type of *maiolica rinascimentale* can generally be dated to the mid- to late 16th century and probably originates from workshops in Faenza (Emilia Romagna). Such imports could have been purchased from traveling peddlers, or in regional market towns and at periodic fairs.[11]

On the other hand, two vessels show that there were imports from Turkey in the Ottoman contexts of the Agora Excavations (Figs. 15a–16b). Among them is a painted 17th-century Iznik ware plate (**9**). The name refers to the pottery production center at Iznik, which functioned mainly in Ottoman times. From the 1470s this distinctly new type of glazed ware began to be produced in north-western Turkey, strongly influenced by Chinese porcelain. Investigations at Iznik have produced evidence for the production of the ware, but Kütahya has also been mentioned as a manufacturing center for similar-looking fritware. Imitations of Iznik ware were moreover made at other Ottoman production centers, as shown by an 18th-century jug (**10**) from the Agora Excavations that was probably manufactured in Istanbul or Kütahya.

A new shape in the glazed tableware repertoire of the 16th and 17th centuries was the large flanged dish with expanded flat rim, sometimes with notches or pie-crust decoration on the lip.[12] These vessels are often monochrome glazed with one color (green, brown, or yellow) in the glaze, although decorated examples in a sgraffito (incised) style also exist (**2**). The proportion of glazed wares at the Saraçhane Excavations in Istanbul, for example, increased substantially during the Ottoman period to around 35–40% of the finds in early Turkish contexts, rising further to 60–80% in the 18th and 19th centuries, when glazed wares became predominant.[13] A similar increase in glazed wares (rising to 32% and 34%, respectively) is visible at Greek sites during the Ottoman and early modern periods.[14]

---

[9] The term "maiolica" is used here to designate painted tin-glazed earthenware from various Renaissance production centers in Italy. In the previous (Late medieval/Latin) period in the Agora, there were more ceramic imports from the West: see Vroom and Tzavella 2017. Numbers in bold refer to the catalogue numbers; see herein, pp. 197–212.
[10] See Vroom 1998a, p. 543; Vroom 2003, p. 287 and table 10.5, for the steadily growing numbers of imported ceramics on rural Boeotian sites in Ottoman times.
[11] Vroom 2003, pp. 255–257.
[12] Vroom 2003, figs. 6.34–36; Vroom 2005, pp. 150–151.
[13] Hayes 1992, p. 233.
[14] See also Vroom 2003, table 7.6, for an increase in glazed products on Boeotian rural sites.

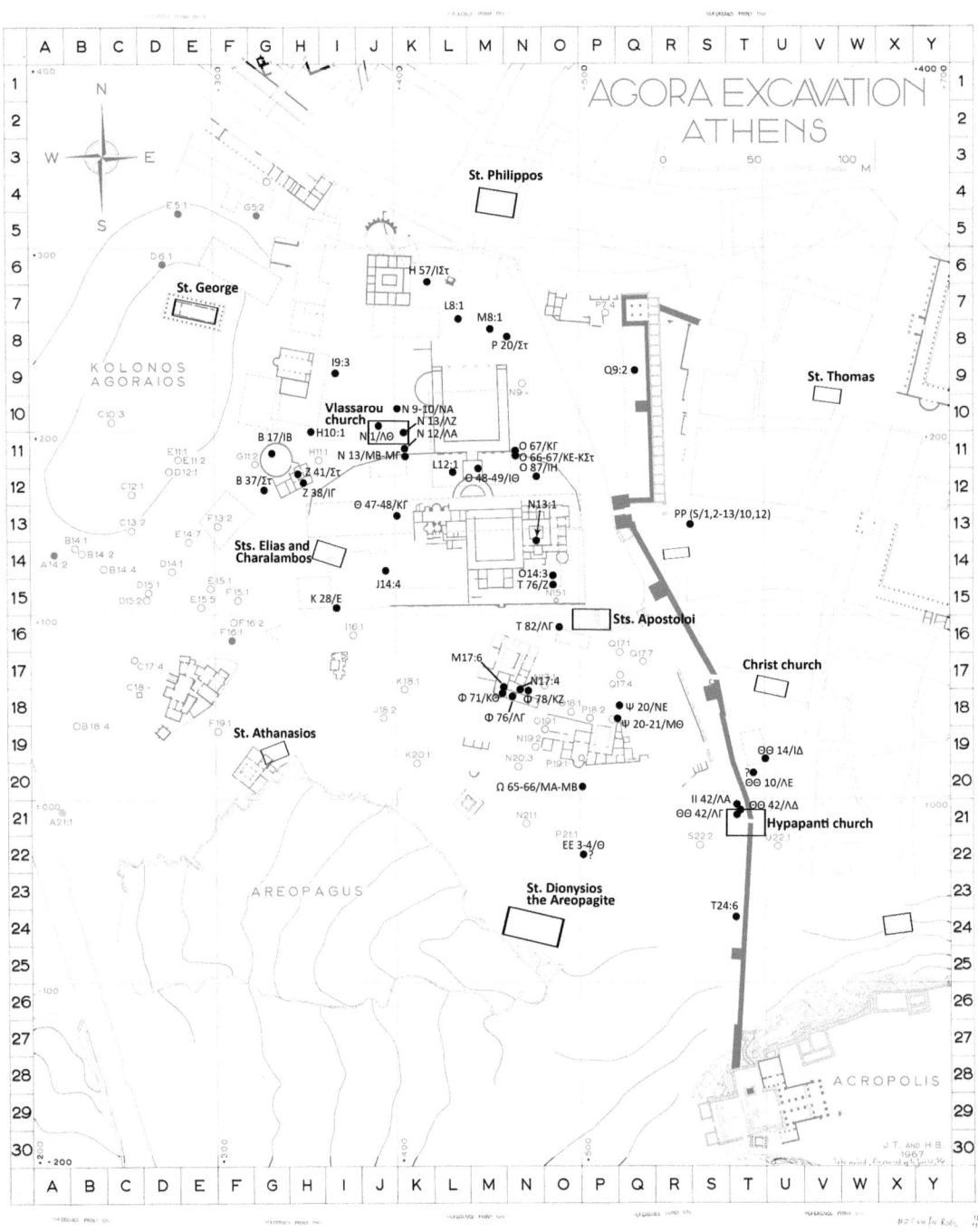

Figure 2. Map of the Athenian Agora with Ottoman wells only. Drawing J. Vroom and E. Tzavella. American School of Classical Studies at Athens, Agora Excavations.

The diameter of the rim of these Early Ottoman glazed dishes varies from 24 to 32 cm, and the increase in average rim width in comparison with glazed bowls of the previous Late Byzantine/Frankish period (17–20 cm) is obvious.[15] These wide dishes were perfect containers for the "Eastern style" of eating, in which a specific dining area and stools or chairs are absent and the diners characteristically sit on the floor around a low, round table [*sini*] eating with their hands from a centrally placed communal vessel shared by all.[16] Such larger dishes may have been used in Ottoman times for preparations containing a lot of fat or oil or for soup, which in the 16th century was one of the most common dishes in the Ottoman Empire.[17] These liquid mixtures were probably eaten from a communal dish into which everybody sitting around dipped his or her spoon.[18]

In Athens, the appearance of these Italian and Turkish imports gave a new impetus to the manufacture of local pottery types (such as Greek imitation maiolica), to new pottery shapes, colors, and painted decorative styles (**4–8**), as well as to incised decorative styles of previous traditions (**2–3**). Innovations were, for instance, the suddenly increased use of trefoil-mouth jugs and spouted jugs (so-called *ibriks*).[19] These jugs became popular in unglazed, plain glazed, painted, and sgraffito forms, but their shapes varied little (**7–8**). They may have been used for serving or pouring liquids, such as water, diluted yoghurt, or sherbets made of fruit juices, known as traditional drinks in Ottoman times.[20] The spouted jug could also have been used for carrying and storing water, or for pouring water into a basin during the hand-washing ceremony before and after meals or for other sanitary reasons.[21]

Italian maiolica imports were definitely imitated in Athens in Early Ottoman times. In the Agora, this type of locally made imitation maiolica was recovered near three excavated kilns of the Early Ottoman period and was first described by Alison Frantz as "blue and white painted ware."[22] Although Frantz presented the Agora material in 1942 with tentative dating suggestions, she proposed that a *terminus ante quem* for the manufacture of this locally made ware (as well as evidence of its Athenian origin) is provided by two potter's kilns (including wasters and tripod stilts) under the paving of the church of Vlassarou.[23] Since this church was seen by Jacob Spon in 1675, Frantz concluded that the latest possible occurrence of this ware must have been the first half of the 17th century.[24]

Apart from locally made imitation maiolica with painted designs, such as the dish with a painted bird (**6**), we can also distinguish a later variant of sgraffito ware that was made locally in Athens in Early Ottoman times (**2**).[25] The polychrome decorated wares of this period have exterior as well as interior designs, often based on spirals and winding lines. The "visual performance" value of the colorful designs must have been significant.[26] We know, for instance, that traditional households

---

[15] Vroom 2003, table 7.3.
[16] Vroom 2003, pp. 335–357, figs. 12.3–5 and table 12.5, matched by pottery assemblages of the same period (Wares 29, 31 and 32).
[17] Babinger 1923, p. 123 (Hans Dernschwam's 1553–1555 travel diary).
[18] Vroom 2000, pp. 209–211; Vroom 2003, p. 349, figs. 12.4–12.5; Vroom 2011, p. 150 and fig. 7.
[19] E.g., Vroom 2005, pp. 176–177 and fig. TUR/VEN 16.2; Vroom 2007a, pp. 323–324, pl. 7c–f.
[20] Scarce 1996, p. 89.
[21] Vroom 2006b.
[22] Frantz 1942, p. 1; for more information on these kilns, see MacKay 2015, pp. 273–277, concerning kilns from section O58:ΚΓ, section N12:ΛΛ–ΛΓ, and section N1–15:ΛΛ–ΛΒ.
[23] Frantz 1942, p. 2. This is not strange, because artisans' workshops in the Stoa of Attalos area can be identified in an early 19th-century engraving by Edward Dodwell; cf. Karidis 2014, fig. II.19. In the meantime, samples of wasters and tripod stilts from two Ottoman-period kilns in the Agora have been taken by J. Vroom and Y. Waksman for further chemical analyses of their provenance.
[24] Spon 1678, p. 331; Frantz 1942, p. 2.
[25] For more examples of this style found in Athens, see Papanikola-Bakirtzi 1999, pp. 100–101, nos. 115–116.

on the Greek islands often had highly decorated wares arranged on wall shelves or mantelpieces to ornament the house and as a display of status, but also used for special occasions.[27]

The repertoire of domestic pottery used in Ottoman Athens differed in significant ways from its Late Byzantine/Frankish predecessors.[28] One of the most striking new features was the total disappearance of large amphorae (ceramic containers for the transport and storage of oil and wine), which were probably replaced by wooden barrels.[29] Noteworthy was also the replacement of thin-walled, unglazed cooking pots by lead-glazed types. The glazes on the locally produced utilitarian wares were generally dark-toned and applied directly to the body clay (though white slip is present on some wares). Decoration was uncommon on these domestic wares; the reasons for glazing were mainly functional, including impermeability and easier cleaning of the pot.[30]

The widespread household practice of using ceramic vessels (for example, in the kitchen as well as on the table) was gradually superseded by a preference for metal pots and dishes.[31] Particularly from the 17th century onward, the demand for ceramic wares (often locally produced) decreased, as non-ceramic materials, such as metal, which is more durable and recyclable, began to be used more often for vessels.[32] Consequently, the role of "missing artifacts" made of silver, pewter, iron, bronze, and wood must be borne in mind when considering the full range of shapes, quantities, and behavioral patterning evident in ceramic assemblages.[33]

1. Polychrome Sgraffito Ware (1)

Ceramic products from northern Italy with incised decoration and added painted colors have sometimes been described in publications as "incised slipwares" [*graffita arcaica*][34] or "North-eastern Italian Painted Sgraffito."[35] This dish found in a well near a burnt building (excavated in 1935 in the Athenian Agora) seems to belong to a more developed style of polychrome sgraffito ware,[36] which is also known in Italy as *graffita arcaica tardiva* and *graffita rinascimentale* (1).[37]

The fabric of the Agora dish is soft, fine, and orange-buff in color (2.5 YR 6/8 to 5 YR 7/6).[38] A white slip covers the interior and exterior surfaces of the open vessel. The incised motifs are enhanced with alternating yellow, brown, green, and blue colors, which tend to run into the transparent lead glaze, so that the washy effect of the color contrasts with the incised design and the orange-buff clay beneath. The outside is covered with a brown color lead glaze.

---

[26] Mills 1999, pp. 112–113.
[27] Vroom 2003, fig. 3.15; Vroom 2005, fig. 13.
[28] See Vroom and Tzavella 2017.
[29] In an early 19th-century drawing in the Eugène Peytier Album, a wooden barrel in an Athenian street can be recognized next to unglazed ceramic jugs used for collecting water; cf. Karidis 2014, fig. II.21.
[30] Vroom 2003, pp. 266–267.
[31] This new cooking trend began in some areas in Europe already before the mid-14th century; cf. Vroom 2003, p. 287. For the growing use of metal dishes on the Ottoman table, see Vroom 2011, fig. 6.
[32] Vroom 2003, p. 287.
[33] Vroom 1998a, p. 541; Vroom 2003, p. 234. See also Vroom 1998b, p. 153, fig. 15, for the display of metal and wooden domestic utensils common in Greek folklore museums.
[34] Cf. Blake 1986.
[35] Gregory 1993, pp. 299–302.
[36] The term "sgraffito" derives from the Italian word *sgraffiare* [to scratch].
[37] Cf. Magnani and Munarini 1998.
[38] The colors of the fabrics are described according to the classification of the *Munsell Soil Color Charts* (1979 edition) in natural light (e.g. 5 YR 6/6 for orange). The colors of the decorations that fall outside the range of the *Munsell Soil Charts* are described according to the *Pantone Matching System* [PMS]; cf. *Pantone Color Formula Guide 747XR* (Moonachie, N.J., 1989).

Common shapes are dishes and bowls with straight plain rims and round lips or with flanged rims. The bases, concave underneath, have ring feet. In general, the decoration of this pottery type consists of elaborate designs of a vegetal and geometric character, such as bands of foliage in combination with a portrait bust. Animals and portrait busts were indeed in fashion by the Early Ottoman period.[39] We note, in the interior of this dish, a human figure with a pointed cap and beard, seated between two spiral fluted columns. The figure has previously been described as a doge because he resembles an unidentified Venetian doge portrayed on a coin found in the Agora.[40] It has been suggested that this image might reflect "trade relations in that time of Athenian merchants with Venice," as Venetian archives show wealthy Athenians vigorously involved in commercial transactions with La Serenissima in Early Ottoman times.[41]

At first glance, the Athenian dish seems to show the distinctive polychrome sgraffito style of the Veneto region and the Lower Po Valley, dating from the 2nd half of the 15th century and the beginning of the 16th.[42] Especially in the late 15th and early 16th centuries, these sgraffito wares, copying Near Eastern and eastern Mediterranean prototypes, were widely produced in northern Italy.[43] When looking at the incised and painted style of decoration in a photograph, I—like Alison Frantz—first assumed that this vessel could be a product of northern Italy; but when I actually had the piece in my hands, I realized that its fabric is not northern Italian but rather of local provenance. In fact, it looks very similar to the fabric of locally made vessels originating from Ottoman kilns recovered in the Athenian Agora.[44] We may conclude that this dish is a local product imitating the 16th-century sgraffito style from northern Italy. Another example of this local "Italian influenced" polychrome sgraffito ware (with similar fabric) appears to be in the Historical Museum of Crete in Heraklion.[45]

2. Local Polychrome Sgraffito Ware (2)

This group can be classified as a later variant of polychrome sgraffito ware (containing brown and green colors) of the Late Byzantine/Frankish period.[46]

The fabric is generally fine and dull orange (5 YR 7/6) in color. It is coated with a transparent or colored lead glaze over a white slip, through which a decorative incised fish is engraved. The white slip, glaze, and incised decoration of these open vessels appear mostly on the interior, merely overlapping onto the rim. The rest of the exterior surface is either unglazed or glazed in green. Scars of tripod stilts can be seen on the vessel's interior.

The engraved decoration on the inside and outside may be enhanced by yellow-brown and green brushstrokes. Iron oxide is used for the yellow-brown, and copper oxide for the green. The incised designs consist of spiral and rosette motifs created by winding lines.[47] Straight or undulating lines, sometimes alternating with pairs of winding lines, can also be discerned. Shapes include large shallow dishes with a ring foot and a broad horizontal rim that forms a ridge where it joins the body.[48]

---

[39] Vroom 2005, pp. 142–143, fig. TUR/VEN 2.2.
[40] Frantz 1961, figs. 62–63.
[41] Karidis 2014, p. 30, n. 175 and fig. I.8.
[42] For a similar decorative technique, see Munarini and Banzato 1993, pp. 99 and 273, cat. no. 244 (beginning of the 16th century, from the Veneto region).
[43] Frantz 1942, p. 17, referring to Arthur Lane's suggestion that the dish might come from one of the factories in Padua; Vroom 2013a, p. 104, fig. 10.
[44] See nn. 23–24 above.
[45] Borboudaki 2007, pp. 98–99, no. 59; see also MacKay 1996, pp. 128–132, for other 15th- to 16th-century ceramic finds on Crete.
[46] Vroom 2005, pp. 144–145.
[47] Borboudaki 2007, pp. 36–42.
[48] Papanikola-Bakirtzi 1999, no. 293.

Because of the fabric, we are dealing here with a local product that was manufactured in one of the three Ottoman pottery kilns recovered in the Agora (**2**).[49] The distinction between local production and imported polychrome sgraffito ware from Italy is not always easy to make yet, because of the flourishing trade in ceramics in the eastern Mediterranean during this period.

3. Maiolica from Italy (3)

This group includes a jug of polychrome painted maiolica from Italy (**3**). The term maiolica is used here as a designation for painted tin-glazed earthenware from various Renaissance production centers in Italy (e.g., Faenza, Deruta, Montelupo).[50] Tin-glazed pottery had its origin in the 9th century in the Near East, from where it spread through the Islamic world to Spain. The word may be derived from Maiolica, the medieval name for the Spanish island of Majorca, which functioned as a major intermediary between the Spanish-Moorish pottery industry in Valencia and Italy.[51] Alternatively it may have been a corruption of the Spanish name for lusterware, *obra de málequa* [Malaga ware].[52]

The fabric of the piece pictured here is soft and fine, with a few lime and sand inclusions. The clay color is generally whitish to pale yellow (2.5 Y 8/3). Its surface is covered with a tin glaze (10 Y 8/3) that provides the foundation for painted designs in dark blue, light blue, green, and yellow. The jug is, for reasons of economy, lead-glazed only on the interior, which gives the white fabric a light bluish tinge. Shapes in the maiolica repertoire seem to be confined to dishes, bowls, and jugs, the last often with flat bases and trefoil spouts.

The majority of the maiolica finds in Greece consists of fragments with painted "ladder-design medallions" in blue.[53] This type of painted decoration is common on Italian maiolica jugs of the so-called *stile severo* from northern Italy (especially from Faenza), but a more simplified version can also be seen on some locally made 16th-century vessels found during the Agora Excavations in Athens.[54] Italian maiolica fragments with a painted "ladder-design medallion" were, for instance, found at six Boeotian sites.[55]

Because of its fabric, glaze, and painted colors, the jug included in this group is clearly an Italian import. This type of *maiolica rinascimentale* probably originates from Faenza and can generally be dated to the mid- to late 16th century.

4. Imitation Maiolica from Athens (4–8)

Italian maiolica imports with blue and white painted decoration were imitated locally in Athens in the Early Ottoman period (**4–8**).[56] During the Athenian Agora Excavations, a type of locally made tin-glazed imitation maiolica first described by Alison Frantz as "blue and white painted ware" was recovered near an Ottoman kiln.[57]

---

[49] See nn. 23–24 above.
[50] See, in general, Wilson 1987, 1989; Poole 1997.
[51] Wilson 1987, p. 28.
[52] Poole 1997, p. 1.
[53] Cf. Vroom 1998a, pp. 531–534; Vroom 2005, pp. 146–147.
[54] Frantz 1942, fig. 5.
[55] Vroom 2003, fig. 6.32: W27.1–7.
[56] Vroom 2005, pp. 148–149.
[57] Frantz 1942, p. 1; see also MacKay 2015.

The fabric is soft, of a medium fineness and pinkish/orange-buff (5 YR 7/4 to 7/6) in color. The glaze, covering a white slip, looks rather dirty white to light green in color.[58] A poorer-quality lead glaze can often be observed on the outside of open vessels. Sometimes the insides of jugs are left unglazed. Both are due to the fact that these expedients were cheaper than using tin or lead glaze all over.

The designs are painted in blue (10 BG 5/1 or PMS 301 U) on a white slip; accessory details are in reddish brown (5 YR 4/6), green (PMS 348/370), or purple (5 R 4/1). The most frequent decorative motifs in the Agora collection are birds, rosettes, and cross-hatchings. The "ladder-design medallions" are painted in a simpler and cruder version than on the Italian original products: the lines are smaller, and spirals and reddish brown dots appear outside the "ladder-design medallion."[59] The most characteristic shapes are small bowls, bowls, dishes, and trefoil-spouted jugs.[60]

Fragments of this type of pottery were also recovered during recent excavations in the eastern part of the peristyle of the Roman Agora at Athens, as well as during earlier excavations at Corinth and at Thebes.[61] Smaller sherds of this type of maiolica from Athens were furthermore found at eight Boeotian sites.[62]

5. Iznik Ware (9–10)

The name refers to the Ottoman pottery production center at Iznik (ancient Nicaea, in north-western Turkey), located about 96.5 km south-east of Istanbul, on the Asian side of the Bosporus.[63]

The fabric of this pottery type is a white body of a fine, hard, and opaque consistency (5 YR 6/3), composed of silica (from sand or quartz), white clay, and lead-rich glass frit. The vessel is covered inside and out with a fine white slip (PMS 9181) that was used as a ground for the painted decoration. The lead glaze, with small additions of tin and alkaline, is colorless and fuses completely with the clay to form a continuous mass. The compact white body sometimes gives the same impression as porcelain.

A three-phase classification has been suggested by John Hayes for this Turkish fine ware, largely on the basis of the decorative color schemes: I. "Abraham of Kütahya Ware," with blue and white patterns only (ca. 1480/90–1525/30); II. "Damascus Ware," in a variety of colors, except red (ca. 1525–1560); III. "Rhodian Ware," with red, green, and blue decoration outlined in black (ca. 1555–1700) (**9**). According to Hayes, the chronology of these phases has been established for the Saraçhane finds in Istanbul on the basis of actual dated specimens and tiles from dated buildings, along with some supporting literary references.[64]

From the 1470s this distinctly new type of tin-glazed ware began to be produced in Turkey, strongly influenced by Chinese porcelain. Investigations at Iznik have uncovered evidence for the production of the ware, but Kütahya has also been mentioned as a manufacturing center for fritware.[65]

---

[58] MacKay (2015, p. 282) says that initial research on the glaze of these locally made vessels using a handheld portable X-ray fluorescence (pXRF) analyzer seems to indicate that no tin is present in the lead glaze. This will be further investigated in samples taken by J. Vroom, V. Kilikoglou, A. Hein, and A. Panagopoulou for XRF and XRD analyses of the fabrics, slips, and glazes of this local pottery type, and as well as in samples taken by J. Vroom and Y. Waksman for WD-XRF analyses of chemical composition.
[59] Borboudaki 2007, pp. 60–72; Vroom 2005, fig. TUR/VEN 5.4.; Vroom 2007b, pp. 75–76, fig. 4.4.
[60] Korre-Zographou 1995, fig. 84; Vroom 2005, pp. 148–149; Borboudaki 2007, pp. 60–73.
[61] For the excavations in the Roman Agora at Athens, see Tsoniotis 2013, fig. 24, and Tsoniotis 2014, fig. 16; for Corinth and Thebes, see *Corinth* XI, fig. 153 below right; Armstrong 1993, p. 319, nos. 201–203, and p. 324, nos. 268, 271–272; Vroom 2006a, figs. 27–28.
[62] Vroom 2003, figs. 6.33 and 6.44: W28.1–7; W28.Ex.
[63] Korre-Zographou 1995, pp. 49–62; Vroom 2005, pp. 158–161; Vroom 2011, pp. 154–156.
[64] Hayes 1992, p. 245.
[65] Carswell 1998, p. 88; Vroom 2005, pp. 158–161; Borboudaki 2007, pp. 138–156.

Before the mid-17th century, Iznik vessels and tiles circulated widely throughout the Ottoman Empire and beyond.[66] At Corinth, for instance, two Iznik fragments were found in the post-Frankish levels of the 1991 excavations and dated to the middle of the second half of the 16th century.[67] At Thebes, fragments of Iznik ware were recovered in some rubbish pits during an excavation in the historic center.[68]

In the 17th century, the Iznik style did continue, but the quality of both the colors and the glaze deteriorated markedly. Some colors are gone or tend to be pale (the red color has lost its luster and can look maroon), while the glaze is poor and more matt. In addition, imitations were made at other Ottoman production centers, such as Istanbul and Kütahya (**10**).

Finds of the Late Ottoman Period (ca. 18th–19th Century)

Let us now move to ceramic finds of the Late Ottoman period (ca. 18th–19th century). Towards the end of the Ottoman period (probably in the 18th century), a new type of glazed tableware made its way to Greece. The type appears mostly in the form of thinly potted small cups made of a fine, buff-colored fabric that were manufactured in Kütahya in north-western Turkey. Their polychrome painted designs, executed in blue, green, red, purple, and yellow, were usually geometric, floral, or figural (**11–15**). This tableware from Kütahya was strongly influenced by Chinese porcelain and is therefore sometimes described as a cheap substitute for real porcelain or as "peasant-porcelain."[69]

A handful of late 18th- and 19th-century decorated Kütahya ware vessels was found in and around the central part of the Athenian Agora, as well as among the refuse in various Ottoman pits, wells, and pithoi (large storage jars). The most common shapes were delicately painted coffee cups, sometimes found with matching saucers. The small cups (the so-called *filcan* or *fincan*, a word of Persian origin) are clearly related to the spread of coffee consumption, and their shape was probably derived from that of porcelain coffee cups made in Vienna and Meissen (Germany) about 1730–1740.[70] A more detailed distribution of these coffee cups in the Agora (especially in and around the so-called "Late Roman Palace" and near the demolished church of Vlassarou) can be seen in a map (Fig. 3), confirming that coffee was consumed on this spot from the 18th century onwards.

After dinner, the diners in well-to-do Athenian households washed their hands and drank a cup of coffee, which aided the digestion. The coffee was served in decorative coffee cups, of porcelain or of Kütahya ware, which were very popular among members of the 18th-century Ottoman elite. The Irish painter Edward Dodwell noted that strong, thick coffee, without sugar, was handed round after dinner: "The cup is not placed in a saucer, but in another cup of metal, which the Turks call '*zarf*', and which defends the fingers from being burnt; for the coffee is served up and drank as hot as possible."[71] In addition, water and sherbets were the only other drinks offered during or after the meal.

---

[66] Hayes 1992, pp. 244–247, with further literature; Vroom 2011, pp. 160–165.
[67] Williams and Zervos 1992, 172, no. 41, pl. 44; see also *Corinth* XI, fig. 153, for more Iznik ware finds in Corinth.
[68] Vroom 2006a, figs. 8–9, 17–18 and 45–46; Vroom 2007b, fig. 4.12.
[69] Lane 1957, p. 65.
[70] Lane 1939, p. 236, 1957, p. 65; in general, see Vroom 1996 for the spread of coffee drinking in the Ottoman Empire.
[71] Dodwell 1819, vol. 1, p. 157.

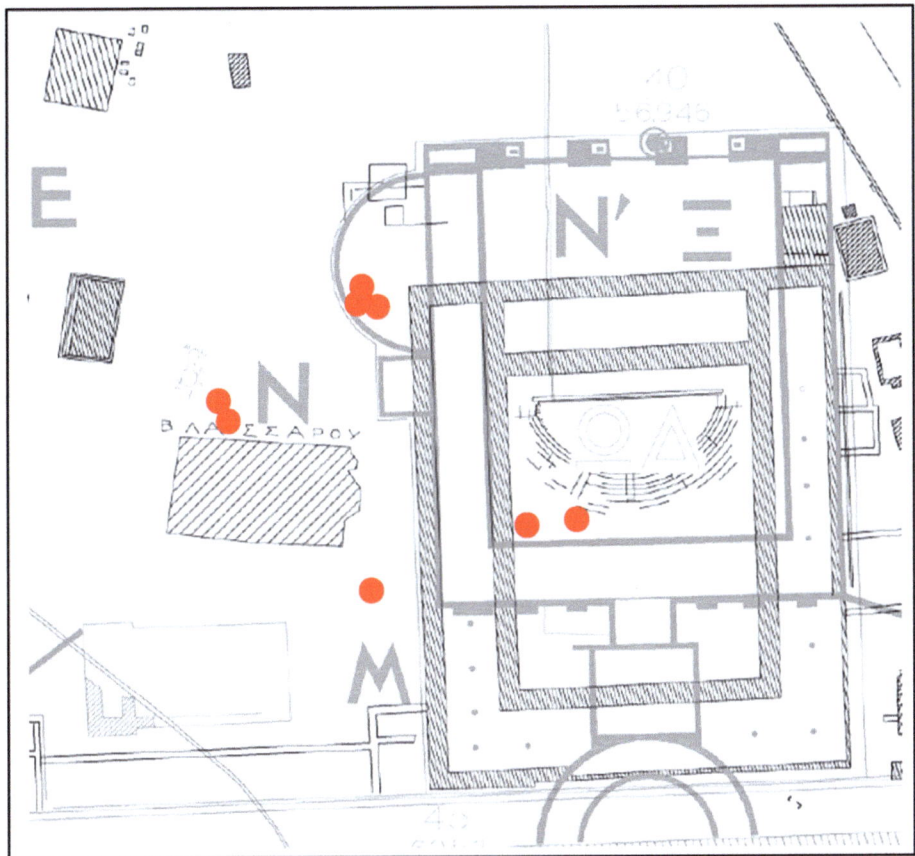

Figure 3. Map of the Athenian Agora with finds of Kütahya ware. Drawing J. Vroom and K. Berghuis. American School of Classical Studies at Athens, Agora Excavations.

The delicacy of the Kütahya cups suggests that they were probably made for intimate gatherings of the Ottoman affluent classes, as well as for more public use in coffee houses and bazaars (Fig. 4). In his traveler's account, Evliya Çelebi recorded at least 300 coffee houses and 500 coffee merchants in Istanbul alone, as well as the coffee cups found in the markets in Istanbul relative to the varying levels of prestige associated with the different types.[72] Imperial edicts were even issued against coffee houses, as these establishments often became places beyond government control for both Muslims and non-Muslims.[73]

Coffee drinking became a sort of national pastime all over the Ottoman Empire during the 18th century.[74] It was drunk not only in coffee houses, but also in the harem, the hammam, and at garden parties and picnics throughout the empire. In a late 18th-century engraving, the British

---

[72] Kut 1996; Baram 1999.
[73] Karababa and Ger 2011.
[74] Vroom 1996.

travelers Nicholas Revett, James Dawkins, and Robert Wood can be discerned studying the monument of Philopappos in Athens, while the janissary who escorts them prepares coffee on a tripod in the open air.[75]

While drinking their coffee, most guests would smoke a pipe in the chibouk style, that is, a long-stemmed Turkish tobacco pipe with a bowl.[76] The introduction of smoking in the Eastern style to Athens as indicated by finds of earthenware bowls of the so-called chibouk tobacco pipe in the Athenian Agora (16–21) is indeed noteworthy in this period.[77] This activity is also confirmed by various contemporary engravings by western travelers depicting people sitting in the streets of Ottoman Athens while smoking the chibouk pipe, among them the famous watercolor of the Athenian bazaar by Dodwell.[78]

A total of 76 chibouk pipe bowls and bowl fragments were excavated in the Athenian Agora, 58 of which could be satisfactorily dated. A little over half of the pipe bowls from the Agora were published by Rebecca Robinson in 1985. Several bowls were found in house fills towards the south, suggesting that tobacco was also enjoyed in domestic settings at the Agora.

A remarkable concentration of these fragments is observable in the northern section of the Agora, perhaps reflecting the consumption of tobacco in a more public context (Fig. 5). The dates of the bowl fragments from Athens vary, from the late 17th century to the 19th (Fig. 6). Their chronology shows that although tobacco was already being used in the Middle East at the beginning of the 17th century, it probably did not become really common in Athens before the late 17th century or the early 18th.

According to Dodwell, "The life of a Turkish gentleman consisted almost entirely of smoking tobacco, drinking coffee, and counting his beads. The former is indispensably necessary for his happiness."[79] Two centuries later, the Ottoman archaeologist Uzi Baram remarked that Kütahya coffee cups and chibouk tobacco pipes in the Ottoman Empire during the 17th and 18th centuries embodied "the new, the modern, the rebellion against the social order."[80] He suggests that by the end of the 19th

Figure 4. Miniature with a depiction of a coffee cup and saucer. Istanbul, Topkapı Palace Museum Library, H. 2164 (fol. 12a), early 18th century. Atasoy and Raby 1989, fig. 26, and Vroom 2003, fig. 12.15.

---

[75] Stuart and Revett 1794, vol. 3, ch. 5, pl. 1.
[76] D'Ohsson 1791, p. 87; Hobhouse 1813, p. 262; see also Gelichi and Sabbionesi 2014.
[77] Vroom 2003, fig. 6.46; on the history of Greek tobacco, see also Balta 2003a.
[78] The painting is in the Benaki Museum, Athens, and dates to ca. 1801–1805/6; see also Vroom 2003, fig. 8.11.
[79] Dodwell 1819, vol. 1, p. 152; see also "Commodities of Pleasure: Tobacco and Coffee in Athens:" http://www.bijleveldbooks.nl/ResearchSeminar/commodities-of-pleasure.html.
[80] Baram 1999, p. 151.

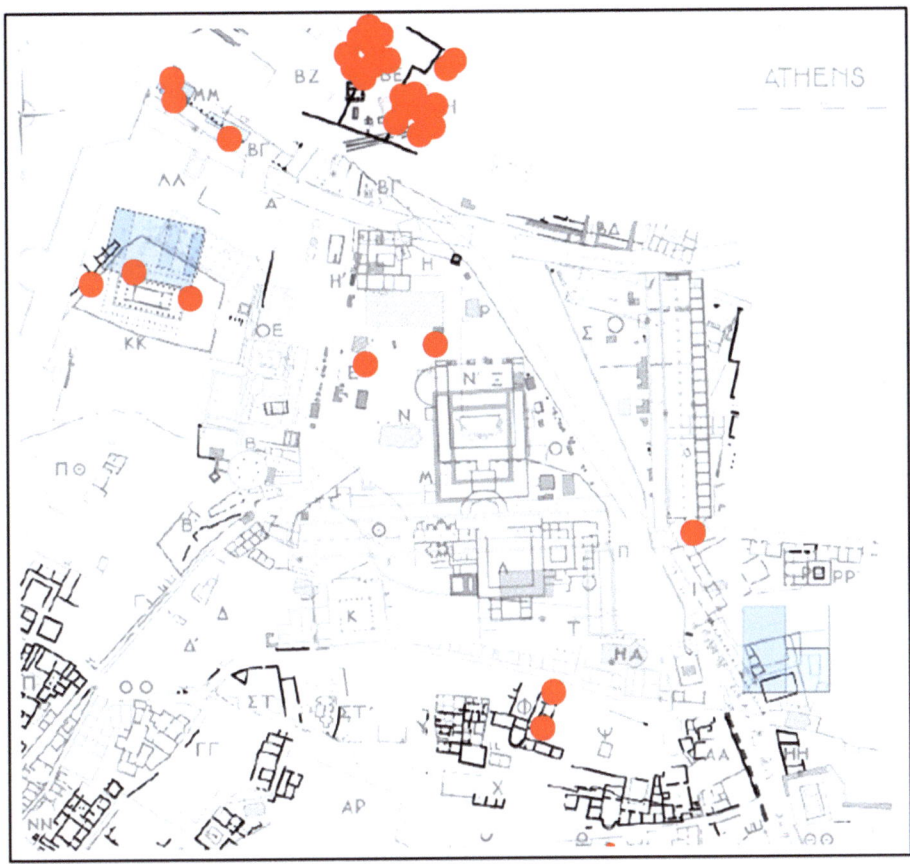

Figure 5. Map of the Athenian Agora with finds of tobacco pipes. Drawing J. Vroom and K. Berghuis. American School of Classical Studies at Athens, Agora Excavations.

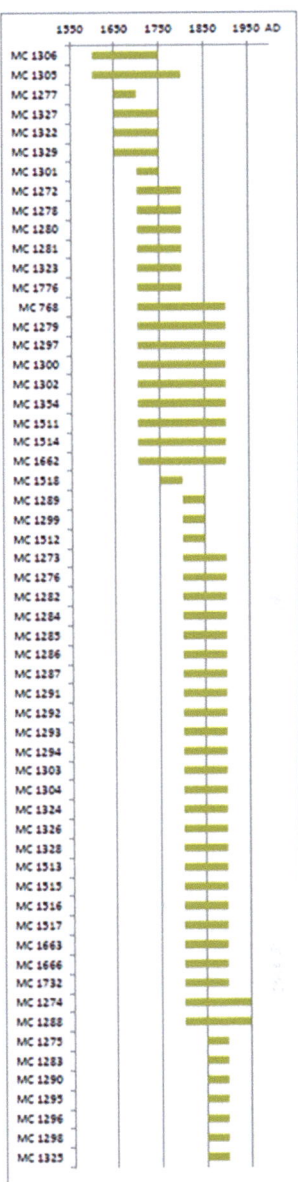

Figure 6. Graph with dates of several tobacco pipes recovered in the Athenian Agora. J. Vroom and K. Berghuis.

century and into the early 20th these items had become old-fashioned, "the vestiges of an old empire," eventually to be "replaced by tea, cigarettes and nationalism" from the West.[81]

Another object from western Europe is an imported glass beaker (**22**) that was recovered in 1971 from a pithos of the "Turkish" period and published in 2010 by Gladys Weinberg and Marianne Stern.[82] When cheap European mass-produced glass appeared in the eastern Mediterranean during the late 18th century and the early 19th, an increase in the use of glass vessels in Ottoman lands can indeed be observed. In a late 19th- to early 20th-century oil painting of a banquet scene at Yıldız Palace in Istanbul, for instance, a variety of wine glasses accompanied by water glasses and glass jugs for each guest dining in a more "western" fashion can be distinguished.[83]

---

[81] Baram 1999, p. 151; see also Vroom 1998b.
[82] *Agora* XXXIV, p. 175, fig. 22, pl. 36.
[83] See Vroom 2003, p. 352 and fig.12.11; this painting is in the Istanbul Museum of Painting and Sculpture.

1. Kütahya Ware (11–15)

This type of pottery was produced mainly during the 18th century in the workshops of Kütahya, a small town in north-western Turkey about 200 km from Istanbul.[84] After the 18th century, this ware was also manufactured in substantial quantities in Iznik,[85] Istanbul, and Jerusalem.

The fabric can be described as a fine whitish or buff-colored fritware (10 YR 8/3) with a granular texture, covered with an irregular glaze. Usually polychrome, the added colors (including blue, green, red, purple, and yellow) are applied on a white slip beneath a transparent glaze on the interior and exterior of the vessel.

The painted designs are usually geometric, floral, or figural, often inspired by Chinese or western motifs. Characteristic are Christian subjects (figures of saints) or depictions of men and women wearing contemporary 18th-century Turkish costume. Some scholars believe that most of the potters in Kütahya were Armenians or Greeks, because the vessels often bear inscriptions in these languages.[86]

The most distinctive products of the Kütahya potters are small, thinly potted vessels, including coffee cups (often with matching saucers), bowls, jugs, and coffee pots (11–15). In particular, the decorated cups were inspired by Chinese, Japanese, and western porcelains (e.g., Meissen, Vienna, Sèvres); the use of saucers is thought to be of western provenance.[87]

In the Aegean area, Kütahya ware has been recovered at Athens, Thebes, Thessaloniki, and Chania (Crete), and at rural sites in eastern Phokis and Boeotia.[88] Again, some examples come from the above-mentioned rubbish pits from an excavation on Pelopidou Street in the city center of Thebes. On Cyprus, Kütahya ware has been recognized during excavations at Kouklia, as well as by surveys in the Troodos Mountains and around Potamia–Agios Sozomenos.[89]

2. Tobacco Pipes (16–21)

This group contains several clay pipe bowls of the typical eastern chibouk-style tobacco pipe.[90] The bowl was used in conjunction with a long tube and with a separate mouth-piece. The chibouk pipe was in fashion throughout the Ottoman Empire from the 17th century onwards.[91] According to Rebecca Robinson's study of tobacco pipes from Corinth and the Athenian Agora, these pipes were first introduced into the Middle East at the beginning of the 17th century.[92] Women as well as men smoked the chibouk pipe in Ottoman times.[93]

In general, the fabric is fine, of a reddish or grayish color (7.5 YR 6/2), with the surface sometimes covered with a burnished slip. The pipes often have a rounded or lily-shaped bowl with a short shank and a developed keel. The shank flares to a simple end, with a slightly convex termination. Molded, stamped, rouletted, and impressed styles of decoration occur on the pipes.

---

[84] Lane 1957, pp. 63–65; Carswell and Dowsett 1972; Korre-Zographou 1995, pp 63–68; Vroom 2005, pp. 168–171; Vroom 2011, pp. 156–160; Borboudaki 2007, pp. 157–167.
[85] A rare example of a 16th-century small cup [fincan] was also recovered at Iznik; cf. Atasoy and Raby 1989, p. 47, fig. 19.
[86] Lane 1939, p. 234, and 1957, pp. 63–66; and especially Kyriazopoulos 1978.
[87] Vroom 2005, pp. 168–171.
[88] E.g., Waagé 1933; Frantz 1942, group 8, nos. 7–8, group 10, nos. 1–3; Vroom 2003, fig. 6.38: W36.1–2, with additional literature; Vroom 2005, pp. 168–171; Vroom 2006a, figs. 19–22, 30–31; Vroom 2007b, fig. 4.13.
[89] Wartburg 2001, p. 367, nos. 6–14, figs. 4 and 9; François and Vallauri 2001, p. 544; Vroom 2011, pp. 160–165; Vroom 2013b, p. 79, TCP325, col. pl. 3.7.
[90] Vroom 2005, pp. 172–175.
[91] Simpson 1990; Simpson 1998; Simpson 2009; Baram 1995; Baram 2000; Ward and Baram 2006.
[92] Robinson 1985.
[93] Robinson 1985, pls. 33–43.

In Greece, fragments of chibouk pipes have thus far been recovered in Athens, Thebes, Chalkis, and Corinth, as well as at a rural site in Boeotia.[94] According to Robinson, the large number of finds in Corinth, compared to the relatively small numbers elsewhere, suggests that they may be a local Corinthian product.[95] The dates of the bowl fragments from Athens range from the 17th to the 19th centuries (**16–21**). Fragments of a later, red-burnished type were also found at excavations in Thebes,[96] in addition to local products made of meerschaum (a soft white clay mineral).[97]

3. Glass Finds (22)

Ottoman-period glass finds are rare in the Agora Excavations, but a nicely enameled piece was recovered in 1971.[98] The piece is a glass beaker, decorated with a simplified floral design in enamel (**22**). The decorative style was common on glass vessels throughout western Europe in the 18th century and the early 19th, but earlier examples exist from the 16th and 17th centuries. The shape and decoration of the Agora piece apparently resemble a beaker in a museum in Geneva and 18th-century drinking glasses from central Germany (from Franconia specifically),[99] suggesting that the Athenian example was probably manufactured in this part of Europe.

Conclusion

The finds from the Agora Excavations give us a glimpse of the activities of daily life in the western lower city of Ottoman Athens. During the 16th and 17th centuries, this part of the city clearly received upmarket imported ceramics from western Europe and the eastern parts of the Ottoman Empire, ranging from colorful maiolica wine jugs from Faenza to large glazed dishes and plates from Iznik. These latter items were appropriate for the communal consumption of semi-liquid or liquid dishes ("Eastern-style" eating), whereas the former undoubtedly influenced the local manufacture of glazed vessels similar in appearance (but with relatively crudely painted motifs) in the Agora.

In fact, the excavation of two pottery kilns under the pavement of the demolished church of Vlassarou yielded much potters' equipment (e.g., tripod stilts), as well as wasters from locally manufactured jugs. Together with other locally made products, these provide evidence for the existence of artisans' workshops in and around the central part of the Agora in Early Ottoman times (during the first half of the 17th century at the latest).

A century later, the same area must have functioned somewhat differently, oriented toward the consumption of coffee, considering that various delicate 18th-century coffee cups and a saucer from Kütahya have been recovered in and around the central part of the Agora. The drinking of coffee in such small cups was often accompanied in Late Ottoman times by the smoking of a long chibouk-style pipe. It is therefore noteworthy that in the northern section of the Agora we can note a cluster of pipe bowls dating to the late 17th century to the 19th. These bowls may reflect the enjoyment of tobacco in a more public context in this part of town.

[94] E.g., Robinson 1983, 1985; Vroom 2003, figs. 6.38 and 6.46: W37.1 and W37.Ex.
[95] Robinson 1985, p. 172.
[96] Koilakou 1994, pl. 48c; Vroom 2006a, p. 214, figs. 23–24 and fig. 35.
[97] Vroom 2006a, p. 233, fig. 66.
[98] Cf. *Agora* XXXIV, p. 175, fig. 22, pl. 36.
[99] Cf. *Agora* XXXIV, p. 175, nn. 93–95.

Kütahya coffee cups and tobacco pipes consequently offer archaeologists more than mere tools for dating—they provide material evidence for the study of the history of consumption patterns (in this case, drinking and smoking) and shed light on the origins, spread, and social acceptance of the use of these stimulants.[100]

In the Ottoman layers of the Agora, we find many bits and pieces of chibouk pipes—but are they just pipes? The pipe seems to have been much more than just a device for smoking tobacco. The French printmaker Honoré Daumier said: "Only a pipe distinguishes man from beast!" and Albert Einstein was no less optimistic in 1950 when he said, "Pipe smoking contributes to a somewhat calm and objective judgement in all human affairs."[101]

Archaeologists are not philosophers and would be better off sticking to those leftovers of the tobacco pipes of the past. And how fruitful this is for the Ottoman period! The broken chibouks of the Ottomans have enabled us to identify a wide range of types and to establish secure dates for these artifacts in Athens, giving us the confidence to conclude that Einstein, in the end, was relatively right.

---

[100] Vroom 2017.
[101] See http://www.smithsonianmag.com/smithsonian-institution/why-albert-einstein-genius-theory-relativity-loved-pipe-180954991/?no-ist.

Catalogue

1 Dish, Italian-influenced sgraffito ware (Agora card P 5673).[102] (Figures 7a–b)
Athenian Agora (Section N, well near south-west corner of burnt building, excavated in 1935).
H. 0.075; Diam. of base 0.100; Diam. 0.240.
Numerous fragments mended into one, preserving about three-quarters of the vessel. Profile complete. Low ring foot; broad convex divergent body; plain rim with round lip. Orange-buff clay. Parts of white slip and transparent lead glaze on the interior. White slip and thin, brownish lead glaze on the exterior (except for ring foot). Painted and incised human figure with pointed cap and beard (previously described as a doge), seated between two spiral fluted columns on the interior, with additional details painted in yellow, brown, green, and blue. The clay between the columns has been scraped away, leaving an unslipped, unglazed surface in the background.
Date: ca. (early) 16th century.

Figures 7a–b. Cat. no. 1, Athenian Agora P 5673. Photo C. Mauzy. American School of Classical Studies at Athens, Agora Excavations.

---

[102] Cf. Frantz 1942, p. 16, fig. 37; Frantz 1961, fig. 62; Thompson 1976, p. 278; MacKay 2007, p. 285, fig. 229.

2 Bowl, locally made (Agora card P 9022).[103] (Figures 8a–b)
Athenian Agora (Section Φ, Turkish pit at 78/KB, excavated in 1937).
H. 0.080; Diam. 0.220.
Mended from several pieces. Complete save for a small body fragment by the fish's head and minor fractures. Ring foot; convex divergent body; sharply offset everted rim, turned in slightly at the outer lip. Three scars from a tripod stilt on the interior of the base. Orange-buff clay. White slip and transparent lead glaze on the interior. Band of brownish yellow paint on interior rim. Incised fish with open mouth on the interior of the base, swimming to the left. Three short sections of an incised vertical undulating line on the interior rim.
Date: ca. 16th century.

Figures 8a–b. Cat. no. 2, Athenian Agora P 9022. Photo C. Mauzy. American School of Classical Studies at Athens, Agora Excavations.

3 Jug, Italian import (Agora card P 7610). (Figures 9a–c)
Athenian Agora (Section Σ, 18–22/KA–IΔ, excavated in 1936).
H. 0.181; Diam. of base 0.102.
Base, most of the body, and part of the rim preserved; handle missing. Flat ring base with rounded transition; convex symmetrical body; straight divergent neck; trefoil mouth. Whitish clay. The base is unglazed, but carries an incised graffito. Elaborate painted decoration of lattice motifs interwoven

[103] Cf. Frantz 1942, pp. 12 and 24–25, fig. 24 (group 8).

with scrolls in blue and white under a tin glaze on the exterior. On one side is a large painted medallion on a blue background with segments of green and yellow. At the center of this medallion is a brown and white dog leaping to the left. On the interior is a light bluish tin glaze.
Date: ca. 16th century.

Figures 9a–c. Cat. no. 3, Athenian Agora P 7610. Photo C. Mauzy. American School of Classical Studies at Athens, Agora Excavations.

4 Small bowl, locally made (Agora card P 6650).[104] (Figures 10a–c)
Athenian Agora (Section N, kiln at 15–15/ A–ΛB, excavated in 1936).
H. 0.043; Diam. 0.095.
One side and fragments from rim missing; profiles of rim, of wall, and of ring foot preserved. One small rim fragment does not join. Ring foot; convex divergent body; plain rim with round lip. Orange-buff clay. White slip and green lead glaze on the exterior, except for ring foot. Two scars from a tripod stilt on the interior. Painted checkerboard and dot decoration on the interior base; painted leaf (?) pattern on the interior body. The decoration is executed in yellow, green, and blue paint on a white slip and under a light greenish glaze.
Date: ca. late 16th – early 17th century.

Figures 10a–c. Cat. no. 4, Athenian Agora P 6650. Photo C. Mauzy. American School of Classical Studies at Athens, Agora Excavations.

5 Small bowl, locally made (Agora card P 2179). (Figures 11a–c)
Athenian Agora (Section Z, square well at 66/B, excavated in 1933).
H. 0.046; est. Diam. 0.095.
Mended from five fragments. Considerable parts of rim and body missing. Small ring foot; convex divergent body; plain rim with round lip. Two scars from a tripod stilt on the interior. Orange-buff clay. White slip and green lead glaze on the exterior, except for the ring foot. Painted decoration of blue spirals on the interior base and of loops outlined in blue under a light greenish glaze on the interior body. The alternating loops are colored, some reddish brown, others green.
Date: ca. late 16th – early 17th century.

---

[104] Cf. Frantz 1942, p. 5, fig. 1; MacKay 2015, figs. 10.1c (kiln) and 10.5 (bowl).

Figures 11a–c. Cat. no. 5, Athenian Agora P 2179. Photo C. Mauzy. American School of Classical Studies at Athens, Agora Excavations.

6 Dish, locally made (Agora card P 12079).[105] (Figures 12a–c)

Athenian Agora (Section Ψ, sandy fill at 16/ΚΘ, excavated in 1938).
H. 0.070; Diam. 0.245.
Mended from a number of fragments; small parts of rim and body missing; minor fractures. Low ring foot; broad convex divergent body; sides rise in a short curve to a plain rim with round lip. Orange-buff clay. White slip and green lead glaze in various shades on the exterior, except for the ring foot. Scars from a tripod stilt on the interior. Painted medallion on the interior, with a bird (looking to the right) in blue with some yellow under a light greenish glaze.
Date: ca. late 16th – early 17th century.

[105] Cf. Frantz 1942, p. 5, fig. 2.

Figures 12a–c. Cat. no. 6, Athenian Agora P 12079. Photo C. Mauzy. American School of Classical Studies at Athens, Agora Excavations.

7 Jug, locally made (Agora card P 7092).[106] (Figures 13a–c)
Athenian Agora (Section T, well at 17/KA, excavated in 1936).
H. 0.226; Diam. 0.159.
Almost complete; parts of handle and rim missing. Flat base with rounded transition; convex symmetrical body; high divergent straight neck; trefoil mouth; one vertical ribbon handle. Orange-buff clay. Central "ladder-design medallion" elaborately painted in light blue and reddish-brown, covered by a glaze on the exterior body (except for the base).
Date: ca. late 16th – early 17th century.

---

[106] Cf. Frantz 1942, p. 6, fig. 5; MacKay 2015, fig. 10.2c.

Figures 13a–c. Cat. no. 7, Athenian Agora P 7092. Photo C. Mauzy. American School of Classical Studies at Athens, Agora Excavations.

Joanita Vroom

8 Jug, locally made (Agora card P 1902).[107] (Figures 14a–d)
Athenian Agora (Section Z, square well at 66/B, excavated in 1933).
H. 0.242; Diam. 0.180.
Almost complete; parts of the rim and neck missing. Flat base with rounded transition; convex symmetrical body; high divergent straight neck; trefoil mouth; one vertical ribbon handle. Orange-buff clay. Decorated with an oval "ladder-design medallion" painted in blue and green under a light greenish glaze on the exterior body. In the center of this medallion is a lion, looking to the right, with an uplifted, curling tail and open mouth with two rows of teeth painted in blue, green, and reddish-brown.[108]
Date: ca. late 16th – early 17th century.

[107] Cf. Frantz 1942, pp. 8 and 20, fig. 12 (group 3); Frantz 1961, fig. 61; Thompson 1976, p. 278; Korre-Zographou 1995, fig. 84; Vroom 2005, fig. TUR/VEN 5.4.; Vroom 2007b, fig. 4.4; MacKay 2007, p. 284, fig. 228.
[108] Karidis (2014, fig. II.9) has suggested that the painted lion on this jug may relate to the "shameful Venetian siege" of 1687, although the jug seems to have been made earlier.

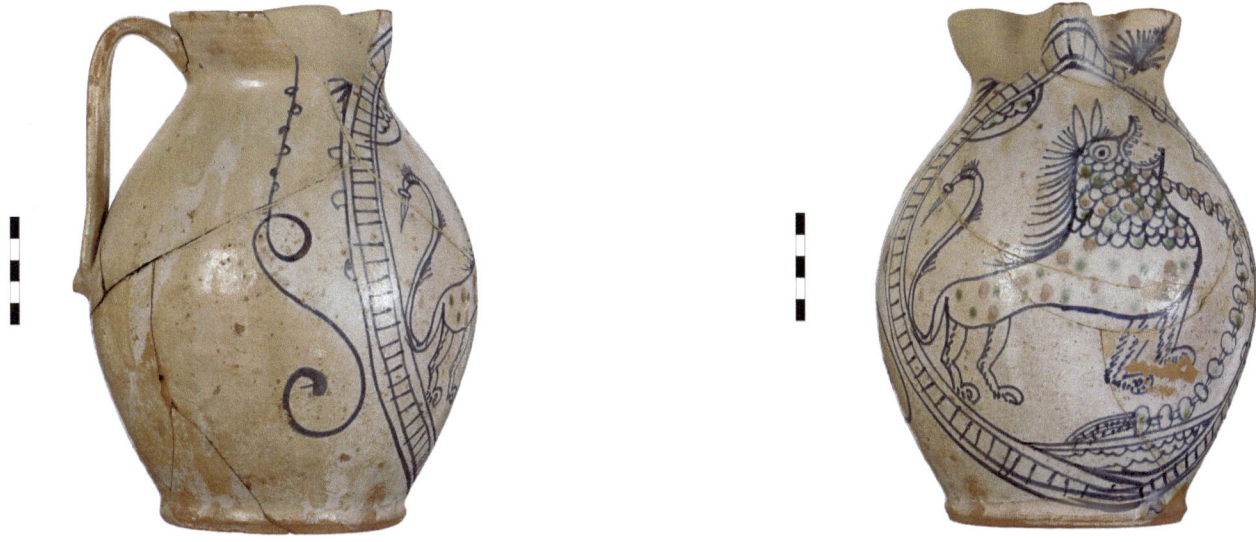

Figures 14a–d. Cat. no. 8, Athenian Agora P 1902. Photo C. Mauzy. American School of Classical Studies at Athens, Agora Excavations.

9 Dish, Iznik ware (Agora card P 10150). (Figures 15a–c)

Athenian Agora (Section ΘΘ, pit at 15/ΙΔ, excavated in 1937).
H. 0.094; est. Diam. 0.285.
Broad low ring foot; broad convex divergent body; plain rim with round lip. Semi-intact. Whitish fritware. Floral design of tulips and carnations painted in blue, green, and red under tin glaze on interior. Alternating dots and plant motifs painted in blue under tin glaze on the exterior.
Date: first half of the 17th century (Iznik III style).

Figures 15a–c. Cat. no. 9, Athenian Agora P 10150. Photo C. Mauzy. American School of Classical Studies at Athens, Agora Excavations.

10 Jug, Iznik ware imitation (Agora card P 12493). (Figures 16a–b)
Athenian Agora (Section Z, well-cesspool at 27/ΠΣΤ, excavated in 1938).
H. 0.204; Diam. 0.139.
Almost complete; except for missing vertical handle, rim, and some chips from the base. High ring foot; convex symmetrical body; high flaring (concave symmetrical) neck. White clay. White slip on the exterior and upper part of the interior. Surface somewhat worn from exposure to the cesspool. Zigzag decoration painted in black between bands above base. Elaborate painted floral decoration (including tulips) in red and blue with green leaves under glaze on the exterior body, which continues on the exterior of the neck. Ring of painted dots between bands in black under the glaze on the lower part of the exterior neck.
Date: 18th century (from Istanbul? or from Kütahya?).

Figures 16a–b. Cat. no. 10, Athenian Agora P 12493. Photo C. Mauzy. American School of Classical Studies at Athens, Agora Excavations.

11 Coffee cup, Kütahya ware (Agora card P 23893). (Figures 17a–c)
Athenian Agora (Section HA, pit against north-west corner of east apse of Church of the Holy Apostles, excavated in 1954).
H. 0.047; Diam. 0.075.
Small low ring foot; thin-walled convex divergent body; plain rim with round lip. Whitish fritware. Floral decoration painted in green, yellow, and purple, outlined in black, on the exterior. Medallion on the interior painted in blue with a blue and yellow flower, outlined in black, at the center. Yellow zone painted on rim.
Date: ca. 18th century.

Figures 17a–c. Cat. no. 11, Athenian Agora P 23893. Photo C. Mauzy. American School of Classical Studies at Athens, Agora Excavations.

12 Coffee cup, Kütahya ware (Agora card P 5517).[109] (Figures 18a–c)
Athenian Agora (Section N, pit at 11/NZ, excavated in 1935).
H. 0.040; est. Diam. 0.070.
Approximately half preserved; profile complete. Small low ring foot; thin-walled convex divergent body; slightly everted rim. Whitish fritware. Transparent, slightly lustrous glaze. Exterior decoration of flowers and leaves painted in yellow, red, and blue, outlined in black. Small blue leaf painted on the inside center of the interior base. Star painted in black on exterior of base.
Date: ca. 18th century.

Figures 18a–c. Cat. no. 12, Athenian Agora P 5517. Photo C. Mauzy. American School of Classical Studies at Athens, Agora Excavations.

13 Coffee cup, Kütahya ware (Agora card P 5518).[110] (Figures 19a–c)
Athenian Agora (Section N, pit at 12/NZ, excavated in 1935).
H. 0.045; est. Diam. 0.070.
Approximately half preserved; profile complete. Small low ring foot; thin-walled convex divergent body; plain rim with round lip. Whitish fritware. Transparent, slightly lustrous glaze. Exterior decorated with flowers and leaves painted in red, yellow, and green, alternating with narrow bands in blue. Two narrow bands painted in blue on the interior rim, and a small green and yellow flower on the interior base.
Date: ca. 18th century.

Figures 19a–c. Cat. no. 13, Athenian Agora P 5518. Photo C. Mauzy. American School of Classical Studies at Athens, Agora Excavations.

[109] Cf. Frantz 1942, p. 16, fig. 35 (group 10).
[110] Cf. Frantz 1942, p. 16, fig. 35 (group 10).

14 Coffee cup, Kütahya ware (Agora card P 34943). (Figures 20a–c)
Athenian Agora (Lot Ψ 158, excavated in 1938).
H. 0.048; Diam. of base 0.038; Diam. of rim 0.074.
One third of wall and entire foot preserved; profile complete. Whitish fritware. Small low ring foot; thin-walled convex divergent body; plain rim with round lip. Thin white glaze inside and out. Decoration on interior and exterior rim of linked recumbent leaves painted in purple. Painted upright triangular leaves with central upright in purple at exterior base. Painted star-pattern with blobs in purple at central interior.
Date: ca. late 18th – early 19th century.

Figures 20a–c. Cat. no. 14, Athenian Agora P 34943. Photo C. Mauzy. American School of Classical Studies at Athens, Agora Excavations.

15 Saucer, Kütahya ware (Agora card P 12475). (Figures 21a–b)
Athenian Agora (Section Ω, pithos at 89/N, excavated in 1938).
H. 0.025; Diam. 0.101.
Small pieces of rim missing; profile complete. Small ring foot; thin-walled flat convex divergent body; upturned plain rim with round lip. Whitish fritware. Thin white glaze inside and out. Painted decoration on the interior, with flowers between blue and dark blue/black circles.
Date: ca. 18th century.

Figures 21a–b. Cat. no. 15, Athenian Agora P 12475. Photo C. Mauzy. American School of Classical Studies at Athens, Agora Excavations.

16 Tobacco pipe (Agora card MC 1277).[111] (Figure 22)
Athenian Agora (Section KK, excavated in 1936).
Pres. L. 0.049; pres. H. (bowl) 0.023; Diam. of shank opening 0.008.
Rim and half of bowl missing; shank chipped. Dark grey clay. Small rounded molded bowl, scored vertically; shank ends in segmented wreath.
Date: ca. late 17th century.

Figure 22. Cat. no. 16, Athenian Agora MC 1277. Photo C. Mauzy. American School of Classical Studies at Athens, Agora Excavations.

17 Tobacco pipe (Agora card MC 1322).[112] (Figure 23)
Athenian Agora (Section E, excavated in 1931).
Pres. L. 0.052; Diam. of bowl 0.029; Diam. of shank opening 0.008.
Rim missing. Reddish-brown clay. Dark to dark grey slip. Small rounded bowl; shank projects directly from bowl, with wreath and stepped ring termination. Stamped band of double triangles around end of shank.
Date: late 17th – early 18th century.

Figure 23. Cat. no. 17, Athenian Agora MC 1322. Photo C. Mauzy. American School of Classical Studies at Athens, Agora Excavations.

18 Tobacco pipe (Agora card MC 1279).[113] (Figure 24)
Athenian Agora (Section KK, excavated in 1936).
L. 0.052; H. 0.040; Diam. of bowl 0.033; Diam. of shank opening 0.012; Diam. of rim 0.029.
Half of rim missing. Light red clay. Burnished slip. Straight plain rim; tall rounded bowl; smooth shank flaring to plain convex end. Various rouletted motifs of different sizes between rim and bowl; on bowl, around keel; and around shank.
Date: 18th–19th century.

Figure 24. Cat. no. 18, Athenian Agora MC 1279. Photo C. Mauzy. American School of Classical Studies at Athens, Agora Excavations.

---

[111] Cf. Robinson 1985, p. 194, A 1, pl. 61, with further parallels; Hayes 1992, fig. 149, type III.
[112] Cf. Robinson 1985, p. 194, A 2, pl. 61, with further parallels; Hayes 1992, fig. 149, type IV.
[113] Cf. Robinson 1985, p. 196, A 14, pl. 61, with further parallels.

19 Tobacco pipe (Agora card MC 1285).[114] (Figure 25)
Athenian Agora (Section MM, excavated in 1936).
Pres. L. 0.059; H. 0.033; Diam. of bowl 0.037; Diam. of rim 0.032.
Shank end broken. Reddish-brown clay. Burnished slip. Straight faceted rim; bowl with carved, incised, and stamped ovals; shank flaring to scalloped termination. Palmettes and floral lozenges on rim; rouletting and stamped triangles between ovals on bowl.
Date: 19th century.

Figure 25. Cat. no. 19, Athenian Agora MC 1285. Photo C. Mauzy. American School of Classical Studies at Athens, Agora Excavations.

20 Tobacco pipe (Agora card MC 1324).[115] (Figure 26)
Athenian Agora (Section KK, excavated in 1936).
Pres. L. 0.061; H. 0.042; Diam. of shank opening 0.014.
Much of rim missing. Reddish-yellow clay. Lily-shaped bowl with deep keel; shank slightly flaring to termination. On each side of the bowl is a cross-hatched circle with a dot in the center, surrounded by 16 dots, the whole surmounted by a pineapple. Dotted triangles and minute rouletting at upper and lower gadroon ends. Seal on right side of shank, bearing the Arabic equivalent of "upsilon."
Date: 19th century.

Figure 26. Cat. no. 20, Athenian Agora MC 1324. Photo C. Mauzy. American School of Classical Studies at Athens, Agora Excavations.

21 Tobacco pipe (Agora card MC 1303).[116] (Figure 27)
Athenian Agora (Section ΠΑ, excavated in 1965).
Pres. L. 0.060; H. 0.042; Diam. of shank opening 0.014.
Pieces missing from rim. Red clay. Burnished slip. Lily-shaped bowl; heavy shank flaring to flat termination. All-over stamped pattern of rayed dots with some reserved zones. Seal beneath end of shank, in reserved zone.
Date: 19th century.

Figure 27. Cat. no. 21, Athenian Agora MC 1303. Photo C. Mauzy. American School of Classical Studies at Athens, Agora Excavations.

---

[114] Cf. Robinson 1985, p. 197, A 21, pl. 62, with further parallels.
[115] Cf. Robinson 1985, p. 198, A 28, pl. 63, with further parallels; Hayes 1992, fig. 149, type VIII.
[116] Cf. Robinson 1985, p. 199, A 31, pl. 63, with further parallels; Hayes 1992, fig. 149, type VIII.

22 Beaker (Agora card G 616).[117] (Figure 28)
Athenian Agora (Section BΔ, Turkish pithos Q5:1, excavated in 1971).
H. 0.070; Diam. 0.060.
Mended from three pieces. About one-third of rim and body missing. Blue-green glass. Straight wall and straight rim. The wall is decorated from top to bottom as follows: wavy white line; straight white line; band of floral design painted in white, yellow, brown, and blue; straight white line.
Date: ca. 18th century.

Figure 28. Cat. no. 22, Athenian Agora G 616. Photo C. Mauzy. American School of Classical Studies at Athens, Agora Excavations.

Putting Athens on the Ottoman Map: Preliminary Observations

Katerina Stathi

Due to the interest of scholars in Classical antiquities, the city of Athens became the object of several descriptions and cartographic attempts from the 17th century onward. Around 1670, Capuchin monks, who had settled in the city some years earlier, made a map of Athens and its surroundings, which, despite its many topographical inaccuracies, was extensively reproduced, in some cases with modifications, by many scholars, among whom were the Frenchmen Georges Guillet de Saint-George and Étienne Gravier d'Ortières.[1] Some years later, this map inspired the French doctor and scholar Jacob Spon (1678), who together with his travel companion, George Wheler, were the first to conduct systematic research on the topography of Athens. Other maps linked directly to the brief Venetian rule of the city (1678–1688) were subsequently created; of these, the one made by Giacomo Verneda is particularly precise.

The next noteworthy map comes from the 18th century. Designed by James Stuart and Nicholas Revett (1751–1753, published 1794), it focused solely on antiquities, disregarding the 18th-century city plan. The same is true of the map by the French architect Julien-David Le Roy (1754, published 1758). In 1781, Jacques Foucherot prepared a map of Athens for the French ambassador to the Sublime Porte, Marie-Gabriel-Florent-Auguste, Comte de Choiseul-Gouffier; and in 1783–1784, Jean-Denis Barbié du Bocage based his map for Jean-Jacques Barthélemy's *Voyage du jeune Anacharsis* (1788) on Foucherot's exemplar. However, the map that represented real progress, as it was the first scientifically executed map of the city of Athens, was the one made by Louis-François-Sébastien Fauvel, which appeared in Guillaume-Antoine Olivier's *Atlas pour servir au voyage dans l'Empire othoman, l'Egypte et la Perse...* (Paris 1801). This map is undated, but it must have been made around 1787 or soon after; it inspired many copies and imitations, such as those by Thomas Burgon, the engineer [François Nicolas Catherine?] Goubault, and others.

William Martin Leake must have drawn his map of Athens around 1806, though it was not published until 1821. It is an exceptional work of scholarship, yet it shows only the ancient city,

---

* This essay is based on ongoing research of the Ottoman map of Athens discovered in the Ottoman State Archives in Istanbul. Its inclusion in this volume will advance further efforts to develop the subject.
[1] For an extensive discussion of the "discovery" of Athens in 1670, see Yakovaki 2006, p. 262 ff.

Katerina Stathi

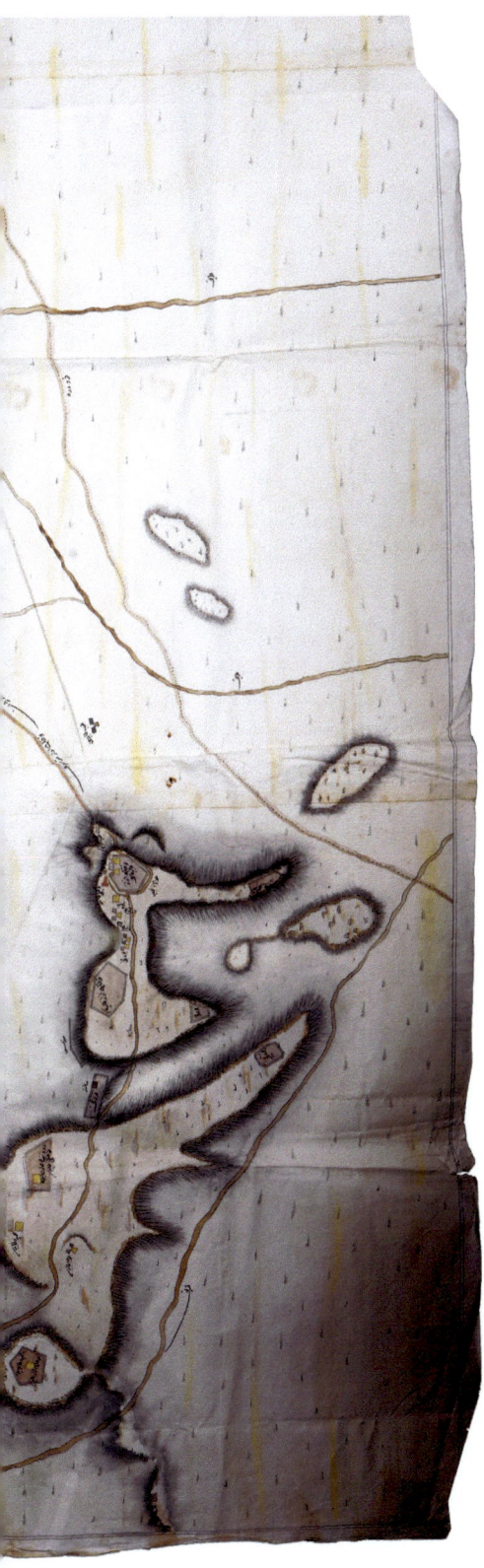

Figure 1. "Atina kalesiyle varoşunun krokisi" [Plan of the castle and "suburb" of Athens]. Istanbul, Başbakanlık Devlet Arşivi Genel Müdürlüğü [General Directorate of State Archives of the Prime Ministry of the Republic of Turkey], Başbakanlık Osmanlı Arşivi [Ottoman State Archives], Hatt-ı Hümayun [Imperial decrees], 946.40721. Photos in Figs. 1-6: Courtesy of the General Directorate of State Archives of the Prime Ministry of the Republic of Turkey, Istanbul.

without including the modern roads. Many other maps were created subsequently, included in travelers' accounts and classicists' books, but these—at least until the declaration of Athens as the capital of the new Greek state—were mainly imitations of the maps made by Stuart, Fauvel, and Leake.[2]

While west European visitors produced and copied many maps and city plans depicting Athens and its antiquities (sometimes meticulously, occasionally naively), similar visual representations cannot be found on the Ottoman side. Even though descriptions of Athens can be traced in various chronicles (fewer in city histories, more often in geographical texts), however exaggerated they can be, as in the case of the Ottoman traveller and writer Evliya Çelebi, there were no known topographical depictions discovered until today. This gap is now filled with an intriguing 19th-century map.

The Ottoman Map of Athens

In the Hatt-ı Hümayun collection of the Ottoman State Archives in Istanbul,[3] squeezed between 19th-century imperial decrees, is a folded manuscript map of Athens in color (Fig. 1). It is catalogued under the title "Atina kalesiyle varoşunun krokisi" [Plan of the castle and "suburb" of Athens].[4] The term *varoş* is taken here to mean the town area—the residential zone—juxtaposed with the citadel [*kale*]. Why this document had not been preserved in the Archives' special section for maps [Plan–Proje–Kroki] is unclear; nevertheless, its unexpected appearance in the Hatt-ı Hümayun collection is astonishing.[5] It was later discovered that other "hidden" maps may be found in the collection of firmans in the Archives. Characterized as sketches [*kroki*, from the French *croquis*, "sketch" or "rough sketch"], 14 further documents, as many plans, and about 100 maps [*harita*] are in the collection, out of a total of 95,134 records.

We can state with certainty that the item we are dealing here with is the only Ottoman map of Athens.[6] Folded a few times to fit into a standard A4-size archival folder (with subsequent humidity stains), the hand-drawn map opens out to 141.5 x 112 cm. The document has been scanned, and the electronic version may be viewed on the Archives' computer terminals. However, the scanned copy is in black-and-white only; the limitations of on-screen viewing significantly diminish the impressive size and colorful details of the original map. With the passage of time, the few basic colors used in the map have faded to a now-predominant brown that matches the yellowing paper and absorbs the red roofs of the buildings depicted. In the upper-left and -right corners are two rectangular legends with inscriptions in Ottoman Turkish. There is a four-point compass rose in a blank area to the right (Fig. 2). All topographical names and indications are written in Ottoman Turkish. Unfortunately, the Archives provide no information about the name of the cartographer.[7] Although we are

---

[2] Leake [1821] 1841; Korres 2010b, p. 6.
[3] Başbakanlık Devlet Arşivi Genel Müdürlüğü [General Directorate of State Archives of the Prime Ministry of the Republic of Turkey], Istanbul, Başbakanlık Osmanlı Arşivi [Ottoman State Archives; hereafter, BOA], Hatt-ı Hümayun [Imperial decrees; hereafter, HAT.].
[4] BOA, HAT., 946.40721.
[5] The documents adjacent to the map in the HAT. collection concern the Ottoman siege of the Acropolis; the map must therefore have been stored with them to preserve its context.
[6] The best collection of modern maps of Athens is the recent lavish publication by Manolis Korres (Korres 2010b).
[7] Following an exhibition in the building of the General Directorate of State Archives of the Prime Ministry of the Republic of Turkey in Istanbul, the map was included in 2016 in a publication concerning maps and plans of Ottoman castles. However useful for the transcriptions it provides, this work does not shed light on the history of the map.

not certain about the initial inspiration, as discussed below, it seems safe to argue that the map was created by an Ottoman draftsman for military purposes.

The map is oriented in a north-east–south-west direction, and the area depicted is the city of Athens within the city walls. This is the so-called Haseki Wall, named after the despotic voivode Hacı Ali Haseki, governor of Athens, with interruptions, during the years 1774–1795. He had it built in 1778 by the forced labor [*angarya*][8] of Athenians over a period that varies from 70 to 108 days, according to which chronicle is consulted.[9] It was approximately 4 km long, 0.80 m thick, and 3 m high.[10] According to other sources (travelers' accounts, chronicles) and archaeological finds, there were seven gates in the walls. This map indicates only six of them.

Figure 2. The compass rose (detail of Fig. 1).

---

[8] Skouzes 1948, p. 43.
[9] Gerontas (1889) and Philadelpheus (1902, vol. 2, p. 132) refer to the differing accounts of the duration of the construction.
[10] Biris 2005, p. 195.

Katerina Stathi

The Gates of Athens

It is remarkable that even though various names for each of the seven gates of the walls of Athens are recorded elsewhere in Greek and Ottoman Turkish—for example, the one at the entrance to the Acropolis rock was called the "Gate of the Castle," or "of the Tombs" (due to the Muslim cemetery nearby), or the "Karababa Gate"—the cartographer seems to have had no knowledge of any of them. Instead, the names we encounter were given arbitrarily, which is intriguing for the topography and place names of Athens, as well as a clue to the cartographer's meager connection with the city. Thus, the aforementioned gate of the castle is simply called a gate [*kapı*].

Progressing clockwise, next to the Temple of Hephaistos (the Theseion), is the *İskele kapısı*, leading to the port, which can be identified with the "Dragon's Gate," also called the "Mandravili Gate" [Πόρτα του Δράκου/Μαντραβίλη] or *Aslan kapısı*. The Morea Gate [*Mora kapısı* or "Gypsy Gate"/Γύφτικη Πόρτα], which led to Eleusis, is missing from the map. The next gate indicated on the map, which was called the "Menidi Gate" or "The Gate of the Holy Apostles" [Αγίων Αποστόλων], or *Grib kapısı*, is the "Islambol Gate." This was, after all, vaguely the direction travelers would take to reach Istanbul.

Moving on, we reach the "Boubounistra" [Μπουμπουνίστρα] or "Mesogeia Gate." At this spot on the map there is a possible indication of a fountain and a name that can be read with some difficulty as *Cengah kapısı*. If the reading is correct, it would mean "Gate of the Field of Battle." Next comes what we know as Hadrian's Gate, or the "Princess's Gate" [Πόρτα Βασιλοπούλας/Καμαρόπορτα] in the sources. On the map it is labelled as *Kebir-i mu'attal kapı* or the "Great Abandoned Gate." The drawing renders the grandeur of the gate, which according to the sources had indeed fallen into disuse.[11] The final gate is the "Gate of the Three Towers," also called "Albanian" [Αρβανίτικη] or *Ide kapısı*; the name on the map is difficult to decipher: it could be *Yatı kapısı*. While one gate is missing, one extra tower is indicated on the map, so that the total number of towers [*kule*] is 23.

Roads, Buildings and Monuments

The road network within the city walls and in the area immediately outside the city is shown in reasonably good detail, with the word road [*tarik*] often scribbled next to the thick lines of the roads. To the south-east, a dotted line is used to indicate the Ilissos River [*Kuru dere*, dry creek, wadi]. Topographical features are shown around the Acropolis rock, the Pnyx, and the Hill of the Muses (Philopappou) in the south-west part of the city. The mapmaker used thick black lines to sketch the rocky hills that sheltered many military redoubts and bastions.

Groups of simple dots and short lines around the city walls are used to indicate vegetation, while inside the walls the map becomes more precise, with housetops and gardens drawn in color. Roofs, gardens, trees, and domes are shown in outline, as circular and rectangular shapes. There is one exception related to the mosques: the drawing indicates all of the architectural parts of a minaret (footing, pulpit, shaft, balcony, upper part of the minaret body, spire) in miniature right next to the mosque buildings.

---

[11] Kambouroglou 1931, p. 60.

Although the outlines of all the buildings, including houses, are sketched in black ink, the non-residential structures, which are indicated as mosques, churches, baths, and so on, have red outlines. More specifically, the Ottoman buildings have red outlines, but are not colored in, while the churches are outlined in red and shaded in gray (Fig. 3). One of this map's intriguing features is that it does not provide the names of the buildings it illustrates. Even though the mapmaker tried to avoid a generic motif for the churches and drew their plans in detail, with variations depending on whether they were domed or had simple roofs, all the churches (60 in number) are invariably indicated as "monasteries" [*manastır*] and the mosques simply as "holy mosques" [*cami-i şerif*].

Figure 3. The center of Athens (detail of Fig. 1).

Besides the monuments on the Acropolis rock, the other two ancient temples present on the map are the Temple of Olympian Zeus and the Temple of Hephaestus, but they are both called "monasteries" or "ruins" of the "40 columns" [*Kırk direkli*]. The number 40, as can be seen elsewhere in reference to temples, was probably given as a generic number to indicate the large number of columns of ancient temples; the Temple of Olympian Zeus, however, at that time had only 16 of its original 104 columns standing, and the Hephaisteion 34.[12]

---

[12] In Ottoman times, 17 of the columns of the Temple of Olympian Zeus were standing. In 1759, the Voivode Tzistarakis removed one column to use in the construction of a mosque in Monastiraki Square, and another fell down during a storm in 1852, leaving 15 columns: Giochalas and Kafetzaki 2013, p. 387.

In the central part of the map, which depicts the Acropolis, the lack of identification of buildings and the disregard for monumental architecture is particularly striking: the rock of the Acropolis is simply called *Atina kalesi*, "the castle of Athens" (Fig. 4). The ground plan of the Parthenon is given simply, with little concern for detail, as well as incorrectly oriented (its east–west axis becomes a north-east–south-west line). In addition, the only inscription provided is for the mosque that was built inside the Parthenon. Unfortunately, no particular name is ascribed to this mosque; it is just another *cami-i şerif*.[13]

Figure 4. The Acropolis rock (detail of Fig. 1).

Apart from the Parthenon, in the location occupied by the Erechtheion is the indication of the Palace of Belkis [*Belkis sarayı*]. Belkis is the name of the Queen of Sheba in the Muslim tradition.[14] However, earlier mentions of a "Palace of Belkis" in Athens usually identify it with the Temple of Olympian Zeus, not the Erechtheion.[15] The name might have been inspired by the statues of the Caryatids that stand in contrapposto on the south porch of the Erechtheion. Some sources also

---

[13] The Parthenon mosque was at that time called Castle Mosque [*Kale camisi*] or Castle Keep Mosque [*İçkale camisi*]: Eyüpgiller 2004, p. 119.
[14] Ullendorff 1991, p. 1220. The queen's name is given there as Bilkis, probably derived from Greek παλλακίς or the Hebraized *pilegesh*, "concubine." See Freytag 1837, p. 44a.
[15] Evliya Çelebi 2003, p. 118.

discuss the use of the Erechtheion to house the female members (in other words, the harem) of the household of the military governor [*dizdar*].¹⁶

Among the other details in the drawing are many small houses, the existence of which is confirmed by travelers' accounts and paintings from the same period. The Acropolis was a small village, where the garrison lived with their families.¹⁷ The person who drew this map put more emphasis on buildings and structures that could be useful for military purposes. Accordingly, every single cistern [*sarnıç*] is clearly shown, as well as the towers for ammunition [*kule, cebe kule*], bastions [*tabya*], storehouses [*anbar*], underground rooms [*zir-i zemin*], a mill [*değirmen*], and gates [*kapı*]. Further indications of structures for military purposes are long trenches for musketeers, labeled *tüfenkendaz metrisi*, as well as bastions for cannons, a small defensive wall [*havale*] facing the entrance of the castle, and a concentration of military bastions, towers, and trenches on the Hill of the Muses and the Pnyx (Fig. 5).

An intriguing detail is the double (parallel) dotted lines that appear to indicate a pathway that starts at the south-west entrance of the rock on the side towards the Propylaea. This is the sole such indication in the map, considering that the only other dotted line is single and used to indicate the river, and all other roads are shown as continuous lines. This way of depicting a path could allude to an underground tunnel, as a document of 1827, the probable date of the map, mentions tunnels/sewers to be constructed by the Ottomans in the citadel of Athens.¹⁸ The mapmaker most probably illustrated

Figure 5. The small defensive wall facing the Propylaea (detail of Fig. 1).

---

¹⁶ Acropolis Restoration Service: see http://www.ysma.gr/en/erechtheion (accessed February 2019); Travlos [1960] 2005, pp. 178, 202.
¹⁷ Evliya Çelebi 2003, p. 117.
¹⁸ BOA, HAT., 943/40675, January 9, 1827: "*Atina kalesi'ne yapılacak lağım için lağımcı ve mühendis izamı ve barut, fişek, humbara ve askerin müterakim ulufesi için para gönderilmesi ve celb edilen ve edilecek olan askere ve eşkıya sergerdelerinin hareketlerine karşılık alınacak tedbirlere dair.*"

Katerina Stathi

the passageway in this specific way to emphasize its importance: this was the entrance to the castle, the only way to gain access to the Acropolis.

Although the map's focus is on military structures, gates, and emplacements, some attention was given to the various garden configurations, shown in green, and the houses in the area.

Chronology

In the upper-right corner of the map is a legend (Fig. 6) with a detailed drawing, in brown and red, showing a side view of the fortifications of the Acropolis, together with a measurement scale. The caption reads: "This is the drawing of the two sides of the castle of Athens—the one side of the bastions facing the defensive wall and the back side facing the suburb—as well as of the banquettes of the fortification, the cistern, and the underground rooms."[19] Underneath this, we read the two sides as *havale tarafı*, "defensive wall side," and *vera tarafı*, "rear/back side." A cistern and two underground rooms are also indicated on the drawing of the Acropolis. Directly below is the elevation scale, marked in gradients of 5 from 5, 10, … to 60.

The legend in the upper-left corner is the main one, as it gives a concise description of the map.[20] It states that it is a level (two-dimensional) drawing (as opposed to the other legend showing the rock in vertical perspective) of the castle of Athens together with its suburb and defensive wall. Underneath is another measurement scale in Ottoman cubits.[21]

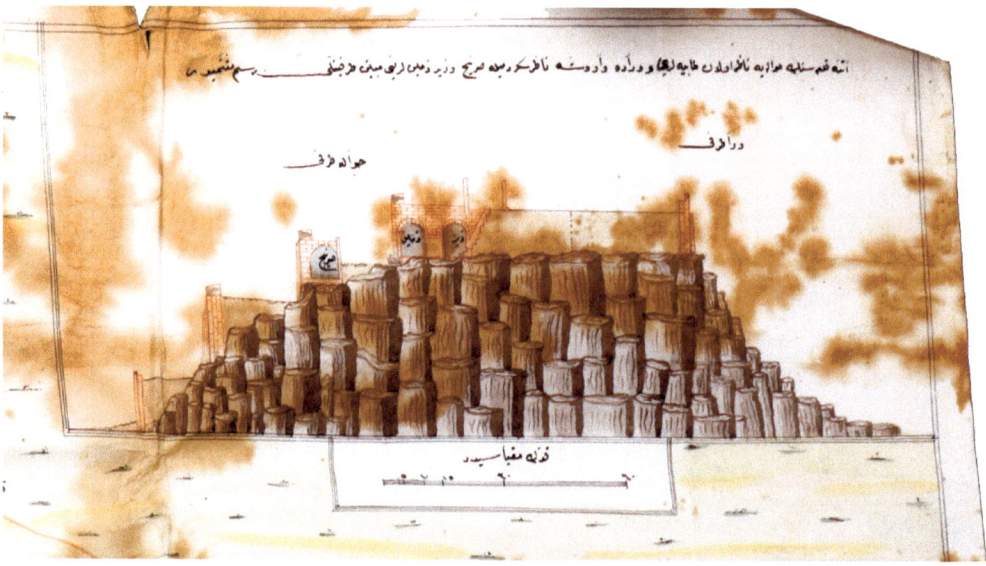

Figure 6. Legend in the upper-right corner (detail of Fig. 1).

[19] "Atina kal'asının havaleye nazır olan tabyaları ve vera'da varoşa nazır segirdimiyle sarnıç ve zir-i zeminlerini mübeyyin tarafeynli resm-i mütenemmidür."
[20] "Begayet allahu te'ala bu def'a fethi müyesser-i hazret-i sübhanî olan Atina kalasının varoşu ve havalisiyle maan bir kıta resim-i musattahidir." I am grateful to Dimitris Loupis and Edhem Eldem for their help with deciphering these inscriptions.
[21] An Ottoman cubit [*zira-i osmani*] is equivalent to 0.56 m.

This inscription on the map also provides us with a date. One particular letter in the inscription has caused some uncertainty, because it is not very clear whether it is an R or a Z, abbreviations for the months of *Rabiülevvel* or *Zilkade*. If it is an R, as it appears to be, because there is no dot over it, then the date would read "*11 Rabiülevvel 1242*" (A.H.), which corresponds to October 13, 1826. This is also the date under which the map has been catalogued at the Ottoman State Archives. If it is a Z, however, without a dot, then the date is "*11 Zilkade,*" corresponding to June 6, 1827. This is a serious chronological discrepancy (as all chronological attributions tend to be!), because it involves seven and a half months in the middle of the turbulent period of the Greek War of Independence. The symbolic castle on the Acropolis was the epicenter of Greek and Ottoman military activity and territorial claims: the castle changed hands three times in a dozen years (1821–1833).

If the date of the map is October 1826, the Ottomans, under their commander-in-chief Reşid Mehmed Pasha (also known as Kütahi in Greek historiography), would already have been besieging the Acropolis for some months, as the final siege began in August.[22] It can thus be argued that this map of Athens was created by an Ottoman draftsman on the orders of military officers who were looking for better ways to bring the difficult siege of the castle on the Acropolis to a successful end. In their efforts to improve their troops' positions in order to attack the heavily fortified castle and control the urban road network around it, the map must have provided valuable aid. This objective could also explain the complete lack of references to Athenian buildings and sites by name: the Ottoman generals who would make use of the map did not need the names of temples or classical ruins, but the locations of gates, main roads, bastions, and underground passages. A simple indication that a building was a mosque—and, if it was, whether it had a visible standing minaret—or a church, or a bath house would have been enough for their purposes.

On the other hand, if it is dated to June 1827, the map might have been sent to Istanbul as a proof/gift of conquest, a sort of *fetihname* for the sultan after the Greeks surrendered the Acropolis on May 25. Looking at the documents in the Hatt-ı Hümayun collection in the Ottoman State Archives, specifically the ones that are catalogued immediately before and after the map, we see that they are concerned with military news and orders during the siege of the Acropolis and date mostly to 1827–1828.[23] This offers a further reason to accept the 1827 dating.

One element that could help to resolve this dating issue is the invocation of God at the beginning of the inscription. "*Begayet allahu teala bu defa fethi*" refers to conquest [*feth*]—but is it the conquest that God has finally granted the Ottomans this time? Or is it the anticipated conquest that God will at last grant them this time? The key word, difficult to decipher, is in the middle; it has been read as *mabed*, meaning "temple," thus referring to the Parthenon, but is more likely to be *müyesser*, which means "facilitated by God." We can therefore arrive at the following translation: "This is a depiction of the castle of Athens together with its suburb and defensive wall, whose conquest this time was enabled by God, May His Name be Exalted …"

What might also be the case is that the map was created with a purely military function and might have been used during the siege; then, after the conquest, the legend on the upper left was filled in, announcing the conquest. On closer examination, the background of the area of the legend is significantly paler, supporting the idea that it was altered at a later stage.

---

[22] Reşid Mehmed Pasha was a prominent Ottoman general who played an important role in the Greek War of Independence and went on to become grand vizier (1829–1833): Danişmend 1971, p. 74. On the sieges of the Acropolis, see also the essay by Ilıcak herein, pp. 243–259.

[23] BOA, HAT., 844/37909 (1827), 847/38048 (1827), 854/38217–A (1828), 887/39197 (1827), 943/40675–A (1827), 943/40675–C (1827), 943/40675–F (1827), 947/40721 (1827), 947/40732–L (1827), 947/40732–Z (1827).

Conclusion

Some winding paths of research that surround this map still beg to be explored. For one, the identity of the mapmaker has been a source of speculation since this map began to attract attention. Given that the map itself does not provide us with a name or signature, we may wonder whether its creator was an Ottoman official or perhaps a foreigner. The cartographic skills, contrasting with a lack of knowledge of the topography, as well as the notation of the measuring scale in the upper-left legend in Ottoman cubits [*zira-i osmani*], are elements that have to be taken into consideration.

As we have seen, plans of the city of Athens were drawn many times until the mid-19th century by travelers and military officers. Closer to the date of the map in question are two other city plans of Athens that were made by French draftsmen,[24] which, although they look like traveler's companions for exploring the monuments of Athens, also point out a gunpowder magazine, cisterns, an artillery battery, and the quarters of both the Greek commander and the Ottoman governor. It would be ideal to have a map of Athens that was made by Greeks during the siege of the city in the years of the War of Independence. We do know, however, that at least one of the French maps (see p. 161, Fig. 7) was commissioned by General Gourrhas, the garrison commander of the Acropolis, in 1826, and that those maps were presumably intended for a wider French or at least francophone public who would be interested in both the ancient past and the contemporary realities of Athens in wartime.[25]

The survival of this beautiful hand-drawn map after so many years and under complicated circumstances is fortuitous. During the long period of Ottoman rule, archival material suffered various reversals of fortune. The passing of time, as well as fire, moisture, and other natural phenomena, inevitably had damaging effects. The worst period for the preservation of archival documents was during the revolutionary period in Greece. From 1821 onwards, with the outbreak of the Greek War of Independence, Ottoman Turks and Greeks alike inflicted terrible damage on archives and public records. Paper, the raw material of archives and libraries, was useful for the production of cartridges.[26] It is for this reason that in those regions which revolted in 1821, where fighting was particularly intense, for example the Peloponnese and central Greece, very few archives survived on account of the hostilities between the Greeks and the Ottoman Turks. Further destruction was also unavoidable in the years following the war, until a proper archival policy was implemented by the Greek state, however late.[27] In Athens, most of the archives were also destroyed. Only the archives of Moni Petraki and some categories of document (*berat*, *ferman*, and *hüccet*) that granted privileges or tax exemptions of one kind or another survived in family archives. Consequently, the survival of this map provides invaluable information to researchers investigating the history and topography of Athens during Ottoman times.

This essay is based on an ongoing examination and analysis of the Ottoman map of Athens. A large part of this research is the technical study of the map using GIS [geographic information systems], an example of which is given below (Fig. 7). Since the Ottoman map lacks geometric accuracy, the Haseki wall line was employed in an attempt to reduce edge effect. The wall line was digitized on the basis of the previous georeferencing[28] of the Stamatis Kleanthis and Eduard Schaubert map of Athens

---

[24] "Plan d'Athènes, levé en 1826 par ordre du Général Gourrhas, par J.-F. Bessan" (Bessan 1835) and "Plan de la ville d'Athènes, avec les monuments antiques et les ruines existantes" of 1826 by Alex de Jaquershind [?] (American School of Classical Studies at Athens, Gennadius Library).
[25] Stathi 2014.
[26] Balta 2003b.
[27] A public records office was not established until 1914, a full 70 years after the creation of the Greek state: Lykouri-Lazarou 1998, p. 71.
[28] I would like to thank my colleagues at the Dipylon Society for the Study of Ancient Topography, especially Dr. Markos Katsianis, for their assistance with georeferencing.

of 1832 (see p. 124, Fig. 1). Points of identifiable locations or monuments were also used (for example, the walls of the Acropolis). On the whole, 37 GCPs [ground control points] were used, with the RMSE [root mean square error] in the affine scale being around 45 m. The spline function was used in order to account for the geometric distortion of the original map. The current attempt can be improved by including more intra-muros GCPs from buildings that can be identified (e.g. churches or mosques); however, even from this test, we can see that the map's value lies in the mode of representation rather than the intended geometrical accuracy.

Further research will allow us to better explore the numerous small urban details that lie hidden beneath the picturesque red house roofs, church domes, and green gardens of this depiction of early 19th-century Athens.

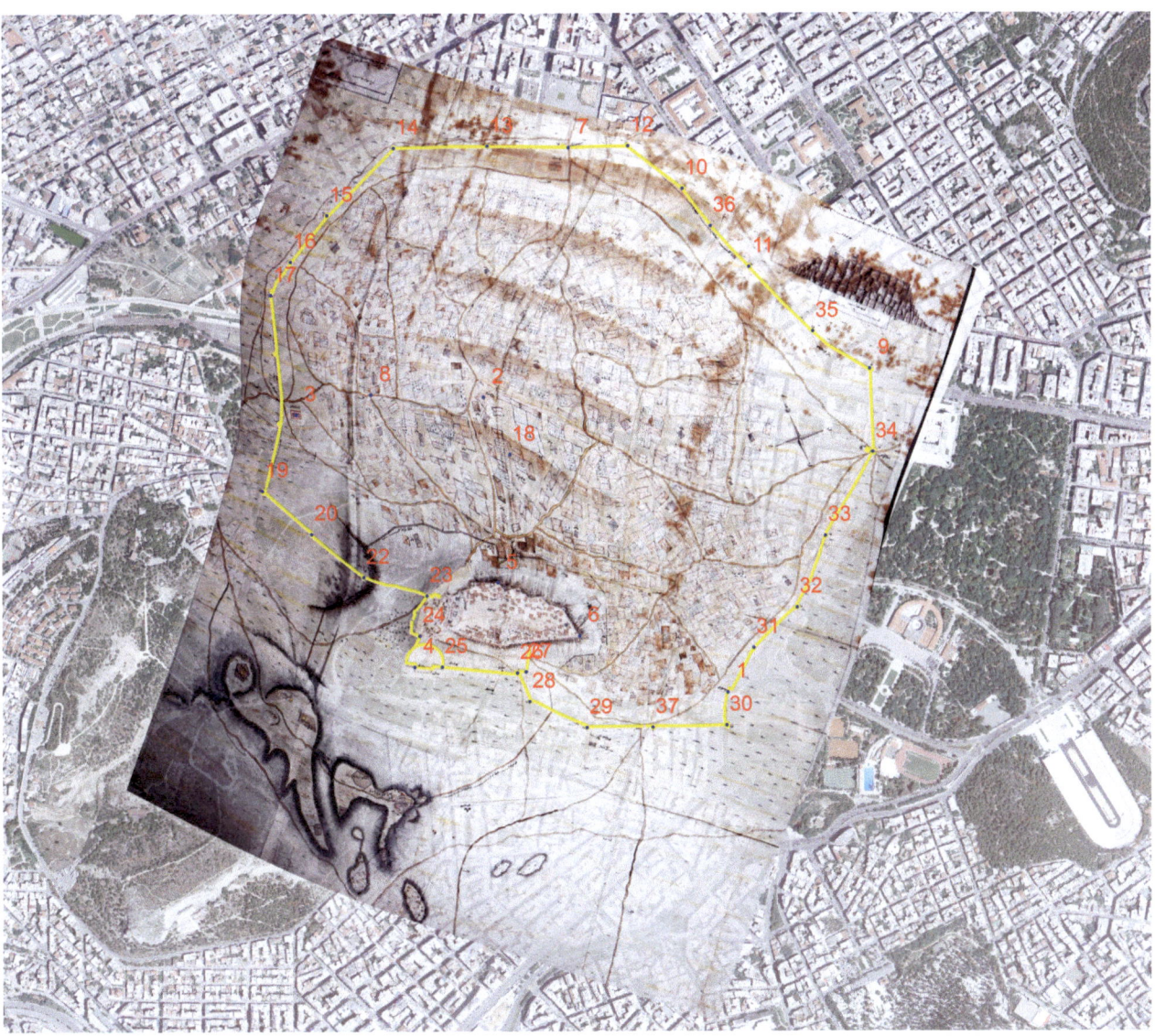

Figure 7. Georeferenced version of the Ottoman map on top of modern satellite imagery of the center of Athens. National Cadastre & Mapping Agency [NCMA] S.A. Photo © Dipylon.

Early 19th-century Athens, the Great Powers, and the Parthenon Sculptures

Elena Korka and
Seyyed Mohammad Taghi Shariat-Panahi

Ottoman history of the 18th century was marked by the increasing intervention of western European states in the empire's economy and politics as a result of the Capitulations granted by the Sublime Porte.[1] Rivalries among these states, particularly France and Britain, often had significant repercussions on the internal political affairs of the Ottoman State and led to open hostilities in order to secure privileges and rights from the sultan. In order to understand the extent to which economic factors influenced politics in those days, we shall examine the case of Athens at the end of the 18th century and the beginning of the 19th, when events ultimately led to the Parthenon being deprived of a major part of its sculptural decoration.

French Cultural Expansionism: Choiseul-Gouffier and Fauvel

The Orlov Revolt in the Peloponnese (1770), a military encounter within the broader context of the Russian–Ottoman War of 1768–1774, led to the Albanian invasion of southern Greece, which was followed by extensive destruction and an unprecedented economic crisis.[2] As a result of this financial situation and the disruption of commerce, a large number of Greek-Orthodox Athenian merchants owed money to their French business partners. The French merchants—several of whom were permanently settled in Athens and owned considerable assets—pleaded with the Ottoman government to intervene. The French ambassador to the Porte, Marie-Gabriel-Florent-Auguste, Count de Choiseul-Gouffier,[3] managed to obtain a firman from the sultan ordering the Athenians to pay their debts to the French under threat of confiscation of their properties.[4] In those days and according to the conditions of the firman, the Greek-

---

[1] For the Capitulations in the Ottoman Empire, see van den Boogert 2005.
[2] For the Orlov Revolt, see Gritsopoulos 1967, 1970; Ragsdale 1988; Vakolopoulos 1973; Rotzokos 2007.
[3] Marie-Gabriel-Florent-Auguste, Comte de Choiseul-Gouffier (1752–1817), was France's ambassador in Istanbul from 1784 to 1791, and upon his eventual return to France became a Senior Minister and a member of the State Council: Simopoulos 1991, vol. 2, pp. 365–439; Grell 1995. The Municipality of Athens has named a street in the Makriyianni neighborhood after him: Samara-Kaufman 2001, pp. 54–55.
[4] Gennadios 1930, pp. 204–205.

Orthodox population as a whole was held responsible when individuals could not meet their obligations. The Ottoman authorities in Athens went so far as to hang three members of the Greek-Orthodox community in order to force the rest to pay, but they failed to achieve their goal because the local economy and its leaders were completely destitute.

The French pursued their financial goals in the period 1780–1790 with persistence, which caused the Athenian population to nurse a grudge against them. This antipathy was probably reinforced by the fact that, during the same period, the French seemed to be following a policy of cultural expansionism in regard to Athenian antiquities. In 1784, Choiseul-Gouffier appointed the artist Louis-François-Sébastien Fauvel[5] as his representative in Athens in order to draw and make casts of sculptures and to collect items of archaeological significance. When Fauvel reached Athens in 1786, the vice-consul of France in the city was Louis-Marie-Dimitri Gaspari, whom Choiseul-Gouffier had admonished "to collaborate" with Fauvel and to facilitate his efforts by negotiating with the local Ottoman authorities to obtain whatever kind of permit might be needed. Indeed, Gaspari did his job well: not only did he acquire a permit for Fauvel to carry out archaeological excavations, but he also persuaded the Ottoman commander [*dizdar*] of the Acropolis (then a military fortress, to which access by non-Muslims was strictly prohibited) to let Fauvel draw the monuments and make casts of ancient sculptures and inscriptions. During his first year in Athens, Fauvel used his permit to enter the fortress and make exact drawings of the architectural remains. Towards the end of 1787, he carried out excavations, all of short duration and of a "hit-and-run" type, in areas far from Athens, such as Polyaegos and Santorini (where he acquired numerous pieces of classical sculpture, including the famous *Chairopoleia*, presently on display at the Louvre), at Cape Zoster, where he excavated a tumulus with no significant results, at Marathon, where he tackled the tomb of the fallen Athenians of the battle of 490 B.C., again to no avail, and in the plain of Brexiza around the villa of Herodes Atticus. Thereafter, as an "experienced" archaeologist, he narrowed his activities to places in and around Athens, excavating in the Kerameikos and on the Acropolis itself. The items he collected were sent to his sponsor, Choiseul-Gouffier. Four times in 1787–1788, cases of antiquities and casts of ancient works of art were loaded on French vessels and transported either directly to France or to other ports within the French sphere of influence, such as Izmir. In all four instances, the sender was not Fauvel, but Gaspari, who had succeeded in obtaining the permits to export the precious contents of these cases. Fauvel himself carried two relief heads, "snatched from the Temple of Minerva," with him to Istanbul, where he met Choiseul-Gouffier at the end of 1787.[6]

Throughout 1788, Fauvel worked on the Acropolis. While digging at the Erechtheion, where he noticed severe damage inflicted by the Early Christians, he discovered an Early Christian mosaic floor with inscriptions. He wrote to Choiseul-Gouffier with the news and received an immediate answer urging him to remove the mosaic and to substitute "other little stones" for it. Choiseul-Gouffier concluded his letter in a manner that reveals his infinite avidity for antiquities: "Remove all that you can, do not neglect any means, my dear Fauvel, of plundering in Athens and its territory, all that is to be plundered [...]; continue, spare neither the dead nor the living."[7] Fauvel followed his

---

[5] The French official Louis-François-Sébastien Fauvel (1753–1838) had first come to Athens in 1780–1782 as a painter working on illustrations for Choiseul-Gouffier's travel book, *Voyage pittoresque de la Grèce* (Choiseul-Gouffier 1782–1809): Gennadios 1930, pp. 15, 238–239. See also Zambon, 2010, 2014.

[6] Zambon 2007, p. 72.

[7] Zambon 2007, p. 76: "*Enlevez tout ce que vous pourrez, ne négligez aucun moyen, mon cher Fauvel, de piller dans Athènes et son territoire, tout ce qu'il y a de pillable [...]; continuez, n'épargnez ni les morts, ni les vivans* [sic]."

advice, taking possession in 1788 of two of the Parthenon metopes (which had already fallen from the monument; he used a Turkish accomplice to take them out of the fortress) and part of the frieze, which he had unearthed after it had fallen to the ground during Morosini's bombardment of the Parthenon and been buried.[8] The latter was so heavy that it took the combined efforts of twenty men and three yokes of oxen to transport it to Piraeus.[9]

Fauvel remained under Choiseul-Gouffier's direct tutelage until 1792, when the French Revolution provoked the latter's downfall; the former ambassador fled to exile in Russia. Fauvel then started collecting antiquities for himself; not only did he appropriate three cases of antiquities meant to be sent to Choiseul-Gouffier as compensation for the three years' worth of salary that his patron owed him, but went on to create a remarkable collection of coins and other precious objects, and even a small museum near the Acropolis. The turn of the French political tide caused by the French Revolution may have affected Choiseul-Gouffier, but not Fauvel, who settled permanently in Athens and pursued his goals unimpeded.

Antagonism against the French: Elgin and Lusieri

The situation changed abruptly towards the end of the next decade, in a way unfavorable to the French. Napoleon Bonaparte's rise to power and subsequent policy caused a rupture in the good relations between France and the Ottoman Empire, as the French became masters of the Ionian Islands in 1797 and invaded Egypt in the following year in an effort to gain a foothold in the Middle East.[10] The Ottomans reacted vehemently, forming an anti-French coalition with the Russians. The British, eager to secure their own position and already waging war against Napoleon, aimed to strengthen their relationship with the Sublime Porte, as British–French antagonism had already reached a peak all over the world.

Meanwhile, in the rather backwater city that was Athens, right after war was declared between the Ottoman Empire and France (September 9, 1798), the local Ottoman administration, by order of the sultan, proceeded to incarcerate French subjects in the town and confiscate their properties.[11] The "painter" [*tesvirci*] Fauvel was among them; an intensive correspondence seeking his release ensued. The Ottoman documents give ample details of these events. At the beginning of October 1799, Fauvel, whom the sources characterize as an instigator, managed to be transported to Istanbul, where he was incarcerated in the prison of Yedikule.[12] The way now lay open for the properties of his compatriots to be confiscated. At the end of December of the same year, an archival source tells us, "Gördöslü [Mehmed] Nuri Bey is appointed as agent [*mübaşir*] for the expropriation and sale of the properties

---

[8] Metope number 10 on the south side of the Parthenon, which portrays a Centauromachy, was discovered during Fauvel's excavations on the Acropolis in 1788. The Centaur's right arm is located in the Acropolis Museum and can be attached to the metope. His excavations on the Acropolis in 1789 also revealed stone number VII from the east frieze of the Parthenon, depicting female weavers of the sacred veil, which could now be reunited with its lower-left corner, containing the toes of the right foot of the master of feasts, in the Acropolis Museum. Fauvel sawed off the back of the stone in order to transport it to Paris. Giovanni Battista Lusieri later followed Fauvel's example in order to transport the stones of the Parthenon that he had detached on behalf of Lord Elgin: Mantis 1986; Berger 1986, p. 166; Korka 2009, pp. 190–192.

[9] Zambon 2007, p. 73.

[10] For the French intervention in Egypt, see Herold 1962; Strathern 2007.

[11] St Clair 1998, p. 77.

[12] A letter signed by the district governor [*kaimakam*] of Athens and sent to the judge [*kadi*] of the city mentions, "As a result of the pleadings of the ambassadors of the governments, it is ordered to release the French painter Fauvel, settled in Athens, who is incarcerated together with other Frenchmen, and to transport him to Istanbul without any hindrance." Başbakanlık Devlet Arşivi Genel Müdürlüğü [General Directorate of State Archives of the Prime Ministry of the Republic of Turkey], Istanbul, Başbakanlık Osmanlı Arşivi [Ottoman State Archives; hereafter, BOA], Cevdet Hariciye [Foreign affairs; hereafter, C.HA.], 18/893.

of the incarcerated French citizens of Athens. The houses and their contents shall be sold. The sums shall be written down and given to the imperial fund."[13] A special accountant was also assigned to record all the properties. The same document that appointed him also stated, "Investigation and inspection should be carried out in person in order to discover the hidden properties of the French as well as their debts. Gördöslü [Mehmed] Nuri Bey or the voivode or the officials of the city and the group of notables of the Christian communities [*kocabaşi*][14] should all contribute to this direction."[15] Indeed, the hunt was successful. Previously unrecorded properties were found to belong to the following French subjects, according to the text: "Monsieur Andrea, Monsieur Roque, Monsieur Gianneto [Gaspari], the deceased Monsieur Jiran and the consul himself."[16] Gördöslü [Mehmed] Nuri Bey was appointed as proxy for the properties of the French, which were handed over to the imperial treasury.[17] The confiscated properties were then auctioned, at prices much lower than their actual value, to Ottoman subjects. Among the buyers were several prominent Greek-Orthodox Christians, including the official interpreters of the British consulate[18] at Athens, Spiros Logothetis and Yorgakis Fotopoulos.[19]

This was the political situation in 1799 when Thomas Bruce, 7th Earl of Elgin, became Britain's ambassador to the Sublime Porte, a position which he held until 1803 in order to help the Ottomans with their campaign against Bonaparte, among other things. Influenced by Sir William Hamilton, Britain's renowned ambassador to the court of Naples, he employed Giovanni Battista Lusieri, a well-regarded Italian artist, to make drawings of the monuments on the Acropolis of Athens, apparently following in Fauvel's footsteps. As no foreigners were officially allowed within Ottoman fortresses, among them the Acropolis, where a Turkish garrison was stationed, Elgin needed to acquire a special permit from the sultan to allow Lusieri and his team to enter this specially protected military zone. Knowing that the French would be a hindrance, Elgin decided to exaggerate the threat to the Ottomans that the French population in Athens represented in order to get rid of them, finally opening the way for Lusieri.[20] The commander of the Acropolis and the voivode, governor of the city of Athens, nevertheless demanded a special firman for Elgin's men to enter the fort.

The history of the removal of the Parthenon Marbles has been and continues to be a long-debated and strongly contentious issue dividing Greece and Britain. This is not the place to analyze it, but it is remarkable to follow the ways and means by which the foreign powers intervened in the political, economic, and social life of small, lowly Athens because of its incomparable antiquities.

Based on the existing material, one thing is certain: uneasiness, uncertainty, and unrest existed among all involved parties in regard to the legality of Lord Elgin's removal of the sculptures. According to the British line of reasoning, the first "firman" of 1801 (in fact an unofficial letter of recommendation, which Elgin exploited in order to remove sculptures from the monument) was followed by other

---

[13] BOA, C.HA., 49/2437.
[14] Papageorgiou 2005; Pylia 2001.
[15] BOA, C.HA., 135/6727.
[16] BOA, C.HA., 52/2596.
[17] BOA, C.HA., 7/344.
[18] These official interpreters of European countries were called *Beratlı* in Ottoman Turkish; for their recruitment, see Kontogiannis 1917; Sonyel 1991; van den Boogert 2005.
[19] This expropriation was short-lived, for upon the signing of the peace treaty between France and the Ottoman Empire in 1803, the Porte asked the buyers of French properties to return them for the same price they had paid. This caused an uproar, as the new owners were of course unwilling to comply; some, like Spiros Logothetis, the official British interpreter, used their political influence to thwart this order.
[20] Unpublished letter, National Archives [hereafter TNA], Kew, UK Foreign Office, 78, vol. 32, pp. 147–149: "The Porte following with me the progress of our intelligence from these has already sent to bring to Constantinople certain French residents at Athens."

documents issued by Ottoman officials of the Sublime Porte in connection with the Marbles that indemnified Elgin for all that he had done on the Acropolis.[21] Yet again, recent archival research has brought to light some significant evidence.

During the early years of Elgin's activity, a few other foreigners were also active in Athens. They included a Dr. Mertrud,[22] who reprimanded Lusieri for his illegal acts, and the transient Russian Prince Dolgorouki,[23] who wished to enter the Acropolis to draw, but was so obstructed by Lusieri, on Lord Elgin's instructions, that in the end he left without understanding what was going on behind the fortress walls. Only the British traveler and artist Edward Dodwell managed to gain access, and

Figure 1. View of the south-east corner of the Parthenon showing the scaffolding for removing the sculptures, drawing by William Gell, 1801. London, British Museum. Photo © Trustees of the British Museum.

---

[21] On this "firman," see Demetriades [1999] 2001 and http://www.parthenon.newmentor.net/illegal.htm. This article was presented by the British Committee for the Return of the Parthenon Marbles along with a memorandum to the Special Examining Committee of the British Parliament in the context of documents deposited in the course of research on Britain's cultural heritage and the issue of the return of cultural heritage assets. Written in Greek by Professor Vassilis Demetriades, the article was submitted to the British Committee and the Ministry of Culture. Demetriades wrote a related paper (Demetriades 2000) analyzing the form that an Ottoman document should have in order to be characterized as a firman and proved that the "firman" that Elgin reportedly acquired, preserved in an Italian translation, does not constitute a genuine firman of the sultan, because it does not fulfill the conditions for such a document. Michaelis 1882; Greenfield 1989, p. 99; Rudenstine 2000, 2001, 2002; Korka 2009, pp. 175–176.

[22] Gennadios 1930, p. 24; Hunt and Smith 1916, pp. 232–234.

[23] Hunt and Smith 1916, p. 230.

his drawings bear testimony to Lusieri's vandalism of the Parthenon.[24] A memorandum delivered by Dr. Philip Hunt,[25] chaplain to Lord Elgin, in the summer of 1801 stated that Elgin had received firmans from the Porte allowing him not only to erect scaffolding (Fig. 1) and make casts of reliefs and sculptures on the Acropolis, but also to "take away pieces of stone with old inscriptions or figures thereon."[26] A generally accepted opinion among anti-Orientalist western Europeans in those days was that the monuments were already being destroyed by the Turks, who were breaking them up and selling fragments to travelers, or shooting at them, or even burning them for lime to use as building material.[27]

Returning to the documents, the line of argument is very long; here, it suffices to say that the original firman that Hunt brought from the Sublime Porte has never been found. It is preserved only in an Italian translation bearing the signature of the district governor [kaimakam], Seyyed Abdullah Pasha. Prosopographic research reveals that his full name was Ömer Paşazade el-Hac Abdullah Pasha, and that he held office from 1799 to 1802, acting on behalf of the Grand Vizier Kör Yusuf Ziyaeddin Pasha. The eminent historian Edhem Eldem has attempted to discover what Ottoman terms lie behind the Italian words in order to determine what precisely the firman permitted Elgin to do. According to Eldem, the five "artists" working on behalf of Elgin had the right to "walk," "view," "contemplate," "fix scaffolding," "mold," and "excavate;" the right to "take" objects with them, as Eldem tellingly remarks, is mentioned only after the official document has ended, "almost as an afterthought."[28] This central fact indicates that the firman was "interpreted" by Elgin himself when he produced the Italian translation. A crucial word in the Italian translation, "*qualche*," seems to refer to the quantity of "stones" that the team could take away: this word can be translated as "any," "some," or "a few" ("and that no one meddle with their scaffolding or implements, nor hinder them from taking away any/some/a few pieces of stone with inscriptions or figures"). In either case, Lusieri's team appears to have violated the terms of the original permit by removing entire sections of the friezes and metopes and effectively dismantling the monument so that the most important architectural sculptures could be taken to Britain.

The Shifting Balance of Power

The removal of the Marbles occurred between 1801 and 1804. When Elgin left office in 1803, he ordered his team to continue its work. Circumstances changed, however, as the ambassadors who succeeded him did not favor continued plunder. Furthermore, the entire political situation was now reversed, because France and the Ottoman Porte concluded a peace treaty in response to the alliance between

---

[24] Edward Dodwell was a British traveler and philhellene who traveled extensively in Greece; his writings, published in 1819, offer a lively description of Lord Elgin's removal of sculptures from the Parthenon; see also Gennadios 1930, pp. 86–93.

[25] Philip Hunt (1772–1838) was a priest of the Anglican Church and an antiquarian who became chaplain to Lord Elgin (1799–1802). Elgin, then ambassador of Great Britain to the Ottoman Empire, assigned him the task of traveling and collecting antiquities. Hunt traveled in the Troad and carried out research in monastic libraries in Istanbul, and on the Princes' Islands and Mt. Athos. He came to Athens in the summer of 1801 in order to supervise the work carried out by Lusieri, bringing with him the informal letter, the so-called firman of the district governor, the Ottoman official who replaced the grand vizier in Istanbul. He realized that the situation offered an unrivaled chance to enhance the efforts of Lord Elgin in Athens with original architectural members from the Parthenon itself. The Ottoman authorities silently acceded to this bold move after a process of bribery and extortion: Korka 2009, p. 176. Cf. Benizelos 1986, p. 464; Angelomatis-Tsougarakis 1990.

[26] Eldem 2011, p. 283; Hunt and Smith 1916, p. 190; but see also Williams 2009, p. 8.

[27] Potter 1837; Great Britain 1816.

[28] Eldem 2011, pp. 285–286.

Russia and Great Britain. After this treaty, all French prisoners were released, and Fauvel was allowed to go back to Athens as a special envoy of the French state (a title accorded to him by Talleyrand, his new protector). He was of course appalled by the fate of the Parthenon Marbles and, despite the dire economic situation that he (and his compatriots) faced, sent a series of letters asking the new French ambassador in Istanbul, Guillaume-Marie-Anne Brune, to exert pressure on the sultan to stop the vandalism. Fauvel had many reasons to be bitter: not only did he consider Elgin responsible for the initial expulsion and incarceration of the French residents of Athens and for the expropriation of their properties, but he was also aware that the pride of his collection, the Parthenon metope, and other objects sent to Choiseul-Gouffier in 1803 on the corvette *L'Arabe* had been seized by the British and ended up in Elgin's collection.[29] They are still in the British Museum.

Sir Robert Adair, chosen as the new British ambassador to Istanbul to succeed Lord Elgin, was posted there in 1808. Some years had passed since Elgin left his position to travel back to England during the Napoleonic Wars. On his return journey, however, he was unexpectedly taken captive by the French and held prisoner in France for three years, not arriving in England until 1806. Through painstaking and outrageously costly efforts, he managed to get hold of the cases and boxes containing the first part of his collection, scattered around various ports in England during his absence and brought up from the *Mentor* shipwreck off the island of Kythera. Furthermore, Elgin was continually looking for a way to bring the second part of his collection to England, as it had been detained in Athens for years and faced immense difficulties leaving Ottoman territory.

Circumstances in Athens had become more complicated since 1806, as the balance of power shifted constantly in the wider Mediterranean. At one point, the Ottomans were allies of the British, at another of the French, while the Russians also switched sides, further confusing matters. This patchwork of interchangeable alliances and enmities had an effect even in out-of-the-way Athens.

The two main powers, France and Britain, embodied by the figures of Fauvel (Fig. 2) and Lusieri, launched a local war, a feud of conflicting personal interests characterized by feverish behind-the-scenes activity. Fauvel, who earlier had to leave Athens, came back in 1803 seeking a chance to seize the reins. From England, Elgin envisaged a raid on Athens with the help of the British navy to spirit the Marbles away.[30] At the same time, Fauvel could not send the Marbles to Paris without the help of a French vessel, even if he finally managed to get his hands on them. The situation remained static, however, until 1808, when Lusieri wrote to tell Sir Robert Adair in Istanbul that he needed firmans in order to ship the Marbles to England. In 1809, Lusieri managed to load the Marbles onto a chartered ship after securing the voivode's consent, but someone apparently informed the Porte, because an order was hastily sent to Athens prohibiting the ship from leaving.[31]

Adair was asked repeatedly to intervene to obtain permission from the Porte for the Marbles to be released, but the Ottomans informed him that Elgin had no right to take the sculptures in the first place. They stated that all the events and actions that took place in Athens, and particularly on the Acropolis, for eight years on Lord Elgin's behalf were totally illegal. This reaction is particularly revealing. The individuals in power in the Ottoman administration had all changed since Elgin's time; their response reveals that no valid authorization was considered to have been granted for the removal of the Marbles, and even that officials in Athens may have had no knowledge of what was going on.

---

[29] Zambon 2007, pp. 73, 75; despite repeated attempts, Choiseul-Gouffier and the French never succeeded in recovering these items.
[30] St Clair 1998, p. 180.
[31] St Clair 1998, p. 183; Hunt and Smith 1916, p. 279.

Figure 2. "The Acropolis as seen from the Home of the French Consul M. Fauvel," engraving after Louis Dupré. Dupré 1825, pl. 19. American School of Classical Studies at Athens, Gennadius Library.

In 1809, Britain and the Sublime Porte signed a peace treaty ending the two-year war. This helped Adair's negotiations for the shipping of the Marbles, but does not seem to have been enough to resolve the issue. In 1810 Adair had to offer gifts to officials in Istanbul amounting to 1480 piasters and 100 pounds sterling, as well as a very generous present to the district governor, the value of which is not mentioned.[32] Adair finally managed to engineer the transport of the antiquities on March 20, 1810, after the district governor sent a suitable document to the voivode in Athens.

[32] Hunt and Smith 1916, p. 280.

The feelings of people in Athens, according to the novelist John Galt, who traveled extensively in Greece in the 1810s, were hostile toward Elgin.[33] Fauvel raised a fuss in order to prevent the departure of the Marbles, stating that no authorization was ever given to Elgin for their removal; his protests were, however, to no avail.[34]

Three Rediscovered Letters

For many years, the latter official documents were considered to be lost. The Greek Ministry of Culture sent Professor Ioannis Alexandropoulos to Istanbul in the late 1990s to search for relevant documents, but to no avail, as the Ottoman State Archives had not yet been reorganized and digitized. Subsequently, we searched the archives again and discovered three letters that are important documents from the second phase of Elgin's collecting efforts. These same letters were later found to have been published in 2011 by Eldem, but without a full analysis of the points important for shedding light on the actual events that led to the removal of the Parthenon Marbles. The scope of this publication was quite different, yet helpful due to the linguistic analysis of the terms used in the letters.[35]

These revealing texts dispel certain theories that had been formulated in their absence. When a document does not exist, researchers tend to speculate on its contents and may impute much more to it than what it actually holds. In the case of the history of the removal of the Parthenon sculptures, every document is considered to be part of the legal record. British arguments have used such non-existent texts as *de facto* instruments to legalize and ratify Elgin's actions retroactively. The difficulty presented by the three newly discovered letters is that the dates attributed to them were probably given by the archivist based on their context, but do not appear to correspond to existing historical evidence.

Document BOA, HAT., 1277/49548,[36] a letter dated April 6, 1810, was probably written to the sultan by the district governor after Adair had offered the latter the aforementioned generous bribe, because it shows great eagerness to persuade the sultan to allow the Marbles to leave Athens:

> My illustrious, awe-inspiring, powerful benefactor, Lord and Emperor,
> As your Highness has been informed, a few days ago during an official conversation with the English ambassador, it was mentioned that he has requested a permit to transport some pieces of stones with images, which the former ambassador of England, Lord Elgin, during his period of office as ambassador had bought in Athens and loaded in crates, which he left there for safekeeping. In his petition is filed and written the official report. We await your order. Along with the official report, I submit to Your Highness my report on the content of the aforementioned conversation. In order to issue the imperial edict, the members of the council have

---

[33] John Galt, a Scottish writer and founder of the city of Guelph in Canada, was concerned with the issue of the Industrial Revolution and the social transformations it brought with it. In the 1810s he journeyed throughout the Levant and became acquainted with Lord Byron and his friend, John Cam Hobhouse. After touring together in Malta, their paths crossed again in Greece. Gant's book *Letters from the Levant* offers interesting glimpses of Athens and expresses the view that had Elgin not removed the Parthenon sculptures, the French would have done so (Letter XIV, March 1, 1810: Galt 1813, p. 112).
[34] St Clair 1998, pp. 187–188.
[35] Bahrani, Çelik, and Eldem 2011; Eldem 2011.
[36] BOA, Hatt-ı Hümayun [Imperial decrees; hereafter, HAT.], 1277/49548.

> convened in order to decide on the issue of the image-bearing stones, and they concluded that these stones had indeed been given to the Englishman, and the fact that the aforementioned ambassador's petition in this respect has not yet been granted is not due to any expected inconvenience, but rather to the intention of letting some time go by so that the matter gained in importance and that in the end it can be said that the imperial permission was obtained as a sign of deference to the ambassador. Thus, the council concluded that the permit for the aforementioned stones should be given, as they saw no harm in that. A letter has been written by your servant [i.e. the undersigned] to the Voivode of Athens and a copy of it is submitted to Your Majesty to be examined by Your Crowned person, and once this has been submitted to Your Imperial knowledge, vested with the wisdom of the world, if it is in accord with Your Majesty's will, it will be for my illustrious, awe-inspiring, powerful benefactor, My Lord and Emperor, to command.[37]

This letter contains many discrepancies in regard to historical truth, such as the statement that Elgin "bought" the Marbles. Since both the sultan and the Ottoman court officials had changed in the meantime, however, they could easily have been persuaded of the contrary.

The text itself is difficult and often unclear, referring to previous events and documents in the convoluted fashion that is common in Ottoman correspondence, which favors rhetoric rather than accuracy. What is clear at least is that this text contains no mention of the Marbles as being from buildings on the Acropolis, giving their removal legality. On the contrary, they are referred to in a derogatory manner, as "stones with images," which may be what Adair told the district governor.

The letter was most probably prepared by the district governor at some time between February 18 and March 20, 1810, when the so-called "firman" from the district governor, Hussein Kâmil, addressed to the voivode in Athens arrived, allowing the Marbles to be taken away. The date of April 6 assigned to the document by the archivist is therefore incorrect.

Two other letters were also discovered, BOA, HAT., 1277/49548–B, and BOA, HAT., 1277/49548–A, both dated by the archivist to January 14, 1812, but probably written much earlier.[38] The former, 1277/49548–B, may perhaps date to 1808, when Lusieri, who had fled Athens in 1806 while the British were at war with the Ottomans, returned to retrieve the Marbles along with the ancient vases he had collected for Elgin.

A copy of an order issued by the grand vizier to the voivode in Athens, the letter specifically mentions the presence of ceramics and that their transport was impeded:

> The ambassador of England, who lives in Istanbul, has asked orally and in writing that a permit for transport of ancient marbles with images and of earthenware vases that are now kept at a location outside the city of Athens be accorded to him. He needs the issuing of an imperial order and the permit for transport and safe passage of these items, which belonged to former ambassador Lord Elgin. The order should

---

[37] Our translation has been greatly improved by comparison with the translation already published by Edhem Eldem, who kindly let us make use of it.
[38] These two letters were appended to the decree; see Eldem 2011, p. 293.

be addressed to the Voivode of Athens, in order that no impediment is caused to the transport and passage of the said pottery by our man, called Luigi.[39]

After this letter, the decree was finally issued and a copy sent to Athens, with text as follows:

Copy of an order by His Excellency the District Governor to the Voivode of Athens.

The Englishman called Lord Elgin lived formerly in the embassy at the Gate of Felicity; when he was in Athens, he loaded some crates with some broken marbles with "images" and some pottery for transport to his country. When the man was sent by the aforementioned ambassador to transport these crates, the transport was hindered, although following your previous communication a report was sent from the Sublime Porte and the High Order [the sultan's firman] was drafted and proclaimed and a letter would be sent in order for permission to be granted for the transport. For the time being, the ambassador of England who dwells at the Gate of Felicity pleads for this letter and for the transport of the aforementioned stones with images. These stones are not acceptable in Islam, but they are acceptable in the European countries. There is no harm in conceding a permit for the transport of the aforementioned stones. The transport and safe passage of the stones that are contained in the boxes should not be hindered.[40]

This letter may be the one that finally allowed the transport of the Marbles in 1810. In any case, the objects referred to in the letter are characterized as some broken pieces of marble with images and certain ceramics that belong to the ambassador. A cover-up is evident, since the Marbles are said to belong to Elgin. What is striking is the choice of words: the vizier [or district governor] refers to these objects as "not acceptable in Islam, but [...] acceptable in the European countries." Reading between the lines, we can trace the vizier's efforts not only to diminish the value of the reliefs and sculptures, but also to stress that they are objects unfit for an Islamic environment, probably the pretext needed in the circumstances.

The latter letter, 1277/49548-A, from the voivode of Athens to the central government, is more difficult to interpret because it mentions the British ambassador, who lives in Istanbul and has "ancient marbles" and "earthenware vases" that should be given back to him and allowed to leave the place outside Athens where they were stored. This letter probably does not come from Elgin's time, but much later, perhaps 1808, when Lusieri was asking Adair for firmans to recover all the confiscated goods and transport them to England. A new letter, so Eldem believes, may have been sent by Adair to the Porte in order that Luiseri's name (the letter simply calls him "Luigi") be specified in the permit enabling the shipment. This document tries to diminish the value of the objects that had to be transported, since at the end it refers only to the shipping of pottery from Athens. Here as well, we find no reference to any permit legitimating the dismantling of the Parthenon.

In any case, for their content to be analyzed and interpreted, these letters should be carefully compared to all the existing material connected with the issue. In no other way can the historical truth

---

[39] BOA, HAT., 1277/49548–A.
[40] BOA, HAT., 1277/49548–B.

be discovered. As regards the transport of antiquities from Athens, a few remaining cases containing parts of the Marbles were also shipped in 1811, although how this was managed is unclear.

In the meantime, many dilettanti and other travelers flocked to Athens and immediately became enmeshed in the Lusieri–Fauvel feud. Almost all vehemently disapproved of the despoilment of the Parthenon. Lusieri in fact used the previous efforts of the French to remove certain Marbles as a pretext for what Elgin finally managed to accomplish.[41] Many texts left by these foreign visitors provide details of their negative stance toward the removals. On the other hand, travelers did catch the fever for collecting antiquities, and many of them departed with ancient souvenirs in their baggage.[42] This was the period when certain individuals from different countries banded together to remove the frieze of the Temple of Apollo Epicurius at Bassae (Arcadia), as well as many of the sculptures from the Temple of Aphaia on Aegina, with the aim of selling them to major European museums.[43] When Lord Byron visited Athens at the time, especially after having travelled on the *Hydra*, the ship that transported the last cases of the Marbles to Malta, he became so sensitive to the issue that he composed his first poem against Elgin.

The existing texts offer useful information about the parochial society of Athens, the behavior of the lowly population of Christians and Muslims, and French–British intrigues over the antiquities. Since both Fauvel and Lusieri lived in Athens even in old age, these agents became part of the city's history, inspiring its inhabitants through the Philomuse Society, which with the help of the patriarch attempted to put an end to the loss of antiquities. Athenian society never forgave Lusieri for his actions, a sentiment Ioannis Benizelos (1735–1807) had been the first to put in writing.[44]

Subsequent Correspondence

Returning to the situation with the Parthenon Marbles, Adair must be said to have succeeded. The Marbles had left, yet the legality of their acquisition was constantly questioned, and Elgin needed even more help from him. Desperate for money, Elgin tried to sell his collection to the British government, which, however, resisted his appeals. A major factor examined in their negotiations was the issue of whether Elgin had made use of his post as ambassador to obtain the collection. Elgin had to prove to the government that the antiquities he collected were the result of a totally private enterprise.

To this end, Elgin had to admit that the Porte never officially authorized the removal of the Parthenon Marbles. Through this admission, he believed that he could prove that he did not use his position to obtain any favors from Ottoman officials and that he succeeded in removing the sculptures

---

[41] Great Britain 1816.
[42] From the Renaissance onwards, particularly from the 15th century, a new, almost systematic manner of stealing cultural heritage assets emerged, not related to wars and other conflicts, but rather to a succession of sales, bribes, and applications of diplomatic and political pressure. Western Europeans, thirsty for knowledge of the past and eager to discover their cultural roots, turned their eyes towards the cradles of civilization. Among them was Greece, suffering under the Ottomans, as well as previously under the Franks and Venetians. Many Europeans, lovers of the classical spirit and its achievements, followed the path to such countries as Italy, Turkey, and Greece, and took some souvenir of their worship of antiquity from the countries they visited. Several of them had an interest in acquiring entire art collections, which they snatched and transported *en masse* to their countries of origin: Gennadios 1930, pp. 167, 174.
[43] The German archaeologist Carl Freiherr Haller von Hallerstein (1774–1817) worked in Greece from 1810 on, participating in the excavations of the Temple of Apollo Epicurius at Bassae (Arcadia) and of the Temple of Aphaia on Aegina; he also bought antiquities on behalf of Ludwig I of Bavaria: Thomson de Grummond 1996, p. 561–562; Bankel 1986, pp. 73–77. See also Kalesopoulou 2015, p. 143. Aside from Ludwig I, Christian VIII of Denmark was particularly interested in Greco-Roman antiquities and the promotion of Neoclassicism in architecture: Haugsted 1996, p. 6; Christiansen 2000, p. 71.
[44] Benizelos 1986.

from the Parthenon as a private individual. Adair's help was required to validate this statement and support Elgin's argument. Elgin needed to have a letter from Adair specifically stating that the Ottomans told him that no official authorization for the removal of the sculptures ever existed, which was in fact the case.

Two letters discovered in the British Library are quite revealing as regards the legality of Elgin's collection. One is from Lord Elgin and the other from Sir Robert Adair; both are dated 1811. Writing to Adair, Elgin made the following request:

> In your letter to me on the subject of your application to the Porte for leave to transmit my Athenian Acquisitions to England your expression is that Mr. Pisani [dragoman to the British embassy][45] more than once assured me that the Porte absolutely denied your having any property on those marbles. Now if you equally conceived Pisani's meaning to be that the Porte denied having given away those Marbles or allowed the removal of those Marbles you would oblige me very much by making that alteration in your letter.[46]

This is where the alteration of meaning and context begins. Adair sent Elgin a draft in which he started to write a sentence, crossed it out, and then wrote a new expression, trying hard to fulfill Elgin's requirements. His difficulties in altering the nuance of the phrases used are easily understood. He starts by writing, "In explanation of the expression in my letter relating to your Marbles, I certainly understood that the Porte in denying your having any property in those marbles meant ["intended" is crossed out] to say that the [originally "those"] persons who sold them to you had no right ["authority" is crossed out] so to dispose of them ["they had given you no authority to make the acquisition of them" is crossed out]". He then continues, "If these additions to my letter will answer your wishes ["can be of any service to" is crossed out] have the goodness to send it to me and I will alter it accordingly ["make the alterations" is crossed out]. Elgin's answer is as follows: "I am extremely sorry to have given you so much trouble about this business. But if you would have the goodness to alter the letter as you propose you would oblige me very much."

This is how the historical record could have been changed. In his desire to comply with Elgin's request, Adair first went so far as to state that the Marbles were sold to Elgin, then, most importantly, changed the meaning of what the Ottoman Porte had in fact told him. He plainly followed Elgin's wishes, since Elgin's purpose was to alter the substance of what the Ottomans had actually said. In order to minimize the Sublime Porte's statement that he had no legal right to the Marbles he put the emphasis on the legal authority of the Turks in Athens and the prospect of their giving him the Marbles. This shift of focus made it seem that Elgin had unknowingly been cheated and could not have known that the Ottoman officials in Athens were unable to dispose of the Marbles according to his wishes. He sought to prove that it was not his fault and that he, for his part, had paid and acted in good faith, whereas the Turks in Athens had exceeded their authority and acted illegally by selling something to which they themselves had no title. The implication was that the sale was completely their doing.

[45] On Pisani, see Cunningham 1993.
[46] Rudenstine 2001.

Finally, he wanted to prove that these transactions could have taken place only in his capacity as a private individual, not as the British ambassador.

Let us now follow what happened next and whether this tampering with the documentary record had any subsequent effect. In 2003, an unpublished letter by Sir Robert Adair was sold at auction to an unknown buyer. It caught the eye of the press and after the sale it was published in a history journal in Athens.[47] This is the letter that Adair sent to Elgin after they reached an agreement concerning the alterations to the text. Dated July 31, 1811, but originally dated July 1, it bears the following note at the head of the page: "corrected and dated [and] altered to July 31st." The text runs as follows:

> In answer to your Lordship's enquiry respecting the marbles collected by your Lordship at Athens, and for leave to transmit which to this country I was directed by the Secretary of State for foreign affairs to apply to the Turkish government, I have to inform your Lordship that Mr. Pisani more than once assured me that the Porte absolutely denied your having any property in those marbles. By this expression I understood the Porte to mean that the persons who had sold the marbles to your Lordship had no right so to dispose of them.
>
> At the same time I beg leave to add that this communication was not made to me in any formal conference with the Turkish Ministers.

Even in this letter, Adair fusses with words and crosses out sentences. He evidently still felt insecure about the letter's content and therefore decided to include the last sentence about all discussions with the Turks having been unofficial.

Elgin waited anxiously for the altered letter, because it would provide the evidence he needed. On the very same date Adair wrote this letter [July 1], Elgin had already prepared a letter addressed to Prime Minister Spencer Perceval that included the following statement: "I had no advantage from the Turkish Government beyond the Firman given equally to other English travelers. My successors in the Embassy could not obtain permission for the removal of what I had not myself taken away. And on Mr. Adair's being officially instructed to apply in my favour, he understood, the Porte denied that the persons who had sold these marbles to me had any right to dispose of them."[48]

What these letters certainly reveal, however, is that Elgin's actions in regard to the removal of the Parthenon sculptures were illegal. Elgin never denied it, nor did he write anything further to Adair that differed from what the latter had been told. The final shipment of the second half of the collection was clearly facilitated by the large bribes given to Ottoman officials.

Conclusion

Newly rediscovered texts, especially documents as important as these, disclose much about the conduct of foreigners in Athens—their mentalities, tendencies, and habits, and the potential extent of their power to influence Athenian society—as well as their actual role concerning the antiquities

---

[47] Theodorou 2003.
[48] TNA, UK Foreign Office, 78/64.

that they supposedly came so far to admire. These texts also illuminate the administrative and bureaucratic legal context of the Ottoman Empire, and the rules of a system that might be followed or sometimes bent by various officials for the sake of personal gain. Above all, such texts shed light on the role of Europe's great powers, France and Britain, as they vied with one another in small, debased Athens to exploit the city's rich yet vulnerable heritage by taking advantage of a decrepit political system and corrupt officialdom in order to enrich their own museums, culturally dominant even today.

Revolutionary Athens through Ottoman Eyes (1821–1828): New Evidence from the Ottoman State Archives

H. Şükrü Ilıcak

Although many scholars have studied the organization and conduct of the Greek War of Independence, serious research based on Ottoman archival documents is extremely limited. This apparent lack of focus on the part of historians is even more curious considering that almost 50,000 archival documents related to this singular event alone exist in the Ottoman State Archives. As such, Ottoman archival documents have much new information to offer on revolutionary Athens.

The most important issue pertaining to Athens in the revolutionary period was, of course, its very possession. In the midst of the revolution, Athens, and more precisely the Acropolis, became the symbol of the Greek struggle for independence. The question of who would possess it came to acquire an importance to both sides of the conflict that was more moral and ideological than military and geopolitical. The answer to this question rested more and more on the discretion of the west European powers, as the forces of the Ottoman ancien régime proved inefficient and untrustworthy allies in fighting the Sublime Porte's battles against the Greek insurgents. In the highly romanticized west European imagination of the early 19th century, the Acropolis became the bastion of the civilized world, and the war was fought between the imaginary descendants of Pericles and those of the barbaric ancient Persians. Official Ottoman documents not only reveal the perceptions and moral universe of state officials, but also illustrate how ferociously this first "clash of civilizations" of the 19th century was fought.[1]

In this essay I examine the struggle for the possession of Athens during the Greek Revolution, based on mostly hitherto unstudied documents from the Ottoman State Archives. Special emphasis is placed on the period 1821–1827, since there are but few Ottoman documents pertaining to Athens after its recapture by the Ottoman forces in June 1827.

---

[1] For the siege of the Acropolis laid by the Greek revolutionaries, see Vakalopoulos 1980, pp. 428–431, 712–714; Gordon 1832, pp. 172–175, 274–283; Finlay 1861, pp. 199–201, 347–350; Waddington 1825, pp. 46–74. For the siege of the Acropolis laid by the Ottoman forces in 1826–1827, see Vakalopoulos 1986, pp. 721–764; St Clair 1972, pp. 314–330; Margaritis 2006, pp. 650–709; Whitcombe 1992.

H. Şükrü Ilıcak

The Outbreak of the Greek Revolution and the First Siege of the Acropolis

On receiving the news of the Greek uprising in the Morea and Livadia, about 1,200 Athenian Muslims[2] sought refuge in the Acropolis, or the "Citadel of Athens" [*Atina kalesi*], as the Ottomans called it. The insurgents immediately laid siege to the citadel. The earliest Ottoman document from revolutionary Athens that is preserved in the archives is a plea for help that was taken to Euboea on June 28, 1821. Written by the deputy judge [*naib*] of Athens, Hacı Halil, the document reported that the insurgent *reaya*[3] of the neighboring villages entered the town on May 8, "became of one heart and one mind with the local ecclesiastics and civilians," and began attacking Muslims. They killed the guards protecting the gates of the citadel, while the deputy judge himself fought against the rebels for two to three hours. The Muslims were forced to withdraw into the citadel, where the insurgents peppered them with bullets and bombarded them from Philopappou Hill and two or three other places.[4] As was customary in public pleas, Islamic scholars, the sheikhs, the descendants of the Prophet, and the rich and the poor of the town all gathered in the courthouse to pen the petition, declaring that their numbers were minimal, whereas the Christians were too many; for this reason they did not have the power to pursue them. They declared that they were in immediate danger and asked that soldiers be dispatched to rescue them.[5]

Hacı Halil's letter points to the main inherent difficulty experienced by the Ottoman administration throughout the years of the revolution. Especially in the Morea and Attica, where the revolt assumed its fiercest form, Muslims comprised a minority, approximately 10% of the population. Most of them were unwarlike common folk, incapable of fighting even to defend themselves. Since the revolution broke out almost simultaneously throughout the Ottoman Empire wherever Greek populations constituted the majority, the Sublime Porte did not know where to deploy its forces first. This was due to the fact that in the decade prior to the Greek Revolution, the Ottoman central state had exhausted its pool of military manpower in its fight against the provincial power brokers in every corner of the empire. Unable to find soldiers to fight its battles, the Sublime Porte was compelled to employ mercenaries to subdue the Greek uprising.[6]

Upon the success of the Ottoman forces in Euboea, Köse Mehmed Pasha, governor of the Morea, was able to spare some troops to help save Athens. He dispatched Ömer Bey of Karystos[7] with 700–800 infantry and Ömer Pasha (Vrioni), the ostensible new leader of the Tosk Albanians after the demise of Tepedelenli Ali Pasha, at the head of 1,500 light cavalry and musketeers. The Ottoman

---

[2] I use the term "Muslim" only nominally, since ethnic Albanians composed a sizable part of the town's Muslim population. Likewise, a considerable number of the Christians of Athens were ethnic Albanians. According to French diplomatic reports, 800 people were besieged, 500 of whom were Albanians. See Archives du Ministère des Affaires étrangères, Paris, Correspondance politique, Turquie 234/164, September 11, 1821; Turquie 233/212, November 10, 1821.

[3] *Reaya*: taxpaying subjects of the Ottoman state. In the 19th century, this term was used exclusively for non-Muslims.

[4] According to Gordon (1832, pp. 276–277), those other places were the batteries raised by the Cefalonians "near the temple of Jupiter Olympius" and the one established by the Zeans "between the theatres of Bacchus and Herodes Atticus."

[5] Deputy Judge of Athens, Hacı Halil, June 28, 1821, Başbakanlık Devlet Arşivi Genel Müdürlüğü [General Directorate of State Archives of the Prime Ministry of the Republic of Turkey], Istanbul, Başbakanlık Osmanlı Arşivi [Ottoman State Archives; hereafter, BOA], Hatt-ı Hümayun [Imperial decrees; hereafter, HAT.], 855/38228–C.

[6] For details of the Sublime Porte's war against the provincial leaders between 1812 and 1821, see Ilıcak 2011, pp. 27–98.

[7] When the revolution broke out, Ömer Bey was the deputy lieutenant governor [*mütesellim*] of Karystos [Kızılhisar]. In a year he was made a vizier of two horsetails [*mir-i miran*] and was appointed castellan [*muhafız*] of the district [*sancak*] of Eğriboz, which encompassed the island of Euboea and the districts [*kazas*] of Athens, Livadia, Thebes, Amfissa, Atalanti, Lamia, and Mendenitsa.

troops lifted the 83-day siege on June 30 without encountering any resistance. They supplied the Athens garrison with enough food, water, and ammunition for a year. In his report to the Sublime Porte, Köse Mehmed Pasha did not forget to mention that the town was recaptured without inflicting any harm on its antiquities.[8]

The ancient monuments of Athens were very unlikely to have been a matter of personal concern to the Ottoman military governor. Yet, he had strict instructions from Istanbul to preserve the antiquities at the request of the British ambassador, Percy Smythe, Viscount Strangford. In an attempt to save the "sacred monuments of antiquity with which that illustrious city abounds" from the fury of the Ottoman forces, Strangford took the initiative of applying to the Sublime Porte.[9] In his letter, the ambassador clearly specified ancient Athens as the originator of modern European civilization, stating that "the famous monuments of antiquity and masterpieces of art made this city the object of Europe's universal admiration for so many centuries." He also invoked his own king into the matter: George IV, who "distinguished himself for his taste and commitment to science and literature, of which Athens was the cradle, would view this proof of a similar sentiment on the part of his old friend and ally, the Ottoman Emperor, with inexpressible satisfaction."[10]

It is not certain, however, whether at this initial stage of the revolution the Ottoman administrators understood how the arts, sciences, and the Greek [*Yunan*] philosophers of ancient Athens were connected with the current Rum *reaya* in the European imagination, or how this cultural legacy might affect the course of the revolution. At this point they were preoccupied by the imminent prospect of war with Russia, so only five days after the Russian ambassador's departure from Istanbul in protest against the Sublime Porte's maltreatment of its Greek subjects, the British ambassador was the last person the Ottoman administrators would risk offending. For this reason, Strangford managed to procure an imperial edict addressed to the Ottoman authorities in Athens, "recommending to their protection the various monuments of art and antiquity that were contained in that city." According to Strangford, "This proceeding was of a character quite unknown to the Ottoman government; and he [Strangford] was perfectly assured that it would never have consented to a demand so foreign to its usages and opinions, had it not been for the sincere desire of doing something that might be agreeable to His Majesty [King George IV of Britain]."[11]

The edict instructed Köse Mehmed Pasha as follows:

> […] as the perfect and sincere affection between the two courts had been increasing day by day; and as the antiquities and ancient monuments in Athens had always deserved the attention of Europe, it befitted the dignity of the Sublime Porte to

---

[8] Governor of the Morea, Köse Mehmed Pasha, to the Sublime Porte, November 17, 1821, BOA, HAT., 1558/0046.
[9] Viscount Strangford to Viscount Castlereagh, August 18, 1821, National Archives [hereafter TNA], Kew, UK Foreign Office [hereafter FO], 78–100/15.
[10] Viscount Strangford to the Sublime Porte, August 15, 1821, TNA, FO, 78–100/15–1: "*L'Ambassadeur d'Angleterre apprenant que les troupes victorieuses de Sa Majesté Impériale sont sur le point d'occuper Athènes, ose recommander à la bienveillance et à la protection du Gouvernement Ottoman les fameux monuments d'antiquité et Chefs d'œuvres d'art qui ont depuis tant de siècles rendu cette ville l'objet de l'admiration universelle de l'Europe. Son Auguste Souverain qui se distingue par son gout et par son attachement aux sciences et à la littérature, dont Athènes fut le berceau, verrait avec une satisfaction inexprimable, cette preuve d'un sentiment analogue, de la part de son Ancien Ami et Allié, l'Empereur Ottoman; et comme l'Ambassadeur se persuade que la Sublime Porte n'a rien de plus à cœur que de faire tout ce qui puisse être agréable à Son Souverain qui de son côté, ne cesse de lui témoigner l'amitié la plus réelle, il a l'honneur de prier Son Excellence le Reis Effendi de vouloir bien faire émaner des Férmans, adressés au Commandant des Troupes Ottomanes, et au Voïvode d'Athènes, pour la conservation de cette Ville, et des beaux monuments de sa gloire antique. L'Ambassadeur saisit cette occasion pour renouveler à Son Excellence l'assurance de sa plus haute considération. Strangford / Au Palais d'Angleterre / Le 15 Aout 1821.*"
[11] Viscount Strangford to Viscount Castlereagh, August 25, 1821, TNA, FO, 78–100/22.

take the necessary measures to retain these ancient monuments in their current state in order to do something agreeable to His Majesty. Thus, due to the sagacity which characterizes you, you shall order all those concerned to spare and preserve the antiquities and monuments in question, so that there should not be any complaint in this regard on the part of anyone.[12]

The patronizing, minatory tone of these instructions was common in Ottoman edicts and thus not guaranteed to generate empathy on the governor's part. As it turned out, the Acropolis was in fact heavily shelled by both the Greek revolutionaries and the Ottoman armies in the following years.

The Second Siege of the Acropolis and the Massacre of Athenian Muslims

As soon as Ömer Vrioni departed from Athens after a three-month stay, the scattered insurgents came down from the mountains and neighboring islands to lay a somewhat loose siege to the Acropolis. The rebels' attempts to take the citadel through open onslaught and surprise attacks proved unsuccessful until the scorching summer of 1822. Running out of water and with no help on the horizon, the besieged asked for the sultan's permission to surrender the citadel. Ömer Bey of Karystos applied to the Sublime Porte on their behalf.[13] The Acropolis was a sultanic fortress, so capitulation was unlawful without the permission of the sultan. The weary Muslims were compelled to enter into negotiations with the insurgents and agreed to capitulate on June 21, 1822, before an answer from the Sublime Porte could arrive. They surrendered the Acropolis the following day, on the condition that the life and honor of every individual belonging to the garrison would be preserved, and that they would be transported to some port on the Anatolian shores of the Aegean. So the Muslims laid down their arms and descended from the Acropolis. Most of them were lodged in the former residence of the voivode, waiting for vessels to take them to safety.[14]

On July 10, 18 days after the garrison's surrender, a rumor reached Athens that the Ottoman army under Dramalı Mahmud Pasha had traversed the pass of Thermopylae and was advancing toward Athens.[15] "The more cruel and treacherous portion of the Athenian people and soldiery," in Thomas

---

[12] The Sublime Porte to the Governor of the Morea, Köse Mehmed Pasha, August 22, 1821, TNA, FO, 78–100/22–1: "*Traduction d'une lettre de S.A. le Grand Vézir au Gouverneur Général de la Morée, ainsi qu'au Commandant et au Juge d'Athènes. L'Ambassadeur de la Cour d'Angleterre résidant près la Sublime Porte, ayant entendu que les Troupes Ottomanes (que la victoire suit partout) sont en marche pour aller purger la Ville d'Athènes des brigands qui s'y sont montrés en force, a présenté une note officielle dans laquelle il a exposé que ce serait faire un plaisir à Sa Majesté le Roi de la Grande Bretagne que d'ordonner, en cette circonstance, qu'on ait à épargner et à conserver les restes d'Antiquités, et les monuments anciens qui existent dans la Ville et dans les environs d'Athènes, de cette Ville à laquelle l'Europe entière a, de tout temps, pris un si vif intérêt. Comme Sa dite Majesté témoigne de l'amitié envers la Sublime Porte, et que la parfaite et sincère affection qui existe entre les deux Cours augmente de jour en jour; et comme les antiquités et les monuments anciens d'Athènes ont, toujours mérité l'attention générale de l'Europe, il appartient à la dignité de la Sublime Porte de prendre les mesures nécessaires pour laisser exister et pour conserver, dans leur état actuel, ces monuments antiques, dans la vue de faire quelques chose d'agréable à Sa dite Majesté. Ainsi vous aurez soin, d'après la sagacité qui vous caractérise, d'ordonner à tous ceux qu'il appartiendra d'épargner et de conserver les antiquités et les monuments dont il s'agit, faisant en sorte qu'il n'y ait pas des plaintes, à ce sujet, de la part de qui que ce soit. C'est à cette fin que la présente Vous est adressée. Le 22 Aout 1821.*"
[13] Deputy Lieutenant Governor of Karystos, Ömer Bey, to the Sublime Porte, June 8, 1822, BOA, HAT., 613/30160.
[14] Gordon 1832, p. 412.
[15] Dramalı Mahmud Pasha had indeed passed through Thermopylae on July 5, 1822, but he apparently had no intention to march on Athens. According to the information gathered by Philip James Green, the British consul in Patras, "Dramali appeared to have been aware of the surrender of the Acropolis, but did not attempt its recapture; preferring to follow his orders, and acting thereon, advanced towards the Isthmus" (Green 1827, p. 116).

Gordon's words, grew agitated and violated the terms of capitulation. Suddenly Athens became the scene of mob violence, and its Muslim residents were massacred regardless of age or sex. The bibliography of sources for these events is ample, including accounts with graphic details.[16] Depending on the source, the number of victims varies from 400 to 800.[17] The remainder survived, thanks to the strenuous efforts of the Austrian, Dutch, and French consulates, which provided shelter to hundreds of survivors before shipping them off to Izmir.

Upon the news of the survivors' arrival in Izmir—270 women and children, along with 30 invalids in 2 French vessels—the sultan remarked, "A major city such as Athens also passed into the hands of the infidels." He then expressed his grief with a sura from the Qur'an (36:38): "That is the determination of the Exalted in Might, the Knowing," and continued, "May God, the Great Avenger and All-Compeller, not deny Muslims revenge, and crush and annihilate [the Greeks] shortly."[18]

The sultan's remarks indicate another prevailing theme of the Greek Revolution: the cycle of violence against noncombatant civilians. The uprising very rapidly turned into a merciless war of religion, basically a vendetta during which indiscriminate massacres were committed by both sides. Although the massacres of the Muslims of Tripoli in 1821 and the Christians of Chios in 1822 were only an iota shy of what might be categorized as genocide today, this label entails a risk of falling into terminological anachronism.

The visit of Georg Christian Gropius, then Austrian consul in Athens, to Istanbul in the summer of 1825 constitutes an interesting footnote to the massacre. Gropius demanded compensation of 20,332 piasters from the Sublime Porte, asserting that he saved 347 Muslims from slaughter, taking care of them at his consulate for a year, securing their exodus from the town on vessels. He claimed to have paid the insurgents a bribe of 7,356 piasters and allocated 12,976 piasters for the hostages' expenses. The Sublime Porte investigated the issue and confirmed that the consul's story was accurate. In his report to the sultan, the grand vizier stated that compensating the consul befitted the Ottoman state's glory. The sultan approved the payment of the sum from the "Brigandry Fund" [Eşkiya Akçesi], a pool of resources reserved specifically for the suppression of the Greek uprising, the main constituent of which was confiscated Greek property.[19]

The Campaigns of 1823 and 1824

In the five years that followed, despite the Sublime Porte's elaborate preparations on paper, the Ottoman military proved hopelessly incompetent in the field, and all efforts to recapture Athens bore no fruit. Strongly recalling the circumstances attending the dissolution of several ancient empires, the Ottoman state was unable to recruit and mobilize soldiers and was obliged to resort to the violence market, whose most important providers were Muslim Albanian warlords. Thus, the overwhelming majority of the soldiers employed to recapture Athens and the Acropolis in subsequent years were ethnic Albanian mercenaries.

---

[16] Waddington 1825, pp. 65–74; Gordon 1832, p. 412; Walsh 1836, pp. 135–145; Finlay 1861, pp. 347–349; St Clair 1972, pp. 104–105.
[17] Viscount Strangford to Viscount Castlereagh, August 10, 1821, TNA, FO, 78–109/21; Green 1827, p. 113; Gordon 1832, p. 413.
[18] Governor of Izmir, Hasan Pasha, to the Sublime Porte, July 26, 1822, BOA, HAT., 877/38855. The same document records that the refugees were fed, clothed, and given shelter in the houses of the wealthy men of Izmir. Among the survivors was the voivode of Athens, Haseki Mehmed Aga.
[19] Grand Vizier Benderli Mehmed Selim Sırrı Pasha to Sultan Mahmud II, July 5, 1825, BOA, HAT., 626/30928.

The reluctance of previous historians to grant the Albanians of the early 19th century the qualities of a people capable of pursuing its own interests—as opposed to being a mere agglomeration of mercenary tribes—has largely prevented a clear understanding of their key role in the Greek Revolution. Amid the murk of revolutionary turmoil, Albanians were at the very heart of the matter, following their own survival instincts and pursuing their agenda while remaining quite unresponsive to the Sublime Porte's demands. Despite the Sublime Porte's reiterated exhortations, Albanian warlords were often tardy in taking to the field and obeying orders; even when they followed through, they were reluctant to fight the Greeks. As William Meyer, the British consul at Preveza and an extremely erudite and intuitive observer of Albanian politics, remarked in the wake of the Greek Revolution: "as to their real national sentiments [the Albanians] were nearly as adverse to the domination of the Porte, as the Greeks themselves," and followed a peculiar policy throughout the insurgency.[20]

The ethnic makeup of the Albanian population proved another matter of concern for the Ottoman state. The two major ethnic groups, the Tosks and the Gegs, the former inhabiting areas south of the Shkumbin River and the latter the northern regions, spoke mutually unintelligible dialects and had different physiognomies and ways of life.[21] They also had a long history of frequent mutual strife that frustrated the Sublime Porte's military efforts during the course of the Greek Revolution.

In the campaign of the summer of 1823, the newly appointed commander-in-chief [*serasker*] of the Morea, Berkofçalı Yusuf Pasha,[22] failed in his assignment to recapture Athens. In their joint report to the Sublime Porte, Yusuf Pasha and Salih Pasha, governor of Ormenio in Thrace, stated that a march on Athens and Euboea necessitated at least 15,000 fresh soldiers, 4,000–5,000 beasts of burden to transport cannons, ammunition, and rations, and an abundant supply of wheat. However, not one Albanian chieftain [*Arnavudbaşı*] or any other official had yet reported for duty at the army's encampment. There were few pastures in the region, and the enemy had scorched the earth, even the reed beds around the lakes. As a result, all pack animals perished, and the army suffered from famine. Despite these inconveniences, they arrived as far as the gates of the Acropolis; around 20 Ottoman soldiers died in the skirmishes. According to information extracted from the captured insurgents, the Greeks had moved all of the provisions in the region to the island of Salamis and into the stronghold of the Acropolis. The pashas were not able to relieve the extreme hunger, distress, and strife in the ranks, so the soldiers who were still able to serve disbanded, and the pashas retired to Lamia with those that remained in their retinues.[23]

The Sublime Porte had no option other than to entrust the suppression of the Greek uprising to the Albanian pashas in the summer campaign of 1824. Geg and Tosk troops were to be sent to different locations in order to avoid contact and prevent contention among them. Buşatlı Mustafa Pasha, governor of Shkodër and patriarch of the leading dynasty of the Geg Albanians, was ordered to capture Missolonghi and quell the revolution in the region of Acarnania. Ömer Vrioni was ordered to lead 8,000–10,000 Tosk Albanians in a march on Athens,[24] but Ebulebud Mehmed Pasha, governor of Rumeli, opposed this decision on the grounds of the utter fiasco caused by these two Albanian chieftains at

---

[20] William Meyer to George Canning, March 31, 1824, TNA, FO, 78–126/7.
[21] See the article "Albania" in the first Turkish encyclopedia, *Kamusu'l Alam*: Şemseddin Sami [Sami Frashëri] 1889.
[22] Berkofçalı Yusuf Pasha was the governor of Salonica at the time of his appointment.
[23] Yusuf and Salih Pashas to the Sublime Porte, July 5, 1823, BOA, HAT., 911/39856; September 21, 1823, BOA, HAT., 838/37787; September 25, 1823, BOA, HAT., 928/40290–A.
[24] Grand Vizier Mehmed Said Galib Pasha to Sultan Mahmud II, undated, BOA, HAT., 1217/47671; BOA, HAT., 845/37954.

Missolonghi in the autumn of 1823.[25] That campaign had failed partly due to the animosity between Gegs and Tosks, and the Sublime Porte was unwilling to risk another failure.

Ebulebud Mehmed Pasha's acrimonious relations with the Albanians necessitated a change in the governorate of Rumeli. Filibeli Şinikzade Derviş Mustafa Pasha was nominated to the position in March 1824 by consensus in the Imperial Council. He adopted a more resolute anti-Albanian position than that of his predecessors. Derviş Pasha became the most strident proponent of an ethnic shift in the composition of the Ottoman military forces; at first, he pursued fairly independent policies without prior authorization from the Sublime Porte. Convinced of the Albanians' lack of religious zeal and consequent uselessness in the field, he discharged his predecessor's sizable mercenary army and stressed the need to employ ethnic Turkish soldiers.[26]

The campaign of 1824 against Athens also resulted in failure. Ömer Pasha of Karystos arrived at the gates of the Acropolis at the beginning of the summer to facilitate the siege until the arrival of the forces of the governor of Rumeli,[27] but that army did not appear. The janissaries had agreed to deploy 6,000 troops,[28] yet not even 3,000 reached Athens. Moreover, the janissaries proved useless; lack of coordination and trust between them and the mercenaries caused disorder in the army. Most of the janissaries fell ill, "furled their banners," abandoned the siege, and left for Istanbul at the end of August without asking permission to do so.[29] Without cannons, mortars, or enough soldiers, Ömer Pasha's base in front of the Acropolis was a waste of resources. He had not paid the mercenaries under his command in the past three months; the soldiers were grumbling. In early September, he quit the siege and retired to Euboea. At the top of the grand vizier's summary report of the events, the sultan asserted that "Ömer Pasha is a zealous vizier. Had he received assistance in time, he would have captured Athens."[30]

Derviş Mustafa Pasha's policies estranged the Albanians to such an extent that the Sublime Porte had to replace him with someone more tactful to prevent an Albanian rebellion. Although frustrated by their independent agenda, the Sublime Porte had no option but to keep the Albanians in check until the arrival of Ibrahim Pasha's army from Egypt. In November 1824 Reşid Mehmed Pasha, governor of Vidin, who was known to have better relations with the Albanians,[31] was named governor of Rumeli and rapidly assuaged the Albanians' discontent.

The Androutsos Affair

For the campaign of the summer of 1825, Reşid Mehmed Pasha considered assigning the subjugation of Athens to Ömer Pasha of Karystos or to an Albanian pasha,[32] but an unexpected development changed the course of events. In the midst of what is called the Second Civil War in Greek historiography,

[25] Governor of Rumeli, Ebulebud Mehmed Emin Pasha, to the Sublime Porte, undated, BOA, HAT., 877/38822.
[26] Governor of Rumeli, Derviş Mustafa Pasha, to the Sublime Porte, April 6, 1824, BOA, HAT., 926/40226; Derviş Mustafa Pasha to his agent at the Sublime Porte [*kapukethüda*], August 27, 1824, BOA, HAT., 906/39723.
[27] Grand Vizier Mehmed Said Galib Pasha to Sultan Mahmud II, undated, BOA, HAT., 846/37981.
[28] Viscount Strangford to George Canning, December 30, 1823, TNA, FO, 78–118/21.
[29] Castellan of Euboea, Ömer Pasha, to the Sublime Porte, August 30, 1824, BOA, HAT., 922/40093; Ömer Pasha to the Sublime Porte, September 1, 1824, BOA, HAT., 510/25048–B.
[30] Grand Vizier Mehmed Said Galib Pasha to Sultan Mahmud II, undated, BOA, HAT., 846/37981.
[31] Grand Vizier Benderli Mehmed Selim Sırrı Pasha to Sultan Mahmud II, undated, BOA, HAT., 919/39988.
[32] Governor of Rumeli, Reşid Mehmed Pasha, to the Sublime Porte, December 28, 1824, BOA, HAT., 880/38944.

Odysseas Androutsos, one of the most renowned heroes of the Greek Revolution and the virtual ruler of Athens and its environs, sought an alliance with the Ottomans.[33] The application of Androutsos—Kapudan Disava, as the Ottomans called him—for amnesty generated a lively correspondence within the Ottoman administration in early 1825.

Distressed by the schism among the contentious revolutionary factions and to avoid anarchy, in the autumn of 1822 Athenians opted for a dictatorship headed by Androutsos. In October 1822, the central Greek government, formed earlier that year, honored this decision by appointing Androutsos captain-general of eastern Greece. In the words of the British consul, Philip Green, he was "one of the most warlike and popular of the Albanian chiefs."[34] Androutsos made Athens his headquarters and became master of the entire Attica region and its environs in the subsequent two years. The British priest and philhellene George Waddington, who was in Greece between 1823 and 1824, wrote that Androutsos, governor of Athens, "possesses, in fact, the whole power, military and civil, legislative and executive, and that he does not appear greatly to abuse it."[35]

When conflict between the Greek revolutionary factions escalated to the proportions of civil war, Androutsos came into contact with Ömer Pasha of Karystos and requested a meeting with a trusted man at a coastal village nine hours distant from Euboea to discuss matters of importance. Ömer sent his secretary [*divan katibi*], who was a Greek speaker. Androutsos demanded amnesty in return for his services to the Ottoman state on several conditions: he should be headquartered in Thebes; the governor of Rumeli should dispatch 1,000 cavalry and 5,000 infantry for the protection of the districts under his rule (Livadia, Thebes, and Atalanti); Androutsos would deploy these troops in numbers necessary for his march on Athens after rendering his services and proving his loyalty; his men should receive a monthly allowance of 40 piasters, with a bonus for provisions; and he should be commander-in-chief of military expeditions against the districts that had not yet requested amnesty.[36] When Ömer Pasha's secretary told him to surrender a castle to the Ottoman state as a sign of goodwill, Androutsos vowed to prove his loyalty and integrity by marching to Athens.[37] A memorandum of agreement was drawn up and sent to the Sublime Porte and the governor of Rumeli for ratification.[38] Ömer Pasha urged Reşid Mehmed Pasha to dispatch the promised troops to Thebes at once, because Androutsos intended to move on to Athens in 15 to 20 days, and it was not proper to give him an excuse to rescind the agreement.[39]

The grand vizier, Benderli Mehmed Sırrı Selim Pasha, found Androutsos's conditions improper, however. Contracting out the recapture of Athens to a dubious infidel who would be put in command of Muslim soldiers and pay his men wages from the imperial coffers was simply unacceptable.

---

[33] For a British account of Androutsos's dealings with the Ottoman officials, see Trelawny 1858, pp. 253–264. Edward John Trelawny was Androutsos's lieutenant and brother-in-law. Trelawny claimed that Androutsos told him that he had made a truce for three months with Ömer Pasha and that "It is the only way in which I could save the people from being massacred ... what I have done, is only to bring the Greek government to terms." See Trelawny 1858, pp. 254-255. For a Greek account of the Androutsos affair, see Spiliadis 1852, pp. 411–414. According to him, it was Trelawny who urged Androutsos to ally with the Ottomans. The 20th-century Greek historian Apostolos Vakalopoulos, who wrote the most comprehensive account of this affair, does not agree with Spiliadis. According to Vakalopoulos, Androutsos's approach to the Ottomans, although borderline treason, was fake and an act of despair, aiming only to scare his enemies in the Greek government. See Vakalopoulos 1986, pp. 205–211; Vakalopoulos 1975, pp. 375–376.
[34] Green 1827, p. 125.
[35] Waddington 1825, p. 77.
[36] Grand Vizier Benderli Mehmed Selim Sırrı Pasha to Sultan Mahmud II, undated, BOA, HAT., 890/39313.
[37] Castellan of Euboea, Ömer Pasha, to the Sublime Porte, February 19, 1825, BOA, HAT., 897/39481–C.
[38] Memorandum of agreement from the Castellan of Euboea, Ömer Pasha, to the Sublime Porte, February 19, 1825, BOA, HAT., 897/39481–H.
[39] Castellan of Euboea, Ömer Pasha, to the Governor of Rumeli, Reşid Mehmed Pasha, February 19, 1825, BOA, HAT., 897/39481–F.

Nonetheless, the Sublime Porte did not spurn the proposal outright, because it was Ömer Pasha who appeared to be pursuing the realization of this agreement. In his report to the sultan, the grand vizier characterized Ömer Pasha as a local man who knew the Greeks and had insight into their deeds and doings. The grand vizier was moreover uncertain whether Ömer Pasha had rushed the draft of the agreement to the Sublime Porte because he was unwilling to let slip the real opportunity of a major Greek chieftain turning against his comrades or had something else in mind.

The sultan, it seems, found Ömer Pasha's project inefficient if not naïve: "Although the castellan of Euboea is a zealous and loyal vizier, due to his gullible disposition I understand that he is not able to contemplate the deep corners [of the issue]."[40] The sultan did not reject the project, however, ordering Reşid Mehmed Pasha, governor of Rumeli, to be in charge of the affair and Ömer Pasha to comply with Reşid Mehmed Pasha's instructions.

While waiting for Reşid Mehmed Pasha's response, the Ottoman administrators made inquiries about Androutsos. The "men of knowledge" in Istanbul did not entertain particularly positive views of him, considering him a "master of deceit and devilry." Yet the *reaya* of the region were in his hands, and he could attract them to the state in the same fashion that he had incited them to rebel.[41]

Reşid Mehmed Pasha's view of the matter was not particularly promising either. He found it blasphemous that the Sublime State should need Androutsos's assistance to capture Athens.[42] He should only be allowed to lead the army. According to Reşid Mehmed Pasha, if Androutsos were sincere in requesting an amnesty, he would have come to Euboea and held a parley with Ömer Pasha in person, or sent his son or brother to the castle of Euboea as hostages. Declarations such as "I will render such and such a service" were simply not credible. If Androutsos was serious about his plea, services such as calling back the scattered *reaya* and repopulating the districts under his rule, which had gone to rack and ruin, and protecting them against the insurgents, undertaking to lead the army expeditions, and assisting in the transport of provisions would be sufficient. Had he done all these things and thus proved his loyalty, all his past crimes would be pardoned.

If we are to believe the account of the imperial courier who returned from Lamia and Larissa in mid-March, Androutsos had promised to remove the Greeks from the Acropolis by whatever means and deliver it to the Muslims. He sent his nephews to Ömer Pasha as pawns, but the pasha wrapped shawls around their heads, gave them compliments, and sent them back to their uncle.[43] Ömer Pasha assured Androutsos that he would urge the Sublime Porte to pardon his crimes if he carried out his promise in 10 to 11 days. The courier reported that he acquired this information from Tahir Aga, the castellan of Trikeri.[44]

The documents preserved in the Ottoman State Archives that have survived to the present day provide no details on the final agreement between Androutsos and Reşid Mehmed Pasha or the process of the negotiations. On March 31 Reşid Mehmed Pasha approved Androutsos's plea for amnesty and sent him a firman. He also noted that he would honor his part of the agreement by sending troops to

---

[40] Grand Vizier Benderli Mehmed Selim Sırrı Pasha to Sultan Mahmud II, undated, BOA, HAT., 890/39313.
[41] The Grand Vizier Mehmed Selim Pasha's commentary on the Castellan of Euboea, Ömer Pasha, to the Sublime Porte, February 19, 1825, BOA, HAT., 897/39481–B.
[42] Governor of Rumeli, Reşid Mehmed Pasha, to the Sublime Porte, March 1, 1825, BOA, HAT., 897/39481–A: "Atina'nın teshiri hususunda Devlet-i Aliyye'nin haşa sümme haşa kapudan-ı mersuma ihtiyacı olmadığı hüveyda olduğundan başka [...]"
[43] The shawl [*şal*] was a fashionable military headdress of the time.
[44] Account of the imperial courier Arnavud Süleyman, March 13, 1825, BOA, HAT., 897/39481.

aid Androutsos. At the head of Reşid Mehmed Pasha's dispatch, the sultan wrote, "May God Almighty allow him to succeed in all his affairs."[45]

The agreement rapidly bore fruit. By April 10, the inhabitants of Livadia, Thebes, and Atalanti, who were mostly Christian Albanians, requested amnesty and reaffirmed Ottoman subjecthood [*ra'iyyet*]. The villages around the Isthmus of Corinth—Koundoura, Vilia, Megara, Pisia, and Perachora—sent representatives to Androutsos and asked him to convey their pleas for amnesty.[46] Androutsos had not yet sent his brother or any other family member to the castle of Euboea as hostage, but asserted that he would do so. He also promised to retrieve the weapons of the *reaya* of Livadia, Thebes, and Atalanti and deliver them to Reşid Pasha, who in turn would send them mandates of pardon.

At this point, matters took a turn for the worse for Androutsos. According to Ömer Pasha's account, when the Greek insurgents in Amfissa began attacking the villages around Livadia Ömer Pasha dispatched his steward [*kethüda*] at the head of 500 cavalry, joined by Androutsos. Intense fighting broke out in the region between Atalanti and Livadia, and 5,000 Greeks came from Athens and the Morea to reinforce the revolutionaries. Androutsos did not leave the steward throughout the 38 days of heavy fighting, but grew anxious when the hostilities intensified and the troops promised by Reşid Mehmed Pasha did not arrive. He wanted to retire to Megara, but the insurgents captured him on the way. Muslim runaways, spies, and Greek informants all confirmed that Androutsos was imprisoned, subjected to all manner of tortures, and eventually executed.[47]

Almost 200 years after this untold episode in the Greek War of Independence, the question of whether Androutsos was an ethnic Albanian or a Greek is now a heated topic of debate only in Internet forums. We will never know if Androutsos's "Albanianness" played any role in his change of heart. At this early point in the Greek nation-building process, however, identities and allegiances were more fluid and subject to rapid change than today. Travel accounts, British consular reports, and official Ottoman documents are moreover rife with examples giving greater importance to tribal identity than to any other form of allegiance among Albanians. Thus, we can see the grandson of Tepedelenli Ali Pasha, Hüseyin Bey, fighting against Ottoman troops at the head of Orthodox Albanians, and Muslim Albanians defending Missolonghi side by side with Orthodox Albanians and Greeks.[48]

The Siege of 1826–1827

After the fall of Missolonghi in April 1826, Reşid Mehmed Pasha's next mission was to capture Amfissa and Athens. During his advance on Athens, 30 to 40 villages in the district of Athens sent their headmen [*kocabaşı*] to beg for quarter. They sent hostages and surrendered their weapons in order to receive certificates of amnesty.[49] Reşid Mehmed Pasha subjugated the town after fierce combat, in which 500 Ottoman soldiers and 400 insurgents died.[50] The siege of the Acropolis began in the third week of August.

---

[45] Governor of Rumeli, Reşid Mehmed Pasha, to the Sublime Porte, March 31, 1825, BOA, HAT., 925/40214.
[46] Governor of Rumeli, Reşid Mehmed Pasha, to the Castellan of Euboea, Ömer Pasha, April 10, 1825, BOA, HAT., 903/39674–A.
[47] Castellan of Euboea, Ömer Pasha, to the Governor of Rumeli, Reşid Mehmed Pasha, September 23, 1825, BOA, HAT., 895/39452–B.
[48] See, for example, Viscount Strangford to Viscount Castlereagh, August 19, 1822, TNA, FO, 78–109/31.
[49] Governor of Rumeli, Reşid Mehmed Pasha, to the Sublime Porte, July 13, 1826, BOA, HAT., 890/39334–A; Report of the imperial couriers Mehmed and Hasan, August 18, 1826, BOA, HAT., 943/40669–A.
[50] Governor of Rumeli, Reşid Mehmed Pasha, to the Sublime Porte, August 27, 1826, BOA, HAT., 943/40671.

At this point, the antiquities of Athens became a diplomatic issue once again. In the summer of 1826 the ambassadors of the European powers took at least two actions for their preservation. Stratford Canning, the British ambassador to Istanbul since 1825, made the first attempt. Canning was "credibly reported" as saying that it was Reşid Pasha's intention "to demolish the monuments of antiquity which still adorn the ancient capital of Attica under a fixed persuasion that those enduring records of the former glory of that country contribute in a great degree to render the present generation of Greeks discontented with the Turkish government."[51] In order to make an effort for the prevention of "so barbarous a design," he addressed a letter to Reşid Pasha. He also enclosed a copy of the imperial edict that had been sent to the governor of the Morea in 1822 at the request of his predecessor.

Although I have yet to find any allusion to the destruction of the antiquities in Reşid Mehmed Pasha's correspondence with the Sublime Porte, it is safe to assume, if the information gathered by Canning was accurate, that of all of the Ottoman administrators Reşid Mehmed Pasha was the most aware of the ideological dimension of the war. During the siege, Ottoman administrators became well aware of the importance of Athens for the west Europeans, although this consuming interest in antiquities did not make much sense to them. While to the grand vizier the antiquities of Athens were mere "stones" and the attempts of the western Europeans to preserve them represented only a reason for irritation, Reşid Mehmed Pasha seems to have grasped the significance of both those stones and the association between the ancient Greeks and the contemporary Greeks better than his peers.[52] He consistently reported that the Europeans' eyes were fixed on Athens and urged the Sublime Porte to take further measures to expedite the subjugation of the Acropolis before a possible European intervention. In any event, Canning informed the minister of foreign affairs [*reis effendi*] about his endeavor, but he was not very hopeful that he would secure an edict this time: "[I]n the present temper of the Turkish government I do not expect to find any disposition in the Porte to repeat its former injunction in favour of an object, which has ever been viewed by Turks even of the higher class with contempt or at best with indifference."[53]

In his letter to Reşid Mehmed Pasha, Canning, just like his predecessor, underlined the importance of the antiquities for the friendly European courts, yet refrained from making references to ancient Greek civilization. He portrayed the monuments as works of supreme beauty in terms that were as neutral as possible:

> It is known to everyone that the citadel and suburbs of Athens contain the ruins of several antique edifices, which though of small importance in the eyes of Reason, or of Religion, and wholly unconnected with affairs of state, have justly fixed the admiration as works of consummate beauty and of perfect architectural skill. In the preservation of these buildings, which are so many memorials of the glory and magnanimity of the Turkish sovereigns who spared them for the benefit of posterity, the governments and nations of Europe in friendship with the Sublime Porte are known to take interest regarding them as models in architecture, whence many of the fairest ornaments of the European capitals have been derived.[54]

---

[51] Stratford Canning to George Canning, June 6, 1826, TNA, FO 78–142/29.
[52] The Grand Vizier Mehmed Selim Pasha's commentary on the Governor of Rumeli, Reşid Mehmed Pasha, to the Sublime Porte, August 27, 1826, BOA, HAT., 943/40671.
[53] Stratford Canning to George Canning, June 6, 1826, TNA, FO 78–142/29.
[54] Stratford Canning to the Governor of Rumeli, Reşid Mehmed Pasha, June 4, 1826, TNA, FO 78–142/29/1. For a very peculiar translation of this letter into Ottoman Turkish, see BOA, HAT., 943/40671–A.

Affecting ignorance of the intelligence he had received, Canning preemptively put the blame of possible injury to the antiquities on "common soldiery," while delivering subtle, flattering, and encouraging remarks to the pasha:

> In all armies of whatever country or of whatever religion, the common soldiery is little capable of appreciating such objects, and the operations of war but too frequently involve the sacrifice of whatever is most beautiful in nature, or admirable in art. The conduct of an army is, however, dependent on the will of its commander, and those commanders who have established the brightest and most enduring reputation for success in arms have alas been distinguished by their humanity, and by their endeavours to mitigate the horrors and destructive consequences of war [...] Their preservation through the various events of the war will greatly redound to your Excellency's fame, and I am well convinced that no one will rejoice at it more than the Gracious Monarch, whom I have the honour to serve as my sovereign and master.[55]

Canning's main argument was, however, that "there was no feeling of national honour, which could suggest to him the idea of their destruction." We do not know if Canning's reasoning aroused any sympathy in Reşid Mehmed Pasha, since his response has not survived. The pasha's reply to the French ambassador two months later exists, however, and exemplifies the mindset of the Ottoman administrators. Apparently having heard about Reşid Mehmed Pasha's designs of destruction, Armand Charles, Count Guilleminot, the French ambassador to Istanbul, also wanted to make an effort. He sent a letter to the pasha with Admiral Henri de Rigny, who reached Athens in mid-August. In a verbal exchange, de Rigny asked the pasha's permission to transfer "the stones in the ancient monasteries" out of the Acropolis, offering a good amount of money to that end. In his turn, Reşid Pasha dismissed the admiral, telling him that "the Sublime State was not distressed for money and such a proposal was unprecedented."[56]

In his official response to the French ambassador, Reşid Mehmed Pasha employed all the topoi and tropes developed by the Ottoman administration throughout the revolution: although the Sublime Sultanate had bestowed so many favors and much benevolence on them, the ungrateful Greeks raised the standard of revolt and declared war. They were "devoid of intelligence and consciousness for entrenching themselves in such an artistically fashioned and beautiful place, and eventually bringing destruction both on themselves and on those such beautiful things."[57] Finally, the pasha stated that he gave orders for the preservation of the monuments only for the sake of the ambassador's friendship. To Reşid Pasha, all these diplomatic maneuvers were aimed at gaining time for the insurgents, and he shelled the Acropolis heavily. According to one count, in August 1826 alone the Ottoman artillery discharged "2,120 cannon balls and 956 bomb and howitzer shells" against the town and fortress.[58]

Although preservation of the antiquities of Athens was a recurring theme in Ottoman correspondence, in all the documents produced by Reşid Mehmed Pasha's secretariat during the siege one theme stands out above all others: the mercenaries' reluctance to fight, coupled with the pasha's

---

[55] Stratford Canning to the Governor of Rumeli, Reşid Mehmed Pasha, June 4, 1826, TNA, FO 78–142/29/1.
[56] Governor of Rumeli, Reşid Mehmed Pasha, to the Sublime Porte, August 27, 1826, BOA, HAT., 943/40671.
[57] Governor of Rumeli, Reşid Mehmed Pasha, to the French ambassador, Armand Charles, Count Guilleminot, August 19, 1826, BOA, HAT., 943/40671-B.
[58] Burgess 1835, vol. 1, p. 292.

lachrymose appeals to the Sublime Porte for payment of their wages. For Albanian mercenaries, fighting was just a part-time profession; they served for only six months and wanted to retire to their hometowns in the winter, or as soon as their contracts expired. Even their own commanders acknowledged that Albanian soldiers were not good for prolonged wars.[59] The Ottoman army was thus in a state of continuous unrest and trouble throughout the siege, especially because of the Tosk mercenaries.

Most of the 7,000 soldiers who laid siege to the Acropolis were Gegs and Tosks. There were only a couple of hundred "Turkish lads" [*Türk uşağı*] at most, under one or two magnates [*ayan*]. The soldiers had been employed for a long time and were tired. Moreover, they carried off a remarkable quantity of booty from Athens and the neighboring districts—20,000 cattle and 300 slaves from Euboea alone.[60] Thus, they looked forward to returning home and were useless in a fight.[61] Having spent all his money at Missolonghi and facing imminent strife among the soldiery due to unpaid wages, Reşid Mehmed Pasha initially wanted to delegate the siege to Ömer Pasha of Karystos. His proposal was rejected by the Sublime Porte, which ordered him to capture the Isthmus of Corinth after subjugating Athens.[62] Several of his dispatches report that he had lost influence with the soldiers and felt personally in danger.[63]

Several items of correspondence reveal that the siege lasted much longer than both Reşid Mehmed Pasha and the Sublime Porte had anticipated, placing an additional burden on the imperial coffers and the Ottoman administrators' nerves. According to the pasha's calculations, the inner fortress could shelter only 800 or at most 1,000 insurgents, so he had expected it to fall soon.[64] He wanted to advance on the Isthmus and leave his steward in charge of the siege. Nevertheless, by late August Reşid Mehmed Pasha must have understood that a successful siege would not be easy because of the determination of the besieged: "The infidels had sworn on their fallacious religion to sacrifice their lives not to abandon the fortress of Athens."[65] In addition, he must have calculated that he could not afford to march on Corinth and therefore stayed and asked the Sublime Porte to send a vizier for the Isthmus.

According to Reşid Mehmed Pasha, the situation of the Acropolis was another reason for the prolonged siege: "The citadel was not comparable to any other," situated on a high, massive rock and with a strongly defended main fortress. Shelling could not wound the besieged, and the infantry could not march into it. The rock beneath the citadel was as hard as flint; it could not be entrenched, and the sappers brought from Istanbul and Albania could not mine it.[66]

An imperial courier who witnessed the siege in January 1827 gave a similar account of the Acropolis. When viewed from Philopappou, the citadel was on top of a massive rock half as tall as a minaret. Cannon fire was ineffectual, as it could not penetrate the walls of the citadel. Half of the walls were solid rock, and the other half were bonded masonry, but the stone walls and the rock appeared to be merged. The sappers dug three tunnels to mine the citadel, but because of the hard rock, mining proved ineffectual. Only mortars, which terrorized and frustrated the insurgents, proved powerful. Hiding

---

[59] See, for example, Governor of Shkodër, Buşatlı Mustafa Pasha, to the Sublime Porte, undated, BOA, HAT., 401/21073.
[60] Kethüda Ibrahim to the Governor of Rumeli, Reşid Mehmed Pasha, July 13, 1826, BOA, HAT., 890/39334–A.
[61] Governor of Rumeli, Reşid Mehmed Pasha, to the Sublime Porte, August 27, 1826, BOA, HAT., 943/40671.
[62] Governor of Rumeli, Reşid Mehmed Pasha, to the Sublime Porte, July 17, 1826, BOA, HAT., 890/39334.
[63] See, for example, Governor of Rumeli, Reşid Mehmed Pasha, to the Sublime Porte, August 9, 1826, BOA, HAT., 854/38217–P.
[64] Governor of Rumeli, Reşid Mehmed Pasha, to the Sublime Porte, August 9, 1826, BOA, HAT., 943/40669.
[65] Governor of Rumeli, Reşid Mehmed Pasha, to the Sublime Porte, August 27, 1826, BOA, HAT., 940/40590.
[66] Governor of Rumeli, Reşid Mehmed Pasha, to the Sublime Porte, October 7, 1826, BOA, HAT., 940/40573.

behind the rock, the infidels were invisible because of the mortar fire. The vents of the insurgents' cannons were broken by frequent pushing and dragging, and their gunpowder turned into sand.[67]

One of the documents dispatched by Reşid Mehmed Pasha provides additional details about the conditions endured by the besieged. The pasha had promised a bonus of 5,000 piasters to a band of Geg mercenaries on the condition that they capture someone from within the citadel and extract information from him. On January 27, 1827, a Geg mercenary captured a rebel who was in command of 20 to 30 insurgents. This captain disclosed that the insurgents were suffering under indescribable conditions. The biggest problem in the citadel was the lack of wood to bake bread, so that many soldiers got sick and died from eating unbaked dough. They had ammunition for 20 days at most. Reşid Mehmed Pasha asked him the reason why they persevered under such conditions instead of fleeing or capitulating. The prisoner's answers pointed to the rapid internationalization of the issue and further alarmed the pasha. Eight months earlier, the insurgents had made a deal with the French and British, who promised them that they would apply to the Sublime Porte on their behalf for better exit conditions if they held out until January. All the captains and headmen of the Morea, Rumeli, and the islands thereupon convened to find a solution. They comprehended that Athens and its citadel were ancient places revered by the west Europeans. If they surrendered the Acropolis to the Muslims, the west Europeans would not support them, and they could not manage the situation by themselves. For this reason, all Greeks united and put every other matter aside to aid the defenders of the citadel, expecting forces to come to their rescue before too long. Unless help arrived within 20 days, they agreed to make a daring sortie from the citadel. Reşid Mehmed Pasha was curious about how the besieged could know that help was on the way, given that no one had broken through the siege in the last two months. The prisoner replied that their vessels were sailing off the coast regularly and communicated with the citadel by use of fire signals.[68]

This was yet another reason for the prolonged siege. The besieged were receiving assistance by sea, especially from the island of Hydra. In his dispatches, Reşid Mehmed Pasha repeatedly urged the Sublime Porte to deploy the Egyptian armada to subjugate the island. He asserted that the Acropolis could be captured from land only if Hydra was subdued and the coastal region of Athens blocked.[69]

The reluctance of the Tosk Albanians to suppress the Greek Revolution was the last item in Reşid Mehmed Pasha's list of reasons for the drawn-out siege. On October 27, 1826, the Tosk soldiers in the army allowed around 450 insurgents to break through the besieging forces and enter the Acropolis. According to Reşid Mehmed Pasha, they fired five or ten bullets for show so that they would not be held responsible for the outcome.[70] In March 1827, he finally dismissed the Tosks from the army and brought in Geg and ethnic Turkish soldiers.[71]

Nevertheless, even these measures did not pan out. By May 1827, not only those on both sides in Athens but also the sultan in Istanbul had grown extremely weary of the siege. Across the top of a report by the grand vizier, the sultan forcefully expressed his frustration: "This matter [the siege] is

---

[67] Report of the imperial courier Mustafa, January 31, 1827, BOA, HAT., 943/40675–F.
[68] Governor of Rumeli, Reşid Mehmed Pasha, to the Sublime Porte, January 29, 1827, BOA, HAT., 938/40528.
[69] Governor of Rumeli, Reşid Mehmed Pasha, to the Sublime Porte, September 16, 1826, BOA, HAT., 942/40665–B; February 10, 1827: BOA, HAT., 882/39010; March 8, 1827, BOA, HAT., 882/38988; April 20, 1827, BOA, HAT., 945/40699; May 10, 1827, BOA, HAT., 886/39164.
[70] Governor of Rumeli, Reşid Mehmed Pasha, to the Sublime Porte, October 27, 1826, BOA, HAT., 943/40674–B.
[71] Report of the courier of Ömer Pasha of Karystos, May 14, 1827, BOA, HAT., 868/38621.

arousing my indignation."⁷² Right before the Greeks on the Acropolis capitulated, Reşid Mehmed Pasha also played his trump card. By early May, he had run out of money, provisions, and munitions. "Leaving aside paying the soldiers' wages," he wrote, "I do not have even a thousand *kurush* for tips."⁷³ He was able to keep the mercenaries in the army encampment only by issuing vouchers stamped with his own seal. Skirmishes with the insurgents occurred on a daily basis, and the army depended on the Albanians. Yet their only concern was money. His debt to the mercenaries built up to 15,000 purses. He was weary of their grumbling for money, but did not know how to present the urgency of the issue to the Sublime Porte.⁷⁴ He reported that he had reached the point of having to kiss the mercenary captains' hands, a gesture of utter humility and submission in Ottoman culture.⁷⁵ Only five days before the capitulation, he was unable even to distribute bread to the soldiers.⁷⁶

With their resources and patience nearly exhausted, and deprived of help by the failure of their comrades' two attempts to raise the siege, the insurgents entered into negotiations for surrender. Reşid Mehmed Pasha informed the Sublime Porte that he had to accept terms from the rebels in order to prevent a possible mutiny in the army. On June 6, 1827, Reşid Mehmed Pasha reported that the Citadel of Athens capitulated, asking for quarter, and "its interior and exterior were cleared and purified from the filth of the brigands' bodies, which were filled with villainy."⁷⁷ The insurgents left unharmed. The same letter did not omit to request money from the Sublime Porte for the mercenaries' wages. Reşid Mehmed Pasha remarked that he was penniless, and if he failed to pay the soldiers would not be able to hold the citadel for long. The sultan was doubly happy about the news, considering it heavenly fortune because it arrived in Istanbul on the same day as the Russian ambassador, against whom he now had a better hand.⁷⁸

After the Fall

Immediately after the capitulation of the Acropolis, the headmen and captains of the villages of Athens, followed by those of many insurgent regions, such as Trikala, Ioannina, Arta, Euboea, and Nafpaktos, requested amnesty.⁷⁹ Reşid Mehmed Pasha sent messengers and recalled Athenians who had scattered all around. Unless they returned within 30 days, their estates and properties would be confiscated. Asking for quarter, Athenians began to return to their hometown in groups. The Sublime Porte ordered Ömer Pasha of Karystos to appoint a charitable voivode to repopulate Athens and decided to send a surveyor to register the land, orchards, olive trees, and other taxable fruit trees.⁸⁰ By late August, 600 Greeks had returned to Athens.⁸¹

---

[72] Sultan Mahmud II's imperial rescript, May 2, 1827, BOA, HAT., 844/37920.
[73] Governor of Rumeli, Reşid Mehmed Pasha, to the Sublime Porte, May 10, 1827, BOA, HAT., 886/39164.
[74] Governor of Rumeli, Reşid Mehmed Pasha, to the Sublime Porte, May 2, 1827, BOA, HAT., 849/38079–A.
[75] Governor of Rumeli, Reşid Mehmed Pasha, to the Sublime Porte, May 14, 1827, BOA, HAT., 879/38900.
[76] Governor of Rumeli, Reşid Mehmed Pasha, to the Sublime Porte, June 1, 1827, BOA, HAT., 846/38017.
[77] Governor of Rumeli, Reşid Mehmed Pasha, to the Sublime Porte, June 6, 1827, BOA, HAT., 844/37909.
[78] Sultan Mahmud II's imperial rescript, June 1, 1827, BOA, HAT., 846/38017.
[79] Joint appeal of the captains of the districts of Trikala, Ioannina, Arta, Euboea, and Nafpaktos, undated, BOA, Cevdet Dahiliye [Internal affairs], undated, 330/16497.
[80] Governor of Rumeli, Reşid Mehmed Pasha, to the Sublime Porte, June 17, 1827, BOA, HAT., 940/40593; August 30, 1827, BOA, HAT., 849/38077.
[81] Governor of Rumeli, Reşid Mehmed Pasha, to the Sublime Porte, August 30, 1827, BOA, HAT., 854/38217–O.

Due to lack of money, soldiers, and a Muslim population in general, Reşid Mehmed Pasha decided to amass the Christians of Athens in a few locations. The largely coastal villages of Athens were scattered and required at least 4,500 soldiers to keep them under control. He could afford to hire only 3,000–4,000 soldiers with his income from the province [*eyalet*] of Rumeli.[82] Thus he suggested transporting residents of the coastal villages to Skala Rapos [Skala Oropou?] and the villagers of the district of Athens to the gardens and orchards around the Acropolis. The pasha reported that he carried out this plan and proposed to do the same in the zone from Arta to Athens.[83] Upon Reşid Pasha's suggestion, the Sublime Porte also decided to resettle the Muslims of Athens, who were scattered in Izmir, Euboea, and other places; however, we do not know if the project proceeded.[84]

In September 1827, Şehla ("cross-eyed") Ibrahim Pasha was appointed as castellan of Athens, lasting less than two months in the position.[85] On October 26, Ibrahim Pasha delivered the Acropolis to Osman Aga, a major in the recently reformed Ottoman army, "The Victorious Soldiers of Muhammad."[86] In November 1827, the Ottoman garrison numbered 544 cavalry and infantry.[87]

The number of documents preserved in the Ottoman State Archives pertaining to Athens decreases sharply after the Battle of Navarino and the ensuing Russian–Ottoman War of 1828–1829. A lively correspondence began again with diplomatic negotiations and conferences that would pave the way for the establishment of the independent Greek Kingdom. The last Ottomans marched out of the Acropolis on March 31, 1833, "in little bands of ten and twelve, with dirty ragged clothes, two richly-caparisoned horses, a mule, and a man pulling a ram by the horns."[88]

Conclusion

Athens constituted one of the many fronts of what was known to the Ottoman administrators as the "Greek sedition" [*Rum Fesadı*], but—militarily speaking—it was not the most important one. Yet, the course of events revolving around Athens was quite exemplary of the revolutionary years. Dehumanization of and indiscriminate violence toward the proverbial other, long and fierce sieges, and pervasive disrespect for historical and cultural heritage were all but commonplace on both sides of the war.

Although caught by surprise and panic, the Ottoman administrators' reaction toward the Greek subjects of the empire was far from monolithic and was shaped by different variables, such as changes in international politics, different cliques vying to dominate the Sublime Porte, and local administrators' own initiatives. Hence, the Ottoman responses to the Greek insurgency ranged from genocidal massacres and pogrom-like events to offering amnesty to the insurgents and protecting noncombatant Greeks against Muslim looters. In order to pursue new policies, different ministers were brought to power; hawks were replaced by doves, or vice versa.

---

[82] Grand Vizier Mehmed Selim Pasha to Mahmud II, undated, BOA, HAT., 890/39302.
[83] Governor of Rumeli, Reşid Mehmed Pasha, to the Sublime Porte, July 17, 1827, BOA, HAT., 940/40592.
[84] The grand vizier's commentary on the Governor of Rumeli, Reşid Mehmed Pasha, to the Sublime Porte, June 16, 1827, BOA, HAT., 940/40605.
[85] Governor of Rumeli, Reşid Mehmed Pasha, to the Sublime Porte, September 9, 1827, BOA, HAT., 940/40608.
[86] Governor of Rumeli, Reşid Mehmed Pasha, to the Sublime Porte, October 26, 1827, BOA, HAT., 1057/43500.
[87] Major Osman Aga to the Sublime Porte, November 20, 1827, BOA, HAT., 1090/44294.
[88] George Finlay's *Journal*, vol. 2, quoted from Mackenzie 1992, p. 124.

Yet, Sultan Mahmud II had one constant policy: categorical refusal to enter into any kind of negotiation with the insurgents or to accept mediation from European states. As the sultan reiterated time and again and as he imposed upon his ministers in his imperial rescripts, he viewed the Greek uprising as an internal security issue of the Ottoman state. Thus, to the sultan and the Ottoman administrators there was only one kind of solution: a forced peace, for which the Greeks of the insurgent provinces were to accept Ottoman subjecthood [*raiyyet*]. Accepting subjecthood would be carried out by Greeks conceding to take poll-tax tickets [*cizye kağıdı*], followed by making a deed—of obedience—[*sened*] and registering it at the local court. In other words, the Greeks' status was to be placed back into its existing legal infrastructure within Islamic laws and Ottoman customs through a bureaucratic process linking the Greek individual to the empire. This could be achieved either by force or by policies of accommodation, namely, coaxing the insurgents and the insurgent provinces through amnesty and tax exemptions. As this essay suggests, both of these policies were tried by the Sublime Porte in and around Athens during the course of the revolution and progressed to a certain extent, while in other provinces they failed to make the Greek insurgents give up their struggle.

Archival Sources

Archives du Ministère des Affaires étrangères, Paris:
    Correspondance politique: Turquie 233/212, November 10, 1821; Turquie 234/164, September 11, 1821.

Başbakanlık Devlet Arşivi Genel Müdürlüğü [General Directorate of State Archives of the Prime Ministry of the Republic of Turkey], Istanbul, Başbakanlık Osmanlı Arşivi [Ottoman State Archives]:
    Cevdet Dahiliye [Internal affairs]: 330/16497.
    Cevdet Hariciye [Foreign affairs]: 7/344, 18/893, 49/2437, 52/2596, 135/6727.
    Hatt-ı Hümayun [Imperial decrees]: 401/21073, 510/25048–B, 613/30160, 626/30928, 838/37787, 844/37909, 844/37920, 845/37954, 846/37981, 846/38017, 847/38048, 849/38077, 849/38079–A, 854/38217–A, 854/38217–O, 854/38217–P, 855/38228–C, 868/38621, 877/38822, 877/38855, 879/38900, 880/38944, 882/38988, 882/39010, 886/39164, 887/39197, 890/39302, 890/39313, 890/39334, 890/39334–A, 895/39452–B, 897/39481, 897/39481–A, 897/39481–B, 897/39481–C, 897/39481–F, 897/39481–H, 903/39674–A, 906/39723, 911/39856, 919/39988, 922/40093, 925/40214, 926/40226, 928/40290–A, 938/40528, 940/40573, 940/40590, 940/40592, 940/40593, 940/40605, 940/40608, 942/40665–B, 943/40669, 943/40669–A, 943/40671, 943/40671–A, 943/40671–B, 943/40674–B, 943/40675–A, 943/40675–C, 943/40675–F, 945/40699, 947/40721, 947/40732–L, 947/40732–Z, 1057/43500, 1090/44294, 1217/47671, 1277/49548, 1277/49548–A, 1277/49548–B, 1558/0046; 946.40721.

National Archives, Kew:
    UK Foreign Office: 78, vol. 32, 78/64, 78–100/15, 78–100/15–1, 78–100/22, 78–100/22–1, 78–109/21, 78–109/31, 78–118/21, 78–126/7, 78–142/29.

Topkapı Sarayı Emanet Hazinesi [Topkapı Palace Library], Istanbul:
    No. 1411: Mahmud Efendi, *Tarih-i Medinetü'l Hukema* [The history of the city of the sages].

Bibliography

Açik, T. 2012. "Evliyâ Çelebi's Ancient World," in Tezcan, Tezcan, and Dankoff 2012, pp. 345–351.

Acropolis Restoration Service. "Erechtheion," accessible online: http://www.ysma.gr/en/erechtheion.

Agora XXXIV = G. Weinberg and M. E. Stern, *Vessel Glass* (*The Athenian Agora* XXXIV), Princeton 2010.

Agostinelli, E., and W. Coleman, eds. 2015. *Giovanni Boccaccio, Teseida delle nozze d' Emilia*, Florence.

Akasoy, A. 2013. "Mehmed II as a Patron of Greek Philosophy: Latin and Byzantine Perspectives," in *The Renaissance and the Ottoman World*, ed. A. Contadini and C. Norton, Farnham, pp. 245–256.

Akerman, J. R. 1984. "Cartography and the Emergence of Territorial States in Western Europe," in *Proceedings of the Tenth Annual Meeting of the Western Society for French History*, ed. J. F. Sweets, Lawrence, Kan., pp. 138–154.

Alexander, P., ed. [1951] 1968. *William Shakespeare, The Complete Works*, London and Glasgow.

Alexopoulos, S. 2015. "When a Column Speaks: The Liturgy of the Christian Parthenon," *Dumbarton Oaks Papers* 69, pp. 159–178.

Anagnostakis, I., and A. Kaldellis 2014. "The Textual Sources for the Peloponnese, A.D. 582–959: Their Creative Engagement with Ancient Literature," *Greek, Roman and Byzantine Studies* 54, pp. 105–135.

Anastasopoulos, A., E. Kolovos, and M. Sariyannis. 2008. "Muslim Cultural Life in the Greek Lands," in *Ottoman Architecture in Greece*, ed. E. Brouskari, Athens, pp. 51–55.

And, M. 1982. *Osmanlı Şenliklerinde Türk Sanatları*, Ankara.

Anderson, B. 2015. "'An Alternative Discourse': Local Interpreters of Antiquities in the Ottoman Empire," *Journal of Field Archaeology* 40, pp. 450–460.

———. 2017a. "Forgetting Athens," in *Antiquarianisms: Contact, Conflict, Comparison*, ed. B. Anderson and F. Rojas, Havertown, Penn., pp. 184–209.

———. 2017b. "The Defacement of the Parthenon Metopes," *Greek, Roman and Byzantine Studies* 57, pp. 248–260.

Angelomatis-Tsougarakis, H. 1990. *The Eve of the Greek Revival: British Travellers' Perceptions of Early Nineteenth-century Greece*, London.

Anghelou, A. 1971. "Private Journal of a Voyage from Smyrna to Venice by J. O. Hanson," *Annual of the British School at Athens* 66, pp. 13–48.

Apostolopoulos, D. G. 2005. "'Νέοι Έλληνες.' Ο νεολογισμός και τα συνδηλούμενά του στα 1675," *Ο Ερανιστής / The Gleaner* 25, pp. 87–99.

Apostolou, I. 2009. "La représentation de soi de l'autre dans le *Seyâhatnâme*, ou Livre de voyages d'Evliya Celebi. Étude comparative avec les voyageurs français du XVIIe siècle," in *L'Ailleurs de l'autre. Récits de voyageurs extra-européens*, ed. C. Le Blanc and J. Weber, Rennes, pp. 125–134.

Armstrong, P. 1993. "Byzantine Thebes: Excavations on the Kadmeia," *Annual of the British School at Athens* 88, pp. 295–335.

Arrigoni, E. 1989. "Fasti attico-Salomonici ed Atene islamica. Il periegeta turco Evliya Celebì (sec. XVII) e la reinterpretazione del paesaggio archeologico della campagna attica," in *Studi geografici sul paesaggio*, ed. G. Botta, Milan, pp. 47–91.

Asvesta, A., and I. Vingopoulou. 2001. "Περιηγητές στα χαμάμ," in *Καθημερινή. 7 Ημέρες*, May 20, 2001, pp. 10–15.

Atasoy, N., and J. Raby. 1989. *Iznik: The Pottery of Ottoman Turkey*, London.

Babin, J.-P. 1674. *Relation de l'état présent de la ville d'Athènes, ancienne capitale de la Grèce, bâtie depuis 3400 ans. Avec un abrégé de son histoire et de ses antiquités*, Lyon.

Babinger, F., ed. 1923. *Hans Dernschwam's Tagebuch einer Reise nach Konstantinopel und Kleinasien (1553–55)*, Munich and Leipzig.

———. 1978. *Mehmed the Conqueror and His Time*, trans. R. Manheim, 2nd ed., rev. F. Babinger and W. C. Hickman, Princeton.

Bacon, E. N. 1967. *Design of Cities*, London.

Bahrani, Z., Z. Çelik, and E. Eldem, eds. 2011. *Scramble for the Past: A Story of Archaeology in the Ottoman Empire, 1753–1914*, Istanbul.

Balta, E. 2003a. "History and Historiography on Greek Tobacco," in *Tütün Kitabı*, ed. E. Gürsoy Naskali, Istanbul, pp. 86–97.

———. 2003b. "Ottoman Archives in Greece," in *Balkanlar ve İtalya'da Şehir ve Manastır Arşivlerindeki Türkçe Belgeler Seminerleri (16–17 Kasım 2000)*, Ankara, pp. 15–24.

Bankel, H., ed. 1986. *Carl Haller von Hallerstein in Griechenland, 1810–1817. Architekt, Zeichner, Bauforscher*, Berlin.

Baram, U. 1995. "Notes on the Preliminary Typologies of Production and Chronology for the Clay Tobacco Pipes of Cyprus," *Report of the Department of Antiquities, Cyprus*, pp. 299–309.

———. 1999. "Clay Tobacco Pipes and Coffee Cup Sherds in the Archaeology of the Middle East: Artifacts of Social Tensions from the Ottoman Past," *International Journal of Historical Archaeology* 3 (3), pp. 137–151.

———. 2000. "Entangled Objects from the Palestinian Past: Archaeological Perspectives for the Ottoman Period, 1500–1900," in *A Historical Archaeology of the Ottoman Empire: Breaking New Ground*, ed. U. Baram and L. Carroll, New York, pp. 137–160.

Barbanera, M., ed. 2009. *Relitti riletti. Metamorfosi delle rovine e identità culturale*, Turin.

Barnard, M. 2009. "Appropriation: A Dynamical Process of Interpretative Action," in *Visual Arts and Religion*, ed. H. Alma, M. Barnard, and V. Küster, Berlin, pp. 3–16.

Bastéa, E. 2000. *The Creation of Modern Athens: Planning the Myth*, Cambridge.

Beard, M. 2002. *The Parthenon*, London.

Belon, P. 1588. *Les observations de plusieurs singularitez et choses memorables, trouvees en Grece, Asie, Judée, Egypte, Arabie, & autres pays estranges*, Paris.

Benizelos, I. 1986. *Ιστορία των Αθηνών*, intro. J. Gennadius, ed. I. Kokkonas, G. Bokos, and M. I. Manoussakas. Athens.

Ben-Tov, A. 2013. "*Turco-Graecia*: German Humanists and the End of Greek Antiquity – Cultural Exchange and Misunderstanding," in *The Renaissance and the Ottoman World*, ed. A. Contadini and C. Norton, Farnham, pp. 181–196.

Berger, A. 2013. *Accounts of Medieval Constantinople: The* Patria, Cambridge, MA.

Berger, E. 1986. *Der Parthenon in Basel. Dokumentation zu den Metopen*, Mainz.

Berlinghieri, F. 1482. *Septe giornate della geographia*, Florence.

Beschi, L. 1956. "Un disegno veneto dell'Acropoli Ateniese nel 1670," *Arte Veneta* 10, pp. 136–141.

———. 1984. "L'anonimo Ambrosiano. Un itinerario in Grecia di Urbano Bolzanio," *Atti dell'Accademia nazionale dei Lincei. Rendiconti* 39, s. 8, fasc. 1–2, pp. 1–22.

———. 1998. "I disegni ateniesi di Ciriaco. Analisi di una tradizione," in *Ciriaco d'Ancona e la cultura antiquaria dell'Umanesimo. Atti del Convegno internazionale di studio (Ancona, 6–9 febbraio 1992)*, ed. G. Paci and S. Sconocchia, Reggio Emilia, pp. 83–102.

——— and T. Tanoulas. 2000–2003. "Ακόμα μια φορά για το σχέδιο της Ακρόπολης του 1670 στο Bassano del Grappa," *Horos* 14–16, pp. 381–394, pls. 91–94.

Bessan, J.-F. 1835. *Souvenirs de l'expédition de Morée en 1828. Suivis d'un mémoire historique sur Athènes, avec le plan de cette ville*, Valognes.

Bierman, I. 1991. "The Ottomanization of Crete," in *The Ottoman City and Its Parts, Urban Structure and Social Order*, ed. I. Bierman et al., New York.

Biggs, M. 1999. "Putting the State on the Map: Cartography, Territory, and European State Formation," *Comparative Studies in Society and History* 41 (2), pp. 374–405.

Biris, K. 1959. *Τα Αττικά του Εβλιά Τσελεμπή. Αι Αθήναι και τα περίχωρά των κατά τον 17ον αι.*, Athens.

———. 2005. *Αι Αθήναι από του 19ου εις τόν 20όν αιώνα*, Athens.

Biris, M. 2010. "Σπίτια της Αθήνας κατά την πρώτη επί Όθωνος δεκαετία," in Korres 2010b, pp. 128–142.

——— and M. Kardamitsi-Adami. 2001. *Νεοκλασική αρχιτεκτονική στην Ελλάδα*, Athens.

Bisaha, N. 2004. *Creating East and West: Renaissance Humanists and the Ottoman Turks*, Philadelphia.

Bisani, A. 1793. *A Picturesque Tour through Part of Europe, Asia, and Africa Containing Many New Remarks on the Present State of Society, Remains of Ancient Edifices, etc.*, London.

Blake, H. 1986. "The Medieval Incised Slipped Pottery of North West Italy," in *La ceramica medievale nel mediterraneo occidentale*, ed. G. Berti et al., Florence, pp. 317–352.

Bodnar, E. W. 1960. *Cyriacus of Ancona and Athens* (Collection Latomus 43), Brussels.

———. 1970. "Athens in April 1436," *Archaeology* 23, pp. 96–105, 188–199.

——— and C. Foss. 2003. *Cyriac of Ancona: Later Travels*, Cambridge, Mass.

Bohrer, F. N. 2015. "Doors into the Past: W. J. Stillman (and Freud) on the Acropolis," in Carabott, Hamilakis, and Papargyriou 2015, pp. 95–112.

Boogert, M. H. van den. 2005. *The Capitulations and the Ottoman Legal System: Qadis, Consuls and Beratlıs in the 18th Century*, Leiden.

Borboudaki, M., ed. 2007. *Πηλός & χρώμα. Νεώτερη κεραμική του ελλαδικού χώρου* (Exhibition catalogue, Byzantine and Christian Museum 2006–2007), Athens.

Borrut, A. 2003. "La Syrie de Salomon. L'appropriation du mythe salomonien dans les sources arabes," *Pallas* 63, pp. 107–120.

———. 2011. *Entre mémoire et pouvoir. L'espace syrien sous les derniers Omeyyades et le premiers Abbassides (v. 72–193/692–809)*, Leiden.

Bouloux, N. 2016. "Ancien et moderne. La géographie de Sebastiano Compagni (1509)," (diss., École pratique des hautes études, Paris).

Bouras, C. 2010. *Βυζαντινή Αθήνα, 10ος-12ος αι.*, Athens [trans. and rev. E. K. Fowden, *Byzantine Athens, 10th–12th Centuries*, Abingdon 2017].

———, M. Ioannidou, and I. Jenkins, eds. 2012. *Acropolis Restored*, London.

Bowie, T., and D. Thimme, eds. 1971. *The Carrey Drawings of the Parthenon Sculptures*, Bloomington.

Branch, J. 2011. "Mapping the Sovereign State: Technology, Authority, and Systemic Change," *International Organization* 63 (1), pp. 1–36.

Briet, P. 1648–1649. *Parallela geographiae veteris et novae*, Paris.

Brown, V., P. O. Kristeller, and F. E. Cranz, eds. 1992. *Catalogus translationum et commentariorum: Mediaeval and Renaissance Latin Translations and Commentaries, Annotated Lists and Guides* 7, Washington, D.C.

Burgess, R. 1835. *Greece and the Levant, or Diary of a Summer's Excursion in 1834*, 2 vols., London.

Burke, P. 2007. "Cultures of Translation in Early Modern Europe," in *Cultural Translation in Early Modern Europe*, ed. P. Burke and R. Po-chia Hsia, Cambridge, pp. 7–38.

Cağman, F. 2013. "Fahri of Bursa," in *Encyclopaedia of Islam Three* 4, ed. M. Gaborieau et al., Leiden, pp. 121–122; accessible online: https://referenceworks.brillonline.com/entries/encyclopaedia-of-islam-3/*-COM_26929.

Calvo Capilla, S. 2014. "The Reuse of Classical Antiquity in the Palace of Madinat al-Zahra' and its Role in the Construction of Caliphal Legitimacy," *Muqarnas* 31, pp. 1–33.

Cameron, A., and J. Herrin. 1984. *Constantinople in the Early Eighth Century: The* Parastaseis Syntomoi Chronikai: *Introduction, Translation, and Commentary*, Leiden.

——— and J. Long, 1993. *Barbarians and Politics at the Court of Arcadius*, Berkeley.

Camp, J. McK., II. 2001. *The Archaeology of Athens*, New Haven and London.

———, ed. 2013. *In Search of Greece: Catalogue of an Exhibit of Drawings at the British Museum by Edward Dodwell and Simone Pomardi from the Collection of the Packard Humanities Institute*, Los Altos.

Carabott, P., Y. Hamilakis, and E. Papargyriou, eds. 2015. *Camera Graeca: Photographs, Narratives, Materialities*, Farnham.

Carswell, J. 1998. *Iznik Pottery*, London.

——— and C. J. F. Dowsett. 1972. *Kütahya Tiles and Pottery from the Armenian Cathedral of St. James*, Jerusalem and Oxford.

Casella, N. [1972] 1974. "Pio II tra geografia e storia. La Cosmografia," *Archivio dell Società romana di storia patria* 26, s. 3, pp. 35–112.

Casson, L. [1974] 1994. *Travel in the Ancient World*, Baltimore and London.

Chabbi, J. 1994. "La représentation du passé aux premiers âges de l'historiographie califale," in *Itinéraires d'Orient. Hommages à Claude Cahen*, ed. R. Curiel and R. Gyselen, Bures-sur-Yvette, pp. 21–47.

Chalkokondyles, L. 1922–1923. Ἀποδείξεις Ἱστοριῶν / *Laonici Chalcocandylae Historiarum demonstrationes*, ed. E. Darkó, Budapest.

———. 2014. *The Histories*, trans. A. Kaldellis, 2 vols., Cambridge, Mass.

Chandler, R. 1776. *Travels in Asia Minor: Or, An Account of a Tour Made at the Expense of the Society of Dilettanti*, London.

Chassagnette, A. 2018. *Savoir géographique et cartographie dans l'espace germanique protestant (1520–1620)*, Geneva.

Choiseul-Gouffier, M.-G.-F.-A. de. 1782–1809. *Voyage pittoresque de la Grèce*, 2 vols., Paris.

Christiansen, J. 2000. *The Rediscovery of Greece: Denmark and Greece in the 19th Century*, Copenhagen.

Clarke, E. D. 1814. *Travels in Various Countries of Europe, Asia and Africa*, 6 vols., London.

Cluverius, P. 1624. *Introductionis in universam geographiam, tam veterem quam novam, libri VI*, Leiden.

Cohen, E. 2018. "Explosions and Expulsions in Ottoman Athens: A Heritage Perspective on the Temple of Olympian Zeus," *International Journal of Islamic Architecture* 7, pp. 85–106.

Colin, J. 1981. *Cyriaque d'Ancône. Le voyageur, le marchand, l'humaniste*, Paris.

Collignon, M. 1897. "Documents du XVIIe siècle relatifs aux antiquités d'Athènes," *Comptes rendus des séances de l'Académie des inscriptions et belles-lettres* 41, pp. 56–71.

Constantine, D. 1984. *In the Footsteps of the Gods: Travellers to Greece and the Quest for the Hellenic Ideal*, rev. 2011, London.

———. 1989. "The Question of Authenticity in Some Early Accounts of Greece," in *Rediscovering Hellenism: The Hellenic Inheritance and the English Imagination*, ed. G. W. Clarke with J. C. Eade, Cambridge, pp. 1–22.

Corinth XI = C. H. Morgan, *The Byzantine Pottery* (*Corinth* XI), Cambridge, Mass., 1942.

Corso, A. 2011. "The Topography of Ancient Athens in the *Mirabilia urbis Athenarum*," *Hyperboreus* 16–17, pp. 69–80.

Cotta-Schönberg, M. von, ed. and trans. 2014. "Oration 'Quamvis omnibus' of Enea Silvio Piccolomini (16 May 1454, Regensburg): Preliminary Edition, 3rd Version." (Orations of Enea Silvio Piccolomini / Pope Pius II; 21); accessible online: https://hal.archives-ouvertes.fr/hal-01086738.

Craven, E. B. 1789. *A Journey through the Crimea to Constantinople in a Series of Letters from the Right Honourable Elizabeth Lady Craven to His Serene Highness the Margrave of Brandenbourg, Anspach, and Bareith Written in the Year MDCCLXXXVI*, London.

Crusius, M. 1584. *Turcograeciae, libri octo … quibus Graecorum status sub imperio Turcico … inde ab amissa Constantinopoli ad haec usque tempora luculenter describitur*, Basel.

Cunningham, A. 1993. "The Dragomans of the British Embassy at Constantinople," in *Eastern Questions in the Nineteenth Century: Collected Essays* 2, ed. E. Ingram, London, pp. 3–9.

Curtius, E., and J. Kaupert. 1903. *Karten von Attika, Bl. 1. Athen mit Umgebung*, Berlin, accessible online: http://digi.ub.uni-heidelberg.de/diglit/curtius1895a/0003.

Dagron, G. 1984. *Constantinople imaginaire. Études sur le recueil des "Patria,"* Paris.

Dainville, F. de. [1940] 1969. *La géographie des humanistes*, repr. Geneva.

Damaskos, D., and D. Plantzos, eds. 2008. *A Singular Antiquity*, Athens.

Dandrow, E. 2017. "Ethnography and Identity in Strabo's Geography," in *The Routledge Companion to Strabo*, ed. D. Dueck, Oxford and New York, pp. 113–124.

Danişmend, I. H. 1971. *Osmanlı Devlet Erkânı*, Istanbul.

Dankoff, R. 2004. *An Ottoman Mentality: The World of Evliya Çelebi*, Leiden.

Darling, L. 2008. "Political Change and Political Discourse in the Early Modern Mediterranean World," *Journal of Interdisciplinary History* 38 (4), pp. 505–531.

Demetriades, V., 1978. *Η κεντρική και δυτική Μακεδονία κατά τον Εβλιγιά Τσελεμπή*, Thessaloniki.

———. 1983. *Τοπογραφία της Θεσσαλονίκης κατά την εποχή της Τουρκοκρατίας, 1430–1912*, Thessaloniki.

———. [1999] 2001. "Was the Removal of the Marbles Illegal?" Appendix A to the Submission of the British Committee for the Restitution of the Parthenon Marbles to the House of Commons Select Committee; accessible online: http://www.parthenon.newmentor.net/illegal.htm.

———. 2000, *The Parthenon Marbles within the EU*, Athens, pp. 5–8.

Desautels, J., ed. 2010. *Pierre-Gustave Joly de Lotbinière, Voyage en Orient (1839–1840). Journal d'un voyageur curieux du monde et d'un pionnier de la daguerréotypie*, Quebec City.

Di Branco, M. 2005. "Atene immaginaria. Il mito di Atene nella letteratura bizantina tra agiografia, teosofia e mirabilia," *Atti dell'Accademia nazionale dei Lincei. Rendiconti* 16, s. 9, fasc. 1, pp. 65–134.

———. 2006. *La città dei filosofi. Storia di Atene da Marco Aurelio a Giustiniano, con un'appendice su "Atene immaginaria" nella letteratura bizantina*, Florence.

Dimakopoulos, I. E. 2001. "Το σχέδιο του Bassano (1670). Η Αθήνα και τα μνημεία της Ακρόπολης," *Ο Μέντωρ* 14 (58), pp. 61–79.

Dodwell, E. 1819. *A Classical and Topographical Tour through Greece, during the Years 1801, 1805, and 1806...*, 2 vols., London.

———. [1819] 1821. *Views in Greece, from Drawings*, London.

Douglas, F. S. N. 1813. *An Essay on Certain Points of Resemblance between the Ancient and Modern Greeks*, London.

Dupré, L. 1825. *Voyage à Athènes et à Constantinople, ou Collection de portraits, de vues et de costumes grecs et ottomans peints sur les lieux, d'après nature, lithographiés et coloriés*, Paris.

Eldem, E. 2011. "From Blissful Indifference to Anguished Concern: Ottoman Perceptions of Antiquities, 1799–1869," in Bahrani, Çelik, and Eldem 2011, pp. 281–330.

Eldem, S. H. 1984. *Turkish Houses: Ottoman Period*, Istanbul.

Ergin, N. 2009. "Architecture and Sociability in Turkish Hamams," *Fürdö Hamam Sauna Symposium (25–26 April 2009)*, Koç University Research Center for Anatolian Civilizations, Istanbul.

———. 2011. "Bathing Business in Istanbul: A Case Study of the Çemberlitaş Hamamı in the Seventeenth and Eighteenth Centuries," in *Bathing Culture of Anatolian Civilization: Architecture, History, and Imagination* (*Ancient Near Eastern Supplement Series* 37), ed. N. Ergin, Louvain, pp. 143–168.

Ertaş, M. Y. 2007. *Sultanın Ordusu: Mora fethi örneği, 1714–1716*, Istanbul.

Erünsal, I. E. 1987. "Şehid Ali Paşa'nın İstanbul'da Kurduğu Kütüphane ve Şehid Ali Paşa'nın Müsadere Edilen Kitapları," *İstanbul Univ. Edebiyat Fakültesi Kütüphanecilik Dergisi* 1, pp. 79–87.

Etienne, R. and F. 1990. *La Grèce antique, archéologie d'une découverte*, Paris.

Evliya Çelebi. 1994. *Οδοιπορικό στην Ελλάδα (1668–1671). Πελοπόννησος, Νησιά Ιονίου, Κρήτη, Κυκλάδες, Νησιά ανατολικού Αιγαίου*, trans. D. Loupis, Athens.

———. 2003. *Seyahatnamesi, 8: Kitap (Topkapı Sarayı Bağdat* 308), ed. S. A. Kahraman, Y. Dağlı, and R. Dankoff, Istanbul.

———. 2010. *An Ottoman Traveller: Selections from the Book of Travels of Evliya Çelebi*, trans. R. Dankoff and S. Kim, London.

———. 2012. *Evliyā Çelebī in Medina: The Relevant Sections of the* Seyāhatnāme, ed. and comm. N. Gemici, trans. R. Dankoff, Leiden.

Eyüpgiller, K. K. 2004. "Atina Akropolünde Bir Cami," *Arredamento Mimarlık* 173, pp. 118–121.

Fanelli, F. 1707. *Atene Attica descritte da suoi principii sino all'acquisto fatto dall'armi Venete nel 1687*, Venice.

Finlay, G. 1836. *The Hellenic Kingdom and the Greek Nation*, London.

———. 1861. *History of the Greek Revolution* 1, Edinburgh and London.

Foerster, R. 1883. "Zum Pariser und Wiener Anonymus über Athen," *Mittheilungen des Kaiserlich Deutschen Archaeologischen Insituts. Athenische Abtheilung* 8, pp. 30–32.

Fowden, E. K., and G. Fowden. 2008. *Contextualizing Late Greek Philosophy*, Athens.

Fowden, G. 2010. Rev. of Kaldellis 2009, in *Journal of Roman Archaeology* 23, pp. 802–810.

François, V., and L. Vallauri. 2001. "Production et consommation de céramiques à Potamia (Chypre) de l'époque franque à l'époque ottomane," *Bulletin de correspondance hellénique* 125, pp. 523–546.

Frantz, A. 1942. "Turkish Pottery from the Agora," *Hesperia* 11, pp. 1–28.

———. 1961. *The Middle Ages in the Athenian Agora*, Princeton.

Freytag, G. 1837. *Lexicon Arabico-Latinum*, Halle.

Galán, Diego. 2001. *Edición crítica de* Cautiverio y trabajos *de Diego Galán*, ed. T. M. Barchino, Cuenca.

———. 2011. *Relación del cautiverio y libertad de Diego Galán*, ed. M. Á. de Bunes and M. Barchino, Seville.

Galland, A. [1699] 1992. *De l'origine et du progrès du café*, Caen and Paris; published in 1997 in Greek as *Περί της προελεύσεως και της εξαπλώσεως του καφέ*, trans. G. Michalos, Athens.

———. 1881. *Journal d'Antoine Galland pendant son séjour a Constantinople (1672–1674)*, ed. C. Schefer, Paris.

Galt, J. 1813. *Letters from the Levant: Containing Views of the State of Society, Manners, Opinions, and Commerce, in Greece, and Several of the Principal Islands of the Archipelago*, London.

Gautier Dalché, P. 2012. "De Pétrarque à Raimondo Marliano. Aux origines de la géographie historique," *Archives d'histoire doctrinale et littéraire du Moyen Age* 79, pp. 161–191.

Gelichi, S., and L. Sabbionesi, eds. 2014. *Bere e fumare ai confine dell'impero. Caffè e tobacco a Stari Bar nel periodo ottoman*, Florence.

Gennadios, I. 1930. *Ο Λόρδος Έλγιν και οι προ αυτού ανά την Ελλάδα και τας Αθήνας ιδίως αρχαιολογήσαντες επιδρομείς, 1440–1837. Ιστορική και αρχαιολογική πραγματεία* (Βιβλιοθήκη της εν Αθήναις Αρχαιολογικής Εταιρείας 25), Athens.

Gennadius–Benaki 1979. *Τόπος και εικόνα. Χαρακτικά ξένων περιηγητών για την Ελλάδα από σπάνια βιβλία της Γενναδείου Βιβλιοθήκης, Μουσείου Μπενάκη, ιδιωτικών συλλογών* 2.1: *18ος αιώνας*, Athens.

Genzmer, F. 1899. *Bade und Schwimmanstalten*, Stuttgart.

Gerbel, N. 1545. *In descriptionem Graeciae Sophiani praefatio ... Eivsdem de situ, nominibus & regionibus Graeciae perbreuis in picturam Sophiani introductio. Item celebrium aliquot urbium descriptions ...*, Basel.

———. 1550. *Nicolai Gerbelij Phorcensis, pro declaratione picturae siue descriptionis Graeciae Sophiani. Libri septem. Quae uerò e singulis libris tractentur ... proprio elencho indicabitur*, Basel.

Gerogiorgi, S., and A. Katselaki, eds. 2005. *Μεταβυζαντινή Αθήνα / Post-Byzantine Athens* [Byzantine and Christian Museum diary], Athens.

Gerontas, A. 1889. "Περί του τείχους της πόλεως Αθηνών και των πυλών αυτού κατά τον ΙΗ΄ αιώνα," in Kambouroglou 1889–1892, 1, pp. 313–314.

Gertz, S. K. 1987. "Translatio studii et imperii: Sir Gawain as Literary Critic," *Semiotica* 63 (1–2), pp. 185–204.

Giakoumis, H. 1997. *Η Ελλάδα. Φωτογραφικό και λογοτεχνικό ταξίδι στον 19ο αιώνα*, Athens.

Giochalas, T., and T. Kafetzaki. 2013. *Αθήνα. Ιχνηλατώντας την πόλη με οδηγό την ιστορία και τη λογοτεχνία*, 3rd ed., Athens.

Gonzalez, V. 2002. *La piège de Salomon. La pensée de l'art dans le Coran*, Paris.

Gordon, T. 1832. *History of the Greek Revolution* 1, Edinburgh and London.

Göyünç, N. 1976. "XVIII. Yüzyılda Türk İdaresinde Nauplia (Anabolu) ve Yapıları," in *İsmail Hakkı Uzunçarşılı'ya Armağan*, Ankara, pp. 461–486.

Great Britain. 1816. *Report from the Select Committee* [of the House of Commons] *on the Earl of Elgin's Collection of Sculptured Marbles*, London.

Green, P. J. 1827. *Sketches of the War in Greece*, London.

Greene, M. 2000. *A Shared World: Christians and Muslims in the Early Modern Mediterranean*, Princeton.

Greenfield, J. 1989. *The Return of Cultural Treasures*, Cambridge.

Gregorovius, F. 1889. *Geschichte der Stadt Athen im Mittelalter, von der Zeit Justinians bis der türkischen Eroberung*, 2 vols., Stuttgart.

Gregory, T. E. 1993. "Local and Imported Medieval Pottery from Isthmia," in *La ceramica nel mondo bizantino tra XI e XV secolo e i suoi rapporti con l'Italia*, ed. S. Gelichi, Florence, pp. 283–306.

Grell, C. 1995. "Les ambigüités du philhellénisme. L'ambassade du comte de Choiseul-Gouffier auprès de la Sublime Porte (1784–1792)," *Dix-huitième Siècle* 27, pp. 223–235.

Grelot, G.-J. 1680. *Relation nouvelle d'un voyage de Constantinople. Enrichie de plans levez par l'auteur sur les lieux, et des figures de tout ce qu'il y a de plus remarquable dans cette ville*, Paris.

Gritsopoulos, T. A. 1967. *Τα Ορλωφικά. Η εν Πελοποννήσω Επανάστασις του 1770 και τα επακόλουθα αυτής*, Athens.

———. 1970. "Οι Ρώσοι εις το Αιγαίον κατά το 1770," *Αθηνά* 71, pp. 85–129.

Guidetti, M. 2016. *In the Shadow of the Church: The Building of Mosques in Early Medieval Syria*, Leiden.

Guillet [Guilletière], G. 1675. *Athènes ancienne et nouvelle, et l'estat present de l'Empire des Turcs, contenant la vie du Sultan Mahomet IV., ministère de Coprogli Achmet Pacha, Grand Vizir, & son campement devant Candie ... avec le plan de la ville d'Athènes, par le Sr. de la Guilletière*, Paris.

———. 1676. *An Account of a Late Voyage to Athens: Containing the Estate Both Ancient and Modern of that Famous City, and of the Present Empire of the Turks: The Life of the Now Sultan Mahomet the IV with the Ministry of the Grand Vizier, Coprogli Achmet Pacha. Also the Most Remarkable Passages in the Turkish Camp at the Siege of Candia. And Divers Other Particularities of the Affairs of the Port, by Monsieur de La Guilletière, A French Gentleman*, London.

Gutas, D. 1994. "Pre-Plotinian Philosophy in Arabic (Other than Platonism and Aristotelianism): A Review of the Sources," *Aufstieg und Niedergang der römischen Welt* II.36.7, ed. W. Haase and H. Temporini, Berlin and New York, pp. 4939–4973.

———. 1998. *Greek Thought, Arabic Culture: The Graeco-Arabic Translation Movement in Baghdad and Early Abbasid Society (2nd–4th/8th–10th c.)*, London.

———. 2015. "The Historical and Ideological Dimensions of Graeco-Arabic Studies: The Conquest of Knowledge from Alexander the Great to Meḥmed the Conqueror," *Intellectual History of the Islamicate World* 3, pp. 326–350.

Guys, P.-A. 1783. *Voyage littéraire de la Grèce, ou, Lettres sur les Grecs, anciens et modernes, avec un parallèle de leurs moeurs* 1, Paris.

Hadjiaslani, C. 1987. *Morosini, the Venetians and the Acropolis* (Exhibition catalogue, American School of Classical Studies, Gennadius Library 1987), Athens.

Hagen, G. 1998. "Kâtib Çelebi and Târîh-i Hind-i Garbî," *Güney-Doğu Avrupa Araştırmaları Dergisi* 12, pp. 101–115.

———. 2004. "Afterword: Ottoman Understandings of the World in the Seventeenth Century," in Dankoff 2004, pp. 215–256.

———. 2006. "Kâtib Çelebi and Sipâhîzâde," in *Essays in Honour of Ekmeleddin İhsanoğlou: Societies, Cultures, Sciences: A Collection of Articles* 1, ed. M. Kaçar and Z. Durukal, Istanbul, pp. 525–542.

Hamilakis, Y. 2007. *The Nation and Its Ruins: Antiquity, Archaeology, and National Imagination in Greece*, Oxford.

———. 2011. "Indigenous Archaeologies in Ottoman Greece," in Bahrani, Çelik, and Eldem, pp. 49–69.

——— and F. Ifantidis 2015. "The Photographic and the Archaeological: The 'Other Acropolis'," in Carabott, Hamilakis, and Papargyriou 2015, pp. 133–157.

Hasluck, F. W. 1929. *Christianity and Islam under the Sultans*, ed. M. M. Hasluck, 2 vols., Oxford.

Hattox, R. S. 1985. *Coffee and Coffeehouses: The Origins of a Social Beverage in the Medieval Near East*, Seattle and London.

Hatzimichali, M. 2017. "Strabo's Philosophy and Stoicism," in *The Routledge Companion to Strabo*, ed. D. Dueck, Oxford and New York, pp. 9–21.

Haugsted, I. 1996. *Dream and Reality: Danish Antiquaries, Architects and Artists in Greece*, London.

Hayes, J. W. 1992. *Excavations at Saraçhane in Istanbul 2: The Pottery*, Washington, D.C.

Heijden, H. A. M. van der. 2002. "Philippus Cluverius and Dutch Cartography: An Introduction," *Quaerendo* 32, pp. 222–244.

Herbelot, B. d'. 1697. *Bibliothéque orientale, ou Dictionnaire universel*, Paris.

Herold, J. C. 1962. *Bonaparte in Egypt*, London.

Hertzberg, G. F. 1885. *Athen. Historisch-topographisch dargestellt*, Halle.

Hobhouse, J. C. [1813] 1817. *A Journey through Albania and Other Provinces of Turkey in Europe and Asia, to Constantinople during the Years 1809 and 1810*, Philadelphia.

Homolle, T. 1894. "Vue d'Athènes en 1674," *Bulletin de correspondance hellénique* 18, pp. 509–528.

Hunt, P., and A. H. Smith. 1916. "Lord Elgin and His Collection," *Journal of Hellenic Studies* 36, pp. 163–372.

Hutchins, R. M. ed. 1952. *Chaucer: The Great Books of the Western World*, 22, Chicago and London.

Iafrate, A. 2016. *The Wandering Throne of Solomon: Objects and Tales of Kingship in the Medieval Mediterranean*, Leiden.

Ilıcak, H. S. 2011. "A Radical Rethinking of Empire: Ottoman State and Society during the Greek War of Independence (1821–1826)" (diss. Harvard University).

Isidore of Seville. 2006. *The Etymologies*, trans. S. A. Barney et al., Cambridge.

Joliffe, T. R. 1827. *Narrative of an Excursion from Corfu to Smyrna*, London.

Judeich, W. 1897. "Athen im Jahre 1395 nach der Beschreibung des Niccolò da Martoni," *Mitteilungen des Deutschen Archäologischen Instituts, Athenische Abteilung* 22, pp. 423–438.

Kafescioğlu, Ç. 1999. "Heavenly and Unblessed, Splendid and Artless: Mehmed II's Mosque Complex in Istanbul in the Eyes of Its Contemporaries," in *Aptullah Kuran için Yazılar*, ed. Ç. Kafescioğlu and L. Thys-Şenocak, Istanbul, pp. 211–222.

Kaldellis, A. 2009. *The Christian Parthenon: Classicism and Pilgrimage in Byzantine Athens*, Cambridge.

———. 2012. "The Date of Laonikos Chalkokondyles' *Histories*," *Greek, Roman and Byzantine Studies* 52, pp. 111–136.

———. 2014. *A New Herodotos: Laonikos Chalkokondyles on the Ottoman Empire, the Fall of Byzantium, and the Emergence of the West*, Cambridge, Mass.

Kalesopoulou, D. 2015. "Περίπατος στην Αθήνα μιας άλλης εποχής. Μια συνοπτική εικόνα της πόλης από τον 17ο έως τον 19ο αι.," in Lagogianni-Georgakarakou and Koutsogiannis 2015, pp. 136–157.

Kambouroglou, D. G. 1889–1892. *Μνημεία της ιστορίας των Αθηναίων*, 3 vols., Athens.

———. 1931. *Αι Αθήναι κατά τα έτη 1775–1795. Επί τη βάσει των πηγών και ιδίως της αυτοβιογραφικής χρονογραφίας του Παναγή Σκουζέ*, Athens.

———. 1934. *Απομνημονεύματα μιας μακράς ζωής (1852–1932)* 1, Athens.

Kanetaki, E. 2004. *Οθωμανικά λουτρά στον ελλαδικό χώρο*, Athens.

———. 2008. "Abid Efendi Bath," in *Ottoman Architecture in Greece*, ed. E. Brouskari, Athens, pp. 79–81.

———. 2011. "Ottoman Baths in Greece," in *Bathing Culture of Anatolian Civilization: Architecture, History, and Imagination* (*Ancient Near Eastern Supplement Series* 37), ed. N. Ergin, Louvain, pp. 221–255.

———. 2014. "In the Bath: A Trip to the Body and the Soul," accessible online: http://www.melt.gr/en/visit/the-bath-house-of-the-winds/in-the-bath-a-trip-to-the-body-and-the-soul/.

Karababa, E., and G. Ger. 2011. "Early Modern Ottoman Coffeehouse Culture and the Formation of the Consumer Subject," *Journal of Consumer Research* 37, pp. 737–760.

Karanasios, C., and K. Petsios. 2004. "Προβλήματα πατρότητας ενός ανώνυμου φιλοσοφικού έργου. Γρηγόριος (Γεώργιος) Κονταρής vel Γεώργιος Σουγδουρής;" in *Βυζάντιο – Βενετία – Νεώτερος Ελληνισμός. Μια περιπλάνηση στον κόσμο της επιστημονικής σκέψης*, ed. N. Efthymios and V. N. Giorgos, Athens, pp. 101–117.

Kardamitsi-Adami, M., and M. Grafakou. [1989] 1999. "Τα 'λουτρά' της Αθήνας," in *Όταν κτιζόταν η Αθήνα. Δημόσια κτίρια 19ου αι.*, ed. M. Kardamitsi-Adami, Athens, pp. 11–36.

Karidis, D. N. 2014. *Athens from 1456 to 1920: The Town under Ottoman Rule and the 19th-century Capital City*, Oxford.

Kazemi, R. S. 2007. *Justice and Remembrance: Introducing the Spirituality of Imam Ali*, London and New York.

Kiel, M. 1991. "Atina," in *Türkiye Diyanet Vakfı İslam Ansiklopedisi* 4, Istanbul, pp. 74–76; accessible online: http://www.tdvia.org/dia/ayrmetin.php?idno=040076&idno2=c040077.

———. 2002. "The Quatrefoil Plan in Ottoman Architecture Reconsidered in Light of the Fethiye Mosque of Athens," *Muqarnas* 19, pp. 109–122.

———. 2008. "Athens," in *Encyclopedia of Islam Three* 2, ed. M. Gaborieau et al., Leiden, pp. 138–141; accessible online: http://referenceworks.brillonline.com/entries/encyclopaedia-of-islam-3/athens-COM_26358.

Kinney, D. 2011. "Spolia as Signifiers in Twelfth-century Rome," *Hortus Artium Medievalium* 17 (*Spolia in Late Antiquity and the Middle Ages: Ideology, Aesthetics and Artistic Practice*), pp. 151–166.

Kizis, Y. 1988. "'Επίσημη' και 'παραδοσιακή' αρχιτεκτονική. Η επιρροή του κέντρου στην επαρχία της Οθωμανικής Αυτοκρατορίας," in *Ελληνική παραδοσιακή αρχιτεκτονική* 6, ed. D. Philippides, Athens, pp. 268–290.

———. 1994. *Πηλιορείτικη οικοδομία*, Athens.

———. 2014. "Τα αρχοντόσπιτα της προεπαναστατικής Αθήνας και το αρχοντικό των Μπενιζέλων," in *Ιστορία και τέχνη, μνήμη Δημήτρη Κωνστάντιου*, ed. G. Mouseidou, Athens, pp. 147–164.

Klenze, L. von. 1834. *Sechs Lithographien zu L. von Klenze's Reise nach Griechenland, Tafel II. Plan der Neustadt Athen*, Athens.

Knithakis, G., F. Mallouchou, and G. Tigginagka. 1986. "Το βοεβοδιλίκι της Αθήνας," in *Επώνυμα αρχοντικά των χρόνων της Τουρκοκρατίας*, Athens, pp. 107–124.

Koilakou, C. 1994. "Θήβα," *Αρχαιολογικόν Δελτίον* 49, Χρονικά, pp. 113–122.

Kokkou, A. 1977. *Η μέριμνα για τις αρχαιότητες στην Ελλάδα και τα πρώτα μουσεία*, Athens.

Kominis, M. 2008. "Η Αθήνα κατά τα τελευταία χρόνια της οθωμανικής διοίκησης (18ος-19ος αιώνας). Η πόλη και το διοικητικό καθεστώς" (diss. Aristotle University of Thessaloniki).

Konstantinides, A. 1950. *Τα παλιά Αθηναϊκά σπίτια*, Athens.

Konstantios, D. 2005. "Πρόλογος," in Gerogiorgi and Katselaki 2005.

Kontares, G. 1675. *Ἱστορίαι παλαιαὶ καὶ πάνυ ὠφέλιμοι τῆς περιφήμου πόλεως Ἀθήνης*, Venice.

Kontogiannis, P. M. 1917. *Οι Προστατευόμενοι*, Athens.

Korka, E. 2009. "Το ζήτημα της επανένωσης των γλυπτών του Παρθενώνα στο πλαίσιο της νέας διεθνούς πρακτικής επιστροφής πολιτιστικών αγαθών" (diss. National and Kapodistrian University of Athens).

Korres, M. 1994. *Μελέτη αποκαταστάσεως του Παρθενώνος, 4: Ο δυτικός τοίχος και άλλα μνημεία*, Athens.

———. 1996. "The Parthenon from Antiquity to the 19th Century," in *The Parthenon and Its Impact in Modern Times*, ed. P. Tournikiotis, Athens, pp. 136–161.

——— ed. 2010a. *Αττικής οδοί, 2: Οι πρώτοι χάρτες της πόλεως των Αθηνών*, Athens.

——— ed. 2010b. *Οι πρώτοι χάρτες της πόλεως των Αθηνών*, Athens.

Korre-Zografou, K. 1995. *Τα κεραμεικά του ελληνικού χώρου*, Athens.

Koumarianou, A. 2005. *Αθήνα, η πόλη – οι άνθρωποι. Αφηγήσεις και μαρτυρίες, 12ος-19ος αιώνας*, Athens.

Kritoboulos of Imbros. 1954. *History of Mehmed the Conqueror by Kritovoulos*, trans. C. T. Riggs, Princeton.

———. 1983. *Critobuli Imbriotae Historiae* (*Corpus Fontium Historiae Byzantinae* 22), ed. D. R. Reinsch, Berlin.

Kuban, D. 1995. *The Turkish Hayat House*, Istanbul.

Küçük, B. H. 2013. "Natural Philosophy and Politics in the Eighteenth Century: Esad of Ioannina and Greek Aristotelianism at the Ottoman Court," *The Journal of Ottoman Studies* 41, pp. 125–158.

Kut, G. 1996. "Turkish Culinary Culture," in *Timeless Tastes: Turkish Culinary Culture*, ed. S. Arsel, Istanbul, pp. 38–61.

Kyriazopoulos, V. D. 1978. "The Contribution of the Christians in Asia Minor Pottery," *Balkan Studies* 19, pp. 77–103.

Labate, M. 1991. "Città morte, città future. Un tema della poesia augustea," *Maia* 43, pp. 167–184.

Laborde, L. E. de. 1854a. *Athènes aux XVe, XVIe et XVIIe siècles*, 2 vols., Paris.

———. 1854b. *Documents inedits ou peu connus sur l'histoire et les antiquités d'Athènes...*, Paris.

Lagogianni-Georgakarakou, M., and T. Koutsogiannis, eds. 2015. *"Ένα όνειρο ανάμεσα σε υπέροχα ερείπια ...". Περίπατος στην Αθήνα των περιηγητών, 17ος-19ος αιώνας / "A Dream among Splendid Ruins...": Strolling through the Athens of Travelers, 17th–19th Century* (Exhibition catalogue, National Archaeological Museum 2015–2016), Athens.

Lambrinou, L. 2015. "Η υστερορωμαϊκή επισκευή του Παρθενώνα και τα χρησιμοποιηθέντα σε αυτήν ελληνιστικά στωικά κτήρια" (diss. National and Kapodistrian University of Athens).

——— and V. Papavasileiou 2013. *Έργο αποκατάστασης Παρθενώνα, 10ο Πρόγραμμα. Μελέτη αποκατάστασης δυτικού τοίχου σηκού*, Athens.

Lamers, H. 2016. *Greece Reinvented: Transformations of Byzantine Hellenism in Renaissance Italy*, Leiden.

Lane, A. 1939. "Turkish Peasant Pottery from Chanak and Kutahia," *The Connoisseur* 104, pp. 232–259.

———. 1957. *Later Islamic Pottery: Persia, Syria, Egypt, Turkey*, 2nd ed., London.

Larzul, S. 2009. "Les premières traductions françaises du Coran (XVIIe-XIXe siècles)," *Archives de sciences sociales des religions* 147, pp. 147–165.

Lauremberg, J. 1622. *Antiquarius, in quo praeter antiqua et obsoleta verba ac voces minùs vsitatas, dicendi formulae insolentes, plurimi ritus Pop. Rom. ac Graecis peculiares exponuntur & en odantur ...*, Lyon.

———. 1660. *Graecia antiqua*, ed. S. Pufendorf, Amsterdam.

Lavedan, O. 1926. *Qu'est-ce que l'urbanisme? Introduction à l'histoire de l'urbanisme*, Paris.

Leake, W. M. [1821] 1841. *The Topography of Athens, with Some Remarks on its Antiquities*, 2nd ed., London.

Legrand, É. 1894. *Bibliographie hellénique, ou Description raisonnée des ouvrages publiés en grec par des Grecs au dix-septième siècle* 2, Paris.

Legrand, L. 1895. "Relation du pèlerinage à Jérusalem de Nicolas de Martoni, notaire italien (1394–1395)," *Revue de l'Orient latin* 3, pp. 566–669; also as an offprint.

Lerebours, N.-M.-P. 1842. *Excursions daguerriennes. Vues et monuments les plus remarquables du globe*, Paris.

Loraux, N. 1996. *Né de la terre. Mythe et politique à Athènes*, Paris.

Lowry, H. W. 2003. *Ottoman Bursa in Travel Accounts*, Bloomington.

Lykouri-Lazarou, E. 1998. *Τα αρχεία στο Νεοελληνικό Κράτος έως την ίδρυση των Γενικών Αρχείων (1821–1914)*, Athens.

MacKay, C. 2007. "The Byzantine and Post-Byzantine Pottery," in *The Art of Antiquity: Piet de Jong and the Athenian Agora*, ed. J. K. Papadopoulos, Princeton, pp. 275–286.

———. 2015. "Three Late Medieval Kilns from the Athenian Agora," in *Cities Called Athens: Studies Honoring John McK. Camp II*, ed. K. F. Daly and L. A. Riccardi, Lewisburg, Penn., pp. 273–288.

MacKay, P. 2011. "Houses," in D. G. Wright's blog "Surprised by Time"; accessible online: http://surprisedbytime.blogspot.gr/2011/01/houses_22.html.

MacKay, T. S. 1996. "A Group of Renaissance Pottery from Heraklion, Crete: Notes and Questions," in *The Archaeology of Medieval Greece* (*Oxbow Monograph* 59), ed. P. Lock and G. D. R. Sanders, Oxford, pp. 127–138.

Mackenzie, M. 1992. *Turkish Athens*, Reading.

Magini, G. A. 1598. *Geografia cioe descrittione universale della terra partita in due volume ...*, Venice.

Magnani, R., and M. Munarini, eds. 1998. *La ceramica graffita del Rinascimento tra Po, Adige e Oglio*, Ferrara.

Mallouchou-Tufano, F. 1998. *Η αναστήλωση των αρχαίων μνημείων στη νεώτερη Ελλάδα (1834–1939). Το έργο της εν Αθήναις Αρχαιολογικής Εταιρείας και της Αρχαιολογικής Υπηρεσίας*, Athens.

Mango, C. 1980. *Byzantium: The Empire of New Rome*, London.

Mantis, A. 1986. "Un nouveau fragment de la 10e métope sud du Parthénon," *Bulletin de correspondance hellénique* 110, pp. 619–624.

Margaritis, Y. 2006. "Η πολιορκία της Ακρόπολης της Αθήνας," in *Ιστορία των Ελλήνων, η Ελληνική Επανάσταση* 11, ed. Y. Margaritis, Athens.

Mavroudi, M. 2013. "Translators from Greek into Arabic at the Court of Mehmet the Conqueror," in *The Byzantine Court: Source of Power and Culture. Papers from the Second International Sevgi Gönül Byzantine Studies Symposium, Istanbul, June 2010*, ed. A. Ödekan, N. Necipoğlu, and E. Akyürek, Istanbul, pp. 195–207.

———. 2014. "Ελληνική φιλοσοφία στην αυλή του Μωάμεθ Β΄," *Byzantina* 33, pp. 151–182.

McKenzie, J. 2007. *The Architecture of Alexandria and Egypt, 300 BC – AD 700*, New Haven.

McNeal, R. A. 1991. "Archaeology and the Destruction of the Later Athenian Acropolis," *Antiquity* 65, pp. 49–63.

Meidanis, C. D. 1820. *Αγγελία. Περί του κατ' Έτος τελουμένου κοινού Μνημοσύνου υπέρ των Συνδρομητών των εν Κοζάνη Σχολείων Ελληνικού ...*, Vienna.

Melanchthon, P. 1844. "Oratio de capta Constantinopoli, recitata a D. Georgio Maiore an. 1556," in *Corpus Reformatorum* XII: *Philippi Melanthonis Opera quae supersunt omnia 12: Declamationes ab anno 1553 usque ad annum 1560. Propositiones et disputationes*, ed. C. G. Bretschneider, Halle, cols. 153–161.

Mercati, S. G. 1964. "Noterella sulla tradizione manoscritta dei *Mirabilia urbis Athenarum*," in *Mélanges Eugène Tisserant* 3 (*Studi e Testi* 233), Vatican City, pp. 77–84.

Meursius, J. 1624. *Athenae atticae, sive, De praecipuis Athenarum antiquitatibus, libri III*, Leiden.

Meyer, G. 2017. "À la recherche d'un portrait d'Antoine Galland. À propos du tableau montrant le marquis de Nointel à Athènes et des peintres à son service," in *Antoine Galland et l'Orient des savants*, ed. P.-S. Filliozat and M. Zink, Paris, pp. 247–314.

Michaelis, A. 1882. *Ancient Marbles in Great Britain*, trans. C. A. M. Fennell, Cambridge.

Milanesi, M. 2001–2002. "Per una storia della geografia storica, versione riveduta e ampliata," *Geographia antiqua* 10–11, pp. 41–57.

Miller, W. 1908. *The Latins in the Levant: A History of Frankish Greece (1204–1566)*, 2 vols., London.

———. 1921. "The Venetian Revival in Greece, 1684–1718," in *Essays on the Latin Orient*, ed. W. Miller, Cambridge, pp. 403–427.

Mills, B. J. 1999. "Ceramics and the Social Contexts of Food Consumption in the Northern Southwest," in *Pottery and People: A Dynamic Interaction*, ed. J. M. Skibo and G. M. Feinman, Salt Lake City, pp. 99–114.

Momigliano, A. [1978] 1980. "After Gibbon's Decline and Fall," *Annali della Scuola normale superiore di Pisa* 8, s. 3, fasc. 2, pp. 435–454, repr. in *Sesto contributo alla storia degli studi classici e del mondo antico* 1, Rome, pp. 265–284.

Moncel, T., du 1845. *Vues pittoresques des monuments d'Athènes*, Paris.

Montagu, M. W. 1763. *Letters of the Right Honourable Lady M--y W---y M----e: Written, during Her Travels in Europe, Asia and Africa, to Persons of Distinction, Men of Letters, &c. in Different Parts of Europe. Which Contain, among Other Curious Relations, Accounts of the Policy and Manners of the Turks*, 3 vols., London; published in 1995 in Greek as *Το οδοιπορικό τριών ηπείρων*, intro. I. Hatzipanagioti, trans. I. Kassesian, Athens.

Moutsopoulos, N. 1986. "Οι περιπέτειες του ναού της Παλλάδος. Ο Παρθενώνας τζαμί," in *Επιστημονική Επετηρίδα της Πολυτεχνικής Σχολής, Αριστοτέλειο Πανεπιστήμιο Θεσσαλονίκης. Τμήμα Αρχιτεκτόνων* 1, Thessaloniki, pp. 1–56.

Mukerji, C. 2006. "Printing, Cartography, and Conceptions of Place in Renaissance Europe," *Media, Culture & Society* 28 (5), pp. 651–669.

Munarini, M., and D. Banzato. 1993. *Ceramiche rinascimentali dei musei civici di Padova*, Milan.

Münster, S. 1552. *La Cosmographie universelle contenant la situation de toutes les parties du monde, avec leurs proprietez & appurtenances ...*, Basel.

Museum of the City of Athens–Vouros-Eutaxias Foundation. 2004. *Great Travellers in Athens*, Athens.

Neander, M. 1586. *Chronicon sive synopsis historiarum. Quae res gestas praecipuarum in orbe gentium a rebus humanis conditis ad hanc usque nostram aetatem ... continet*, Leipzig.

———. 1589. *Orbis terrae partium succincta explicatio, seu simplex enumeratio, distributa in singularum partium regiones: ubi singulis regionibus suae urbes, elogia, et praeces ... maria item, littora, marium sinus, peninsulae, et insulae maris magni ...*, Leipzig.

Necipoğlu, G. 1992. "The Life of an Imperial Monument: Hagia Sophia after Byzantium," in *Hagia Sophia: From the Age of Justinian to the Present*, ed. R. Mark and A. Ş. Çakmak, Cambridge, pp. 195–225.

———. 2008. "The Dome of the Rock as Palimpsest: 'Abd al-Malik's Grand Narrative and Sultan Süleyman's Glosses," *Muqarnas* 25, pp. 17–105.

———. 2010. "From Byzantine Constantinople to Ottoman Kostantiniyye: Creation of a Cosmopolitan Capital and Visual Culture under Sultan Mehmed II," in *From Byzantion to Istanbul: 8000 Years of a Capital, June 5 – Sept. 4, 2010, Sabancı University Sakıp Sabancı Museum, Istanbul* (Exhibition catalogue, Sakıp Sabancı Museum 2010), pp. 262–278.

———. 2012. "Visual Cosmopolitanism and Creative Translation: Artistic Conversations with Renaissance Italy in Mehmed II's Constantinople," *Muqarnas* 29, pp. 1–82.

———. 2014. "Connectivity, Mobility and 'Portable Archaeology:' Pashas from the Dalmatian Hinterland as Cultural Mediators," in *Dalmatia and the Mediterranean: Portable Archaeology and the Poetics of Influence*, ed. A. Payne, Leiden, pp. 313–381.

Nicolay, N. de. 1577. *Les navigations, peregrinations et voyages, faicts en la Tvrqvie... contenants plusieurs singularitez que l'autheur y a veu & oseruẻ*, Antwerp.

Niger, D. M. [S. Compagni] 1557. *Geographiae commentariorum, libri XI ...*, Basel.

Nikoloudis, N. G. 2017. "The Conversion of [the] Parthenon into a Mosque," *Post Augustum* 1, pp. 33–38.

Nixon, L. 2004. "Chronologies of Desire and the Uses of Monuments: Eflatunpinar to Çatalhöyük and beyond," in *Archaeology, Anthropology and Heritage in the Balkans and Anatolia: The Life and Times of F. W. Hasluck, 1878–1920* 2, ed. D. Shankland, Istanbul, pp. 429–452.

Norre, A. D. 1966. "Studies in the History of the Parthenon" (diss. Univ. of California, Los Angeles).

Ohsson, I. M. d'. 1788–1820. *Tableau général de l'Empire othoman, divisé en deux parties, dont l'une comprend la législation mahométane; l'autre, l'histoire de l'Empire othoman*, 3 vols., Paris.

Olivier, G.-A. 1800. *Voyage dans l'Empire othoman, l'Égypte et la Perse. Fait pendant les six premières années de la République...* 1, Paris.

Omont, H. A. 1898. *Athènes au XVIe siècle. Dessins des sculptures du Parthénon, attribués à J. Carrey, et onservées à la Bibliothèque nationale, accompagnés de vues et plans d'Athènes et de l'Acropole*, 2 vols., Paris.

Orhonlu, C. 1972. "The History of Athens (Tarikh-i medînetül hukema) Written by a Turkish Kadi," in *Actes du IIe Congrés International des Études du Sud-Est Européen (Athènes, 7–13 Mai 1970)* 2, Athens, pp. 529–533.

———. 1973–1974. "Bir Türk Kadısının Yazdığı Atina Tarihi," *Güney-Doğu Avrupa Araştırmaları Dergisi* 2–3, pp. 119–136.

Orlandos, A. K. 1923. *Μεσαιωνικά μνημεία της πεδιάδος των Αθηνών και των κλιτύων Υμηττού – Πεντελικού, Πάρνηθος και Αιγάλεω*, Athens.

———. 1936. "Παλαιά αστικά σπίτια της Άρτης," *Αρχείον Βυζαντινών Μνημείων της Ελλάδος* 2, pp. 183–194.

———. 1939–1940. "Αθηναϊκόν Αρχοντόσπιτο της Τουρκοκρατίας," *Αρχείον Βυζαντινών Μνημείων της Ελλάδος* 5, pp. 198–205.

Ortelius, A. 1596. *Thesaurus geographicus ...*, Antwerp.

———. 1598. *Theatrum orbis terrarum*, Antwerp.

Ousterhout, R. 2005. "'Bestride the Very Peak of Heaven': The Parthenon after Antiquity," in *The Parthenon: From Antiquity to the Present*, ed. J. Neils, Cambridge, pp. 317–324.

———. 2008. *Master Builders of Byzantium*, Philadelphia.

Pagonis, K. 1993. *Κτηριακό συγκρότημα της μονής των Καπουκίνων στην Αθήνα και η περιοχή του*, Athens.

Palerne, J. 1606. *Peregrinations du S. Jean Palerne. Où est traicté de plusieurs singularités, & antiquités remarquées és prouinces d'Egypte, Arabie deserte, & pierreuse, Terre Saincte, Surie, Natolie, Grèce, & plusieurs isles...*, Lyon.

Papageorgiou, S. 2005. *Από το γένος στο έθνος. Η θεμελίωση του ελληνικού κράτους, 1821–1862*, Athens.

Papageorgiou-Venetas, A. 1999. *Εδουάρδος Σάουμπερτ, 1804–1860. Συλλογή τεκμηρίων για τον σχεδιασμό της Αθήνας και του Πειραιά*, Athens.

Papalexandrou, A. 2003. "Memory Tattered and Torn: Spolia in the Heartland of Byzantine Hellenism," in *Archaeologies of Memory*, ed. R. M. van Dyke and S. E. Alcock, Malden, Mass., pp. 56–80.

Papanikola-Bakirtzi, D., ed. 1999. *Byzantine Glazed Ceramics: The Art of Sgraffito* (Exhibition catalogue, Museum of Byzantine Culture, Thessaloniki, 2006–2007), Athens.

Pardoe, J. 1838. *The Beauties of the Bosphorus... Illustrated in a Series of Views of Constantinople and Its Environs, from Original Drawings by W. H. Bartlett*, London.

Pastoureau, M. 1984. *Les atlas français, XVIe-XVIIe siècle. Répertoire bibliographique et étude*, Paris.

Paton, J. M. 1951. *Chapters on Medieval and Renaissance Visitors to Greek Lands* (*Gennadeion Mongraphs* 3), Princeton.

Patrinelis, C. G. 1997. "Γεώργιος Κονταρής, λόγιος του ΙΖ' αιώνα άπο τα Σέρβια," in *Η Κοζάνη και η περιοχή της. Ιστορία – Πολιτισμός*, Kozani, pp. 459–470.

Pausanias. 1550. *Pausaniae de tota Graecia libri decem ... hactenus a nemine in linguam latinam conuersi, nuncque primum in lucem editi*, trans. A. Loescher, Basel.

Péret, B. 1939. "Ruines. Ruine de ruines," *Minotaure* 12–13, pp. 57–65.

Perocco, G., and A. Salvadori. 1976. *Civiltà di Venezia, 3: L'età moderna*, Venice.

Pertusi, A. [1976] 2007. *La caduta di Costantinopoli, 1: Le testimonianze dei contemporanei; 2: L'eco nel mondo*, repr. Milan.

Philadelpheus, T. N. 1902. *Ιστορία των Αθηνών επί Τουρκοκρατίας από του 1400 μέχρι του 1800*, 2 vols., Athens.

Piccolomini, E. S. 1509. *Cosmographia Pii Papae in Asiae et Europae eleganti descriptione. Asia historias rerum ubique gestarum cum locorum descriptione complectitur. Europa temporum authoris varias continet historias ...*, Paris.

———. 2001. *Enee Silvii Piccolominei postea Pii PP.II de Europa* (*Studi e Testi* 398), ed. A. van Heck, Vatican City.

———. 2004. *De Asia*, ed. N. Casella, Rome.

Pinet, A. du 1564. *Plantz, pourtraitz et descriptions de plusieurs villes et forteresses, tant de l'Europe, Asie, & Afrique, que des Indes, & terres neuves. Leurs fondations, antiquitez, & manieres de vivre. Avec plusieurs cartes generales & particulieres, servans à las Cosmographie ... Le tout mis par ordre, region par region*, Lyon.

Pitsos, N. 2013. "La ville d'Athènes dans les mémoires de voyage d'Evliyâ Çelebi et de Jacob Spon. Représentations croisées de l'Ailleurs," *Cahiers balkaniques* 41, pp. 99–116.

Pitton de Tournefort, J. 1717. *Relation d'un voyage du Levant, fait par ordre du roy... 2*, Paris.

Pococke, R. 1745. *A Description of the East, and Some Other Countries*, 2 vols., London.

Pollard, L. 2015. *The Quest for Classical Greece: Early Modern Travel to the Greek World*, London.

Pomardi, S. 1820. *Viaggio nella Grecia fatto... negli anni 1804, 1805, e 1806* 1, Rome.

Poole, J. E. 1997. *Italian Maiolica*, Cambridge.

Postel, G. 1560. *De la Republique des Turcs, & là où l'occassion s'offrera, des meurs & loy de tous Muhamedistes*, Poitiers.

Potter, J. 1837. *Archaeologia Graeca, or The Antiquities of Greece*, 3rd ed., London.

Prokopiou, G. 2001. *Το αρχοντικό του Γ. Βούλγαρη στην Ύδρα*, Athens.

Ptolemy. 1548. *La Geografia di Claudio Ptolemeo Alessandrino*, trans. P. A. Mattioli, Venice.

Pylia, M. 2001. "Λειτουργίες και αυτονομία των κοινοτήτων της Πελοποννήσου κατά τη δεύτερη Τουρκοκρατία (1715–1821)," *Μνήμων* 23, pp. 67–98.

Raby, J. 1982. "A Sultan of Paradox: Mehmed the Conqueror as a Patron of the Arts," *Oxford Art Journal* 5, pp. 3–8.

———. 1983. "Mehmed the Conqueror's Greek Scriptorium," *Dumbarton Oaks Papers* 37, pp. 15–34.

Ragsdale, H. 1988. "Evaluating the Traditions of Russian Aggression: Catherine II and the Greek Project," *Slavonic and East European Review* 66, pp. 91–117.

———. 1993. "Russian Projects of Conquest in the Eighteenth Century," in *Imperial Russian Foreign Policy*, ed. H. Ragsdale, Washington, D.C., pp. 75–102.

Rat, M., and A. Thibaudet, eds. 1962. *Montaigne. Œuvres complètes*, Paris.

Robinson, R. C. W. 1983. "Clay Tobacco Pipes from the Kerameikos," *Mitteilungen des Deutschen Archäologischen Instituts, Athenische Abteilung* 98, pp. 265–285.

———. 1985. "Tobacco Pipes of Corinth and of the Athenian Agora," *Hesperia* 54, pp. 149–203.

Rohn, A. H., E. Barnes, and G. D. R. Sanders. 2009. "An Early Ottoman Cemetery at Ancient Corinth," *Hesperia* 78, pp. 501–615.

Rojas, F., and V. Sergueenkova, 2017. "The Smell of Time: Olfactory Associations with the Past in Pre-Modern Greece," in *Knowing Bodies, Passionate Souls: Sense Perceptions in Byzantium*, ed. S. A. Harvey and M. Mullett, Washington, D.C., pp. 144–151.

Rosenthal, F. 2002. "Yūnān," in *Encyclopaedia of Islam* 11, 2nd ed., rev. H. A. R. Gibb et al., Leiden, pp. 343–345.

Ross, L. 1855. "Zur Geschichte der Topographie und Denkmäler Athens," in *Archäologische Aufsätze, Erste Sammlung*, Leipzig, pp. 245–281.

Rotzokos, N. V. 2007. *Εθναφύπνιση και εθνογένεση. Ορλωφικά και ελληνική ιστοριογραφία*, Athens.

Rubio y Lluch, A. 1908. *La Acrópolis de Atenas en la época catalana*, Barcelona.

Rudenstine, D. 2000. "Did Elgin Cheat at Marbles?" *The Nation* (May 29, 2000), pp. 30–35.

———. 2001. "A Tale of Three Documents: Lord Elgin and the Missing, Historic 1801 Ottoman Document," *Cardozo Law Review* 22 (5–6), pp. 1853–1883.

———. 2002. "Lord Elgin and the Ottomans: The Question of Permission," *Cardozo Law Review* 23 (1), pp. 449–471.

Samara-Kaufman, A. 2001. *Ελληνικές αρχαιότητες στο Μουσείο του Λούβρου. Εκατόν πενήντα ένα έργα τέχνης και η ιστορία τους*, Athens.

Sandwich, J. [Montagu, 4th Earl of]. 1799. *A Voyage Performed by the Late Earl of Sandwich round the Mediterranean in the Years 1738 and 1739 Written by Himself*, London.

Sandys, G. 1673. *Sandys Travels: Containing an History of the Original and Present State of the Turkish Empire...* London.

Saradi, H. 2011. "The Antiquities in Constructing Byzantine Identity: Literary Tradition versus Aesthetic Appreciation," *Hortus Artium Medievalium* 17 (*Spolia in Late Antiquity and the Middle Ages: Ideology, Aesthetics and Artistic Practice*), pp. 95–113.

Savant, S. B. 2013. "Forgetting Ctesiphon: Iran's Pre-Islamic Past, c. 800–1100," in *History and Identity in the Late Antique Near East*, ed. P. Wood, Oxford, pp. 169–186.

Scarce, J. 1996. *Domestic Culture in the Middle East: An Exploration of the Household Interior*, Edinburgh.

Schimmel, A. 1975. *Mystical Dimensions of Islam*. Chapel Hill.

Schleyer, W. 1909. *Bäder und Badeanstalten*, Leipzig.

Schnapp, A. 1993. *La conquête du passé. Aux origines de l'archéologie*, Paris.

———. 2015. *Une histoire comparée des ruines est-elle possible? / Είναι δυνατή μια συγκριτική ιστορία των ερειπίων;*, Athens.

Şemseddin Sami [Sami Frashëri]. 1889. "Arnavudluk," *Kamusu'l Alam* 1, pp. 149–153, Istanbul.

Setton, K. M. [1948] 1975. *Catalan Domination of Athens*, 1311–1388, rev. ed., London.

Shanks, M. 1996. *Classical Archaeology of Greece: Experiences of the Discipline*, London and New York.

Shaw, W. M. K. 2003. *Possessors and Possessed: Museums, Archaeology, and the Visualization of History in the Late Ottoman Empire*, Berkeley.

Sicilianos, D. 1960. *Old and New Athens*, trans. R. Liddell, London.

Simopoulos, K. 1991. Ξένοι ταξιδιώτες στην Ελλάδα, 1700–1800. Δημόσιος και ιδιωτικός βίος, λαϊκός πολιτισμός, εκκλησία και οικονομική ζωή, από τα περιηγητικά χρονικά 2, Athens.

Simpson, St J. 1990. "Ottoman Clay Pipes from Jerusalem and the Levant: A Critical Review of the Published Evidence," *Society for Clay Pipe Research Newsletter* 27, pp. 6–16.

———. 1998. "'Where There's Smoke, There's Fire…': Pipe-Smoking in the Ottoman Empire," *British Museum Magazine* 31, pp. 15–17.

———. 2009. "The Archaeology of the Clay Pipe in the Near East," *Al-Rāfidān* 30, pp. 67–75.

Skouzes, P. 1948. Χρονικό της σκλαβωμένης Αθήνας στα χρόνια της τυραννίας του Χατζή Αλή γραμμένο στα 1841, ed. G. Valetas, 2nd ed., Athens.

Sonyel, S. R. 1991. "The Protégé System in the Ottoman Empire," *Journal of Islamic Studies* 2, pp. 56–66.

Soucek, P. P. 1993. "Solomon's Throne / Solomon's Bath: Model or Metaphor?" *Ars Orientalis* 23, pp. 109–134.

Soysal, Y. N., and V. L. Antoniou. 2002. "A Common Regional Past? Portrayals of the Byzantine and Ottoman Heritages from Within and Without," in *Clio in the Balkans*, ed. C. Koulouri, Thessaloniki, pp. 53–72.

———. 2004. "Nation and the Other in Greek and Turkish History Textbooks," in *The Nation, Europe, and the World: Textbooks and Curricula in Transition*, ed. H. Schissler and Y. N. Soysal, New York, pp. 105–121.

Spiliadis, N. 1852. Απομνημονεύματα διά να χρησιμεύσωσιν εις τη νέα ελληνικήν ιστορίαν 2, Athens.

Spon, J. 1678. *Voyage d'Italie, de Dalmatie, de Grèce, et du Levant, fait aux années 1675 & 1676*, 2 vols., Amsterdam.

Starkey, J., and O. El Daly, eds. 2000. *Desert Travellers: From Herodotus to T. E. Lawrence*, Durham.

Stathi, K. 2014. "The Carta Incognita of Ottoman Athens," in *Frontiers of the Ottoman Imagination: Studies in Honour of Rhoads Murphey*, ed. M. Hadjianastasis, Leiden, pp. 168–184.

St Clair, W. 1972. *That Greece Might Still Be Free: The Philhellenes in the War of Independence*, London and New York.

———. 1998. *Lord Elgin and the Marbles: The Controversial History of the Parthenon Sculptures*, 3rd rev. ed., Oxford.

Stierle, K. 1996. "Translatio Studii and Renaissance: From Vertical to Horizontal Translation," in *The Translatability of Cultures: Figurations of the Space Between*, ed. S. Budick and W. Iser, Stanford, pp. 55–67.

Stockhammer, P. W., ed. 2012. *Conceptualizing Cultural Hybridization: A Transdisciplinary Approach*, Berlin and Heidelberg.

Stoneman, R. 2010. *Land of Lost Gods: The Search for Classical Greece*, London and New York.

Strabo. 1469. *Geographia, libri XVI*, trans. G. Veronese and G. Tifernate, Rome.

Strathern, P. 2007. *Napoleon in Egypt: The Greatest Glory*, London.

Strauss, G. 1958. "Topographical-Historical Method in Sixteenth-century German Scholarship," *Studies in the Renaissance* 5, pp. 87–101.

Strauss, J. 1992. "*Aretos yacni Sevdâ*: The Nineteenth Century Ottoman Translation of the 'Erotokritos'," *Byzantine and Modern Greek Studies* 16, pp. 189–202.

———. 2002. "Ottoman Rule Experienced and Remembered: Remarks on Some Local Greek Chronicles of the Tourkokratia," in *The Ottomans and the Balkans: A Discussion of Historiography*, ed. F. Adanır and S. Faroqhi, Leiden, pp. 194–221.

———. 2003. "The Greek Connection in Nineteenth-century Ottoman Intellectual History," in *Greece and the Balkans: Identities, Perceptions and Cultural Encounters since the Enlightenment*, ed. D. Tziovas, Aldershot and Burlington, Vt., pp. 47–67.

Stuart, J., and N. Revett. 1762–1830. *The Antiquities of Athens: Measured and Delineated by James Stuart F.R.S. and F.S.A. and Nicholas Revett Painters and Architects*, 5 vols., London.

———. 1827. *The Antiquities of Athens Measured and Delineated* 3, 2nd ed., London.

Szegedy-Maszak, A. 1987. "True Illusions: Early Photographs of Athens," *The J. Paul Getty Museum Journal* 15, pp. 125–138.

Tanoulas, T. 1987. "The Propylaea of the Acropolis at Athens since the Seventeenth Century: Their Decay and Restoration," *Jahrbuch des Deutschen Archäologischen Instituts* 102, pp. 413–483.

———. 1997a. *Τα Προπύλαια της Αθηναϊκής Ακρόπολης κατά τον Μεσαίωνα*, 2 vols., Athens.

———. 1997b. "Through the Broken Looking Glass: The Acciaiuoli Palace in the Propylaea Reflected in the Villa of Lorenzo il Magnifico at Poggio a Caiano," *Bollettino d'arte* 100, pp. 1–32.

———. 2004. "'Ὁραμ' ἐρατεινὸν: Architecture and Rhetoric (Eleventh–Fifteenth Centuries)," in *Byzantium Matures: Choices, Sensitivities, and Modes of Expression (Eleventh to Fifteenth Centuries)*, ed. C. Angelidi, Athens, pp. 313–338.

———. 2005. "Ο Ludwig Ross και τα Προπύλαια," in *Ludwig Ross und Griechenland. Akten des internationalen Kolloquiums, Athen 2.–3. Oktober 2002 (Internationale Archäologie, Studia Honoraria 24)*, ed. H. R. Goette and O. Palagia, Athens, pp. 85–96.

———. 2011. "Τα ερείπια των Αθηνών και οι περιηγητές," in *Έπαινος Luigi Beschi (Μουσείο Μπενάκη, 7ο Παράρτημα)*, ed. A. Delivorrias, G. Despinis, and A. Zarkadas, Athens, pp. 335–347.

———. 2012. "'Το πολυτιμότερο στολίδι του κόσμου' στο στέμμα της Αραγωνίας. Η αθηναϊκή Ακρόπολη υπό καταλανική κυριαρχία (1311–1388)," in *Η Καταλάνο-Αραγωνική κυριαρχία στον ελληνικό χώρο*, Athens, pp. 23–65.

Taşçioglu, T. 1998. *The Turkish Hamam*, Istanbul.

Tezcan, N., S. Tezcan, and R. Dankoff, eds. 2012. *Evliyâ Çelebi: Studies and Essays Commemorating the 400th Anniversary of His Birth*, Istanbul.

Theodorou, T. 2003. "Η επιστολή του R. Adair στον Λόρδο Έλγιν," *Ιστορικά* 20, pp. 509–517.

Thévenot, J. 1725. *Voyage du Levant* 1, Paris.

Thevet, A. 1554. *Cosmographie du Levant*, Lyon.

———. 1575. *La Cosmographie universelle d'André Thevet Cosmographe du Roy. Illustree de diverses figures des choses plus remarquables veües par l'auteur, & incogneuës de noz Anciens & Modernes …*, 4 vols. in 2, Paris.

Thompson, H. A. [1962] 1976. *The Athenian Agora: A Guide to the Excavation and Museum*, 3rd ed., Princeton.

Thomson de Grummond, N. 1996. "Haller von Hallerstein, Carl Christoph, Baron," in *Encyclopedia of the History of Classical Archaeology* 1, ed. N. Thomson de Grummond, Westport, Conn., pp. 561–562.

Tolias, G. 2006. "Nikolaos Sophianos's *Totius Graeciae Descriptio*: The Resources, Diffusion and Function of a Sixteenth-century Antiquarian Map of Greece," *Imago Mundi* 58, pp. 150–182.

———. 2007. "Mourning Greece: Cartographic Allegories of Melancholy in the Late Renaissance," in *Ausdrucksformen des europäischen und internationalen Philhellenismus vom 17.-19. Jahrhundert*, ed. E. Konstantinou, Frankfurt, pp. 305–318.

———. 2012. *Mapping Greece, 1420–1800: A History. Maps in the Margarita Samourkas Collection*, New Castle, Del., and 't Goy-Houten.

———. 2014–2015. "Penser les régions. Histoire brève d'une conception cosmographique," *Geographia antiqua* 23–24, pp. 139–150.

———. 2017. "Géographie comparée et mémoire locale au XVIIe siècle. Les *Parallela geographiae veteris et novae* de Philippe Briet," in *Orbis disciplinae. Hommages en l'honneur de Patrick Gautier Dalché*, ed. N. Bouloux, A. Dan, and G. Tolias, Turnhout, pp. 763–777.

Travlos, I. [1960] [1993] 2005. *Πολεοδομική εξέλιξις των Αθηνών*, Athens.

——— and G. Manousakis. 1967. *Νεοκλασσική αρχιτεκτονική στην Ελλάδα*, Athens.

Travlos, J. 1971. *Bildlexikon zur Topographie des Antiken Athen*, Tübingen [English ed. as *Pictorial Dictionary of Ancient Athens*, London 1971].

Trelawny, E. J. 1858. *Recollections of the Last Days of Shelley and Byron*, London.

Tsigakou, F.-M. 2000. "Η επανακάλυψη της Αθήνας από τους ζωγράφους περιηγητές," in *Αθήναι, από την Κλασική εποχή έως Σήμερα (5ος αι. π.Χ. – 2000 μ.Χ.)*, ed. C. Bouras et al., Athens, pp. 284–287.

———. 2007. *Η Αθήνα με τα μάτια των ζωγράφων–περιηγητών, 16ος-19ος αιώνας / Athens through the Eyes of Artists-Travellers, 16th-19th Centuries*, Athens.

Tsirgialou, A. 2015. "Photographing Greece in the Nineteenth Century: An Overview," in Carabott, Hamilakis, and Papargyriou 2015, pp. 77–93.

Tsoniotis, N. 2013. "Η Ρωμαϊκή Αγορά της Αθήνας, από την Ύστερη Αρχαιότητα έως την Τουρκοκρατία. Αρχαιολογική έρευνα – ανασκαφικά δεδομένα," in Αρχαιολογικές συμβουλές, 2: Αττική ed. S. Oikonomou and M. Douka-Toli, Athens, pp. 169–192.

———. 2014. "Lo scavo del lato est dell'Agora Romana di Atene (2000–2003). Dati stratigrafici e risultati," in Gli Ateniensi e il loro modello di città. Seminari di Storia e Archeologia greca 1 (Thiasos Monografie 5), ed. L. M. Caliò, E. Lippolis, and V. Parisi, Rome, pp. 323–336.

Tunalı, G. 2013a. "Another Kind of Hellenism? Appropriation of Ancient Athens via Greek Channels for the Sake of Good Advice as Reflected in Tarih-i Medinetü'l-Hukema" (diss. Ruhr-Universität Bochum).

———. 2013b. "'Seseya': Representation of Theseus by the Ottoman Mufti of Athens at the Beginning of the Eigthteenth [sic] Century," in Das osmanische Europa. Methoden und Perspektiven der Frühneuzeitforschung zu Südosteuropa, ed. A. Helmedach et al., Leipzig, pp. 487–506.

Ullendorff, E. 1991. "Bilkīs," in Encyclopaedia of Islam 2, 2nd ed., rev. H. A. R. Gibb et al., Leiden, pp. 1219–1220.

Vadianus, J. 1534. Epitome trium terrae partium, Asiae, Africae et Europae compendiariam locorum descriptionem continens, Zurich.

Vakalopoulos, A. E. 1973. Ιστορία του Νέου Ελληνισμού, 4: Τουρκοκρατία, 1669–1812. Η οικονομική άνοδος και ο φωτισμός του γένους, Thessaloniki.

———. 1975. "Σύλληψη και θανάτωση του Ανδρούτσου," in Ιστορία του Ελληνικού Έθνους 12, Athens.

———. 1980. Ιστορία του νέου ελληνισμού, 5: Η μεγάλη Ελληνική Επανάσταση, 1821–1829. Οι προϋποθέσεις και οι βάσεις της, 1813–1822, Thessaloniki.

———. 1986. Ιστορία του νέου ελληνισμού, 7: Η μεγάλη Ελληνική Επανάσταση, 1821–1829. Ο αφρικανικός Σιμούν ή η επιδρομή του Ιμπραΐμ στην Ελλάδα, Thessaloniki.

Vandelli, G., and L. Polacco, eds. 1974. Dante Alighieri, La Divina Commedia, Milan.

Van Steen, G. 2014. "Sin and the City: A Mid-fifteenth-century Lament for the Fall of Athens to the 'Persians'," in Re-Imagining the Past: Antiquity and Modern Greek Culture, ed. D. Tziovas, Oxford, pp. 229–252.

Vatin, V., and N. Déroche. 2016. Constantinople, 1453. Des Byzantins aux Ottomans, textes et documents, Toulouse.

Velmos, N., and S. Doukas. 1931. Παλιά Αθήνα (Φύλλα τέχνης του Φραγγελίου 12), Athens.

Vernon, F. 1676. "Mr. Francis Vernon's Letter, Written to the Publisher January. 10th. 1675/6 Giving a Short Account of Some of His Observations in His Travels from Venice through Istria, Dalmatia, Greece, and the Archipelago, to Smyrna, where This Letter was Written," Philosophical Transactions 11, pp. 575–582.

Vigarello, G. 1985. *Le propre et le sale. L'hygiène du corps depuis le Moyen Âge*, Paris; published in 2000 in Greek as *Το καθαρό και το βρώμικο*, trans. S. Marketos, Athens.

Vingopoulou, I. 2004. *Le monde grec vu par les voyageurs du XVIe siècle*, Athens.

Vlachos, M., ed. 1994. *Louis Dupré. Ταξίδι στην Αθήνα και στην Κωνσταντινούπολη*, Athens.

Vroom, J. 1996. "Coffee and Archaeology: A Note on a Kütahya Ware Find in Boeotia, Greece," *Pharos* 4, pp. 5–19.

———. 1998a. "Medieval and Post-Medieval Pottery from a Site in Boeotia: A Case Study Example of Post-Classical Archaeology in Greece," *Annual of the British School at Athens* 93, pp. 513–546.

———. 1998b. "Early Modern Archaeology in Central Greece: The Contrast of Artefact-rich and Sherdless Sites," *Journal of Mediterranean Archaeology* 11 (2), pp. 131–164.

———. 2000. "Byzantine Garlic and Turkish Delight: Dining Habits and Cultural Change in Central Greece from Byzantine to Ottoman Times," *Archaeological Dialogues* 7, pp. 199–216.

———. 2003. *After Antiquity: Ceramics and Society in the Aegean from the 7th to the 20th Centuries A.C.: A Case Study from Boeotia, Central Greece* (Archaeological Studies Leiden University 10), Leiden.

———. 2005. *Byzantine to Modern Pottery in the Aegean: An Introduction and Field Guide*, Utrecht; 2nd rev. ed., Turnhout 2014.

———. 2006a. "Byzantine Garbage and Ottoman Waste," in *Thèbes. Fouilles de la Cadmée II.2. Les tablettes en linéaire B de la "Odos Pelopidou". La céramique de la Odos Pelopidou et la chronologie du Linéaire B*, ed. E. Andrikou et al., Pisa and Rome, pp. 181–233.

———. 2006b. "Durrës Amphitheatre's Afterlife: The Medieval and Post-Medieval Ceramics," in *New Directions in Albanian Archaeology: Studies Presented to Muzafer Korkuti* (International Centre for Albanian Archaeology Monograph Series 1), ed. L. Bejko and R. Hodges, Tirana, pp. 303–308.

———. 2007a. "Pottery Finds from a 'Cess-pit' at the Southern Wall in Durrës, Central Albania," in *Çanak: Late Antique and Medieval Pottery and Tiles in Mediterranean Archaeological Contexts, Çanakkale, 1–3 June 2005* (Byzas 7, Veröffentlichen des Deutschen Archäologischen Instituts Istanbul), ed. B. Böhlendorf-Arslan, A. O. Uysal, and J. Witte-Orr, Istanbul, pp. 319–334.

———. 2007b. "Kütahya between the Lines: Post-Medieval Ceramics as Historical Information," in *Between Venice and Istanbul: Colonial Landscapes in Early Modern Greece* (Hesperia Supplement 40), ed. S. Davies and J. Davis, Princeton, pp. 71–93.

———. 2011. "'Mr. Turkey Goes to Turkey', Or: How an Eighteenth-century Dutch Diplomat Lunched at Topkapı Palace," *Princeton Papers: Interdisciplinary Journal of Middle Eastern Studies* 16, pp. 139–175.

———. 2013a. "'Digging for the 'Byz': Adventures into Byzantine and Ottoman Archaeology in the Eastern Mediterranean," *Pharos* 19 (2), pp. 79–110.

———. 2013b. "Medieval – Modern Fine Wares," in *Landscape and Interaction: The Troodos Archaeological and Environmental Survey Project, Cyprus* 1: *Methodology, Analysis and Interpretation*, ed. M. Given et al., Oxford, pp. 74–80.

———. 2017. "The Global Ottomans," in *The Routledge Handbook of Archaeology and Globalization*, ed. T. Hodos, Abingdon and New York, pp. 899–917.

——— and E. Tzavella. 2017. "Dinner Time in Athens: Eating and Drinking in the Medieval Agora," in *Medieval MasterChef: Archaeological and Historical Perspectives on Eastern Cuisine and Western Foodways*, ed. J. Vroom, Y. Waksman, and R. van Oosten, Turnhout, pp. 145–180, 378–380.

——— and Y. Boswinkel. 2019. "New Dimensions in Archaeology: 2D and 3D Visualisations of Byzantine Structures and their Contents in the Athenian Agora," *Pharos* 22 (2) [2016], pp. 87–114.

Vryonis, S. 2002. "The Ghost of Athens in Byzantine and Ottoman Times," *Balkan Studies* 43, pp. 5–115.

Waagé, F. O. 1933. "Excavations in the Athenian Agora: The Roman and Byzantine Pottery," *Hesperia* 2, pp. 279–328.

Wachsmuth, C. 1874. *Die Stadt Athen im Altertum* 1, Leipzig.

Waddington, G. 1825. *A Visit to Greece in 1823 and 1824*, London.

Walbridge, J. 1998. "Explaining away the Greek Gods in Islam," *Journal of the History of Ideas* 59 (3), pp. 389–403.

Walker, M. 2013. "Francis Vernon, the Early Royal Society and the First English Encounter with Ancient Greek Architecture," *Architectural History* 56, pp. 29–61.

Walsh, R. 1836. *A Residence at Constantinople, during a Period Including the Commencement, Progress, and Termination of the Greek and Turkish Revolutions* 1, London.

Ward, C., and U. Baram. 2006. "Global Markets, Local Practice: Ottoman-period Clay Pipes and Smoking Paraphernalia from the Red Sea Shipwreck at Sadana Island, Egypt," *International Journal of Historical Archaeology* 10 (2), pp. 135–158.

Wartburg, M.-L. von. 2001. "Types of Imported Table Ware at Kouklia in the Ottoman Period," *Report of the Department of Antiquities, Cyprus*, pp. 361–396.

Watts, E. J. 2006. *City and School in Late Antique Athens and Alexandria*, Berkeley, Los Angeles, and London.

Weiss, R. 1969. *The Renaissance Discovery of Classical Antiquity*, Oxford.

Welsch, W. 1999. "Transculturality: The Puzzling Form of Cultures Today," in *Spaces of Culture: City, Nation, World*, ed. M. Featherstone and S. Lash, London, pp. 194–213.

Wheler, G. 1682. *A Journey into Greece, by George Wheler Esq.; in Company of Dr. Spon of Lyons…*, London.

Whitcombe, T. D. 1992. *The Campaign of the Falieri and Piraeus in the Year 1827* (Gennadeion Monographs 5), Princeton.

Williams, C. K., II, and O. H. Zervos. 1992. "Frankish Corinth, 1991," *Hesperia* 61, pp. 133–191.

Williams, D. 2009. "Lord Elgin's *Firman*," *Journal of the History of Collections* 21, pp. 1–28.

Wilson, T. 1987. *Ceramic Art of the Italian Renaissance*, London.

———. 1989. *Maiolica: Italian Renaissance Ceramics in the Ashmolean Museum*, Oxford.

Woods, J. 1828. *Letters of an Architect, from France, Italy, and Greece* 2, London.

Xyngopoulos, A. 1960. "Ὁ μεσαιωνικός πύργος τοῦ Παρθενῶνος," Ἀρχαιολογική Ἐφημερίς, pp. 1–16.

Yakovaki, N. 2006. *Ευρώπη μέσω Ελλάδας. Μια καμπή στην ευρωπαϊκή αυτοσυνείδηση, 17ος-18ος αιώνας*, Athens.

Yatromanolakis, D. 2012. *Greek Mythologies: Antiquity and Surrealism*, Cambridge, Mass.

Yegül, F. 2010. *Bathing in the Roman World*, Cambridge.

Yerasimos, S. 1990. *La fondation de Constantinople et de Sainte-Sophie dans les traditions turques. Légendes d'Empire*, Istanbul and Paris.

Zacharakis, C. G. 2009. *A Catalogue of Printed Maps of Greece, 1477–1800*, Athens.

Zambon, A. 2007. "Louis-François-Sébastien Fauvel et la constitution de la collection Choiseul-Gouffier," in *Le voyage en Grèce du comte de Choiseul-Gouffier*, ed. O. Cavalier, Avignon Le Pontet, pp. 62–83.

———. 2010. "Louis François Sébastien Fauvel, le consul antiquaire (1753–1838)," in *Consuls et services consulaires au XIXe siècle / Consulship in the 19th Century / Die Welt der Konsulate im 19. Jahrhundert*, ed. J. Ulbert and L. Prijac, Hamburg, pp. 139–156.

———. 2014. *Aux origines de l'archéologie en Grèce. Fauvel et sa méthode*, Paris.

Ziebarth, E. 1899. "Ein griechischer Reisebericht des XV. Jahrhunderts," *Mitteilungen des Deutschen Archäologischen Instituts, Athenische Abteilung* 24, pp. 72–88.

Zorzi, G. 1959. *I disegni delle antichità di Andrea Palladio*, Venice.

Zosimus [1971] 2000. *Νέα ιστορία / Histoire nouvelle* 1, ed. and trans. F. Paschoud, 2nd ed., Paris.